PRAISE FOR GERALD ASTOR

# BATTLING BUZZARDS

"ABSORBING, INFORMATIVE ... TELLINGLY DETAILED."—*Kirkus Reviews*

"Superior as an example of oral history."—*Booklist*

"QUICK AND WELL-PACED, this will please even the most jaded of readers."—*Army* Magazine

# THE MIGHTY EIGHTH

"No one does oral history better than Gerald Astor.... Here the men of the mightiest air force ever built, tell their story in their own words—of trials, tribulations, triumphs, terror, and tedium."
—Stephen Ambrose

"FASCINATING ... invaluable in terms of understanding both the process of protracted war and its effect on the human spirit. Excellent in weaving these stories into a broader analysis of the Eighth's role in the air war with Germany, Astor demonstrates once again that he's one of the most accomplished oral historians at work today."
—*Publishers Weekly*

*Please turn the page for more extraordinary acclaim....*

"Revealing and vivid . . . His many interviews of American airmen turn up some fascinating anecdotes, catching the grim realities of air combat in a way that more conventional histories cannot." —*Kirkus Reviews*

## A BLOOD-DIMMED TIDE

"ORIGINAL . . . EVOCATIVE . . . BRILLIANT . . ."
—*Publishers Weekly*

"Consistently gripping . . . a vivid vision of warfare from the foxhole." —*Newport News Daily Press*

"A GRIPPING STORY . . . will no doubt take its place as a classic." —*Troy Record*

"The immediacy and clarity of enlisted men's accounts form the core reality here, giving a palpable sense of infantry and tank warfare. Strong narrative, sound history, and a good read." —*Kirkus Reviews*

"AN ABSORBING BOOK, fascinating for its first-person detail." —*Richmond Times-Dispatch*

"A compelling, effective contribution to World War II history." —*Booklist*

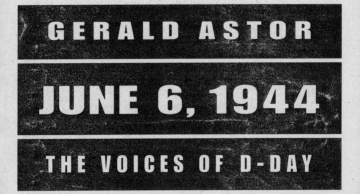

# GERALD ASTOR

# JUNE 6, 1944

## THE VOICES OF D-DAY

A DELL BOOK

Published by
Dell Publishing
a division of
Random House, Inc.
1540 Broadway
New York, New York 10036

Dell® is a registered trademark of Random House, Inc., and
the colophon is a trademark of Random House, Inc.

Dell books may be purchased for business or promotional use
or for special sales. For information please write to: Special
Markets Department, Random House, Inc., 1540 Broadway,
New York, N.Y. 10036.

Library of Congress Catalog Card Number: 94-2041

ISBN: 0-440-23697-5

Reprinted by arrangement with St. Martin's Press

Printed in the United States of America
Published simultaneously in Canada

May 2002

OPM      10  9  8  7  6  5  4

# CONTENTS

# ACKNOWLEDGMENTS

This book could not have been written without the cooperation of the men who so patiently responded to my interviews and whose words encapsulate so much of what went into June 6, 1944. Their names appear throughout the text, and I am grateful for their help.

I received valuable assistance in locating British soldiers from Henry Brown, vice president, Commando Association, and Eddie Hannath, president, Normandy Veterans Association.

The Archives Branch of the U.S. Army Military History Institute, Carlisle Barracks, Pennsylvania, under the direction of Dr. Richard J. Sommers, provided documents and leads to valuable sources. The United States Naval Institute at Annapolis, Maryland, through its publication *Naval Proceedings*, informed its audience of my interest in sailors who were present on D-Day, and Paul Stillwell, director of oral history at the Naval Institute, was helpful in finding useful material. Bob Busch advised readers of the *Scuttlebutt*, the publication for U.S. Navy amphibious forces, of my hunt for men aboard landing craft.

Col. Donald Van Roosen of the National Order of Battlefield Commissions supplied a roster in whose ranks I discovered a number of my respondents. *Legion* magazine in Canada advised its readers of my interest in D-Day vets. Len Milkovics supplied me with a copy of his history of the 508th Parachute Regiment, *The Devils Have Landed*.

Donald McKee, national senior vice commander of the 29th Division Association, gave me a list of potential sources. Ralph Lingert arranged for the 4th Division's publication *Ivy Leaves* to publish a notice that invited men from that outfit to contact me. Ivan Worrell of the 101st

Airborne Division spread the word of my project and offered names. Arthur Chaitt from the Society of the 1st Division helped me locate former wearers of the Big Red One. Jake Waldstein arranged for a notice of my interests to appear in the 1st Combat Engineer Battalion newsletter. Don Lassen carried an item in the *Static Line*, the newspaper for members of the airborne. Jim Allardyce printed my request for volunteers from the 508th PR in the newsletter for vets of that organization.

I also want to express my appreciation of the efforts of my editor, Jared Kieling.

# PREFACE

This is my third book dealing with events in World War II. In all of them I have relied heavily upon the men who were onstage. Their memories and their voices provide the continuity for what happened before they put on uniforms and what happened over the years they served their country.

I make no claim that I present a definitive study of strategy, tactics, and the "big picture," and I am aware that my sampling of people may be distorted by the effects of time on memories and limited by the vantage points of the individuals. Possibly, with fifty years gone by, a few may inflate their own roles or accomplishments. On the other hand, attainment of the age of retirement also removes the curse of ambition that so often colors a remembrance of past events.

Modern generals do not fight battles. Men of much lesser rank engage one another with shot, shell, and missile. With their staffs, the high commanders draft the scenarios, pick the settings, choose the actors, issue the props, and then hope the performance follows the script. Unfortunately, the stage for the drama of war is always beset with unexpected "technical" problems and the conflict takes on a life of its own.

After the pileup of bodies, the shedding of blood, the authors of the tragedy and their academic interpreters offer exegesis. Those who wore stars on their shoulders review their plan drafts, go back to their journals and their diaries (records that lower echelons are usually enjoined from keeping for fear of their use if captured) and to the official documents.

Among the basic tools for writing these accounts are After-Action Reports, filed by company-grade officers as soon as possible after an engagement, and Combat Interviews. The first of these attempts to lay out what happened in terms of the units involved, the time and location, the disposition of forces, and the results. The AAR is often skewed. The writer may not have been on the scene, and his information depends upon the point of view of his sources. Those who provide descriptions of their organizations' achievements are susceptible to self-serving aims.

Combat Interviews go into more depth about individual or small-unit experiences of a situation. During World War II they were conducted on a catch-them-when-you-can basis. In some instances the wounded provided information fairly soon after the battle, although casualties, having been hit and removed from the field, had only a partial view. In other cases, the debriefings were held many months after the engagement, when memories may have faded.

An unfortunate result of this form of historical record is countless books that accept AARs and Combat Interviews unquestioningly and perpetuate the errors of fact contained in them. But perhaps a worse aspect of histories that depend only upon official records and the memories of the highest echelons is that they tend to ignore the presence of the actors who lived the parts. There is no voice, only an abstraction graced by rank and name.

Oral histories, the personalized statements of participants, interviews, and diaries offer redress. The stories related here challenge a number of the accepted versions of events that occurred on June 6, 1944. For example, histories relating the Ranger assault on Pointe du Hoc have frequently misreported the details. The soldiers who climbed that cliff remember what actually happened. Similarly, others correctly identify who was responsible for success in a significant skirmish at the vital La Fière Causeway, which has been credited to the wrong parties in a number of books. And the accident that killed the highest-ranking officer participating in the Normandy invasion is, as it turns out, best explained by those who were there.

Only through the words and memories of the men who fought that day does one grasp a sense of what war is about, how it consumes human lives, and what is masked by the dry term "casualties."

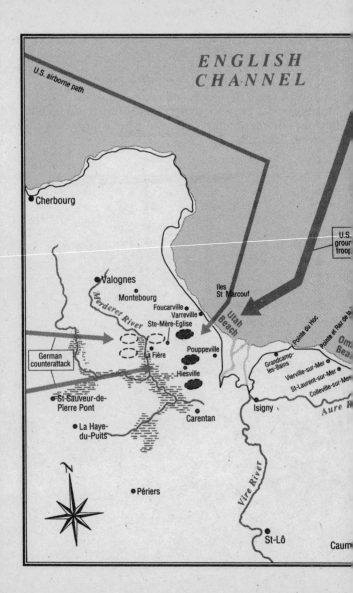

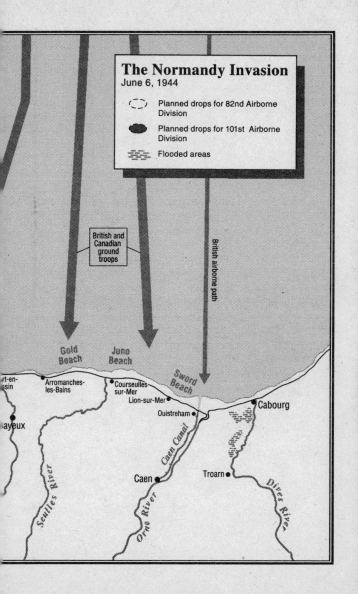

# The Normandy Invasion
June 6, 1944

○ Planned drops for 82nd Airborne Division

● Planned drops for 101st Airborne Division

Flooded areas

British and Canadian ground troops

British airborne path

Gold Beach

Juno Beach

Sword Beach

rt-en-ssin

Arromanches-les-Bains

Courseulles-sur-Mer

Lion-sur-Mer

Ouistreham

Cabourg

ayeux

Caen Canal

Caen

Troarn

Seulles River

Orne River

Dives River

# THE BEGINNING
# OF THE END

"IT WOULD HAVE killed us not to go," says John R. "Bob" Slaughter, a machine gun section sergeant with the 29th Infantry Division, referring to that gray, windswept morning of June 6, 1944. "Raymond Hoback suffered from bad nosebleeds but he would not accept a discharge. Russell Ingram went AWOL from the hospital with his broken vertebrae. Jack Simms ate bananas to gain enough weight so he wouldn't be left behind. We felt we were as good as any soldiers in the world."

"I was proud to be a part of this," says then T/Sgt. Felix Branham of the 116th Infantry Regiment. "My dad, twenty-seven years before, had gotten off a ship, walked down a gangplank to France. And here I was, about to fight for every little grain of sand on that beach."

"Neal Beaver, our platoon leader who would jump our stick, and I looked at some aerial photos," says Bill Lord, an 81mm mortar sergeant with the 508th Parachute Regiment. "Neal told me this was going to be the greatest thing I ever did in my life. If we survived, we would have something to talk about to our grandchildren. I told him that was pretty much word for word what Yale coach Ducky Pond used to tell his football players on the day of the Harvard game."

"Things were a bit tight for us that night," says Robert Kiel, a sergeant with the 101st Airborne Division. "But this was what we trained for for so long. I had a box of Fannie Farmer chocolates I passed around, but only a few pieces were taken."

"There is no greater bore than waiting around to go back into combat," says Bill Dunfee, an 82nd Airborne trooper who already had jumped into battle in Sicily and Italy. "You know damn well there is nothing you can do to change anything. Everyone sweats it out in his own way. We all put on happy faces for appearance' sake. I saw one young replacement who was really down. I got the company barber kit and trimmed his hair. I told him I wanted him to look good when we entered Paris. I was able to talk him out of his funk. I assured him that every man in that hangar was as scared as he was, including myself. I feel I relieved him of some of his anxiety. I hope so; he was one of the first killed."

"I still can remember the disbelief I felt, that within a few hours we would be facing the enemy," says Jack Kuhn, a sergeant with the 2nd Ranger Battalion. "I could not envision myself going into combat. It all seemed so detached, as if happening to someone else. The only thing I was afraid of was not being able to face the test. I didn't want to coward out. Then everybody else said the same thing, and I was okay. For some reason, I didn't have the feeling I would be killed or injured. But I prayed as never before, not only for myself but for my buddies."

"We were quite proud that we were to be the leaders of the Glider Phase," says George "Pete" Buckley, a glider flight officer in the 74th Squadron, "but some of us, I'm sure, secretly wished we hadn't been so good on our training operations. The thought of a night landing, in enemy territory, in strange fields with a heavily loaded glider, sounded like a recipe for disaster.

"Takeoff was scheduled for approximately 12:30 A.M. on the 6th. Our glider was no. 49 at the tail end of the fifty-two-ship formation. Bill Bruner, my copilot, and I went to the mess hall for the proverbial last meal. Those of us who felt the need went to see the chaplain. His tent was jammed."

"I don't recall anybody who was eager to see combat," says Richard H. Conley, a 1st Division platoon leader. "I would have been apprehensive if anybody with that attitude had been close to me. Nobody but a nut wants to be shot at."

"We had a Lt. Leo Van de Voort," says erstwhile anti-tank squad leader Bill Lewis. "He had been in the Canadian Army. He had seen actual combat, and he would talk to us about the horrors we would see, how it would be and it wouldn't be, even though they talked about these great waves of men and things."

"Reveille was at 3:30 A.M. on June 6," remembers Bill Bidmead, who describes himself as a "twenty-year-old virgin soldier" in the British Army's No. 4 Commando. " 'Get dressed' was the order from the sergeant major that disturbed the butterflies in my stomach, but they were quickly dispersed by pangs of seasickness and nervous excitement. We never knew what a nightmare it was all going to be."

Lt. Homer Jones's platoon prepared to board its aircraft after a message from Supreme Commander Gen. Dwight D. Eisenhower was read to them. Lt. Jones felt impelled to address the men himself. "I had tremendous respect and feeling for them," he recalls. "In the paratroops, the normal walls between officers and enlisted men broke down. You did everything the men did, and I often finished marches carrying a mortar or machine gun. In the entire platoon, there was only one man who I believed didn't belong. There were a lot of country boys, poor kids, ones with different backgrounds, and they'd all become close.

"I looked at them and realized there were a lot I wasn't ever going to see again. This would be a final goodbye. I said, 'I'd like to add a few words.' I began, 'We've been together a long time . . .' and then it got to me. 'Oh shit!' is what I said.

"Trooper Japhet Alphonso said, 'That's okay, lieutenant. We know what you mean.' "

"The navy had opened up. It seemed like the whole world exploded," says then Lt. Robert Edlin, with the 2nd Ranger Battalion. "There was gunfire from battleships, destroyers, and cruisers. The bombers were still hitting the beachers. There didn't seem to be any way that anyone could live on the beaches with the amount of firepower that was being laid down by the American forces. As we went in, we could see small craft from the 116th Infantry that had gone in ahead, sunk. There were a few bodies bobbing in the water, even out three or four miles.

"I took stock of the men in my boat. They were vomiting on each other's feet and on their clothing. It was just a terrible sight. They were so sick from the action of the waves. There was a deep silence. All the gunfire had lifted for a very short time. The navy was giving way to let the troops get on the beaches. The only thing I could hear was the motor of the boat. It was dawn. The sun was just coming up over the French coast. I saw a bird, a seagull I guess, fly across the front of the boat, just like life was going on as normal.

"Then there came something like a peppering of hail, heavy hail on the front of the ramp. I realized it was enemy machine gun fire. All hell broke loose from the other side, German artillery, rockets, and mortars. It was just unbelievable that anybody could have lived under that barrage. It came in through our boat and the other boats. We crouched in the bottom of the boat in the vomit, urine, and seawater and whatever else was there.

"The assault boat hit a sandbar. We were at least seventy-five yards from shore. I told the coxswain, the operator of the boat, 'Try to get it in further.' That British seaman had all the guts in the world, but he couldn't get the assault craft off the sandbar. So, I told him to drop the ramp or we were going to die right there."

THUS, SOME EARLY moments and sentiments of the most celebrated occasion of World War II, D-Day, Operation Overlord—the invasion of Normandy on the French coast. Winston Churchill called it "not the end, but the beginning of the end." To the thunderous clamor of twentieth-century warfare, the curtain rose on the last bloody acts in the conflict between the Western democracies and Adolf Hitler's Third Reich.

It was such a mammoth enterprise that U.S. admiral

Morton L. Deyo, attending a briefing three weeks before the start of Overlord, remarked, "It seemed to us that the proper meshing of so many gears would need nothing less than divine guidance."

The sachems of Overlord—the strategists, technicians, intelligence specialists, scientists, engineers, and inventors involved in preparations for the invasion—labored mightily and meticulously to ensure that all those gears meshed. The technology of the day, the latest mechanical and electronic wizardry, seduced the powerful into the belief that they could readily overwhelm an enemy crumpling from the blows of the Soviet armies in the east, the Allied push through Italy, and the constant aerial attacks that had reduced the once-vaunted Luftwaffe to hit-and-run strikes.

To be sure, substantial casualties were anticipated, but the men at the top were convinced that when night fell on June 6, their forces would control a solid stretch of waterfront property forty miles wide and as much as ten miles deep.

But for all of the enterprise, effort, men, and money that had been invested, nature, human fallibility, and chance conspired to create a massive breakdown. By midnight of D-Day, less than twenty-four hours after Sgt. Kiel had passed around his box of candy, the invaders barely clung to small strips of territory along the edge of Western Europe. Two or three miles beyond the shore—or in places as little as a few hundred yards inland—isolated bands of Allied soldiers hunkered down beside hedgerows in desperate skirmishes for survival.

With the smugness of hindsight, history labels the landings of June 6, 1944, as a mighty victory. As a signal event in history, the invasion resonates with the glory inscribed in Shakespeare's tale of Henry V and his army, also in France, at Agincourt.

> *He that outlives this day and comes safe home*
> *Will stand a tiptoe when this day is named.*

In reality, the assault, more than five hundred years after British yeomen destroyed the French, verged on catastrophic defeat for hours. Despite the grand Allied armada hurling huge shells from miles offshore, despite the fleets of aircraft dumping thousands of tons of explosives from two miles overhead, there was no magic weapon like the longbow that had enabled the English archers to down the foe at long range with only a handful of casualties.

The 1944 invaders paid a fearsome price for their small holdings of French turf. As June 7 began, the hammer of war had, in a mere twenty-four hours, killed about 2,500 Americans, Britons, Canadians, and a smattering of fighters from captive nations. Medics and doctors tended 6,500 wounded. Roughly 2,000 men were listed as missing. Some would show up subsequently after having been isolated from their units; others had been taken prisoner. A significant number would never be found, their bodies disappearing forever into the murk of the English Channel or man-made swamps, a defensive tactic employed by the Germans. Estimates of the losses among the German defenders ranged from 4,000 to 9,000.

Bloody as the landings on Tarawa (1,500 casualties), Iwo Jima (2,000), and Peleliu (1,000) were in the South Pacific, the dead and wounded there number far less than those struck down on June 6, 1944.

Statistics serve as a palliative, covering the dead with a blanket of anonymity. But they were young, vibrant men whose torn flesh spilled their lifeblood that day. They had names, homes, and hopes. They had kinfolk, loved ones, and friends, some of whom saw them die. And fifty years later, only monuments and fading memories attest to their sacrifice.

The largest American gathering of World War II dead is the huge U.S. military cemetery on a Normandy bluff. It overlooks the shale-and-sand strand known on D-Day as Omaha Beach, a site of much of the carnage. Row on row of white crosses, with an occasional Star of David, mark thousands of graves. Included are not only the fallen from Overlord but others killed during World War II.

A far less conspicuous, almost hidden reminder of June 6, 1944, stands in the hamlet of Bedford, Virginia. Beside the old courthouse on Main Street there are actually three memorials for fighting men. The biggest, an obelisk dedicated to the Confederacy, towers over a pair of tombstone-like monuments that honor local sons from more recent wars.

Facing the old Bedford courthouse, a person gazes on a stone tablet mined from quarries at Vierville-sur-Mer, one of the Normandy villages that witnessed Overlord. Alphabetically, the inscription lists a series of names: "Leslie C. Abbott, Jr., Wallace R. Carter, John D. Clifton, Frank P. Draper, Jr., Taylor M. Fellers," and on and on through Bedford T. Hoback, Raymond S. Hoback, Ray O. Stevens, ending with Grant C. Yopp—twenty-three in all. Every one of them died on June 6, 1944, probably within the space of two or three hours.

The total population of Bedford in 1944 numbered well under four thousand, and the young men, drawn from farms, timber-cutting gangs, and a tiny manufacturing plant, represent an enormous demographic loss. Had such a cataclysm of death struck New York City, for example, 45,000 young men would have been wiped out in that fraction of time.

The monument beside that aged building provides a way to begin the story of the men who participated in Overlord. The backgrounds of those who happened to be there and what befell them before, during, and after June 6, 1944, are a mosaic portrait of white American men—African-Americans were almost entirely excluded from combat roles until late in the war—stretching from colonial days down through the Great Depression of the 1930s. It is a tale of sons of the American Revolution, waves of immigrants to the United States, military institutions ill prepared for World War II, and the baggage of tradition, belief, education, and experience carried along with rifles and ammunition. While details differ for participants from the United Kingdom and Canada, the commonality with their American cousins breeds a similar story line. As the set piece of the last war that fully engaged the West, the Normandy invasion embodies an enormous amount of human experience.

# PART I

# PREPARATIONS

# CHAPTER 1

# THE PREWAR SOLDIERS

THE CALAMITY VISITED upon the Bedford community rose from the American tradition of home militia—National Guard units formed in states or regions and then in wartime federalized intact into the United States Army. The young men from Bedford belonged to the 116th Infantry Regiment of the 29th Division. They were enlistees from Bedford, Charlottesville, Roanoke (Bob Slaughter's hometown), and other places toward the southwestern part of the state.

The regiment's origins lie in the American Revolution of the 1770s, when George Washington and Patrick Henry led the early militia. The outfit later stood with Gen. Thomas "Stonewall" Jackson as part of the Confederacy in what some still call the War Between the States. As "doughboys" in the 116th, fathers of those who would slosh ashore on Omaha Beach had fought in France with the 1917 American Expeditionary Forces (AEF).

Well before the first Japanese bomb fell on Pearl Harbor, the 116th filled its ranks with earnest local youths as well as, according to Bob Slaughter, "thugs and drunks." The original roster of Slaughter's D Company, like the memorial at Bedford, speaks of a homogeneous population—Smith, Slaughter, Lancaster, Boyd, Jones, Baker, Croft, Atkins,

and the like—an Americanized Anglo-Saxon, Scotch-Irish
replica of those who accompanied Henry V into France for
St. Crispin's Day.

"We grew up together, went to school together, played
together, worked together, and went to church together,"
says Bob Slaughter. "We were all Baptists; we didn't know
what a Jew was. I never met a Roman Catholic until after
the war started."

A notable exception to the common strain is one of the
names on the Bedford monument, that of Weldon A.
Rosazza, dimly remembered fifty years later in the local di-
alect as "an Eyetalian boy" who worked at a small manufacturing plant.

By contrast, the Normandy adventure of 1944 brought to
bear almost all of the ethnic elements of America, with much
of the homogeneous quality of the 116th vanishing under
the influx of manpower demands. Slaughter notes that once
war reached the States, attrition and authorities weeded out
most of the misfits he originally encountered. Draftees from
neighboring states like Pennsylvania and Maryland sewed on
the circle-shaped blue-and-gray patch of the 29th Division.
Thus, Frustoso Chavez, Jacob Osofsky, Francis Malinowski,
John DiBeneditti, and Edward Berghoff also died wearing it
on the Normandy shores.

Still, the 116th started out as a homegrown Virginia
product. Slaughter traces his history with the unit. "My
father was a construction company vice president in
Tennessee, but during the Depression he lost his job and
we moved to Virginia, where he caught on as a warehouse
foreman. We had current events in school, but I didn't
know or care anything about the war in Europe or the Far
East. The propaganda films were very popular—*For Whom
the Bell Tolls, Sergeant York, A Yank in the RAF*.

"One of my neighborhood buddies, Medron R. 'Nudy'
Patterson, came by the house one night on his way to
National Guard drill. He was all decked out in an immacu-
late uniform with brass insignias shining. He was a well-
built lad, very impressive-looking in his olive-drab wool
dress uniform. I secretly admired his military demeanor."

Slaughter also was attracted for financial reasons. "You received a whopping dollar per drill, and during the summer the outfit spent two weeks at Virginia Beach. We didn't have enough money for the family to vacation, and the Guard trained in the morning and gave you the afternoon off."

Presenting himself as a year older than he was for an interview with a Guard captain—Slaughter, only sixteen, was big for his age and eventually would reach six feet five—he learned that if his folks signed he might be accepted. "My parents had a fit. They tried to explain that I should first finish school, then go into the service."

Slaughter won that skirmish and became a member of Company D, a heavy weapons unit with .30 caliber water-cooled Browning machine guns and 81mm mortars in support of rifle companies. "Our National Guard uniforms were hand-me-downs from World War I doughboys—Smokey the Bear hats, wrap leggings, soup-bowl helmets, blue denim fatigues, and cavalry breeches that usually didn't fit. The rifles were the old Springfields." Within a few months, in February 1941, President Franklin D. Roosevelt directed the 29th Infantry Division to report for a year's training. Slaughter welcomed federalization. "I could send at least half my thirty dollars a month home to help with the household expenses. Besides, there was one less mouth to feed."

Born in 1921, farmboy Felix Branham grew up in Charlottesville, Virginia, a hoot and a loud holler from Thomas Jefferson's Monticello home. "I didn't care nothing about the situation in the Far East," says Branham. "But I was concerned with things in Europe because my daddy had served in Europe in World War I with the 1st Infantry Division, 'the Big Red One.' My uncles had also been in the army, and there was a lot of talk while I was growing up about the Great War. Naturally I learned to hate the Germans, whether it was Hitler or who. Before 1933 it was Kaiser Wilhelm. Everyone felt Hitler was a dog. Anything that stood for Germany I hated, anything that looked German, whether human or made by Germans, I hated.

"It was expected in Virginia that young fellows, when they became of age, would join the National Guard, which was also known as the Virginia Militia. I enlisted in 1939 and was assigned to Company K, which was also known as the Monticello Guard. It got that name when Lafayette visited Mr. Thomas Jefferson.

"When we were called up for federal service in 1941, we were sent to Fort Meade, Maryland. We traded in our riding britches, wrap leggings, campaign hats, and old World War I flat-type helmets for new clothes and equipment. For the start, though, we received six M-1 rifles to the entire company."

Roy Stephens was from Bedford. His family operated a farm. "My twin brother Ray and I were talked into joining the Guard. We was all like one big family. In A Company we had three sets of brothers."

Bob Sales hailed from Lynchburg, Virginia, and was even younger than Slaughter. "I was tired of school. I wanted to get on with my life, and somebody said I could get in the Guard if I would tell them I was eighteen. So I signed up."

During the Great Depression, the pittance paid by the National Guard drew enlistments across the country. In California, Harold Oliver Isaac Kulju, born in 1924, started on the path to Normandy in his home state's National Guard. Unlike the men of the 116th, he could not stretch his ancestry back to colonial times. "My grandparents were Finnish immigrants, and Finnish was the language spoken until I was five years old, at which time I learned English in order to go to school." Eventually, he Americanized his surname to Canyon.

Harold Canyon lived mostly on a farm, but life was hardly pastoral. "I saw my grandparents killed when a Southern Pacific passenger train hit their Model A Ford. They were on their way to church. After that, I lived alternately with an uncle, a couple of aunts, and with my mother when I was not living alone. While on my own, I had a paper route that paid fifteen dollars a month. I could get a one-pound loaf of bread for nine cents and a quart of raw milk for a nickel that would last me all day. Sleeping quarters would be an alfalfa field one night, a eucalyptus orchard another, and a tree house on the east bank of the Kings River until my aunt let me use her barn.

"My goal in life was to make the army my career. In high school I took cadets, which was combined with gym class. I signed up for the draft in Martinez, California, but at the time only twenty-one-year-olds were being drafted. I was called up, but they noticed I was only seventeen. I then joined the California State Guard, lying about my age. They were still inactive, and I went into the Civilian Conservation Corps. After three months with the CCC, the Guard was activated and I reported for duty at the fairgrounds in Napa."

Bernard McKearney, born in Camden, New Jersey, in 1917, was another national guardsman, with slightly different reasons for his enlistment. "My parents were Irish immigrants. My father was a railroad man all of his life. My mother went to the fifth grade before she was forced to quit school to raise four brothers and a sister.

"I was an altar boy until I graduated from high school. Later, in the 101st Airborne, I often served mass for Father Andy, the chaplain for the 502nd Regiment. In high school, I was a poor student who graduated in the lower fifth of my class. I was lousy in baseball and basketball but was a good boxer and a better than good football player. I eventually became the starting guard for the Screaming Eagles, the 502nd Parachute Regiment team.

"There was nothing to rebel about when I was a youngster. I loved my family, my church, and my boyhood friends. The family never had any discretionary money before, during, or after the Great Depression, but my father worked every day and we had enough. My concerns as a teenager were to be good in sports, learn to dance, and get up enough nerve to ask a girl for a date. To me, German and Japanese aggression were a world apart.

"I joined the Howitzer Company, 114th Infantry, New Jersey National Guard, when I was a senior in high school. This meant I could play basketball in the Armory, and we received one dollar a drill. When the Guard was called into active service in September 1940, many old-timers flunked their physical. I was made first sergeant of the antitank company, at twenty-three, the youngest in the regiment."

Robert Edlin was a seventeen-year-old "country boy" in 1939 when he entered the Indiana National Guard, where, like his Virginia contemporaries, he was instructed in the barest essentials of military duties. "We went to drill one night a week, receiving a dollar for each night paid quarterly. That twelve dollars made us feel we were rich. These were the days of piss-pot helmets, 1903 rifles, stovepipe mortars, and a few old-time sergeants who trained us in the World War I tradition. But what could you teach a bunch of green-ass rookies who were interested only in baseball, boxing, basketball, and girls, not necessarily in that order? We went to Fort Knox, Kentucky, for two weeks' summer training. That '03 rifle kicked like a mule, and wrap leggings were a mystery I never solved.

"In November of 1940 we were told to get our affairs in order. We were going on active duty for one year. Drastic changes took place. Many of the older, married men with children were released. The draft started and some younger fellows enlisted to be with friends.

"On January 17, 1941, a very nondescript group of civilians reported to the National Guard Armory. I was promoted to the heady rank of corporal and given command of a 60mm mortar squad. Even Gen. MacArthur had never received such an honor, two stripes and command of four men, even though I had never seen a mortar and didn't even have a weapon of any kind. I was a soldier—damn. I could hardly wait to get on that train. Look out, Hitler, here we come.

"After we were activated, we prepared for the train ride to Camp Shelby, Mississippi. Hundreds of people lined the streets of New Albany, Indiana, to see these elite units, B Company and D Company of the 152nd Infantry, 38th Division, following the high school band to the depot. Wrap leggings proudly flapping in the breeze, full field packs falling apart, dropping blankets and mess gear in the streets—little did we know it would be more than five years before some of us would return. Many still lie in countries and places we didn't even know existed."

Bill Lewis, originally from Altus, Oklahoma, was born in 1921. The family migrated to Wichita Falls, Texas, when his father, a conductor for the railroad, moved his home base to accommodate his run. "I finished high school, put in one semester at Hardin College in Wichita Falls, and joined the Texas National Guard, the 36th Infantry Division." The vagaries of military bureaucracy would eventually join Lewis's fortunes with those of Bob Slaughter and Felix Branham in the 116th Infantry Regiment.

In Connecticut, Chester B. McCoid, better known either as C.B. or Mac, lied enough to gain admission to Company B, 169th Infantry, the local National Guard unit, although he was only a sixteen-year-old high school student. "Adding a couple of years was in no way unusual at a time when size and seeming maturity were all the commander and first sergeant used when gauging a recruit's potential. My motivation came from a lifelong interest in all matters military [McCoid's father, divorced from his mother, was a regular army officer] and a growing awareness that a world war was an approaching certainty. An additional consideration was the prospect of an easy dollar per week drill money along with the pay from annual summer training or maneuvers, fifteen dollars.

"When the 43rd Division was federalized in February 1941, I was the recently promoted sergeant of the light machine gun section of our company's newly formed weapons platoon, which was without either mortars or machine guns at that juncture. I was still in high school but left without too many regrets. The academic authorities very kindly graduated me in absentia, five months later."

On New York's Long Island near the village of West Freehold, the family of Edward Jeziorski grew potatoes. "Money was always tight," says Jeziorski, who was born in 1920. "We worked with horse teams until the early 1930s, when we got our first tractor. A friend of mine, who would later become my brother-in-law, convinced me to join him in the National Guard, the 119th Quartermaster Regiment, in April 1940. The extra dollars for drills were welcome. We were federalized in September for a one-year period."

The Illinois National Guard attracted a Norwegian

immigrant, Raider Nelson. "I was born in Oslo in 1921 and came to the U.S. when I was four. My mother was a homemaker, and my father worked in Chicago for a large dairy company.

"I was an athletic and adventurous kid. I traveled all over the city riding the bumpers of cars or the tailgates of trucks. I hopped freight cars and earned pocket money selling coal I borrowed from coal cars to our neighbors. I used bushel baskets and gunny sacks hauled by sled. It was the adventure rather than the money that attracted me. I had very good parents. They didn't care if I went to China so long as I came home at suppertime.

"I followed events in Europe. Whenever I went to the movies and watched the Pathé News I saw that no army in the world could beat the French with its Maginot Line that housed an army of soldiers with their elevators, trucks, armament, et cetera. When the German Army conquered all of France, I was devastated. Then again when they invaded Norway, I couldn't believe it. From then on I certainly had no love for the Germans and especially Hitler.

"I completed four years of high school but never graduated. While in high school, I belonged to the National Guard. In March of '41, I went to Camp Forrest, Tennessee, for basic training, but after Pearl Harbor, I was placed in the 136th Infantry Regiment. A notice went up on the bulletin board that paratroopers were needed. Wow, that's for me, I thought. If I'm lucky, I might even get to jump into Norway. I volunteered for paratroop school in July 1942."

While the National Guard outfits attracted young men impressed with uniforms or the modest rewards for service, the 1st and 4th Infantry Divisions, old-line regular army units, also drew volunteers. Both divisions had served with the AEF in battle against the Germans during 1917–18 and continued as active military organizations, albeit on the meager budgets allotted during the years between the great wars.

Even here, geography initially stamped its imprint on the soldiers. The 1st Division, with one regiment quartered at Governors Island in the New York City harbor and another at Fort Devens, Massachusetts, included mostly New Yorkers, Pennsylvanians, New Jerseyites, and New Englanders.

George Zenie's parents, like Bernard McKearney's, were immigrants. The Zenie clan's roots were in Beirut, Lebanon. "My father had actually joined the U.S. Army, serving from 1913 to 1914, at which time he was honorably discharged. He worked at a series of jobs, sales, delivery, and as a streetcar conductor. But he was killed in an accident when I, born in 1920, was only eight months old and my brother was two.

"My mother was a fine seamstress and worked in the garment industry to provide for my brother and me, as well as my father's mother, who lived with us in our cold-water flat.

"When I was seven, a local grocer hired me to work in his store and to make liquor deliveries—this was during Prohibition—because he felt no one would suspect a young boy. I was given lunch, seventy-five cents a week, and tips. In high school I worked in a record store and as a soda fountain clerk and delivered newspapers. I played basketball on the church team. I wasn't interested in world events; my concerns were the 1939 World's Fair, basketball and girl-friends."

Zenie graduated from high school in 1938, but one job in a lingerie business vanished when the firm folded, and his next position with a sweater manufacturer also ended.

"Since I had no luck finding employment, I enlisted in October 1940. Because I requested a post close to home, I was sent to Fort Hamilton, Brooklyn, where a new unit was being organized, the antitank company of the 18th Infantry Regiment in the 1st Infantry Division.

"When I enlisted, my original company officers and indeed the officers of the 1st Infantry Division were, for the most part, West Point graduates. They ran their outfits by the book, but we expected that, and we respected them. Our division commander, Maj. Gen. Terry Allen, and Brig. Gen. Teddy Roosevelt, Jr., the assistant division commander, were revered. Our noncoms were also old army. They enjoyed telling us what a sad state the army had come to, to have people like us in it. They drilled us and worked us very hard. Later in North Africa, Sicily, France, and Germany, I thanked God they had pushed us.

"I was made a driver on the half-ton truck that pulled the 37mm antitank gun. I had to care for my truck, protect the gun crew—I carried a BAR, a Browning Automatic Rifle—help position the gun, and, when necessary, work as a gun crew member, leading or even firing the gun. I was taught to use the BAR, M-1, .45 pistol, and .30 and .50 caliber machine guns also."

Fred Erben, a native of Brooklyn, grew up in the shadow of the huge Brooklyn Navy Yard. "I dropped out of high school after three years and joined the Civilian Conservation Corps. We built roads, cut down trees, planted new ones. We also fought forest fires. I was stationed in a camp at Elk City, Idaho, a summer camp, then Riggins, Idaho, for the winter. The difference was that in one we lived in tents while the other had barracks. The pay was a dollar a day, more than I got when I enlisted in the army in January 1941 as a private at twenty-one dollars a month. I was seventeen years old, and I joined the 16th Regiment of the 1st Division to train at Governors Island."

A third New Yorker who chose military service in peacetime America was Bronx-born Bill Wills. "My father was the chief engineer of the New York Botanical Gardens, and my mother was a housewife and the best mother in the world.

"I was a scrappy kid who liked to fight, also a pretty good ball player. When I graduated from De Witt Clinton High in 1938, I worked part-time at the A&P, at gas stations, at the Botanical Gardens, and even on a farm in up-state Sullivan County.

"I was twenty-one when I enlisted in the regular army in October of 1940. [The peacetime draft was about to begin.] I was assigned to the 1st Engineer Battalion, part of the 1st Division, at Fort Dupont, Delaware. We lived in a tent city for about three weeks while receiving shots, clothing, and equipment, some of which dated back to World War I. There was never a real boot camp training program. Instead, you were put in a squad and a corporal taught you close-order drill and similar stuff. Then we went into the field and received on-the-job training in bridge building, demolition—we blew up the old fort's gun emplacements.

"We did a lot of marching and exercising to get into shape. We qualified on the rifle range with the Springfield '03. There was only one .30 caliber, water-cooled machine gun available, and it was passed from company to company.

"The outfit shipped to Fort Devens, where the entire division got together for the first time. Training intensified, emphasizing bridge building, river crossings, and weapons."

The 4th Division, with a home base at Fort Benning, Georgia, originally drew its prewar men from the South and Southwest. Ollie Clark, a farmboy from Kemper County, Mississippi, born in 1913, says, "I worked for the WPA [Works Progress Administration] in Noxubee County during the Depression. I made fifteen dollars a week, using a mule and a wagon to haul gravel and dirt for the county roads. I enlisted in the army when I was twenty-five and took my basic training at Fort Benning."

Not all who enlisted before the United States entered World War II sprang from poverty. David Thomas, a Cleartown, Pennsylvania, baby of 1912, grew up in Cleveland, Ohio. "My dad came to this country at age four. Neither he nor my mother went past the third grade, and at an early age he went to work in the coal mines. He did pretty well, because he was a canny sort and invested well in the stock market.

"I wasn't much of an athlete; when I finished high school I still weighed only 105 to 110 pounds. I was more of an outdoors kid, hunting and fishing. I was studious, not a hellraiser, but I took no crap from anyone and had a lot of fights.

"I was always very independent, and when I was nine I decided I wanted to go to medical school. I started to sell magazines, *Saturday Evening Post, Ladies' Home Journal, Country Gentleman,* and when I was thirteen I would ride to the end of the line in Cleveland and bum rides thirteen miles to the country club, to caddie. I made one hundred bucks over the course of summer, stuck it all in the bank. I sold peanuts and cold drinks at the racetrack, worked at steel plants as a laborer while I attended college. My last two years in medical school I worked the 11:00-P.M.-to-7:00-A.M. shift as a policeman. That was pretty good duty, worth $1,651 a year. I bought a secondhand car and lived high on the hog without any scholarship for my three years as an undergraduate and medical school. I wound up less than $1,000 in debt to my parents when I completed medical school at what was then Western Reserve in Cleveland.

"I graduated twenty-sixth of a fifty-two-man class. Didn't join a fraternity for two reasons. I couldn't afford it, and anybody that hit me in the ass with a paddle was going to get decked.

"I interned at Charity Hospital and was a surgical resident. I knew what was happening; I read the newspapers. I joined the army early in 1939 because a war was coming and the best place to be was the regular army.

"There was no training for being a battalion surgeon. I started out stationed at Fort Devens hospital, then attended the Carlisle Barracks Medical Field Service School for five weeks of instruction. I spent nine weeks on maneuvers with infantry units at Camp Polk and Fort Benning. Then I was posted to Fort Knox as assistant to the armored force surgeon, an old boy named Bob Dunner. Bob didn't do anything, and I helped him. I got to be a helluva pool shooter in the officers' club during duty time.

"In the spring of 1941, a notice in the *Army-Navy Journal* said they were looking for regular army officers to join the parachute troops. I thought, that'll get me the hell out of where I was. I couldn't sit there and take the boredom. Action was something I had to have."

The gathering of war clouds that impelled David Thomas to join the army also lured others, less interested in a vocation than excitement. Vic Warriner grew up on farms in upstate New York. "My early years were happy ones," says Warriner. "I had to work long hours, and so did my parents. During the Depression years we were almost penniless. But living on a farm had its advantages: we were never hungry.

"My mother encouraged me to read, and I devoured

every book within reach. I always received high marks in school and graduated from Waterville Central School as a member of the National Honor Society. I lettered in baseball and basketball and enjoyed all sports activities. In spite of a latent urge towards rebellion, I did stick to the rules and retained a deep-seated respect for authority.

"I entered the University of Michigan, Class of '42, and survived with surprising ease the change from small-town, small-school life to the frenzy of a campus with 25,000 students. I was a slightly above average student and thought I might go to South America after graduation to pursue a career in government service.

"In the spring of my junior year, events in Europe were supplying all the headlines, and I began to think seriously about my future, the draft, and the excitement of war. Life had become dull and routine, and when one afternoon a flight of fighter planes buzzed the roof of the dorm where a bunch of us were sunbathing, I knew what I wanted to do.

"The next day I was at the office of the air corps recruiting staff, passed the exams, and was accepted as a flying cadet. The following day I hitchhiked home for what was one of life's more unpleasant tasks, telling my mother what I had done. I broke her heart, then hitched back to Michigan to finish my junior year.

"In August 1941, I was called into active duty, and my first station was primary cadet training at Hicks Field, Fort Worth. There was only one other Yankee in the whole class; everyone else was from the South, the Deep South. In spite of all the ribbing, hazing, and other unpleasantries, I completed the first part of training and became an upperclassman. I got even for all the crap I had endured.

"After graduation, we were sent to Randolph Field for basic training. I still hate the place. The field had recently received wide publicity as 'the West Point of the Air,' and the staff took it literally. Life for a cadet at that time was pure hell. I loathed it enough to try to wash out purposely, and succeeded.

"My plan was to return to college, but the Japs took care of my future with that episode at Pearl Harbor even before I could complete the paperwork for my discharge. I was transferred to a pool with other washouts from the cadet program, and just before Christmas was sent to Lowry Field in Denver to attend armament school.

"Everything that was distasteful at Randolph Field was the opposite at Lowry. I loved it there. I was named cadet captain of my class and upon graduation received a commission as a second lieutenant. I was chosen to remain as part of the permanent staff, given the job of armament supply officer with a staff of old army NCOs who knew everything about supply and whose only desire was to have green second lieutenants mind their own business.

"This was a dream assignment that many officers would have loved. But I began to get a little bored. When one day a notice appeared on the company bulletin board about glider training, I was interested. Here was something that certainly sounded exciting, involved flying, and—except for having to leave Lowry—was everything I wanted. So I volunteered."

While American youths voluntarily trickled into the military toward the close of the decade and as war edged closer, Great Britain, much closer to the shadow cast by the rise of Nazi Germany, still scarred by the losses of the Great War and struggling with the worldwide economic slump, was slow to mobilize and was hardly better prepared than the United States. During the period before the fighting began, there were marked similarities in the attitudes and experiences of the prewar enlistees.

Briton Alfred W. "Bill" Sadler, born one year after the war to end all wars concluded, had ambitions to rise from his working-class background. "My formal education in an elementary school during the twenties and thirties was dismal, albeit thorough in the three R's. I bitterly resented, and still do, the fact that my academic future was decided by one examination on one day in a strange school. I was virtually defeated in advance by the sizable inferiority complex I carried around with me. I failed that examination, which was called 'the Scholarship,' and so my dreams of wearing the posh uniform and attending Ilford High were dashed. Under the system, I was required to leave school at the age of fourteen and find work. I endeavored to improve things by attending night school."

Like so many of his countrymen, Sadler confesses to a lifelong fondness for ceremonial Britain. "Perhaps I always had a hankering after uniforms. I was always mad about brass and military bands. Having joined the Lifeboys, the junior arm of the Boys' Brigade, at age nine and transferred to the brigade proper at twelve, my main ambition was to get into the band. How I envied that select few as we paraded on Sundays and marched with drums and bugles playing.

"At long last I made it, but only as far as being given the triangle. Of course, apprenticeships have to be served, but it was somewhat demeaning, that everlasting ting! ting! ting! However, time came when I graduated to the cymbals, slightly better, but it was those bugles and drums I lusted after. Tragedy—at sixteen I was passed over for either drum or bugle. That broke my spirit and I left the BB."

By this time, Sadler says, he was aware that " 'that Hitler person' was gaining his ground in Europe as the news filtered through to us ordinary mortals via radio and the cinema newsreels. At seventeen, I was keen to be a fighter pilot. My parents objected, but it would have made no difference even if they were rooting for me. I knew in my heart my hopelessness at math would probably have prevented me from being allowed to pull the chocks away, let alone fly the thing.

"My mind turned to another lifelong craze, motor vehicles. Hitler by then was getting louder and stronger, and my best friend had joined a Royal Signals unit of the Territorial Army because he loved their uniform, which included riding breeches, spurs, and very macho leather bandolier. He was convinced girls would go a bundle on it, and it certainly helped.

"I knew my mother in particular would be upset at the thought of her only child, her beloved little boy, going into the rough and licentious army, but in my mind was the somewhat vague thought that if there was going to be a war, I wanted to drive my way through it."

The Territorial Army unit which accepted Sadler was an antiaircraft brigade of the Royal Army Service Corps. When he joined, however, it possessed no trucks but only a single dual-control utility van.

"Suddenly came the Munich crisis of 1938 and Neville Chamberlain with his pathetic little piece of paper. In a way I was relieved, and yet my inner voice told me Hitler was not going to go away just like that. We were 'stood by' and issued a complete uniform of 1914–1918 vintage. My poor mother nearly died on the spot when I arrived on the doorstep lugging that stuff. Up to then, brown overalls and a peaked cap had hardly suggested military gear to her. But puttees and webbing brought her thoughts of the trenches, the mud, and the blood.

"The crisis faded, and eventually four or five wonderful brand-new army lorries were delivered to our unit. What a scramble there was to get to drive one. As a relative kiddy, I was way down the list, because the unit included many bus drivers from nearby garages, and they were, naturally enough, trusted not to break the expensive and precious vehicles which had been so kindly provided by the benevolent taxpayers of the United Kingdom.

"However, came the Sunday morning when I got the chance to come hurtling down Whalebone Lane towards the A127 Southend Road, fighting with a multigeared monster and terrifying everybody else in that spacious cab until, by what seems now to be a miracle, I actually found a gear and got things under control just before a roundabout."

Sadler had completed his motor school course and passed his army driving test by mid-August of 1939. "My TA unit was scheduled to go away to annual camp as usual, but this time it was for a month instead of the usual two weeks. I reported at the drill hall and checked in, and I will always remember the exact words uttered individually to us: 'You are now embodied until further notice.' At that time I didn't really know what the word 'embodied' meant, but I soon found out." It meant absorbed as a member of the British Army.

Another Territorial Army recruit was Horace Wright.

Born in Bournemouth in 1918, George Edward Wright, son of an electrical contractor, completed his schooling at age eighteen and worked as a clerk in London. "I initially favored Neville Chamberlain and his policies, but by 1939, I sensed these would not succeed. I realized we were likely to become involved. I volunteered for a regiment of the Territorial Army. We were called up immediately upon the outbreak of hostilities."

"I left school at fourteen years of age, in 1927," says Liverpudlian James Murray. "These were Depression years in England, and most boys of my age had to go to work as soon as possible. I joined the army on September 4, 1939, as soon as the recruiting office was open." Murray had responded to the declarations of war between his homeland and Germany, after Hitler sent his legions over the Polish border.

June 6, 1944, lay almost five years ahead, but overnight, while the Americans still prepared for the possibility of a war, the forces of the United Kingdom had been committed to one. The pace of preparations for the U.S. soldiers remained slow, however. Most Americans hoped to avoid participation in a second world war, and there was active opposition to becoming involved. Although England was now at war with Nazi Germany, the military effort was sluggish and defensive; Britons were seemingly unaware of how powerful a force the Third Reich could muster.

# CHAPTER 2

# WAR IN EARNEST

GERMAN TROOPS FIRED the first shots of World War II on September 1, as the Wehrmacht launched its Blitzkrieg against Poland shortly after Bill Sadler was "embodied." The speed of the Nazi conquest surprised much of the world, but most Americans believed the combined strength of the British and French forces blocked any German drive to the west. The French Maginot Line, an intricate series of bunkers and walls featured in newspaper stories and newsreels of the day, seemed impregnable. It was the latest advance in the trench warfare that had marked the war to end all wars more than twenty years earlier. Military experts for the Western democracies drew upon the only experience they had. They relied on the equipment that had served them the last time, and they clung to the old traditions of class, discipline, and proper combat conduct.

The Germans digested Poland during the "phony war" that followed through the autumn, winter, and first months of spring into 1940 as hundreds of thousands of United Kingdom soldiers joined the *poilus* (French enlisted men) guarding the frontier.

The slow pace and hoary customs of the British Army,

however, gnawed at Bill Sadler. Having achieved his dream of getting behind the wheel of a motor vehicle, he languished in the post of batman for a lieutenant. "I hated it, every single minute. I had to iron shirts, polish his Sam Browne belt and his shoes, make his bed, bring him tea, and suffer his criticism over many of those tasks."

By January 1940, Sadler had joined the British Expeditionary Force in France. "The estaminet was the village bar, the nearest equivalent to a British pub and where, with our sudden wealth of two hundred francs a week, we could go raving mad. Liquors cost seventy-five centimes a go; that was the pay of a French soldier per day! For that relatively short period of time we were the GIs of France. Hardly surprising that the *poilu* did not go a bundle on us."

The idyll in France ended on the morning of May 10. "I looked out the window and saw a Lewis machine gun lorry passing by, with a soldier firing into the air. Gradually, the news filtered through—the balloon had gone up, the Germans were attacking, and the phony war was at an end.

"Before long the refugees started to pour onto the roads. Progress was nearly impossible. I had to weave my way between pedestrians, the cars, the carts, and the bicycles. Then the German bombers would come, the road would clear as if by magic. I would put my foot down and we would approach one hundred miles per hour while the going was good."

Sadler and his mates joined a general movement forward into Belgium. "We were kept in complete ignorance. In the absence of information, we fondly imagined we were at least holding our own. During the phony war we had been fed tales about the Germans' having cardboard tanks and the like. But the Blitzkrieg they launched on countries such as Poland and now Holland didn't seem to be carried out with cardboard. We felt rather uneasy."

Suddenly, Sadler became part of a retreat degenerating into a rout. He and his fellow drivers were appalled at orders to destroy their vehicles. They smashed the cylinder blocks with sledgehammers, dumped bulk rations such as entire pig carcasses into pits, then piled into a handful of trucks, only to abandon them after being told, "It's every man for himself. If you walk in that direction you will reach the coast."

Sadler hiked on until he breasted a rise and beheld the scene near Dunkirk. "The dunes and the flat sand behind were completely covered in a hellish mixture of abandoned equipment, vehicles, and many lines of soldiers, a lot wearing greatcoats and steel helmets, snaking out into the sea." They were waiting for vessels to carry them off. Some soldiers had driven their vehicles out into the sea to form a pier. Men reached the small boats by scrambling along the tops of trucks.

Periodically, the enemy tormented those on the beach with air strikes. "The major part was the dive-bombing by the hated Stukas. When they began their dive and turned on their terrifying sirens, we pressed our faces to the sand, flattened our bodies, and endeavored to become invisible. To each individual it seemed that the whole aircraft was making for a spot on the back of his head."

On the early evening of May 31, Sadler, with a group of about fifty, formed up by a noncom, went to the water's edge. Bodies rolled about as the tide shifted and he tripped over them in the twilight. "We must have walked several miles when we came to the dock area of Dunkirk. Amidst the intermittent shelling from Germans sat an officer at a small table lit by a shaded lamp. He said, and these words are burned in my brain, 'Right, men, I want you to run up this slope and along the jetty. There's a ship at the end, but there's not much tide left and you are the last group, so, run! Run!'

"We ran. I had my rifle, two canvas bandoliers of .303 ammunition, and a full Lewis gun pan of ammo. There were gaps in the decking of the mole [the jetty], and we were forced to jump these. At least one did not jump far enough and went down. There was nothing we could do, although I experienced an awful feeling of selfishness, as if I should have stopped to see if I could help.

"We reached the ship at the very end of the mole. There was the strong, friendly hand of a seaman who said things like 'Come on, me lucky lads.' " Headed for England,

Sadler says, "The feeling of relief was sublime. I was four days away from my twentieth birthday. I experienced the thrill of seeing the White Cliffs of Dover. I was like a small child who pulls the bedcover over to keep out the bogey man, but I knew the bogey man wasn't dead."

His fellow Briton Jim Murray also served with the BEF in France during the phony war. As a member of the Royal Engineers, he "made bomb stores and camouflaged hangars for the RAF. I was stationed in Rheims and life was pleasant enough until May 1940, when, in the words of my colonel, 'The balloon has gone up and we can't hold them.'

"We packed up and were chased across France, destroying our stores and bases as we went. I was in the lead on a motorcycle and heading for Cherbourg. Some miles away I saw a tank column, definitely not ours. We changed tack and went to Saint-Malo, where we got away on a destroyer."

Unlike Bill Sadler, Horace Wright, another graduate of the Territorials, had not been posted to France. Instead, he guarded areas of Great Britain deemed vulnerable to surprise attacks. In September 1940, while Sadler and the other remnants of the BEF nursed their memories of the Dunkirk evacuation, Wright was selected for officer training. Upon receiving his commission he was posted to the prestigious Hampshire Regiment (Princess Di was the honorary commander at one time) as an infantry platoon leader with the 2nd Battalion.

"In the early days," says Wright, "we were training according to the last war. The criticism can be applied to officer training also. But the Hampshire Regiment had come back from France, and the training now became progressively better due to the combat experience."

Following the disaster that culminated at Dunkirk in 1940, Great Britain, as the sole active opponent of the Rome-Berlin Axis, could barely muster the strength to ward off an invasion. While the Royal Air Force managed to stave off the German Luftwaffe, enemy submarines crippled efforts at resupply from the United States. Hitler's decision to turn on the Soviet Union in June 1941 eliminated the prospect of a German assault upon England itself. Still, the only offensive actions by the U.K. lay in an occasional aerial raid and the elite Commandos.

The birth of the Commandos dates back to the darkest period of the war. On June 4, 1940, only four days after the rescue of Bill Sadler from France, Winston Churchill declared to the House of Commons, "We shall not be content with a defensive war." To back his words, the Prime Minister, with a lifelong infatuation for derring-do, directed, "We should immediately set to work to organize self-contained, thoroughly equipped raiding units." Subsequently he added, "Enterprises must be prepared with specially trained troops of the hunter class who can develop a reign of terror down the enemy coasts . . . leaving a trail of German corpses behind them."

The plans called for ten commandos (the word applied both to individuals and to units) of five hundred men each. Since the "enterprises" usually involved naval or RAF support, the Commandos became part of Combined Operations, a fief eventually headed by Lord Louis Mountbatten.

Among the first recruits was Bob Cubitt, born in 1921 and a youth whose poverty background had even drawn him into the Young Communist League. "It was more a matter that I could play a drum in the fife-and-drum band," says Cubitt, who had worked as an electrician's assistant after leaving school at age fourteen. Still shy of his eighteenth birthday, Cubitt volunteered for army service. He had trained with a heavy weapons unit, and was among those who escaped through Dunkirk.

"The Commandos did most of the training within the unit itself," recalls Cubitt. "The discipline and training in the Commandos made you feel you could take on anything. We worked on the principle of me-and-my-pal. You matched up with someone and went through everything with him. You relied on him and he on you. We trained very hard and we played very hard. Col. Durnford Slater [a career military man appointed first to head No. 3 Commando] was a very good, well-respected commander. He had a most calm nature considering how we had people on the wild side, who went over the top on occasion."

Others in the British forces engaged in more humdrum activities. Saved by a destroyer that ferried him to England, Bill Murray as a member of the Royal Engineers now helped construct camps to house and train the British forces struggling to recover from their losses in France or to relieve suffering when cities like Coventry were bombed.

The swift series of German victories in Western Europe had led to the first peacetime military draft in the United States. Young men entered the service by that route starting in November 1940. Part of the American drift toward preparedness also involved the call-up of others who had signed up with the Reserve Officers Training Corps while attending college. Horace Wright observed that his country filled its commissioned ranks with university graduates, and higher education in the United States also served as a breeding ground for officers.

Wallace Swanson enrolled in an ROTC program at Kansas State University. Growing up on a farm-ranch near Sharon Springs, Kansas, Swanson says, "I had always been interested in military preparedness. Way back in my high school days, I tried to join the Civilian Military Training Corps but was rejected because of an ear infection and some color blindness."

As a halfback for the Kansas State football team, Swanson flashed enough talent for the Philadelphia Eagles of the National Football League to offer a contract. However, in July 1941, shortly after he completed four years at KSU and his ROTC course, he was summoned to active duty as an infantry lieutenant.

He leaped at the opportunity to become a paratrooper. "While in college in a pilot training program, I had wondered what it would be like to jump with a parachute. The airborne troops were receiving PR as an elite army unit, special physically and mentally. The pay was better than in other outfits. And I concluded I'd rather jump into a battle situation than have to walk or ride in with more danger because of confronting the enemy real estate by real estate." Swanson eventually was assigned to the 1st Battalion of the 502nd Parachute Regiment, affectionately known to its members as "the Deuce" or even "the Duck."

John Hanlon, a native of a Boston suburb, Winchester, Massachusetts, would also jump into France as a member of that organization. "I was born in 1917," says Hanlon. "My father, an Irish immigrant, was a cop in a town of twelve thousand which was quite rich, although we didn't contribute much to the wealth of the town. My mother was Anglican and I was raised a WASP.

"I was a jock. I didn't pay much attention to world events. I went to the University of New Hampshire, where I played on the football team and took ROTC.

"When I graduated in 1940, I was aware the British were getting clobbered, but that hadn't affected our ROTC training. Someone remarked to me, 'Why don't you go in now, spend a year doing your service, and you'll be out in '41 and then you can get on with whatever the hell you're going to do with your life?'

"I was granted a Thomas Act commission. That meant you went on active duty for a year and after that period the army had the option of offering you a regular commission. I was assigned to the 26th Infantry Regiment, part of the 1st Division at Fort Devens.

"Teddy Roosevelt, the son of the President in the early 1900s, was the regimental commander. He was a great leader. Our equipment was all right; we had Springfield rifles, but ROTC had been a joke. I knew nothing. But the division in 1940 was being brought up to snuff. Our regiment had a lot of West Pointers and old-timers like our first sergeant, Jake Sadoski. He had nine reenlistments, all with the same company. He scared the shit out of everybody, including the junior officers like me. My platoon sergeant was another old-timer who knew what the army was about. I learned something about military procedure from them, and when I completed that year I knew something about being a soldier.

"In September of 1941 I had to choose whether to accept a commission. My decision was no, but then Pearl Harbor came, and that settled where I'd spend the next few years.

"I didn't have the guts to try for the air corps, but when I saw the notice for paratrooper volunteers I applied immediately. I still owed money for my scholarship at the university, and there was a hundred dollars a month extra for a paratroop officer. I also was caught up in the glamour that went with jumping. The few troopers I saw in their boots struck me as ten feet tall. My battalion CO refused to endorse my first application. A month or two later, in March or April, they took away the ability of a CO to turn down such a request."

"I was an army brat," says Homer Jones, another D-Day paratrooper. "My father had graduated from Annapolis, but when he got seasick he transferred to the army. My Dad had been on Corregidor, and when we were in the Philippines everyone took it for granted that there would be war with Japan. I was a normal teenager, physically active but mentally a bit lazy. I did a lot of reading of pulp magazines—they were usually stories about World War I.

"I had two brothers, and we all became career army. My eyesight wasn't good enough for me to enter West Point, so I enrolled in the Citadel [a private military college]. I graduated in 1942 and almost immediately volunteered for paratroop training."

Morgan C. Adair, a native of Marietta, Georgia, also followed the route from a college reserve program into the army. "My father was a graduate of Georgia Tech and worked as an engineer for AT&T for forty years. I was not very athletic but studied hard and was salutatorian for my 1932 graduating class at Druid Hills High School.

"While I was working as an extern in Georgia Baptist Hospital, Hitler marched into the Sudetenland [Czechoslovakia, 1938] and I thought this might eventually involve me. In 1939, I graduated from Emory University Medical School, and then I interned at Grady Memorial Hospital in Atlanta for two years. In the summer of 1941, I enlisted in the Army Reserve Medical Corps, with the commission of a first lieutenant. I went on active duty in September of 1941 as a hand surgeon at the Fort Bragg Station Hospital No. 3. In August of 1942, I was transferred to Fort Gordon, Georgia, and assigned to the 4th Division. I trained with the troops and never attended the Medical Field Service School."

Other U.S. military arms also enhanced themselves

through college reserve programs. For example, Harvey Bennett of New York City earned his degree from Yale in 1940. Shortly thereafter, he enrolled in the Navy V-7 program. Following a ninety-day course at the United States Naval Academy at Annapolis and postgraduate instruction, Bennett served a brief tour with the Marine Corps learning more about the specialty of naval gunfire liaison officer. The role would be critical when the invasion forces grappled with the enemy on the Normandy coast.

Richard Willstatter's direct paternal antecedents lay in enemy territory. His father had been born in Karlsruhe, Germany, and emigrated to New York City in 1889 at eighteen. Starting at the bottom in Wall Street, the elder Willstatter bought a seat on the New York Stock Exchange when he was thirty. Although he died in 1931, when Richard was only ten, the family affluence allowed the boy to attend the Riverdale Country School from the sixth through twelfth grade and then, on the same path as Harvey Bennett, enter Yale in September 1939, while the German armies crushed Poland.

"We were very pro-English and anti-German," remarks Willstatter. "Most of us assumed the U.S. would eventually be involved. As a budding engineer, I thought volunteering for the navy made sense. I believed I would do engineering, and I had always enjoyed nautical things—small-boat sailing for example. In late 1941, I signed up with the navy, and my commission was dated March 3, 1942, while I was still a junior at Yale. My commission, and thousands like it, was probationary, good until successful graduation from college and going on active duty."

For Ken Almy, the Naval Reserve program probably postponed his active duty by several years. Of Irish descent and originally from San Francisco, Almy attended schools in California until the family moved east in 1937.

"I was an average student, not motivated academically, who really loved outdoors activities like hunting and fishing, and I was a good golfer. This was a time of early laid-back California. I mixed stints at public schools with three years at a military academy in Palo Alto and three years in a Jesuit prep school.

"My father was an executive for a large insurance company, and during the period of 1920–39 you could call us affluent. The Depression to us on the West Coast seemed only hearsay. We had paid a good deal of attention to happenings in Europe during the thirties, but on the West Coast it was the Japanese that we considered our principal threat. Not until I was back East did Germany become more worrisome to me.

"I had enjoyed my military school experience. I liked the discipline, the regimentation, and always loved a parade. We played war games in the next-door lot, using dirt clods as hand grenades. My brother and his older friends were always the Yanks.

"I entered Moravian College in Bethlehem, Pennsylvania, in 1940 and in '42 enlisted in the Naval Reserve. They returned me to the college under the V-7 program. I don't know why I joined the navy except that I was never one to slog in the trenches."

The training and call-up of reserve officers was one factor affecting the overall character of U.S. military forces. More profound change came with the influx of newcomers via the draft, which drastically altered the insular personality of the National Guard.

"The first draftees assigned to the company," says Bob Slaughter of the 29th Division, "arrived in the early spring of 1941. These men were from southwest Virginia, east Tennessee, and western Kentucky. A few weeks later a second group of 'selectees' were integrated into the company, and these men were from north of the Mason-Dixon line, Pennsylvania and Maryland, and gave real meaning to the motto of the 29th, 'the Blue and Gray Division.' The ethnic origins included Irish, Polish, and Italian, and most of them were Roman Catholic.

"They laughed at the thick-tongued drawl of the mountaineers from Appalachia. And the southern rednecks had to strain their ears to understand them. When I went on a pass with an Italian boy, he took me to a restaurant where I had spaghetti for the first time in my life."

As 1941 drew to a close, Slaughter and his fellows in the 116th Regiment mucked about in war games. On

December 7, Slaughter's battalion paused in Virginia, en route to Fort Meade, Maryland, where the men, having fulfilled their obligation for service, expected separation from the army.

"It was a chilly night and the first platoon was huddled around a blazing campfire. Some men were playing cards, others just watching the blaze. I was lying on a blanket on the ground, almost asleep. Motor Sergeant Bill Hurd burst into the area screaming, 'The Japs have bombed Pearl Harbor!' I remember saying, 'Shut up, Bill! We're trying to sleep.'

"Hurd yelled, 'I'll swear it's the truth!' The attack had occurred in the morning, Pacific time, but due to our isolation and lack of communication, it was late afternoon before we heard. Anger and frustration overcame us at such a cowardly act. Then we realized we were not going home after all."

Richard Conley, with Pennsylvania's National Guard 28th Division on its return from maneuvers in the Carolinas, remembers a similar reaction to the events at Pearl Harbor. The outfit had paused to bivouac when the attack was announced. "There was total silence for about a minute and then Sgt. McDermott said in a loud, clear voice, 'There goes me fucking furlough.' "

The U.S. 1st Infantry Division, in which Northerners Fred Erben and George Zenie enlisted, also added a more cosmopolitan touch with men originally put in uniform by the draft. From his home in Charleston, South Carolina, in August 1941, twenty-two-year-old Bill Behlmer rode a Greyhound bus to Fort Jackson in his home state with five other draftees. "I was asked what branch of service I preferred. I answered that it didn't matter, since it was only for a year. I had thirteen weeks of basic infantry training at Camp Croft, South Carolina, and I loved every minute of it—manual of arms, close-order drill, long hikes, marching, even the food. We were issued blue denim fatigues, and no one advised me to wash them first. After a day in the sun I was purple for three days."

Behlmer was on KP, peeling potatoes while awaiting assignment, on December 7. "We were listening to music played by Sammy Kaye when the news broke about Pearl Harbor. We were immediately issued rifles and live ammo and then walked guard duty around the camp. Before, the rifles were always locked up.

"Attitudes changed, those of the civilians and us. Before then, civilians would not speak to soldiers on the street, ignoring us completely. Now, they became friendly and treated us with respect.

"I had a ten-day furlough, and when I returned to Camp Croft, the other fellows had already been shipped out. The CO said the 1st Division needed replacements immediately and they would be one of the first units shipped over. About five hundred of us went by troop train to join the 1st Division at Fort Devens.

"When we arrived, the regular army treated us coldly, because we were draftees. I was issued an M-1 rifle, live ammo, and a pair of skis. I had never seen a pair before, and that made me nervous. But after about a week, we turned in the skis.

"The 16th Infantry Regiment was a spit-and-polish outfit. The regulars taught me how to shine my shoes, iron creases in shirts, polish brass buttons. I ate it up. It didn't take long for the regulars to realize that us draftees were going to be good soldiers and pretty savvy. They began to warm up to us and take us under their wings. When I sewed on my 1st Division patch and put the 16th Regiment insignia on my uniform, I stood tall and proud. I was where I belonged. One of the regulars even let me wear his dress blues uniform to a dance on the base. It was the only dress uniform I ever saw.

"Most of our officers were West Pointers and very knowledgeable. Our CO, 1st Lt. Charles Denholm, a West Pointer who made captain shortly after I arrived, was one of the finest soldiers I ever met. He really cared for his men; we called him Mother Denholm."

The Japanese attack on Pearl Harbor had brought the war to America, albeit via a series of Pacific outposts. Meanwhile, in Europe, the British pricked the skin of Hitler's empire through the Commandos. Bob Cubitt, the erstwhile Young Communist drummer boy, participated in the first significant Commando thrust, the raid on Vaagso, a port on a Norwegian fjord. The results were eminently satisfactory with about 150 Germans killed and another ninety-eight captured. Several vessels were sunk, some heavy guns were destroyed, and a number of factories went up in smoke, thanks to the demolition team of which Cubitt was a member. Seventy-seven Norwegians boarded the small fleet for the return to Britain and to join the Free Forces. The Commandos lost twenty killed, fifty-seven wounded. The threat of similar attacks forced the enemy to spread its troops over a much wider coastline.

While Vaagso could be counted a success, the Dieppe operation later in 1942 was an unmitigated fiasco, with enormous losses, 4,300 casualties among the 5,000 men, most of whom were Canadian. A German E-boat (the Teutonic equivalent of the American PT boat) patrol dispersed the landing craft flotilla designated for some Commando units. "My troop was in reserve, waiting to go in as part of the second wave," says Cubitt. "It was very frustrating because there were no landing craft to take us. We never even made it ashore." Memories of Dieppe would influence Allied planning for the invasion of Normandy.

The entry of the United States into the shooting war quickly altered the circumstances of army life for the youthful 43rd Division machine gun sergeant C. B. McCoid. "Our division was gutted to furnish a regimental combat team for the Pacific. Those of us left behind faced month after month of training raw recruits, not a particularly happy prospect if you wanted to get overseas. Then came a means of exit, Officer Candidate School at Fort Benning.

"Upon graduation, I entered the parachute school. There was no screening other than a face-to-face interview, since those at OCS were presumed to be in reasonably good physical and emotional shape. With activation of several new parachute regiments scheduled soon, there was a need for second lieutenants.

"I'd always been fascinated with the idea of parachuting ever since watching a single jumper at a country fair in 1928—he broke his leg. The incentive pay, an extra $100 for an officer, when second lieutenants only earned $150 a month, would boost one's means nicely. Finally, the shiny boots, the jump wings, the parachute shoulder patch, and the swagger were the source of envy among the un-anointed. Troopers felt these special items, and the money, attracted the girls."

Added to the mix of the 4th Division by dint of his draft board had been Charles A. Mastro, son of an immigrant from Italy who settled in White Plains, New York. "When they started the draft in October of 1940, I was at the top of the list. By February 1941 I was at Fort Benning, enter-ing the 22nd Infantry Regiment of the 4th Division. We were in what's called the Harmony Church area, with no paved roads and plenty of mud. I got married in May, and in November my wife came down for a visit. Along with my buddies Vic and Pete, I was getting ready to go on reserve status. On December 6, I was made a sergeant. We had rented a house off post, and an MP came around a day later. He asked, 'Don't you guys listen to the radio?' When we got the news, the reaction was 'Oh, shit!'

"Almost immediately, we got rid of the old Springfield rifles and were issued new M-1s and air-cooled machine guns. Everything was full of Cosmoline, the grease they used to prevent rust, and the weapons all required hours to clean.

"My first post–Pearl Harbor assignment was to take a platoon down to a railroad trestle over the Chattahoochie River which the residents used as a shortcut to the brick mills. Our orders were to keep anyone from using it; they were afraid of sabotage, I guess. But it meant an extra one-and-a-half-mile hike for the people."

Bob Meyer, a precocious Illinois youngster, quit high school at sixteen to clear snow from state highways. His ab-breviated education later cost him opportunities in the air corps and OCS.

"When I was called up by the draft [while the United States was still at peace] I was probably in some sort of mi-nority in that I was pleased when I was accepted. The ex-planation for my attitude goes back to years of being belittled by my father, who, although he loved me, wasn't sure if I was worth anything at all. I was very subordinate to my older brother, who was athletically inclined. I did not shine in that area at all, and in school and at church picnics I was always the last chosen when they played ball."

On December 7, 1941, Meyer was at Camp Croft, South Carolina, undergoing special training in auto mechanics. He ran afoul of an administrative officer and was booted out of the program. Meyer joined the 4th Infantry Division.

"This was an eye-opener. These were real soldiers of the regular army. It was being used as a feeder division. Men were assigned, trained, perhaps made noncommissioned officers and then dispatched to new divisions. Because of the transient nature, morale was not high. However, I thought the outfit was great. In fact, we began to keep our men shortly after I got there.

"I was assigned to G Company of the 2nd Battalion, 22nd Regiment. Because I had been pushed ahead in school, I had grown up with no peer group of my own. Company G became my peer group, which probably accounts for the psychological difficulties I experienced later when combat began to thin out the group."

Fred Tannery had hardly cleared the induction center for his one-year term of peacetime service before the United States became a full-fledged participant in World War II. Just shy of his twenty-second birthday, Tannery arrived at Fort Bragg, North Carolina, on November 25, 1941. From there he traveled to Fort Monmouth, New Jersey, for basic training and instruction from cadre of the Signal Corps. When he completed his course, he joined Mastro, Meyer, and others from the 4th Division at Camp Gordon.

Inductee John Barner, a railroad man's son from Albany, New York, reacted both to peer pressure and the conviction that he might as well serve his year and then get on with his future. "I finished high school in 1937 and worked at a number of jobs. Whenever I looked for a better position, the first question they would ask was my draft status. When I said 1-A, they turned me down. In November 1941, I went to the draft board and volunteered."

Shipped to Fort Knox, Kentucky, Barner learned the

rudiments of armor. His group was formed into companies, tank crews, and support units, and then taken to Fort Meade to become part of the newly activated 741st Tank Battalion. To prepare the 741st for fighting in the desert sands of North Africa, Barner's outfit traveled across the country to the California desert at Indio.

Bill Lewis, who had started his military career as part of his Texas National Guard division, followed a more bizarre pathway toward Normandy. "I was part of a group of 185 enlisted men chosen while in Maryland to impersonate Germans, demonstrating their tactics and equipment. We had German uniforms, motorcycles, even horse-drawn equipment—they had to go to the Smithsonian Institution to get the right harnesses. On one occasion we were on a motorcycle, with Ernest Lee driving and me in the sidecar. At Gettysburg we pulled into a drive-in hamburger joint in full German uniform, jackboots, helmet, swastikas all over us. We ordered something to eat, and they brought it to us; nobody asked what the hell you Germans are doing here.

"Then I made the only mistake I made in the war, asking for a transfer. We could have remained there for the duration. But we wanted to go fight, which is dumb, but that's what we did. An officer promised us we could go with him to England, and we went as part of a hundred-ship convoy.

"In England we were assigned to work with a bunch of linguists, mostly German Jewish refugees who would be used as interpreters. They had been made noncoms, but none of them knew close-order drill or even how to salute and stand at attention."

It is apparent that the massive mobilization triggered by the Japanese sneak attack on Pearl Harbor and subsequent declarations of war by both Germany and Italy was accompanied by confusion over the enemy's potential for further blows. At the same time, the authorities were uncertain over Allied objectives and strategy. And even with the draft in effect for more than a year, the military establishment faltered in efforts to fill the ranks of both specialists and front-line troops.

# CHAPTER 3

# VOLUNTEERS AND ASSIGNEES

IN THE FIRST flush of patriotism after the declaration of war, many Americans enlisted. Among them was a sixteen-year-old high school senior from Salem, Massachusetts, George "Pete" Buckley. "I hated school. I was bored, always looking out the window and a terrible student. I was a kid who always got into trouble. My old man used to whack me and then I'd go out and get in trouble again. My old man would say, 'Jesus, Pete and Repeat.' That's how I got my nickname.

"I dreamt of getting away. So I forged my birth certificate," says Buckley. "It was a crude job, but this was three days after Pearl Harbor, December 10th. The recruiting sergeant at Fort Devens glanced at the birth certificate, looked up at me, and said, 'This looks okay.' My mother could have got me out if she had protested, but I told her it was too late and that there was a war on.

"I had asked for the air corps, and he told me I'd go to Biloxi, Mississippi, for basic. He said it was beautiful down there and I should take my bathing suit. It turned out to be a hellhole. When I finished basic, they sent me to Dow Field, near Bangor, Maine. I always wanted to fly, but there was no way I could qualify for pilot training, because of the educational requirements—you had to have a college degree at the time. But I saw a notice which called for volunteers to become glider pilots. They guaranteed your wings and a staff sergeant's stripes within ten weeks. The rating and the chance to fly were all I needed to hear. But it took me a helluva lot longer than ten weeks to get them."

Some three thousand miles west of Buckley's hometown, Irwin Morales, a Native American who had a degree from Oceanside Junior College and already held both primary and secondary certification for powered flight, enlisted in the air corps. "I picked the gliders," says Morales, "because enrollment was open. Immediately after I completed the course I became a staff sergeant, and then in November of '42 I was made a flight officer. My instruction also included weapons like the M-1, Thompson submachine gun, .45 caliber pistol, .30 caliber machine gun, and even the 37mm cannon." Morales's familiarity with infantry firepower would become crucial to his survival in Normandy.

Like Morales, S. Tipton "Tip" Randolph already had a flier's license, obtained while in college through the Civilian Pilots Training Program, when he entered the glider program. Son of an educator, Randolph spent his formative years in the mountains of North Carolina, where his father served as dean of a Presbyterian-sponsored institution originally catering to high school youths.

In June 1942, the twenty-year-old Randolph enlisted at the post office in Asheville, North Carolina. "You went down this alley and the air corps had the first little office. They were pushing for glider pilots. I wanted to fly and didn't care that it was not a power plane.

"You couldn't be over twenty-eight or twenty-nine, and originally you had to have a pilot's license. That last requirement was dropped because most of those who'd gone through the CPT Program were already in and they needed more people. When they put together one hundred of us from the Carolinas and Georgia, we went to Goodland, Kansas, for primary training. The instructors were hired through contracts with private flying schools all over the Midwest and Texas. We used Piper Cubs, and a big part of the training was dead-stick flying—a few thousand feet up you cut the engine.

"You developed a sense of distance and learned the feeling of dropping out of the air, what you had to do to get over to a certain place. We went to basic at Amarillo, Texas. There we used sailplanes, two-place jobs. It was a completely different sensation, flying like a bird. There were lots of thermals, and you could stay up half a day. Sometimes when they complained, you'd say, 'Hey, I got disoriented and just got lost.'

"They washed out a lot, guys who couldn't adjust to how far to turn in order to hit the right place, even though they passed the depth-perception tests. We had lots of little, quick exams in depth perception, lining up two sticks on strings. They gave you little leeway.

"Night flights knocked out a lot of people who would go all to pieces in the dark. They set out a smudge pot in front of you and you were supposed to set down close to it.

"We moved on to the actual gliders in advanced training. The CG-4A Waco with a steel frame was the American-made glider, and the all-wood Horsa, which was British, was twice as big. When fully loaded, a Waco had a twelve-to-one glide ratio. Compare that with a sailplane with a forty-to-one ratio. You could forget about thermals with the Waco or Horsa.

"While we had to be able to use a weapon and fight as an infantry soldier, the British system was different. Their pilot was integrated into the unit. He flew his people and when they landed he became part of the group, as the radio operator or whatever. It was expected that as soon as possible our pilots would return to the job of flying gliders."

Chicago-area native Eddie Ireland signed up immediately after he completed high school in 1942. By enlisting he obtained some choice in his assignment. "I didn't want to do a lot of walking, so I chose the armored forces. I went to Camp Bowie, Texas, to B Company of the 745th Tank Battalion. They made me a driver, and within three weeks I was a technician fifth grade. Other guys went to Fort Knox, Kentucky, for radio school."

Bill Dunfee, after dropping out of high school in Columbus, Ohio, occupied a number of blue-collar slots—running a filling station, driving a truck for a lumber company. He volunteered in 1942 and elected to become a paratrooper.

"I spent ten days at Fort Benjamin Harrison in Indiana," says Dunfee, "before they shipped me to Camp Roberts, California, for my basic training, infantry heavy weapons. When I completed the course, it was on to Fort Benning, Georgia, for parachute school."

Bill Lord, a Philadelphia Main Liner until the family moved to Norfolk, Virginia, while he was attending the prestigious private academy Hotchkiss, had engaged in the customary pursuits of the well-bred preppie. "I was reasonably athletic, played football and baseball all my life, began skiing in 1932, which was about as early as anyone we knew in those days.

"I wasn't studious but liked school enough to do pretty well. My father was a member of a fairly prominent textile family, and while we weren't wealthy, we were certainly reasonably comfortable. Every summer from the time I was eight until I went away to school, I either went to summer camp or traveled with the family to places like Wyoming or Bermuda.

"After I graduated from Hotchkiss, *cum laude* on June 6th, of all days, I moved on to Yale. There I enjoyed the freedom, something I didn't have any of at Hotchkiss. I took my studies less seriously. I had been at Yale only three months when Pearl Harbor came along. My studies meant less and less. I managed to fail an exam for the first time in my life at the end of my first year.

"I got through the first half of my sophomore year in an accelerated program during the summer of '42, but I then failed all of my courses except military science in the ROTC program. I decided God was trying to send me a message. I enlisted at Norfolk in October of 1942.

"Originally, I thought after basic training I would apply for artillery and get a commission because of the Yale ROTC program. But at the reception center at Fort Lee, Virginia, they asked anyone interested in joining the parachute troops to hold up his hand. I did."

Another paratrooper recruit, Lou Merlano, grew up under less comfortable circumstances in Manhattan. "You could probably have called me a feisty kid. I was more street-smart than studious. I was a junior in high school when I enlisted.

"Much to my dismay, I was sent to Fort Lee for training in the Medical Corps. I naturally disliked it, since the work had to do with books and I had joined the service with the intention of being involved in a shooting war. Furthermore, while the medical training was way over my head, everything was true military style, spit and polish.

"I played for the battalion basketball and softball teams, joined the boxing team, anything to avoid classes. In March I discovered a poster which said anyone who was single could join the paratroopers. I immediately asked for a transfer."

Sid Salomon spent his formative years in Newark, New Jersey, where his father supervised a manufacturing plant. Big and strong even as a youngster, Salomon, born in 1913, was very involved in athletics but also academically ambitious. He graduated from New York University in 1937 with a degree in business administration.

"I was working for a Wisconsin paper mill, selling packing materials used for feed. Right after Pearl Harbor I enlisted. I asked the recruiting officer how do I get to be an officer. He explained that I'd have to go through basic training and then OCS, which I did.

"After receiving my commission, I was assigned to the 100th Infantry Division. It seemed like a joke to me. We had no manual. We would stay up nights and try to figure out what to do. There was a British book about Commando activities which we used, but it was all so haphazard. I was fed up with the infantry division and applied for the paratroopers. I couldn't pass the physical. Then I had an opportunity to volunteer for the Rangers. The 2nd Ranger Battalion was being formed under Rudder [James], who was still a captain and just getting his majority. He interviewed me, and my interest in sports meant something to him, since he was a former football coach. I was accepted and we were stationed at Camp Forrest, Tennessee."

Harper Coleman of Shippensburg, Pennsylvania, attempted to enlist. "Two or three months prior to being drafted, I went to Harrisburg to enlist in the Army Air Forces. When I brought the papers home, my parents would not sign, and being only twenty years old, I could not enlist without their consent."

Drafted, Coleman traveled by bus to the induction center and from there to Camp Atterbury, Indiana, home of the 83rd Infantry Division. "The camp wasn't completed. Most of the buildings were finished but the streets were mud."

Like Harper Coleman, Nathan Fellman of Omaha also thought he might anticipate the draft through enlistment. "My best friend and I decided to volunteer after Pearl Harbor. But my mother cried and carried on so much that I waited until I was drafted, about six weeks later.

"As a kid, I had a kind of dual personality. I grew up in a neighborhood that was fifty percent black. I had many fist-fights at school. Then when I was ten, we moved to an all-white area and I had several fights with white boys. I didn't do very well. As a matter of fact, I was badly beaten. I decided to stick to studying and made the honor roll.

"I graduated from Omaha Central High in 1934 and wanted to go to college, but I had no money. My dad, in the coal business then, asked me to work for a year or two until times got better. It turned out to be six years that I worked in the coal yard and also a year owning and operating a service station.

"I had previously tried to enter the flying cadet program. I was taking private flying lessons, but in the air force physical I learned I was color-blind. That really broke my heart. When I was inducted in February '42 I was sent to Fort Jackson, South Carolina, for thirteen weeks of very rugged basic training."

High school graduate Malcolm Williams, raised in Edgecomb County, North Carolina, by an aunt after the deaths of his parents, jerked sodas, then went on the road as a candy salesman. Married in March 1942, he hoped to serve in the coast guard, "but the army got me first, in June '42." He settled in with the 12th Infantry Regiment of the 4th Division.

The son of a highway patrolman, even as a schoolboy in Richfield, Utah, Reed Jensen developed an animosity toward the Axis nations. "I felt like killing them all, but I didn't think we'd go to war. I really followed events. After high school I worked for the Union Pacific Railroad until I was drafted in September 1942, when I was twenty-one."

Jensen was chosen for service with a medical unit in the 4th Division. "Most of the men in my unit were from New York. All of us resented being medics rather than fighting soldiers. Everyone wanted to be a flyboy. They sneered at us back in camp. But when on the front lines we received respect and were called 'Doc.' "

Frank J. Wawrynovic was one of those draftees who added ethnic and geographic diversity to the 29th Division. "My parents were both Polish immigrants, and my father worked as a coal miner in Pennsylvania, as I did from 1936 to 1942, when at age twenty-four I was drafted. I had graduated from high school in the top fifth of my class and spent a year in the CCC. The time there was good preparation for later army life, for the CCC camps were administered by army officers."

John Beck, a Philadelphian, put aside his knickers and long stockings to dress in his first pair of long trousers for his graduation from a Philadelphia parochial school in 1932. "If I could have gone to college I would have wanted to study law. But when I finished high school in 1936, my father became ill with tuberculosis, and I had to go to work for twenty-six cents an hour with Westinghouse Electric. I became the main support of a family of eight, my father in the sanitarium, my mother, brother, and sisters.

"When the draft started in 1940, my brother and I registered. In a family decision, it was decided that my brother would go into the army, as I was making good money and could support the family in a better fashion.

"In 1943, I told my mother I wanted to enter the service, since some of my sisters now earned paychecks. I was assigned to Company A of the 87th Chemical Mortar Battalion, which fired a 4.2 mortar shell weighing twenty-six pounds. The battalion was considered a 'bastard' outfit with its six hundred men unattached to any regiment or division.

"The men in my unit, being drafted in '43, were either

right out of high school and eighteen or nineteen, or else in their thirties. I became a kind of big brother to a lot of the young boys, helping them to adjust to army life. In six weeks I became a pfc, corporal in eight weeks, and finally staff sergeant in four months."

Leo Des Champs grew up nine miles north of Albany, New York, in the town of Cohoes, "the Spindle City." His father, a harness and shoe maker, died in 1927 when Leo was only seven.

"The sisters at my parochial school were considerate of my mother's position as a widow. They overlooked a lot of my shenanigans. As a child I did not care for sports but enjoyed reading anything and everything. I remember the Hearst papers ran a series of articles on World War I, showing pictures of casualties. They were graphic, and not meant to glorify war but to show the horror and devastation.

"After I graduated from the parochial school system in 1934 I entered the public schools. I was strong-willed and feisty and didn't take well to the public school ways. I resisted following the herd, and in 1936, the principal suggested I leave school on my own.

"I entered the CCC and worked on soil erosion, building drainage ditches and removing stone walls that dated from the Revolutionary War. I was honorably discharged after fifteen months, just before my eighteenth birthday.

"I returned home, got a job in the mills as a vat dyer, then applied for a spot at the Watervliet Arsenal. I was hired to work with the plumbing gang and ran a jackhammer for eight hours a day. I had been classified as 3-A because my mother was a widow with a dependent son. [Des Champs' brother was five years his junior.] In March of 1942 I asked my mother to waive my status, and I volunteered to go with the April draft contingent. At Camp Upton [Long Island, New York] we were given our AGCT [military intelligence exam] and Mechanical Aptitude Test. Based on the score of those tests I was assigned to the Corps of Engineers."

Leonard Lomell was the adopted son of Scandinavian immigrants who settled first in Brooklyn. "Their children were all grown, but they had lost their firstborn, a boy who was six when he died. One of their married daughters knew a salesgirl who had just borne an infant, and so I was adopted. My new parents were in their fifties. I didn't find this out until I was twenty-two years old while looking for a birth certificate so I could enlist.

"We had moved to New Jersey, where my parents ran a rooming house. Things were tough, but we lived out of the ocean and river, clamming, fishing, doing odd jobs. In high school and later on vacations from college I worked in the post office.

"I was an athletic kid, high school baseball, boxing, golf, football. I begged the coaches to find me a scholarship. I got a football one to Tennessee Wesleyan College. I was a halfback but not a star. At college, I worked in the mess hall, sold sandwiches in the dorms at night, drove a truck weekends. When I graduated in 1941, I worked for the Pennsylvania Railroad as a brakeman on freight trains out of Jersey City.

"In June 1942 I was drafted. I expected that with my background I'd be assigned to a transportation unit. Instead, I was sent to the 76th Infantry Division. I loved military life; I've always loved competition. It didn't take long for me to work up to the rank of tech sergeant in charge of the intelligence and reconnaissance platoon of the 417th Regiment.

"My CO informed me that if my performance continued to improve, I was first in line to become first sergeant of the company. Meanwhile, he told me he was sending me to a divisional Ranger school at Fort Meade. Upon completion, I would organize and give Ranger training to the regiment with other graduates assisting me.

"I became one of sixty-five from the original two hundred trainees to finish the course. The division's exec, a brigadier general, called me and asked if I'd like to be a Ranger first sergeant. I talked it over with my CO and my platoon leader. After meeting with them, I realized I could get my promotion faster in the Rangers and earn more money quicker.

"I'm no Rambo. I didn't join the Rangers because I wanted to fight and to kill Germans. I went into the

Rangers for the money. I was always a money guy, and I had been helping to support my parents. I was drawing only ten dollars a month from my pay; my parents lived on my allotment and whatever else I could send them."

Jack Kuhn was destined to become a close associate of Lomell's. "We really had it rough during the Depression," says Kuhn, born in Altoona, Pennsylvania, in 1919. "I was aware of my poverty and hated it. Dad had only attended school to the sixth grade, when his father put him to work. As a kid I was not aggressive. I would walk a mile to stay out of a fight. I did not like controversy and avoided any violence, but I enjoyed individual sports—boxing, fencing, wrestling.

"I went to work for my cousins when I was a junior in high school, receiving five cents for every ton of coal we unloaded from a delivery truck. On a Saturday, I could earn a dollar. I also sold magazines and did odd jobs.

"Throughout my youth, I had a burning desire to be in the military. While in grade school, I joined a military group in Altoona known as the Boys' Brigade. We had a drum-and-bugle corps, carried real rifles. In 1935, when I was sixteen, I signed up for thirty days at the Citizens Military Training Camp, Fort Meade, Maryland. You were paid a dollar a day, and issued uniforms including a Springfield .30 caliber rifle. I loved every minute of the thirty days.

"The CMTC was designed as part of a four-year course to prepare you for a second lieutenant's commission. But I attended only the one session, because when I was sixteen, I joined Troop C of the 104th Horse Cavalry in the Pennsylvania National Guard. You were supposed to be eighteen, but we all lied about our ages. I spent four years in the Guard, receiving a discharge in 1940. After I graduated from high school, on my eighteenth birthday in 1937, I went to Pittsburgh to enlist in the U.S. Marine Corps. I failed the color-blind test and was very discouraged."

Kuhn married in September 1941 and obtained a job at the railroad shops in Altoona; he was employed there on December 7, 1941. "I was called up to serve in the army in March 1942. My wife was expecting our first child, and the

separation was hard to accept. But however difficult it was
to go into the service, I looked forward to the experience
with excitement. I know this was selfish, since it was tough
on my wife, but I wanted to be part of the picture."

Through contact with a colonel from the horse cavalry,
Kuhn gained assignment to Fort Riley, Kansas, where he
taught horsemanship to recruits, at a time when German
armor had rolled through the low countries and France two
years before and the panzers now threatened the British
holdings in North Africa. Offered an opportunity to attend
OCS right at Riley, Kuhn eagerly applied.

"I was told to be ready for a transfer, and the next day I
found that the army in all its wisdom had decided that after
my four years of guard training in the horse cavalry and in-
structional duty at Riley, I should attend the Camp Davis
Antiaircraft OCS school in North Carolina. To say I was
disgusted is to be kind. I was really pissed off.

"I spent eight weeks at Camp Davis, and it was eight
weeks of hell. I was never good at math, which the equipment required. Even with a full week of tutoring I washed
out, and I was transferred to Fort Meade. This proved a
huge break, because one day I read on the bulletin board
that the army wanted volunteers for the Rangers. I had seen
the movie *Rogers' Rangers* [a film set in colonial America]
years before, and the memory lingered. I signed up and arrived at the barracks designated for the volunteers. There
were about six others there. The first soldier I met was the
one in charge, Len Lomell, the acting first sergeant."

Frank South, a Nebraskan by birth in 1924, entered the
army toward the end of his first year at Bradley University
in Peoria, Illinois. "Knowing I would probably be drafted
before the end of the term—and the football season was
over—I decided to volunteer for induction. I was beginning to feel guilty about remaining a student in view of the
world situation. And there was something of a family tradition to enter the service during time of war."

South underwent basic training at Fort Jackson, as a
medic in the 106th Division, an outfit that later would be
all but destroyed during the German breakthrough known
as the Battle of the Bulge.

"We were on maneuvers in a wooded area when a notice stated a team on the base was interviewing individuals interested in becoming a Ranger. I was bored with the lusterless life in which I was involved. The very idea of joining such a unit, of which I knew precious little, seemed exciting.

"About twenty or thirty men went before a pair of officers and a noncom. They had our training records, our intelligence and aptitude tests, and queried us on whether we could swim, whether we had participated in team sports, and why we volunteered." South passed muster; he too headed for Camp Forrest and instruction in the arts of a Ranger.


AS THE DRAFT and enlistments filled their ranks, the 1st, 4th, and 29th Divisions, three of the better-established organizations, executed the march orders that would eventually land them on the Normandy beaches. The 1st Division, with antitank squad men George Zenie and Bill Behlmer, rifle platoon sergeant Fred Erben, the 1st Engineer Combat Battalion's Charles Murphy, and others, shipped first to England before assignment to Operation Torch, the Allied landings in North Africa designed to trap Gen. Erwin Rommel and his Afrika Korps in a pincers.

The 4th Infantry Division prepared itself in a series of U.S. encampments, including Camp Gordon Johnston on the Gulf of Mexico, where the GIs practiced amphibious maneuvers.

The Virginia-dominated 29th Division, including Bob Slaughter, the lanky Roanoke youth; Felix Branham, from Thomas Jefferson's Charlottesville turf; and a total of forty-three men from the hamlet of Bedford, augmented by draftees like Frank Wawrynovic, was selected as one of the first American outfits to reach Great Britain.

Following a spring and summer in the red-clay dust of the Carolinas and a more pleasant stay at Camp Blanding, Florida, Bob Slaughter and his comrades boarded trains that rattled north to Camp Kilmer, New Jersey, an embarkation post. Although barbed wire enclosed the installation and

MPs patrolled to keep everyone out and everyone in, Slaughter succumbed to the promise of another corporal for a night on the town in nearby Newark. "I will never forget that miserable night of eating, drinking, and wandering around downtown, lost and almost broke. We climbed the barrier back into camp and tiptoed into the barracks—where 1st Sgt. Obenshain was waiting."

Slaughter and his fellow corporal lost their stripes. "I don't believe Schilling [Walter O., the company commander] ever forgave me. Going overseas saved us."

The troops loaded aboard the HMS *Queen Mary*. Speeding at twenty-one knots, and escorted by the light cruiser HMS *Curaçao* and six destroyers to thwart German U-boats, the ship steamed along smoothly until about two hundred miles from the British coast. Although visibility extended for miles and the weather was good, the zigzag course taken by the *Curaçao* somehow brought it across the path of the *Queen Mary*.

Slaughter remembers, "There was a distinct bump that caused many of us to run to the rail, just in time to see the bow of the *Curaçao*, nose up, scraping our starboard side. There was little we could do except throw life preservers. Endangering the fifteen thousand men on our ship to save a few hundred was out of the question. The cruiser, cut in half, sank within six minutes. Of the *Curaçao*'s 430 officers and men, 332 were lost.

"The liner slowed to ten knots and limped towards port. Orders came for all Browning Automatic Rifle men to assemble on deck. Pfc Curtis Moore was assigned duty on one of the upper decks, armed with his loaded rifle against possible attacks of the Luftwaffe or a U-boat. It was reported that Capt. Schilling had directed Company D's .30 caliber machine guns be uncrated and manned."

The *Queen Mary* docked in Scotland without further incident. Within a few weeks the division settled in at Tidworth Barracks, a former British cavalry base near Salisbury Plain.

"For a short while," says Slaughter, "sightseeing the English countryside through twenty-five-mile hikes kept the newcomers occupied. Once a month, forty-eight-hour passes were given. Stonehenge and Salisbury Cathedral were landmarks seen, but under the circumstances not appreciated.

"Food was scarce. Typical fare consisted of Australian mutton, Spam, cabbage, brussels sprouts, potatoes, powdered eggs and milk, brown bread, bitter marmalade, and tea. Portions were small and waste not allowed. Sleeping quarters were similarly austere. Narrow, short double-decker bunks with straw mattresses and only two GI woolen blankets, minus a pillow, made sleeping in the unheated Victorian barracks very uncomfortable. My six-foot-five-inch frame didn't fit. If I assumed the fetal position, my rear end and knees hung over the side. If I straightened out, a couple of feet were exposed. I was so tired, though, I had no trouble sleeping."

Morale rose, and fell. Maj. Gen. Charles Gerhardt became division commander and instituted a tougher regimen of training. But eight-day passes to London salved some of the complaints, and organized sports boosted some flagging spirits. Food improved as the shipments from the States increased, but homesickness, dreary weather, and the never-ending cycle of preparing for war inevitably drained enthusiasm.

To persuade the troops that their countrymen held them in high esteem, First Lady Eleanor Roosevelt accepted an invitation to visit them at Tidworth. An orgy of scrubbing, polishing, painting, and planting preceded the much-publicized appearance. Some grumbling ensued when the men learned Mrs. Roosevelt would come on a Sunday, their usual day off.

"After an inordinately strict inspection by Schilling," recalls Slaughter, "the company marched to the church, where the First Lady awaited them. The chaplain introduced Mrs. Roosevelt, inviting her to speak to 'her boys.' Lady Eleanor, in her high-pitched voice, expressed good wishes from her husband and the nation. Her brief message was cordial and uninformative. Concluding her remarks, she asked what she could do on our behalf. A private from one of the rifle companies jumped to his feet and said very distinctly, 'Mrs. Roosevelt, ma'am, wouldn't it be better for the taxpayer and for *our* morale to send one of us home rather than sending you over here?' We almost choked."

Among those added to the Blue and Gray Division in England was Bill Lewis, who had swapped his disguise as the enemy for an opportunity to see combat. Having completed his tutoring of interpreters in the basics of army life, Lewis returned to the role of an antitank squad leader as a member of the 29th Division. "In the beginning, they didn't have any landing craft for us to practice with. They would dig a hole the shape of the inside of one, and on a given signal, we would charge out." But within several months, more earnest drill with genuine equipment began.

The flow of Americans to the United Kingdom included naval units. Ken Almy, studying under the navy's V-7 accelerated program, graduated from college in August 1943. Less than a month later he enrolled at the Naval Reserve Midshipman School in Chicago, where he was commissioned as an ensign. "A few weeks later, I was at sea, en route to England and the war."

By 1943, the army was obtaining the bulk of the draftees. Bill Hughes, a Norwalk, Connecticut, native, avoided that fate by enlisting in the navy ten days before his eighteenth birthday in June 1943. "I had one year of high school before I started work as an electrician's helper. The navy sent me to boot camp at Sampson, New York, for a few weeks, and then I reported to Pier 92, New York City. Our crew picked up LCI [Landing Craft Infantry] 491 at a yard in New Jersey. We had filled out forms about our previous experience at home and at work. As an electrician's helper, I was designated the ship's only electrician. I had tried to go to electrician school, but there was no time for that. From being a bulb changer in civilian life, I became the only electrician on a 250-foot-long ship. I had to learn on the job."

Hughes exercised a choice open to those not already in uniform. But within the U.S. Army, only two major options remained open to those seeking a change of assignment: the paratroops and the Rangers accepted qualified applicants.

# CHAPTER 4

# AIRBORNE

ALTHOUGH NOT EVEN American aviators in World War I wore parachutes, as early as 1918, a foresighted American colonel, Billy Mitchell, plotted a dramatic parachute drop of well-armed infantrymen against the Germans. His vision, left on the drawing board by the Armistice, eventually attracted Soviet, French, and Italian forces but was most fully exploited by the resurgent military under Adolf Hitler.

On June 25, 1940, the day that the French signed the papers for their surrender, an order to the commandant at Fort Benning, Georgia, directed a platoon of volunteers from the 29th Infantry Regiment to undergo parachute training.

While the theories and practices of airborne infantry have a number of sires, probably the most eloquent spokesman was James M. Gavin, whose background and personality exemplifies the label "trooper."

An orphan, adopted by Irish-born parents, he was raised in a Pennsylvania coal-mining town. Despairing of ever getting the education he desired, Gavin, in 1924, enlisted in the regular army. He became a "mustang"—a soldier who won an appointment to the U.S. Military Academy, graduating with his gold bars in 1929.

While a member of the faculty in the tactics department at West Point, Gavin volunteered for the embryonic paratroop forces, going through jump school in August 1941. Put in charge of development, doctrine, and training for the Provisional Parachute Group, Gavin studied the German tactics in Crete and Holland while formulating a philosophy to govern paratrooper selection and instruction.

Although the Germans conquered Crete, the losses among the paratroopers and glider-borne soldiers so shocked Hitler that he severely curtailed the airborne role. Gavin, however, detected a tactical failure by the Germans: they had dropped their forces directly upon the sites held by the British. The defenders slaughtered the attackers before they could man their weapons. Gavin and his associates saw the value in landing behind rather than on enemy positions.

At least as important was Gavin's determination to create an elite fighting force, superior even when involved in the tasks of infantry. "We had an idea. We wanted to tell these guys that they were the most capable guys on earth. And when they land, it doesn't matter who they meet; they can really lick them under any circumstances. And any parachute squad is worth a platoon of anybody else. We wanted these guys to find out that there's nothing too good for them; no bed too soft, no food too good, no conditions too good for them. But, by God, when combat comes, then there's not too much to ask from them. We really expected to ask anything of them and we expected them to come through.

"We tried to give a whole dimension of how to train human beings and how to get them committed and dedicated to believing in what they were doing and how to make them very combat-effective, consistent with trying to find the kind of leadership that could lead these guys. You had to be as good at anything as they were, and oftentimes better, and quite willing to do anything you ask them to do."

From the start, all paratroopers were volunteers. (Glider-borne soldiers often did not enjoy any choice, and when the men in the 82nd Airborne Division were given the opportunity to attend jump school, those who decided against it became glider passengers.) To draw men with the right stuff, Gavin and company embarked on a shrewd public relations campaign.

"We handpicked our recruiters," said Gavin. "We'd put up publicity on the bulletin boards when the new trainees were brought in. These very alert, sharp-looking guys, our airborne recruiters, would walk around for a day or so when they got there, be seen at the NCO club and the PX."

During interviews with the candidates, a recruiter might perform a series of tumbles and ask the potential trooper if he could manage a similar stunt. That provided insight into physical abilities, but according to Gavin, the gymnastics were really designed to show off the élan of a trooper. "It impressed young kids, who thought if a guy can do that and with that sharp look, it must be a pretty good outfit."

As C. B. McCoid observed, the shiny, high leather boots, the silver parachute wings, the airborne shoulder patch, the extra pay, and the publicity in the media added to the lure of the paratroopers. But once a man was accepted, the notion of being special took a tangible turn. During preliminary training, the recruits double-timed everywhere, even when visiting the latrine. They marched farther, faster, and with heavier loads than the ordinary infantry rookie. The word was "If you fall out, you drop out." They learned to use a variety of weapons and practiced small-unit tactics endlessly, because of expectations that they would fight in fractionated groups behind enemy lines.

It became a matter of pride to remain a paratrooper. To maintain that sense of an elite, ouster for a major breach of discipline or loss of nerve often meant public humiliation, with boots removed in front of the entire company or shoulder patches ripped off. The sense of brotherhood was fostered by the requirement that everyone, from general officer through chaplain, down to the cooks and bakers, was expected to jump. Typically, Gavin stressed the status of an officer when he instructed a newcomer reporting for duty, "Lieutenant, in this outfit, you'll jump first and eat last."

Gavin, perhaps more than any other man of his rank,

inspired enormous loyalty. One member of the airborne family said, "There wasn't a 505er who wouldn't follow him through hell, if he so ordered it, and they would have the colors flying over Satan's command post hours ahead of schedule."

Among the earliest to pass through the newly formed parachute school at Fort Benning was Bernard McKearney, the New Jersey National Guard member who signed up for the twin lures of basketball at the Armory and the dollar per drill.

"I dumbed my way into the paratroopers," confesses McKearney. "I had been sent to OCS Class 2 at Benning before Pearl Harbor. I stayed at the Infantry School as an instructor on the M-1 Rifle Committee. Part of my duty was working a rifle range.

"Just after Pearl Harbor, I was given a lot of cheap crap from two captains out of a new unit called the paratroopers. They were really just ragging a second lieutenant. One of them later blew up himself and members of his demolition team in Holland. The other was relieved of duty while in the States for jumping his company over the barracks area. Lots of broken limbs.

"Stupidly, I reacted to their hassling by saying, 'Any nut with balls could jump out of an airplane.' They called me; I raised them, and I was in the paratroopers. There was no screening process for transfer to the airborne. The division history says no unit CO could turn down a request for transfer to airborne units. [Actually, the power to deny volunteers existed briefly, as John Hanlon, who came to jump school later, attests.]

"My jump school training was grueling but not difficult. This was before the days of the 'mock tower' and other devices. [The very first troopers in 1940 traveled to New Jersey for several days of work on towers made by the company that installed one at the New York World's Fair in 1939.]

"Our physical conditioning consisted of running around Lawson Field until someone dropped. Then we would get a break and start all over again. Then there was a damnable rope that went up into the recesses of a hangar. Since I weighed 185 pounds, I had trouble getting to the top. We did knee-popping duck walks until it was agony to stand up straight. Capt. Jim Hatch remarked in later years that we probably lost a lot of good men by breaking down their 'hinges' with exercises that have since been discredited.

"A few days before our first jump, I fell from a parallel ladder device where we had to hand-over-hand and landed flat on my back. I was black and blue all over. The doctor said I could rest a few days but would have to repeat jump school. I said to hell with that and with the help of friends made the five jumps and graduated.

"I regale my grandsons with the statement that I was in a plane seven times before I ever landed in one. But in 1941 few working-class men had ever been in an airplane. I once asked a platoon of men if any had ever been up before their first jump; none had. I think it is fair to say that ninety-eight out of a hundred enlisted men had never flown before jump school."

Another early matriculant at the parachute school was David Thomas, the regular army physician whose sojourn with the armored forces mostly honed his skills at the pool table. "I became battalion surgeon for the 503rd in August of '41, but not until October did I enter a class at the parachute school. I thought jumping was fun, and eventually I became a Master Military Parachutist, although along the way I broke an ankle and received two lumbar fractures."

Jim Irvin, son of a West Virginia electrician, enrolled in ROTC while in college and around his twenty-second birthday, in October 1941, became a GI. "I entered the army by popular request, the draft. Because of my ROTC I was selected to do guard duty by my training instructor at Camp Walters, Texas. When I pulled that duty in excess of regulations, I requested to see the captain to express my rights. I was then relieved of guard duty and given a weekend pass by the captain.

"To my amazement, I was promoted to corporal, but the training instructor informed me I would remain under his command the remainder of my time in the army, since I was so smart. I told the sergeant I was a helluva lot smarter than he was and there was no way he could keep me. The paratroopers were recruiting in December 1941. The challenge, the extra fifty dollars a month in jump pay, and getting away from my mentor was all the incentive I needed.

"At jump school in those days we didn't even have football helmets. We wore a cloth liner with a chin strap, had no boots but jumped in our GI shoes. Only the noncoms wore sidearms. By the time I finished I had made sergeant and in April 1942 attended OCS. Commissioned a lieutenant, I was assigned to Company B, 505th Parachute Regiment, as a platoon leader."

A contemporary of Irvin's at the Fort Benning "Frying Pan" area, the desolate, sun-baked site of the paratrooper course, was a former country boy, Tom Graham. "I was a typical farm kid, occasionally spent time in the hay with a neighborhood girl, rolled cigarettes with corn silk in newspaper, and swam in the crick. I left the land to work in a five-and-dime store and then in construction.

"I was finishing basic training, learning my right foot from my left, how to make my bunk, how to march, and that the military has its own method for punishment when Doc Alden [Capt. Carlos] came to the base. He convinced a lot of us we should join the airborne. It sounded real good. The enlisted men Doc Alden had with him wore leather jackets and shiny boots, and Doc himself looked great in his outfit. [Alden, of course, epitomized the missionary project described by Gavin.]

"I ended up on a train to Fort Benning. I had mixed feelings about my first jump, especially when I looked down and saw the meat wagon with the big red cross on top which was parked by the drop zone. Doc Alden was right about the fifty dollars additional pay, which caught up with us about three months later. The parachute boots also finally came through, but the leather jackets were for officers only, not enlisted men." Subsequently, Graham followed the same route as Irvin through OCS and then into the 505th PR.

Irvin "Turk" Seelye from Pekin, Illinois, a typical Midwestern, blue-collar son, washed out of the U.S. Army Flying Cadet program in 1940. Before that, Seelye, a high school band trombonist, sandlot ballplayer, newspaper delivery boy, and car hop at a hamburger stand, squeezed in two years at Illinois State. In 1942, he enlisted, choosing jump school because he still wished to be "involved in flying" and because of the extra fifty dollars a month.

"The paratroop training was much more vigorous, hazardous, strenuous, and energetic and more frightening than what I'd had in my three months with the cadet program." Turk Seelye as a private first class became a lead scout with the 505th's Company E, third platoon.

Bill Dunfee, a Columbus, Ohio, high school dropout, had been among those enticed by Gavin's reruiters. "The 505 was in its formative stage in the Frying Pan under then Lt. Col. Gavin. The paratroopers were tough kids. Initially, my group came from the Canton-Youngstown area, western Pennsylvania and West Virginia. They were from coalmine and steel-mill backgrounds. Boozing and brawling was an accepted way of life and a form of recreation.

"You were stretched to your maximum physical and emotional endurance. In parachute school and subsequently in the 505, you were allowed only two positions, attention or parade rest. No leaning on anything or hands in your pockets. Any minor deviation from the rules meant punishment by additional push-ups.

"During July 1942 in Georgia, it was very, very hot. While in ranks, if a man fell over from heat exhaustion and you bent over to assist him, you were told, 'Leave him lay, soldier. He ain't dead.' They wanted to wash out as many faint hearts as possible before the jump stage."

Bob Kiel, who offered Fannie Farmer chocolates to his platoon on the eve of the Normandy drop, had teamed up with a buddy to seek membership in the airborne fraternity. "The first physical screening was on the lax side, but at Benning the tough stuff caught up with us in a hurry. Had I not informed my parents I was airborne-bound, I'd have dropped out, because the facilities were so bad. The training was plenty tough, with the road runs the worst. Most of the discipline meted out meant extra marching with full field packs. That got your attention."

Lou Merlano, the escapee from duty as a medic, entered the Fort Benning parachute establishment in May 1942. "I found a whole different way of life. The officers were West Pointers and gave you the feeling that they were going to take care of you. The noncoms were true physical disciplinarians. They tore you down and then rebuilt you. They made every one of us feel we were going to be in tremendous condition when they finished with us.

"I was prepared to make the first jump after three weeks of strenuous training. When I boarded the plane I had that empty feeling in the pit of my stomach. There's no question that a lot of anxiety lay behind the whole venture. After the jumpmaster said, 'Stand up and hook up,' then 'Stand in the door,' and finally 'Go!' I hit the silk. My chute opened above me and I felt great jubilation. I laughed and hollered at fellows alongside. I tried climbing the risers to see if I could spill air from the chute. I tried all the things the instructors taught us. All of the training far exceeded the needs of the jump. It was a piece of cake. From then on, I jumped every time I could. I volunteered numerous times to make practice and pattern jumps.

"I had heard that if half of our class came through to graduation, that would be an accomplishment. I didn't believe it until, sure enough, less than fifty percent of the four hundred actually made it. That in itself helped create the tremendous esprit de corps that the paratroopers possessed.

"There's no question that the paratroopers were cocky and loved to visit Columbus and Phoenix City and have a good time. We cherished brawling with other units."

For John Hanlon, the University of New Hampshire jock who switched from the 1st Infantry Division after eighteen months, the four-week course went smoothly. "The training was such that I had no trepidation at the first jump. It went easily. If there was any apprehension it came with my second one, but after that I had no problems. When I was posted to Fort Bragg with the 502nd Regiment, on weekends we'd go to the airfield where the pilots wanted experience and make extra jumps."

While the earliest graduates of the Frying Pan academy came singly or in small groups to Fort Benning, authorization for added airborne forces led to activation of entire regiments that would attend jump school en masse. In

October 1942, the 508th Parachute Infantry set up for business at Camp Blanding, Florida. The shoulder patch led to the nickname "Red Devils," but members rarely referred to themselves by that label. To lead the outfit, the upper echelons appointed Lt. Col. Roy Lindquist.

"He was a very competent soldier," says Dave Thomas, who had been named a battalion surgeon for the 508th. "He was an entirely different fellow from Jimmy Gavin. Lindquist's forte was personnel. He knew how to pick people and was ruthless in getting rid of officers if they didn't measure up to his standards. Unlike Gavin, who always dressed in fatigues during duty hours, Roy would go out to check the training while wearing his Class A uniform." Among the handful of officers and noncoms who met Lindquist's high standards was Lt. Homer Jones, the Citadel graduate who had qualified to wear the silver wings only a month earlier and completed a course at the parachute demolition school.

The draft caught Chicago stockyards worker Adolph "Bud" Warnecke a few weeks shy of his twenty-first birthday. Originally a farmboy from downstate Illinois, Warnecke says, "When I first learned to talk, I would pester my mother for buddy bread and she nicknamed me Buddy, later shortened to Bud. That was a blessing, because when World War II broke out, Adolph was not a popular name.

"My parents tried to make a living off about sixty acres of land, fruit trees, a couple of cows, horses, and chickens. I played in a barn full of burlap bags with sugar lumps. One day, three men came to the house and my father went off with them. Years later I learned the reason for that sugar. My father had allowed bootleggers from East St. Louis to operate a still on the property. The three nice men were revenue agents, and Dad served thirty days.

"After I started school with a two-mile walk each way, I became agile and liked any kind of sport. One day I got into a fight with a bigger kid and beat him. My oldest brother watched and became my fight promoter. Almost every day he had me fight some kid, behind the board fence that hid the school outhouse. When the principal found out, I was taken off the hook."

Warnecke left school after nine years of education and held a series of odd jobs before becoming a paint mixer and packer in a straw-hat factory. "My pay was twenty-five cents an hour for a forty-hour week. My take-home pay was nine-ninety a week.

"By this time Hitler had a lock on Germany and caused a lot of arguments in our German community. Some thought he was the greatest. I didn't give him much thought. I had never been any further from home than St. Louis. My current events were limited to a ten-square-mile area—who took whom to the Lakeside dance, who got drunk, and how many fights took place."

In search of economic improvement, Warnecke rode a bus to Chicago. He hired on at Swift & Co. and earned twenty-eight dollars a week for his forty-hour week. He discovered burlesque featuring two-hundred-pound strippers, and the Aragon Ballroom, with "hundreds of young girls who would dance with you for one ticket that cost ten cents." He also expanded his knowledge of current events. "The majority of people who worked in and lived near the stockyards were Polish. I really learned about Hitler from the Poles. He had invaded their homeland and I felt like they did, that Hitler was an evil son of a bitch and sooner or later we'd have to deal with him."

After Pearl Harbor, Warnecke tried to enlist in the merchant marine but was rejected because of his 1-A draft status. When Warnecke reported to Camp Grant, Illinois, a corporal interviewed him, asking what kind of unit he would prefer. "My reply was any that would help get the war over quicker. He said, 'Why don't you volunteer for the parachute troops?' My reaction was, who the hell are they? He answered they'd be in the thick of things soon. I said fine and he told me where to sign."

Warnecke celebrated his twenty-first birthday aboard a train bound for Camp Blanding and the 508th. "I was assigned to Company B, first platoon. My platoon leader was Lt. Homer Jones. His assistant was Lt. Lee Frigo, and the platoon sergeant was Forrest 'Lefty' Brewer. Our CO, Lt. Royal Taylor, whom I soon idolized, had been a first sergeant before graduating from OCS. Taylor set an example by not asking anyone to do anything he couldn't do himself. He was always in the lead during our runs and endurance marches. He taught me the first thing is to take care of your men and they will take care of you. If you get that right, you won't have time to worry about yourself. The other lesson was you must prove your loyalty to your men before you can expect theirs.

"I adapted to the discipline quickly. I did not have a problem adjusting to living in close quarters with different personalities and did more listening than talking. I thought then, and still do, that the best soldiers came from farmlands and small towns, because of having responsibilities during their childhood. Many of the big-city recruits were know-it-alls and not ready to accept the discipline demanded.

"It seemed crazy to me when they tested your mental fitness and fired questions like a machine gun—'What's your name? Why? Is Mickey Mouse a boy or girl? Lift your left foot off the ground.' By the time the interview ended I was not sure exactly what I had gotten into, but I knew I had the best squad, in the best platoon, in the best company and best regiment in the U.S. Army. We were told, and believed, that one trooper could whip five 'legs'—the term used for non-airborne soldiers.

"I was promoted to corporal, and in February '43 we moved to Fort Benning for jump school. We were in such good condition that we skipped the A stage—physical training. We were so brainwashed that jump school was a breeze. I heard that only one man in the entire regiment quit or refused to jump.

"We were the first troops to move into the tar-paper shacks at Camp Mackall, North Carolina, for advanced instruction. We trained six days a week and on Sundays, cut weeds, brush, and cleared the woods. That continued until one Monday morning there were a large number of AWOLs (not me). Thereafter, we had Saturday afternoons and Sundays off. The AWOLs were not court-martialed. Instead, they received severe and humiliating company punishment. I saw the first sergeant make one man crawl on his belly with his face in the sand to kiss his boots, while the sergeant backed up, until he figured the trooper had enough.

"The work was hard, with many forced marches in full field gear. It was tough marching in loose sand. We also practiced water discipline; a number of times I would take my helmet off, scoop water out of a stream, and drink it. Our canteens had to be full when we returned, just as when we left.

"We participated in live-fire exercise, became efficient in all weapons available to paratroopers, and learned to operate all vehicles, including armor, although there were no vehicles in an airborne infantry company. We jumped when aircraft were available, and when not we jumped from the tailgate of a truck, simulating the dispersion of a stick."

Among those in the same company as Warnecke was a Pennsylvania steelworker's son, Bill Dean. He had graduated from the CCC and enlisted at nineteen, volunteering for airborne because of "peer pressure and the recruitment propaganda."

Also joining the 508th was Jim Kurz, the offspring of a patent attorney. Kurz abandoned his student deferment and football scholarship at the University of Maryland. "I asked to be drafted in early 1943 but figured I would miss the action, so I volunteered for the paratroopers. During an interview, they warned that if I didn't keep up in the drills and runs, I could be kicked out. My attitude was that if the man next to me could do it, then so could I."

Bill Lord, the preppie and Yale flunkee, traveled from the induction center to Camp Toccoa, Georgia, before ultimately shipping out for the 508th. "At Toccoa, we were taken right from the train in trucks to a field with a mock tower. We still wore our Class A [dress uniforms] with overcoats and carried barracks bags. We put the bags down, folded the coats over them, and lined up to jump from the mock tower, which was thirty-four feet high. Theoretically, if you would jump from it, you would jump from an airplane. It was free-fall for the first fifteen feet. Then you slid down a wire to what was like a high-jump pit. Anyone who refused to jump was out, immediately.

"Then we went to the obstacle course, still in our Class

A uniforms. It was rainy, cold, and the red mud was a river of red. The first obstacle was a horizontal ladder. As a left-hander, I grabbed first with that hand, swung out and reached with my right. I slipped, falling into the red running water.

"I was asked to give the sergeant twenty-five push-ups for falling. After I finished, he told me to double-time to the latrine, get under a shower, wash my uniform, and double-time back, all in five minutes. I said, 'Sergeant, there's no way I can get the uniform dry in five minutes.' He said, 'I didn't say dry. I said clean.'

"I made it back in five minutes. When I tried the ladder again, I fell at the second rung. The sergeant asked if there was something wrong with my hand. I explained I had broken it playing football and the cast had been removed a few days before. I said I didn't want to wash out and he excused me from the rest of the obstacle course."

The brass suddenly decided Camp Toccoa was not ready to handle the influx of would-be troopers and dispatched Lord with others to Camp Blanding, where he joined the 508th's 3rd Battalion under Captain Louis G. Mendez, Jr., a "mustang" like Gavin. "Mendez interviewed every one of us. He asked me to take my left foot off the ground, which I did, and then to take my right one off the ground, and finally both feet. I jumped. He asked whether Mickey Mouse was a boy or a girl. I said, 'He's a mouse.' "

Having satisfied Mendez as to his mental acuity, Lord plunged into the regimen. "The physical training was fun. They ran your ass off, everything done on the double. Some guys did fall out, but most of us were young and in pretty good shape. We had exercises with Indian clubs, where you held them with your arms stretched out until it felt as if they would fall off.

"Discipline was basically physical. If someone went AWOL briefly, he might have to dig a hole six foot by six foot using a mess-kit spoon and then fill it. If you looked cross-eyed at a noncom, that could bring push-ups. In basic training, there was a punishment squad that met every night after dinner. They wore full field packs and tossed twenty- or thirty-foot logs around. They double-timed

with logs. It was punishment, but it helped get them in
better condition. It was not chickenshit stuff."

"Mendez was an exceptionally fine officer, very strict,
absolutely no nonsense, completely devoted to training as
well. He took the attitude that because we came from all
over, a lot of us didn't know how to take care of each other.
Very early on he used an expression, 'combat morale,'
which he told us had nothing to do with movies at the
USO. He said it was a spirit among us where everybody re-
alizes nobody can win a war or battle alone. You're
completely interdependent. He taught us the necessity to
respect those people we might command and to obey those
who led us. He later told me he was much tougher on
his officers. Generally, they were very good. Those who
weren't stayed only a short time. They showed a minimum
of compassion while trying to make us self-reliant."

"After high school in New Jersey," says Frank McKee,
another 508th member, "I had a job paying fifty dollars a
month. I had it made. We were too busy surviving to have
an interest in world affairs. I knew very little about what
was happening. One of the neighborhood guys had made it
to the Golden Gloves finals. All us young guys were interested in boxing and body building. We fashioned a boxing
ring in my yard and had regular bouts.

"Some months after Pearl Harbor I enlisted. I liked the
posters, the pep talk from the paratrooper recruiter, and the
added money, so I volunteered. We were locked in at
Blanding for about six or seven weeks and became physically tough. The outfit was a cross section of America with
good men from all segments of the population—farmboys,
woodsmen, city boys from the East, rebels from the South,
Indians and Mexican transplants from the Southwest. The
officers were mainly from colleges and military schools,
many of them from the South."

Former California state guardsman Harold Canyon,
while at the Presidio of Monterey, met another draftee who
sold him on the idea of volunteering for airborne. "I hadn't
thought of their existence, but it sounded like a good
idea." His group of recruits traveled first to Fort Benning
and temporarily received assignment to a casualty company.

"Those already in it told us horror stories about jumping from airplanes, about injuries and chickening out." Canyon squelched second thoughts and soon surfaced at Camp Blanding as another member of the 508th.

"The doctor who examined me there thought I was a little puny to be a paratrooper, but after some discussion he said he would pass me. But if I failed just once, I would be disqualified." Canyon survived to reach jump school. "When the jumpmaster tapped me on the leg and said 'Go!' the thought flashed through my mind, 'You've got to be kidding.' But I went, counting, 'One thousand, two thousand,' and at that point, the opening shock knocked the wind out of me. When I regained my breath, I finished the count—'three thousand.' I was trained to count to three thousand and that's what I did.

"I checked my chute, and from there down, I was on an incredible high. Our first two jumps were at twelve hundred feet and thereafter at seven hundred feet. The second jump was much more frightening because now I had some idea what I was doing. Most men sweated out their third jump. The sixth was again terrifying because of the long period of time since the previous one."

A product of Canton, Ohio, Elek Hartman, a fledgling actor who "lived in the wonderful world of books where I learned that to defend one's country was noble," enlisted "because we were at war and I didn't want to wait to be drafted." He too volunteered for parachute training and joined the 508th.

C. B. McCoid, who stayed within the confines of Fort Benning as he moved directly from OCS to the paratroop course, became a company commander in the 507th PR. "The senior officers were seasoned professionals. Most were regulars. They were conscientious, tough, demanding, and they did like to party. They could be compassionate but would not tolerate professional lapses on the part of their commissioned subordinates.

"Discipline was rigid. Punishment was meted out without too much reference to the manual for courts-martial. Too many courts-martial, too many AWOLs, too high a venereal rate would get commanders relieved as quickly as tactical incompetence. Most resorted to non-judicial measures"—ditch digging, extra marching tours, restriction to barracks. "The troops didn't feel abused if they had committed some offense. Most were inured to hardship and glad to avoid a loss of pay, not to mention the stockade."

Former Long Island national guardsman Ed Jeziorski, bored with patrolling the Atlantic shoreline, applied for airborne and came to the 507th. "There were no trucks available when we reached Fort Benning. We'd have to march carrying the bulky barracks bags with all our worldly possessions. It was tough in the heat. My friend Bill Poole, dragging his bag up that last long grade, said, 'Jeziorski, if I ever get to the top of this hill with this bag, I'm going to kick the shit out of you for getting us into this.' " Both men qualified as troopers.

Gavin's dream was being realized. Airborne figured prominently in operational plans for the future. But the paratroopers would still have to prove themselves under combat conditions.

# CHAPTER 5

# THE RANGERS

THE BRITISH STRATEGISTS had perceived Commando raids as an opportunity to build home morale; indeed, newsreel and still photographers accompanied the Commandos on risky adventures like Vaagso. The publicity and the modest successes inflamed American appetites for similar exploits. The experiences and the knowledge of the British raiders eventually helped shape an American counterpart, the Rangers, albeit with subtle changes as the purposes of the small, elite units shifted with the flow of the war.

While the airborne grew outsize in numbers and glamour, the U.S. Rangers remained a much smaller elite. They faced even tougher acceptance as an effective force than paratroopers and glider soldiers. Except for the modest shoulder and cap insignia, the Rangers never flourished any special trappings—burnished boots, shiny breast insignia, or distinctive headgear. The only tangible inducement lay in the additional stipend. While the apparent model for the Rangers was the British Commandos, the top U.S. strategists were not intent on raids to maintain morale and disrupt enemy operations. Instead, as Len Lomell's first experience indicated, army chief of staff Gen. George C. Marshall wanted to develop a body of well-trained, highly

motivated, combat-experienced soldiers to bring leadership
to regular units.

The original plan envisioned the assignment of Rangers
to Commando units in order to gain experience under
fire, and the very first Rangers learned their trade from
Commandos. A handful of them from the 1st Ranger
Battalion—forty-six all told—participated in the ill-fated
raid at Dieppe. Lt. Edwin Loustalot, cut down a few yards
beyond the beach, became the first American soldier of
World War II to fight on foreign soil and become a KIA.

Subsequently, the 1st, 3rd, and 4th Ranger Battalions
engaged the enemy in North Africa and Italy. Rather than
the traditional hit-and-run missions of the earlier
Commandos, the Rangers took on special tactical missions,
destruction of particularly difficult defenses or surprise assaults upon topographically impregnable objectives.

Rangers led by Col. William O. Darby first achieved notable success in North Africa. The 1st Battalion was split up
to become the cadre for the 3rd and 4th, with some veterans sent back to the United States to assist in developing
2nd and 5th Battalions. A Ranger training school opened at
Fort Meade in 1942. Len Lomell, who volunteered for
Ranger training because of the possible extra money and
promotion to first sergeant, matriculated at this institution.

"The colonel in charge was a former wrestling coach at
Columbia University, and his staff included Asian and
Caucasian experts in both boxing and judo. There were
two hundred of us, unknown to one another. We wore coveralls without any indication of rank. We went through an
awful lot of physical training and simulated hand-to-hand
combat. They would blow a whistle and shout, 'Take 'em
down!' I usually did okay, but there was one guy with
whom I had a helluva battle and who really beat me up.

"The weeding-out process at Meade left sixty-five guys
from the original two hundred. Promised my first sergeant
stripes, I was given travel orders to take them by bus
to Tullahoma, Tennessee, where a permanent school for
Rangers was opening at Camp Forrest. I had hardly arrived
when the brass canceled out the Ranger school and instead

activated the 2nd Battalion. The sixty-five guys became Company D with me as first sergeant from day one, April 1, 1943."

Jack Kuhn also began his Ranger career at Fort Meade. "The screening was done by Ranger officers. When asked why I wanted to be one, I didn't talk about God and country but that I did not want to be an ordinary dogface. I said I wanted the adventure and excitement the name of the outfit implied.

"They asked me what I would do if I had a small patrol out and came under machine-gun fire. I said if I knew our Ranger outfit had a mortar in the rear I would contain the machine gun from a safe distance with my patrol, call for mortar support, and then follow up by attacking. Then someone asked what I would do if no mortar support was available. I answered I'd flank the gun, have the men throw grenades, and then assault the position. That satisfied them.

"When a man arrived by truck, he put his barracks bag on the ground and immediately went on a five-mile speed march with one of us who had been accepted. If you covered the distance in the allotted time and appeared in good enough shape to then attack the enemy, you underwent further tests. If you failed that speed march, you picked up your bags, got back on the truck, and returned to your unit. There were no exceptions or second chances."

Initially, when Lomell, Kuhn, and the rest of the group from Meade reached Tennessee, they found the proposed new unit a shambles. A series of COs came and left, leaving a ragtag, poorly equipped, untrained band of eager volunteers. But in June 1943, James Earl Rudder, a former Texas A&M football star, college coach, and teacher, took over. Rudder moved the men from tents into barracks with indoor plumbing, improved the food, and instituted stern discipline modified by genuine compassion. When the sloppiness of a group brought disgrace upon him during a pass-in-review parade, Rudder chewed out the entire battalion, finishing his tirade with a challenge to any man who thought he could lick him.

"He was a big man, maybe a little overweight,"

remembers Lomell, "and had played center for Texas A&M. What I liked about him was that he would listen, to privates, even to the troublemakers. He was the big brother for everyone."

"Rudder brought tremendous enthusiasm," says Sid Salomon, the New York University graduate. "He was just what we needed. He knew how to organize the training, how to pick the right man for each niche and whip the battalion into shape. At the same time he went through channels and maintained the fine line between officers and men."

Lomell was temporarily discomfited when he was confronted by a new arrival, a lieutenant. "I recognized him as the man from Fort Meade who'd whipped me. 'You!' is all he could say. 'Yes sir' was all I could answer. In time, Duke Slater, who rose to captain, and I, who was his first sergeant, became strong friends."

Slater became the CO of D Company. Jack Kuhn, assigned to that unit along with Lomell, describes Slater as "the most remarkable man and officer I had the good fortune to serve with. He led by example. Everything he did produced excellent results. He was strong, fearless, and in perfect physical condition.

"He lived for today, and each day was a challenge he had to conquer in order to be happy. Whatever he started he carried to the finish, never leaving anything hanging. His presence gave us the feeling that everything was and would be okay."

But it was Rudder who put his stamp on the entire battalion. Testifies Kuhn, "None of those commanders who came before him measured up. He had a steely-eyed look when he was not pleased. There was also a look of pride when we were successful at some training exercise. In spite of his rank, he was always friendly towards the troops. He knew I was married and always asked me how Mary and our baby were doing. One day during a bull session in the field—Rudder made it a habit of holding informal gripe sessions to learn the feelings of the men—a fellow mentioned that the colonel had said every man would be issued a wristwatch. This young Ranger remarked he had never been given one. Col. Rudder declared that would be corrected immediately. He walked over to the soldier, took his own wristwatch off, and gave it to the Ranger."

Under Rudder the newly formed 2nd Battalion underwent the same sort of intensive conditioning as the paratroopers. They developed expertise in all of the weaponry available, learned the arts of demolition, drilled in house-to-house combat, and practiced assaults upon cliffs.

"As an elite volunteer unit," says Lomell, "we gave up all privileges. Rudder was extraordinarily sensitive to what was going on. He felt there were cliques developing in certain companies. He rotated one platoon from each, shipping it to another company. No wives were around, because we kept moving so fast. The training was so tough that I saw All-American football players as well as tough guys drop out."

Jack Kuhn recalls one particularly grueling kind of drill. "Anytime we worked on high places, we lost men because of their fear of heights. We trained on an apparatus where you climbed a ladder to forty or fifty feet above the ground. Then you were on a narrow walkway, facing long steel poles approximately four feet away. On command, you propelled your body into space, grabbed the metal poles, which were about four inches around, and slid to the ground. That brought numerous dropouts and injuries."

Frank South, as a medic, learned the skills of a medical and surgical technician, perfected his first-aid, bandaging, and evacuation skills, and also studied marksmanship, tactics, map-reading, and other infantry skills. "Scaling cliffs I loved, regardless of whether it was freehand, smooth or knotted rope, or rope ladder. Who ever thought the army could be such fun?

"Like everyone else we were thoroughly trained in all infantry weapons, M-1, submachine gun, light and heavy .30 and .50 caliber machine guns, BAR, 60, and 81mm mortars, .45 pistol, bazooka and demolition with gelignite, nitrostarch, and TNT. This was to make it possible for medics to act as Ranger infantry either on an 'as needed' basis or to transfer over to a line company.

"It proved to be an effective policy," says South. "We

had one man who went back and forth two or three times and another, a crack shot, who transferred to the medics for religious reasons. He was later paralyzed from a sniper's bullet. I became an active combatant several times during the war. However, whenever we were armed with anything beyond our fighting knives, we *never* wore a Red Cross brassard or carried our International Red Cross ID cards, although we would lug along our aid kits. In our battalion, we did not have those atrocious helmets with huge red crosses painted on them. No one would have allowed us on night patrols with them."

In November 1943, the 2nd Ranger Battalion boarded the *Queen Elizabeth* and sailed for England, debarking as tens of thousands of other American troops would in Scotland. "From the start," says Len Lomell with D Company, "we were billeted with local families, both while at Dartmouth, where we got both room and board, and at Bude, where we had our own mess hall. We had expected to sleep out in the open, in tents, and hadn't known this would be the situation until Slater informed us. He said, 'Think how you would feel if Englishmen moved in with your family back home. Treat the women as mothers, daughters as sisters, and the boys as brothers.'

"The British people were wonderful, and I'm proud to say our Rangers always behaved like gentlemen. There was no resentment towards us and I think the people responded to us the way we did to them. Everybody got along in the pubs."

"They accepted us," says Jack Kuhn, "as the sons and husbands they had lost or who were serving elsewhere. In Bude, we threw a Christmas party for the children. They put on a Christmas show and dance for the Rangers, and it helped get us through our first holidays away from home."

Lt. Sid Salomon arranged the lodgings for C Company. "I had a list with all of my men, and usually two were put in a house. I told them to go to the door and introduce themselves. Some of the kids from Appalachia were timid, but the people were extremely hospitable.

"When we were at Bude, the battalion took over a public garage for a mess hall. There was no reveille like at an army camp, and we couldn't blow a whistle for people. Instead, they were on their own to get up, meet in town, and form with mess gear to march the mile or so to the mess hall."

Sharing rooms in civilian houses added to the sense of brotherhood in the Rangers, as it had with the Commandos. Furthermore, Lomell notes, "Training constantly stressed the need to be on time—you better be there because lives may depend on it." Because the men were expected to show up without the usual sound and urgency of a formal reveille, self-discipline grew.

In England, the Rangers endured a punishing series of exercises. "We often marched twenty-five miles," says Lomell. "We would be sweaty, chafed between the legs, and then have to climb cliffs." Although the Rangers did not know their assignment yet, they worked constantly at ascending ever steeper obstacles.

"There were no safety ropes," recalls Lomell. "And the climbs became higher and higher. You'd get to the top and there would be Duke Slater waiting for you. You would have to go down and start up again. By the third time, you'd be exhausted, your hands sore, psychologically ready to drop out. That was the most troublesome moment, when you had approached the limits of physical exhaustion, thinking, I'm not even there, I feel a cramp coming. But Ranger pride said never give up. We had some who did fall, they died or were severely injured by the drop or when rocks fell on them."

The 2nd Rangers gained a new member in Lt. Robert Edlin, the Albany, Indiana, youth with an OCS commission. Edlin, a platoon leader with the National Guard 28th Infantry Division, had arrived in England a month earlier than Rudder's band. "I had a run-in with a major that persuaded me to look for other employment. Sitting in the mountains of southern Wales, ten miles from the nearest pub with an infantry unit destined for bad times, with a battalion commander who disliked ex-sergeants with OCS commissions, I wondered how the hell I could get out, since he wouldn't transfer me. When I saw a bulletin about volunteers for the Rangers must be transferred, I thought it worth a try.

"There were hundreds of volunteers. I figured, ain't no way I can make it. I passed the first interview with a first sergeant and then a sharp-looking captain passed me on to the finest officer and man I've ever come in contact with, Lt. Col. James Earl Rudder.

" 'I have just two questions,' he said. 'Why do you want in the Rangers?' I figured I better tell the truth. I told him my battalion commander is going to get a lot of people hurt and I need to be with an outfit that believes in itself.

" 'What would you do if your unit was surrounded by Germans and you were out of ammo?'

"I said, 'I would surrender to save my men, and besides, we would tie up a lot of them guarding us.' I thought, well, at least I got to see the top man.

"Rudder shook my hand. 'You're the first SOB that hasn't said, "Fix bayonets and charge." Report back to your battalion, get your gear, and see Max Schneider,' CO of the 5th Rangers at the assault training center.* After I spent a few days with Schneider I headed for Bude in Cornwall.

"I found the Rangers warm, very intelligent, athletic, and high-spirited. They were the best and knew it. Morale was very high. They would fight anyone, anytime, anywhere. We were convinced we were better than the British Commandos or the American paratroopers. I'm sure we didn't win all the battles but we sure as hell tried. Rank didn't mean much. Junior officers were usually called by their first names, even by the lowest privates.

"Most of the lieutenants did not wear bars. Your men knew you and you had to prove yourself to the rest of the battalion. I was a pretty fair boxer at five foot nine and 145 pounds, except a tall stringbean knocked me on my ass regularly and there was a first sergeant from C Company whom I couldn't handle either. I believe we lost both of them on D-Day.

* Max Schneider as a lieutenant had been among the earliest Rangers and served with the original battalion led by William O. Darby. As a member of Darby's Rangers he saw combat in North Africa and Italy and was one of the few battle-experienced Rangers to participate in Overlord. He survived World War II, only to die from enemy fire in Korea.

"The first time I stood on the beach and looked up at those ninety-foot-high cliffs it scared the crap out of me. I had mountain-climbing training back in West Virginia, but nothing like this. Some of those monkeys were even free-climbing, going up without a rope or ladder, just natural handholds plus some chopping with a fighting knife.

"We started with a six-foot section of ladder. After you climbed that, you added a section until you reached the top. Then we went to ropes. Climbing ninety feet on a wet, muddy rope will pucker you a little. There was no rank here, either. Bars or stripes meant nothing. If you couldn't make it you were gone. It seemed like senseless, stupid bullshit. When would you ever need to climb ninety-foot cliffs under fire? Some people quit; they were gone the next day.

"After two or three speed five-mile marches," remembers Edlin, "I developed shin splints. I would start at the front of the column and come in at the rear. The pain was so terrible I couldn't kick it and I couldn't keep up. I saw Dr. [Walter] Block, our battalion medic. 'What the hell's wrong, Doc? I could always keep up.' He explained about the muscles swelling, pinching a nerve, and told me I would need to rest for a few days.

"I said I couldn't do that. The company will think I'm goldbricking. The colonel will kick me out. On the second run that day I was sure I couldn't make it. Guys were dropping out, but I can't. I've got to stay with my platoon. Sgt. White carried my rifle, Sgt. Courtney my pack, and I still can't make it. Dreher wanted to carry me on his back. What the hell kind of a platoon leader can't keep up? On the last trip of the day I was crawling part of the time. The damn battalion was an hour ahead of me. Shit, I hated to wash out. But I will finish anyway, I thought. All of A Company was standing at the edge of the road, waiting for me. Lt. Rafferty, our company commander, slapped me on the back. 'You're the biggest goldbrick I've ever seen.'

"Now I had to face Rudder. He grinned and said, 'Rest your damn leg. The invasion ain't tomorrow.' "

George Kerchner came to the Rangers as a replacement platoon leader for B Company of the 2nd Battalion. "After

Bude early in January," says Kerchner, "we moved to various places, with scouts trying to locate the highest, most difficult cliffs. At the Isle of Wight, we worked with landing craft manned by British sailors. On the Isle of Wight there were the Needles by an entrance to the Solent [the channel between the island and the rest of Britain], lovely chalk cliffs two hundred to three hundred feet up. On the other side we climbed the Tennyson Cliffs, named for the poet, which were the tallest we worked on, 350 feet.

"We practiced coming in to the beaches by landing craft, with live-fire exercises and then climbing to simulate what was expected. On the west coast of England we went through fire-team training, assaulting pillboxes and fortified areas. We engaged in a full-dress rehearsal, with the same time schedule expected for Normandy. A lot of things went wrong, but the whole idea of the exercise was to iron out the kinks.

"They issued special equipment. A lot of very deep thinking had gone into this gear. Our British assault craft, LCAs [Landing Craft, Assault], which were like an American Higgins boat, carried twenty-five to thirty men. They mounted six rocket projectors on each of the landing craft. Two boxes behind a pair of rocket projectors held rope ladders, two others had toggle ropes—these had wooden pieces at intervals on the ropes—and then another pair contained smooth climbing ropes.

"The LCA was to be pointed like a weapon at the cliffs from offshore. When it came within seventy-five yards of the base of the cliff, the rockets would be electrically fired. The rocket head carried a grappling iron with a hook and a lead wire that led back to the rope. The wire avoided the problem of the rocket burning the rope. Fired in a high trajectory—the arc was expected to go three or four hundred feet in the air—the rocket would come down fifty to a hundred feet inland from the edge of the precipice. As soon as we left our landing craft, we would cross the beach, pull on the rope, taking up slack, until the grappling iron dug into the ground. We'd give it a number of tugs to make certain it was well seated and then start climbing.

"We practiced this many times in England, working on it

until a man carrying normal combat gear could scale a severe cliff, such as we expected to climb, within a minute. You could get up a sheer wall fairly easily so long as you could find a foothold and use your feet to assist you.

"When I joined the Rangers, I could probably not have made it up twenty feet of slope because of a lack of experience. But by the time D-Day rolled around, all of us could climb extremely high cliffs rather easily."

Kerchner and Edlin had been posted to the 2nd Ranger Battalion. The other Ranger unit scheduled for the D-Day landings, the 5th Battalion, also added personnel. Frank Dawson, a Branchville, South Carolina, native born in 1919, completed high school but could not afford college.

"I enrolled in the Palmetto School of Aeronautics," says Dawson, "and stayed with it until the Japs bombed Pearl Harbor. I received orders to report for active duty at Fort Benning in early January 1942. I held a second lieutenant's reserve commission from attendance at the Citizens Military Training Camp for thirty days each of four years and with extension courses."

Although Dawson had begun as an infantry officer, by then he was a tank platoon leader with the 3rd Armored Division in Warminster, England. When the call for Ranger volunteers came, Dawson says, "I had infantry experience and felt I was more suited for ground pounding than that hunk of metal called a tank."

Along with a number of other applicants from the 3rd Armored Division, Dawson became a member of the 5th Ranger Battalion, joining the outfit for drills in Scotland. "I was a platoon leader in D Company, but for some reason, we replacement officers never did fit into the clique of officers who had been with the battalion during their training in the States. I only saw Rudder several times and never had a conversation with him. I didn't know Max Schneider either. As a platoon leader, I tried to stay away from headquarters."

Apart from Edlin, Kerchner, and Dawson, who augmented the Rangers in the United Kingdom, one important addition actually entered the ranks between the time at the amphibious school in Florida and the move overseas.

Captain Walter Block, a pediatrician in civilian life and about forty years old, became an almost instant favorite.

"Our previous medical officer," says Frank South, the Ranger aidman, "was too old and too often either drunk or hungover to continue on with us. Block had tried to join the airborne but was deemed to be too old, and his wife, Alice, objected strongly to the idea. The Ranger battalion was desperate for a medical officer, and he was the only one to volunteer. He told Alice he was going to join the Rangers, leaving her with the general impression that this would have something to do with either law enforcement or tending the nation's forests.

"He was obviously much older than we were and rather slight of stature. It amused us but gained him some respect when we saw that every morning and night, he would retire to his tent or room and do countless push-ups, as well as join us on some Ranger marches, fifty minutes double-time and ten minutes route step. He did all he could to keep up with the youngsters.

"As soon as he came on board he started to give us additional and very practical instruction, 'always anticipate what the man who is doing the actual surgery will require next'; how to perform various types of suturing; how to handle an open belly wound or a pneumothorax [injury in the respiratory system]. He took every opportunity to teach us drug therapies, read X-rays, and educate his men to the fullest.

"As an instructor he was very patient, direct, and as thorough as possible. He listened to his medics and respected what they had to say. He gave some of us wide latitude in our action in our treatment of men and our decisions affecting their health. He was, however, short-tempered, especially if his personal authority or integrity were questioned.

"When a staff sergeant, his second in command, began to undermine his authority and decision on several issues, Block warned him once. The second time he was summarily demoted to private and allowed to transfer into a line company as a BAR man. He was killed on D plus one. My closest friend, then T/4 William Clark, and Block got into a silly dispute as to whether Willy should carry his aid kit with him at all times. The final exchanges were, 'Well, for Christ's sake, do you want me to sleep with the damned thing?' Block responded, 'From now on, you will report to Sgt. Bayer, Pvt. Clark.'

As the Rangers concentrated on assaulting ever steeper terrain, Jack Kuhn was at a local pub enjoying an evening of dart games when a Ranger brought him the message to see Duke Slater immediately. "He told me to get my gear together and report tomorrow morning. I was moving out. There was no explanation and I knew better than to ask."

The following day, Kuhn and Pfc Peter Korpalo loaded themselves on a jeep driven by Slater. As they neared London, Slater informed them of their mission. Amphibious trucks (officially listed as DUKW* and in GI parlance called ducks) were being fitted with hundred-foot extension ladders. The intention was to mount a machine gun atop the ladder. When the DUKW pulled onto the beach, it would raise and extend the ladder, lifting a Ranger manning the weapon on a small platform at the top. The machine gun would provide covering fire for Rangers during their ascents up cliffs.

Says Kuhn, "I was taken to a large factory where I met with firefighters, military personnel from the British forces, and two British soldiers who would drive the DUKWs. I learned the fundamentals of the ladders and the British Lewis machine gun. The British were very high on the concept, and we worked together with great enthusiasm, through trial and error, to make the systems operate.

"In the first experiments I walked up to get acquainted. I had climbed cliffs from one hundred to three hundred feet, and this was a scary proposition. I would much prefer to hold a rope. Then I stood on the platform while the ladder was extending, giving me a hundred-foot free ride. We had a communication system so that I could speak to those on the DUKW and they could answer.

"On a cloudy, cold day with a pretty heavy sea running in the Channel we gave the vehicle a trial run. The two

---

* The initials are a descriptive code: *D* means 1942; *U* indicates amphibian; *K* signifies all-wheel drive; and *W* is for dual rear axles.

British soldiers and I went out on the water, turned about, and came ashore. That answered my first question, whether the duck would float. Then the Lewis gun was mounted, and with me on the platform they raised the ladder, extending it to its full hundred feet. I fired the machine gun and everything worked to perfection.

"While we were testing the system in the water, I spotted an English major whom I recognized as Sir Malcolm Campbell. As a boy I remembered seeing him in the newsreels, driving his racing car, the *Bluebird*, over the Salt Flats at Utah to set the world's land speed record. Campbell taught us how to inflate or deflate the tires of the DUKW so it wouldn't stick in the sand.

"Feeling the experiments were successful, Korpalo and I returned to the battalion with our DUKW, and I believe altogether we had four of them on D-Day."

While neither the paratroop nor the Ranger organizations knew their precise missions for D-Day, both had done their best to recruit the most capable and motivated soldiers. The training regimens honed bodies, taught weaponry and tactics. But drills and exercises, however rigorous, can never match the conditions of combat. Only a handful of those destined for the Normandy beaches knew firsthand what a shooting war was like.

# CHAPTER 6

# BAPTISMS OF FIRE

DURING THE EARLY stages of the mobilization of the Allied armies, there was a desperate need to block further enemy expansion rather than take the offensive. Into the maw went the few refitted United Kingdom organizations after Dunkirk. In 1942, with the Germans attempting to expand their conquests in North Africa, Horace Wright as part of the Hampshire Regiment sailed to Algeria to join the British First Army trying to advance eastward while the Eighth Army under Gen. Bernard Montgomery fought off the Nazi panzers led by Gen. Erwin Rommel in Egypt.

As a platoon leader in the Hampshire Regiment, Wright with the troops then moved toward Tunisia as part of the British First Army advancing east, while Montgomery with the Eighth Army fought Rommel's Afrika Korps in Egypt.

"There was a buildup over the winter, and then we confronted the enemy," says Wright. "This led to the Battle of Tébourba in Tunisia. Our supply line had been extended to the point where we ran out of momentum. The Germans, drawing their materials from Sicily, could obtain what they needed more quickly. The Germans had tanks; we didn't. The Germans had air support; we didn't.

"The battalion engaged in a five-day holding action. We lost quite a lot of men, perhaps two hundred out of a total of six hundred. Eventually, we started to withdraw in small parties. A shell from an 88 exploded in a tree over my head. The wounds I received temporarily incapacitated me and I was taken prisoner.

"They evacuated me first to a Tunis hospital, where I was treated quite decently. Then I went to a hospital in Sicily before being shipped to a prisoner-of-war camp northeast of Rome on the Adriatic side of Italy."

North Africa would also serve as the baptismal caldron for Americans serving in the 1st Division and provide vital lessons in survival. For the totally inexperienced GIs there was an enormous amount to learn on the job about tactics and weaponry. But in the months before the Big Red One underwent its introduction to combat, even as Horace Wright languished in a POW camp, the shooting war still seemed far off.

In the States, Bill Behlmer had continued to enjoy the new attitude of civilians toward GIs. "Girls would run up to the backs of trucks in a convoy, give us cookies, cake, candy, sometimes a kiss and hug." Less inspiring were maneuvers on the outskirts of Fort Benning, in the Harmony Hills area. "It was pitiful. We lacked everything. A stick in the ground marked a tank. Another stick stood for a 75 or 105mm gun. They'd call out, 'Look up. We're being bombed.' But nothing was in sight.

"I had gained a new squad leader, Cpl. Swede Johnstone. We became fast friends, and he always told me that if anything happened to him, he wanted me to have his stripes.

"We pulled into Indiantown Gap, Pennsylvania. We had no idea where, but we knew we were leaving for overseas. We removed the 1st Division and 16th Regiment insignia from our uniforms and were told to send any valuables home. We were issued passports and then sailed on the *Queen Mary*.

"We didn't like the English when we first came, but our attitudes changed as we saw the old men and kids drilling with the home guards. We knew that if Hitler invaded England, the old men, kids, and women would fight with sticks, stones, and bare fists if necessary. We warmed up to them and they to us."

Behlmer and the others in the division soon embarked on British ships as part of a convoy bound for North Africa. "We were briefed that we'd land at a seaside resort, Arzew, and our objective was the railroad station in Oran. The English crews dropped some of the trucks and guns in deep water and it was a mess, but we made it to the beach. This was the real thing, artillery shells, machine guns, mortars, small arms. We had our first taste of the gnawing feeling in the pit of the stomach. Fear!

"We secured the beach, but that first night was terrible. Everybody had an itchy trigger finger and fired at anything that moved, shot up half of the grapevines in North Africa. The corporal of the guard shot one of our sentries in the stomach.

"In mid-January we moved into a pass or valley called Ousseltia under cover of darkness. We were told we were to stop Rommel and his Afrika Korps from breaking out. We dug in our guns all night long. Other guys dug in machine guns, mortars, etc. At dawn we decided to light up a cigarette. A few minutes later, a mortar shell hit behind us. Then another in front of us. We dove for cover, because we knew where the next would land. All hell broke loose, and we didn't stand a chance. The Germans had gotten there first and were dug in on the slope ahead of us.

"The out-of-action signal came and we took off, leaving everything behind. Gen. Rommel had won round one. A few days later, we returned and recovered our guns and equipment intact. We were losers again at Kasserine Pass, but we were getting smarter. 'Old Blood and Guts' Gen. Patton took command of the II Corps, and we knew he was there to win even if he had us all killed doing it. We got the Afrika Korps out of Gafsa, Feriana, and El Guettar. But we also found out our 37mm antitank guns were peashooters and ineffective against the big Tiger tanks. We played hit-and-run, aiming for the treads and exhaust pipes.

"On Easter Sunday, we were in a command car looking for a gun position. The lieutenant, platoon sergeant, and another corporal were in the backseat, the driver, Swede Johnstone, and myself in the front. I was on the outside and the lieutenant told me to jump out and find company headquarters and report back. I had gone about fifteen yards when I heard a loud explosion and something hit me in the back. I turned and the command car was smoking. The right front wheel had hit a land mine. A piece of tire had struck me in the back. I ran to the car and started pulling them out as an ambulance showed up to help. Swede was lying next to the wheel, blown open and dead. The lieutenant and platoon sergeant were just shook up. The driver had a broken leg, and the corporal in the back died on the way to the hospital.

"It was a horrible sight and a narrow escape for me. Swede's wish came true. I got his corporal stripes and his squad, but at a terrible cost.

"The Afrika Korps was bottled up and surrendered. The Germans marched in, stacked their arms, and sat by the railroad tracks waiting for boxcars to haul them out as POWs. They were very orderly and made no waves. We offered cigarettes and smoked with them. We didn't hate them, nor did they hate us. We were soldiers with a job to do and they had lost."

After maneuvers in North Carolina and the swamplands of Florida, Fred Erben with the 16th Infantry Regiment was under the impression his unit was to fight in the tropics.

"On August 1, 1942, we left for England on the *Queen Mary*. Then we trained with the British, who showed us the wrongs and rights of beach landings. We boarded troopships, and I was on the HMS *Duchess of Bedford*, part of a fifty-vessel convoy. We headed west, then south, and finally learned our destination, North Africa.

"While we originally trained with the Springfield bolt-action rifles, we had been issued the M-1 Garand just before leaving the States. Our uniforms were combat OD, dress khaki. They issued all new vehicles; this was to be the first test under combat. It was easy to land in North Africa. The Vichy French were literally caught with their pants down, asleep. We awakened them, assembled them in the town square. They were genuinely surprised that the Americans had invaded. We took the town of La Macta. We moved on to the city of Oran, and then heavy fighting started on our way to Algiers.

"The first death I saw was the result of an ambush. A friend named Bob Katz was shot while on a jeep patrol. The men became very angry and wanted to go on a patrol to retaliate. We later caught up with those responsible for his death. We shot them because they would not give up. I never knew I could actually shoot somebody. I was remorseful—I felt taking a life was wrong. But it was kill or be killed. I felt it was my duty and I was here for a reason. Many men felt as I did, but we had some who did not care to take prisoners unless ordered. Many of the men had family in Europe who were persecuted by the enemy.

"The ordinary barriers between officers and enlisted men tended to fade in combat. The sirs and salutes were used only while in rear areas. Officers preferred it that way, figuring if you saluted them on the line, the enemy would pick them off as leaders. What the enemy did not realize was that any one of the enlisted men could take over because of the training received. Many enlisted men would receive combat commissions.

"The men felt they were good. We were cocky because it was instilled in us we were number one. Each man backed up his partner. We got to know about each other and the problems at home. We became like family."

George Zenie, as a member of the 18th Regiment in the 1st Division, traveled much the same path as Fred Erben. "After Pearl Harbor," says Zenie, "we were certain we would be shipped to the Pacific because of our amphibious training. We had made many practice landings in Puerto Rico and Buzzards Bay, Massachusetts. Instead, we became a cadre for some other division, and we lost many good officers and noncoms. The new officers were a mixed bag. Our new platoon leader was arrogant, pompous, stubborn, and refused to consider any suggestions from men who had been with the outfit since its inception. After a rough day with the lieutenant in England, several men wrecked his tent and scattered his equipment. Since no one would confess, he punished the entire platoon, telling us we would march with full pack and rifle until we dropped or informed on the guilty ones. No one would do so. After we walked thirty-one miles, the company commander called a halt, telling the lieutenant he was destroying the entire platoon. Soon after he was transferred out.

"Our landing at Arzew, North Africa, was fairly easy. At Medjez-el-Bab we learned to dig foxholes in the sides of hills and cover the tops for protection against artillery fire. We learned never to flash a mess kit in the sun, because the reflection would bring enemy artillery fire. When we went on patrols to gather information or capture a prisoner we learned to stay quiet, wear dark clothes, and blacken our faces. Sometimes there were assault patrols that used automatic weapons and grenades. Here the purpose was to make a lot of noise and trouble before returning to our units.

"At El Guettar, we discovered how inadequate our antitank guns were against German armor. [Both the 37mm and the successor 57mm cannons were incapable of penetrating the heavily armored enemy tanks, yet six months after the Normandy invasion and two years after Zenie and his crew learned the facts of antitank life, U.S. replacements continued to train with them.] "The Stuka dive-bombers proved to be mostly noise, and except for a very close hit, we were safe in our foxholes. [A view in sharp contrast to that of Bill Sadler at Dunkirk.] The most important thing we learned was how to react under enemy fire." Zenie reacted well enough to earn a Bronze Star.

From North Africa, Zenie and the 18th Infantry Regiment participated in the landings on Sicily. "Everyone in our LCI [Landing Craft Infantry] was seasick and miserable. We were constantly under enemy air strafing and bombing attacks. They sank the cargo ship containing all of the heavy weapons for our company. We had only the weapons we carried ashore, rifles and hand grenades, to fight off an attack by forty to fifty enemy tanks.

"We helped the artillery move their pieces to positions where the armor would be under direct fire. Many tanks were destroyed and the rest retreated. We fought with a rifle company while we waited for the heavy equipment. The combat in Sicily was strictly an infantry war—up and down mountains, across ravines, rivers, and draws. At Troina we repelled attack after attack. I added an Oak Leaf Cluster to my Bronze Star from North Africa."

Bill Behlmer endured yet another defeat in Sicily. "We moved inland after the first day and the Hermann Goering Panzer Division encircled us. Tanks everywhere. We stood our ground and thought we could outlast them. The 57s which had replaced our 37mm cannons performed beautifully. Finally their big guns had us zeroed in and the German armored infantry was advancing. We knew we had to change our positions, but we couldn't get the trucks up the hill to move our guns. I could see we were surrounded and got going. The Germans captured our guns and spiked them. The heavy cruiser *Savannah* and our own artillery saved the day. The *Savannah* steaming back and forth off the beach knocked out the tanks."

Bill Wills, who entered the regular army in 1940 from New York City, led a squad of engineers with the 1st Division. "Each squad had two mine detection teams and a machine gun crew, and all were qualified riflemen. We did not have much mine training in the States. I never saw a Teller mine or a Bouncing Betty [when a Bouncing Betty was tripped, a small charge boosted the device into the air before it exploded] until North Africa. I learned from British training books how to take them out and disarm them. Italian box mines were very dangerous; they were four feet long and about eight inches wide, and there were three ways to trip them. We removed them by a hook and rope, pulling them out until they went off. We also learned a great deal in Sicily about booby traps, trip wires, and bridge demolitions. We became familiar with some of the German weapons, the rockets, 88s, their tanks, and how effective their machine guns and machine pistols were. We also discovered some of their weaknesses.

"The first man I saw killed was a good friend, a sergeant shot through his helmet by a French soldier when we were going into St. Cloud in North Africa in November of 1942. After North Africa, there were always rumors of the unit being sent back to the States, but after a while no one believed them. The men I enlisted with that weren't wounded or killed would spend thirty-five months overseas covering eight campaigns."

After the fighting in North Africa, the 1st Division received its first replacements. Among the newcomers was Dick Biehl, a former part-time clerk at the post office in his hometown of Temple, Pennsylvania.

After induction in February of 1943, Biehl arrived at Fort McClellan, Alabama, to be inserted into a thirteen-week basic training cycle already in its third week. He lost more time with ten days of hospitalization for pneumonia. "I barely qualified firing the M-1 rifle and avoided repeating the training cycle. In total I had about nine weeks of training, certainly not nearly sufficient to go into combat against the experienced veterans of the German Army, and about half of my company was sent to North Africa as replacements.

"I joined B Company of the 26th Infantry Regiment, 1st Division, and I quickly learned to respect the noncoms who had been with the company through North Africa and then led us in Sicily. These fellows were GI [strict, by the book] when necessary, and most were of good character."

Biehl absorbed the essential facts of combat infantry life. "Always spread out; never bunch up. Night patrols are necessary. Artillery fire can be used effectively as close support for advancing foot soldiers. Air superiority was crucial. Communications were vital for command and control, from the CO through the platoon to the squad level. Tanks were very effective when available, but on the other hand they could also draw enemy fire."

The American forces still struggled with shortages and disadvantages in their arsenal. "I carried an '03 in Sicily—not every GI had an M-1. The '03 was clip-fed, five rounds, bolt-action. [An M-1 held an eight-round clip and fired semiautomatically.] German weaponry was good, lots of automatic weapons.

"In Sicily, my initial assignment was that of first scout, what today is called the point man. In any event, it's lonely out front. Our last battle in Sicily was taking the town of

Troina, astride a hilltop. The German Hermann Goering Division used terrain and buildings to great advantage, even concealing tanks inside houses and firing through windows and doorways.

"One sunny, hot afternoon, another young GI and I were on outpost, a couple of hundred yards beyond the company position, lying on either side of a huge rock. We were to remain there, observe and report any enemy activity in the valley below until relieved. After an hour or so, an artillery shell landed nearby with a large BANG! The other soldier took off and ran to the company area. I remained.

"A few weeks later I was promoted to corporal. My former companion 'accidentally' shot himself in his left ankle while cleaning a pistol. Staying by the rock brought my stripes."

Cpl. Thomas R. McCann, son of a Mississippi railroad switchman, was another replacement who caught up with the 1st Division in time for operations in Sicily. "I graduated from Mississippi State in 1942," says McCann, "where as a land-grant college, freshmen were required to enroll in ROTC. But I failed to pass the physical examination because of a heart condition."

Drafted, McCann qualified for OCS, but flunked out. "Later, I was grateful, since second lieutenants did not last long in the front lines of an infantry company."

From a replacement camp in Oran, Algeria, McCann was assigned to the 18th Infantry Regiment of the 1st Division. He became a member of an intelligence and reconnaissance platoon.

"Our platoon leader had come from a National Guard unit and believed in going by the book. He told us how to fall by the numbers. When we reached Sicily with shells falling around, I was interested to see how he hit the ground; it wasn't by the numbers.

"All of the noncommissioned officers whom I came in contact with were very nice fellows. Most were what we called 'old soldiers.' They were always talking about taking the next hill and then they would go home. Very few from the 1st Division got to go home before the war ended unless they were wounded or ill."

Among the Americans who would be involved in Overlord, one other organization besides the 1st Division
claimed extensive combat experience: the 505th Parachute
Infantry of the 82nd Airborne Division. One member was
Bill Dunfee, the Columbus, Ohio, native.

Flying from North Africa, Dunfee, assigned to Company
I, 3rd Battalion, in the 505th, made his first combat leap
near Gela, Sicily. Forced by the invasion schedule to jump
in winds hovering around thirty-five miles an hour—practice missions were canceled if the velocity reached fifteen
miles an hour—the 505th suffered, notes Dunfee, "a dis-
proportionate number of jump injuries. A man with a broken leg is a liability you cannot afford in combat. This was
our first exposure to the German SS troops, the Hermann
Goering SS Panzer Division. I did not find them supermen.
They were well trained, armed, and led, but they bled and
died just like us."

After hard fighting to wrest Sicily from the Germans, the
505th jumped near the town of Paestum, close to Salerno
on the Italian mainland. "From the two experiences," says
Dunfee, "I learned how to stay alive, when to hit the deck.
I knew the sounds of incoming artillery and mortar rounds
before they hit and explode, the sounds of small-arms fire
aimed in your direction, the popping and cracking sound of
a bullet passing near you. When you are in a static position,
*always* dig a foxhole! And I prayed very sincerely."

The 82nd Airborne also acquired replacements. Vic
Allegretti, son of a barber in a suburb of New York City,
enlisted after his eighteenth birthday, exactly one year after
Pearl Harbor. "I asked for the paratroopers, but they said I
was too light, too small," says Allegretti. "In Casablanca, I
became a gliderman with the 80th Antiaircraft and Antitank Battalion, which was part of the 82nd Airborne. We
went to Sicily, landed by sea rather than in gliders."

Although the Germans had been defeated in Sicily, the
airborne aspect of the battle for that island raised serious
concerns about such operations. Not only did the troopers
suffer heavy casualties from enemy guns, but an episode of
deadly friendly fire shattered the 504th Regiment during a
night drop in an area secured by Dunfee and his fellow

troopers from the 505th. The transport pilots sought to
use the invasion fleet offshore as a marker for navigation.
When they flew over the ships, the warship crews identified them as enemy bombers and opened fire. The fliers
switched on their running lights, thinking the sailors would
then recognize them. Instead, they only enhanced the aim.
Twenty-three planes were shot down; as many as four hundred troopers were lost.

What happened to the airdrop in Sicily would affect
planning and tactics for the invasion of France. Based on
the results, some strategists argued against the use of airborne soldiers. And adherents tinkered with modifications
in equipment and techniques.

In spite of the severe loss both from enemy and friendly
fire during this phase of the Italian campaign, the Allies
slowly pushed the Germans ever farther north. Horace
Wright, lodged in POW camps for nine months, became involved in an escape-tunnel plot. "When the Italians capitulated and the Germans moved in," says Wright, "I used the
tunnel for a hidey hole. The place was abandoned while
they evacuated the camp and moved its inhabitants further
north. I walked south, until I met the British forces
not far from Foggia [close to one hundred miles from the
POW camp]. I was sent back to the U.K. to rejoin the
Hampshires, and the 1st Battalion. We were to take part in
the invasion of France."

Other combat-experienced British soldiers also plunged
into invasion preparations. Bill Murray, who'd been run out
of France in 1940, sought both revenge and an opportunity to carry on family tradition. "By 1941 and '42, I was
involved in putting up POW camps for Italian prisoners. I
got bored. I joined the army to fight the Germans and
Italians, not nurse them. I applied for a transfer to the infantry, in the King's Regiment, a Liverpool organization.
My father had been in the 8th Battalion in World War I.
My younger brother was in India with the 1st Battalion.

"When I was informed there were no vacancies at my
rank in the 8th, which was the only battalion still in
England, I became so desperate to get away from the depressing surroundings of the POW camps I requested a

reduction to the rank of private. I then realized my ambition to serve in an infantry regiment.

"I was good at sketching and map drawing, and it didn't take long before I chose intelligence, where I soon learned codes and ciphers. From then on, it was rigorous training and exercises."

By the time Wright returned to his old regiment and Murray joined the King's Regiment, an enormous jumble of men, arms, and equipment packed the U.K. Among the arrivals was the U.S. 1st Infantry Division, which returned from Sicily.

The able-bodied men from the Big Red One stepped off the gangplank at Liverpool in November 1943. The outfit set up housekeeping at "Puddletown." There was little doubt in the minds of most that they would join the burgeoning ranks of those to be committed to an invasion of France. "Arriving in England from Sicily," says Dick Biehl, "was sort of like coming home. Hills and fields were green; people spoke a like language; there were smiles, greetings, questions about our homes, 'back home.' We were introduced to fields divided by small trees and shrubs rather than fences as we knew them. That is how we first came across hedgerows, which were to become our nemesis in France."

The depleted ranks of Biehl's unit received replacements. "There were twenty-two men left of the original company [approximately two hundred] that had landed in North Africa. The old-timers never complained, but I'm sure they were not pleased about being called upon for a third landing against enemy-held positions."

Tom McCann quickly found rapport with the host people. "I met a village policeman who informed me we were in Thomas Hardy's country. He introduced me to Hardy's first cousin's widow, Mrs. Antell, a lady in her seventies who lived in a thatched cottage. She took care of an eight-year-old boy from London who had been brought to the rural area for safety. Mrs. Antell always had fresh eggs for me, which were rationed, and I learned a lot about Hardy. She gave me one of his childhood books with his autograph and a photograph of Hardy with the former Prince of

Wales, the Duke of Windsor. I had my mother send gifts to her and the boy.

"I met many local people and was invited into their homes. I played bridge and made a foursome with the village doctor, the headmaster of the local school, and the canon of the church. One night at the canon's home he expressed regret for not having any alcoholic beverage to serve. It shocked me, a minister who drank.

"At the village church, a family invited me to sit in their pew. On Christmas Day, a doctor asked me to dinner. The policeman offered me a bath in his home anytime, since we had to travel a distance from our billet to the bathhouse.

"We took part in the invasion practice maneuvers at Slapton Sands. We were told not to say or talk about what we had seen during the exercise. The secret weapon we saw was the DD [Duplex Drive] tank, which was a tank covered with canvas and rubber which would allow it to float. The tank was to head into the shore firing." There were two versions of the DD tanks. In addition to those that were fully amphibious, others were designed to be waterproofed but launched in shallow enough water for them to track across the sea bottom until they climbed up onto the beach.

The Fort Garry Horse or 10th Canadian Armored Regiment was among the units chosen to operate the amphibious versions. Gunner Earl Kitching remembers, "We heard for the first time about such tanks in January 1944. We were taken to a lake in England where we learned how they worked in a sixteen-ton Valentine tank. After a week of instruction, we moved to the south of England, where we trained with the thirty-ton Shermans.

"The exercises were all conducted at night to maintain secrecy and run between Portsmouth and the Isle of Wight. The main concern was the rubber tubes, filled with compressed air, attached to the canvas wrapping of the Sherman. We were issued oxygen masks, and if a tank sank, you were supposed to wait until the thing settled to the bottom and then go out through the hatch. We did not, however, lose a single tank during the training period."

Among the Americans learning to operate DD tanks

scheduled to participate in the landings was the 741st Tank Battalion's John Barner, who had decided to accept early induction into the service after job interviews began with questions on his draft status.

"After winter training and working with English soldiers during the spring, we went near Weymouth Harbor. I was with A Company and we waterproofed our tanks to the turrets. Air ducts to and from the engine were installed. Both B and C Company had the DD tanks which could float and propel themselves.

"At night we watched the spectacular antiaircraft fire against the Jerry planes. The light from all the tracers was enough to read the newspaper. Until they locked the gates to our camp, we could walk on the beach there, buy fish and chips or visit the local pubs."

In the 745th Tank Battalion, Eddie Ireland, the Chicago youth who elected the armored forces because he didn't fancy walking to war, also learned to waterproof his tank. "We filled every crack or crevice with a heavy clay, like putty, up to the top of the turret. We practiced, loading up on LCMs, going around a peninsula to make beach landings and then drive back to our base. The LCM [Landing Craft Mechanized] was a little guy; it held just one tank. An LSD [Landing Ship Dock] could carry eighteen of them. The LSD would take on water until the LCMs could float off."

Separated from the 504th Parachute Regiment of the 82nd Airborne, which continued to fight in Italy, the 505th Parachute Regiment with Bill Dunfee now took up residence in the U.K., where the division added a brigade composed of the 507th and 508th Parachute Regiments. The 101st Airborne Division arrived, and both the 4th Infantry and 29th Infantry Divisions moved about the British Isles for various phases of training. Both the 2nd and 5th Ranger Battalions had become part of the forces committed to Overlord.

All of the ground forces practiced beach assaults. The nature of their training left little doubt of the mission ahead. And in March 1944, Felix Branham with the 29th Division in Devon stood at parade rest awaiting an important visitor. "Suddenly a jeep drove up. It was Gen. Bernard

Montgomery. He got on top of the jeep, gave us a little talk, told us how glad he was to see us and that he'd just come from London, where he met our boss, Ike. He said, 'You know you're going to be landing in France, and I will be your immediate commander. I am sure that when the time comes, you will be outstanding in any task laid before you. Good hunting, lads.'

"That evening back at the barracks and during chow, the conversation was all about what he said. We didn't care to be under his command, preferring an American to lead us. But we agreed that Montgomery does not visit occupation troops; he comes to see combat troops."

Although the GIs knew their role and that the time for the invasion was approaching, they did not know the details, where and exactly when. Additional organizations expected to reinforce the U.S. invaders, starting on D plus one, spread out over Great Britain. Vast numbers of trucks, jeeps, and armor transformed the meadows and fields into an enormous parking lot. The requisite ammunition and other supplies choked all available storage space.

# CHAPTER 7

# LAST REHEARSALS FOR THE BIG SHOW

WHILE HOMEGROWN UNITS of the British Isles prepared for their role, Canadian troops were also readying themselves. The North Shore Regiment drawn basically from the New Brunswick area of the country and composed largely of nine hundred young volunteers from farming and fishing communities had shipped its 1st Battalion to England.

One of the platoon commanders for D Company was Everett Gorman, son of a pulp-mill worker, born in 1919. "I was always inclined toward the military and was a member of the nonpermanent militia during the mid-1930s, as a signalman, first-aid person, and in the regimental band.

"I first thought I should go with the rest of the unit, since I had been with them even before the war. I talked to the good Padre Hickey, who taught at the university. He told me that the war would last a long time and I should graduate, get my degree first. Father Hickey would become Major Hickey and win a Military Cross for his D-Day work.

"I graduated from college, St. Thomas in Chatham, in 1942, and the next day, July 4th, I joined up. I was a provisional second lieutenant and after a three-months course I was confirmed as a one-pip wonder. Then I got my second pip and went to England to join the regiment, which had been there since 1941.

"They were getting ready for the big show. Most of them were fed up with going through the schemes [training exercises], which had begun with the outline of the landing craft taped on a field and progressed through actual boats at Slapton Sands."

Both the U.S. airborne forces and the Rangers continued to cope with ambivalence or downright hostility from certain circles within the military establishment. On the heels of the airborne troubles in Sicily, three Ranger battalions had suffered extensive casualties while slugging it out with the Germans between Rome and the infamous Anzio beachhead.

The airborne ranks, however, had grown to the point where professional officers saw the chutes as an asset to one's career. Division-size units required tables of organization that included ample field-grade rank and the stars of a general. Powerful voices could plead the case for airborne.

But the small battalion-size segments of the Rangers meant the top job carried only the silver leaf of a lieutenant colonel. Furthermore, those wise in the ways of the military bureaucracy knew that small unattached units usually draw the dirty end of the stick in assignments and have few champions or clout when commendations or medals are passed around. As a consequence, there was a conspicuous absence of West Pointers among the Rangers.

Still, someone had initially thought enough of the Ranger way of doing things to create a program in which soldiers from a variety of units would take Ranger training and then bring it back to their old units. Bob Slaughter eagerly volunteered for such an opportunity. As a member of a National Guard division, Slaughter may have been discomfited by the attitude toward such organizations. "The National Guard units," says Slaughter, "were initially derided as not fit for combat. We were called 'the home guard' or 'home nannies,' not only by the regular army people but even by some draftees.

"Approximately five hundred zealots [including Bob

Sales, a fellow Virginian from the 116th, and Frank Wawrynovic, the Pennsylvania draftee in the 115th Regiment] and I were selected after passing rigid physical and mental examinations," says Slaughter. "One of the questions I was asked was whether I could stick my knife into a man's belly and then twist it. Of course I said yes.

"Training was at Tidworth, Scotland, the rugged British Commando Depot at Achnacarry House. This was the Highlands, blue lochs between low mountains, green heather on desolate, craggy, waterlogged moors. Herds of wild deer roamed in relative peace. It rained often and a biting wind was constant. The scenery was beautiful to the eye but unpleasant to the skin.

"The instructors from Lord Lovat's No. 4 Commando were old-school, ruthlessly harsh, strict disciplinarians. Grueling speed marches, mountain and cliff climbing, unarmed combat, boat drills, exercise with logs, finding one's way on the desolate Scottish moors with nothing but a compass and map made one wonder if he had miscalculated his ability. The obstacle course followed a five-mile climb up a steady grade. It had every diabolical obstacle the British could devise; there were ten-foot walls to negotiate, log and rope bridges, steep ravines to traverse, rope swings over water hazards. Umpires stationed along the route graded the contestants. Life-size targets popped up, requiring snap judgment. One had to decide quickly whether to shoot [live ammunition] at the target or bayonet it. A miss or wrong decision could be judged fatal. It was imperative that weapons were in good working order. The entire team was required to finish on time. If an umpire judged a squad member neutralized, his squad was obligated to carry him to the finish. The last squad member to finish was timed, and if he didn't come within the deadline, the entire team had to run the 'black mile'—do the course on our only day off, Sunday.

"Our Commando instructor, Capt. Hoar, a veteran of the Dieppe raid, carried a foot-long leather baton or swagger stick. During one speed march a man dropped out. Capt. Hoar ordered him to his feet. When the soldier refused, the stick flailed the shoulders of the 'yellow-bellied coward unfit to breathe fresh air!' He also rib-kicked another slacker.

"Near the conclusion of the debilitating speed marches just before rounding the curve up the last hill to camp, Capt. Hoar would yell in his curt English brogue, 'Straighten up, mytees! Get in step!' Although camp was still a mile away, the wail of bagpipes could be heard in the distance. The kilted pipers, standing at the entrance, greeted us with one of their traditional Highland tunes. It did wonders for morale. No matter how tired the soldiers were, the bagpipe music set adrenaline flowing. With pride we marched into camp in step, heads high.

"Half the candidates threw in the towel and returned to their outfits. Those completing the training were dubbed 29th Provisional Rangers. Our reward was a pair of paratrooper boots and a three-inch felt patch to sew on our jackets. The rainbow-shaped patch bore blue lettering, '29th Rangers,' over a red background."

Bob Slaughter put in eleven months as a 29th Ranger. But after they had prepared for a raid-in-force, the brass disbanded the outfit in November 1943. The 2nd and 5th Ranger Battalions were now in residence in the British Isles. Strategists decided they would provide sufficient men for the special assignments plotted for D-Day.

During the time Slaughter pursued the role of a Ranger, Felix Branham began his ultimate preparations for the Normandy invasion at Tidworth Barracks, near Salisbury. "The training was hard, the weather miserable, and the food was half rations. We trained seven days a week and many times at night. Until we arrived in the British Isles we had never seen grenade launchers or bazookas, but now we learned how to use every infantry weapon and explosives of all types. I became a demolition man.

"We tried to outdo everyone else. We competed against other divisions, other regiments, other battalions, other companies. We went on twenty-five-mile hikes, and guys would drop out all over the place. We would try to come in with more men, fewer falling out. We wanted to be special; we were proud to trace ourselves back to Stonewall Jackson and even George Washington.

"A lot of guys had joined the air corps and we envied their flashy boots, flying jackets, and the real eggs they ate. They were hotshots. But at an air base, we saw a flight of planes come in. They started to hose down the tail of the plane and chunks of stuff started to fall off. We said, what was this here? They told us we were looking at what was left of the tail gunner. Their food was better, they were paid more, but when we saw the tail gunner being washed out, we said no thanks, we don't need the real eggs and the money.

"The majority of people didn't seem to like us to be over there. We had cigarettes, chewing gum, chocolate, made more money, were better dressed, and every place we went, we paid top pound. There were catcalls—'What are you doing over here, Yank? We didn't send for you.' We answered, 'If we weren't here, you guys would be running around hollering Heil Hitler.'

"Pocahontas, the Indian princess from Virginia, was buried at Winchester, which was near Salisbury. I visited her grave, saw Stonehenge, and had forty-eight-hour passes to London. Lady Astor, who was Nancy Langhorne from Virginia and had lived thirteen miles west of Charlottesville, came to our regimental area many times. When a group of us Virginia fellows were her guests at her home for a luncheon and a swim in her pool, she said, 'Boys, if you are out on the town and have too much to drink and any English people ask you where you are from, tell them New York, New Jersey, or anyplace but Virginia. I have told the English people that Virginia boys don't drink and rough it up.' "

Bob Slaughter rejoined D Company, the heavy weapons unit of the 116th Infantry Regiment, as it labored to improve physical power while studying the techniques of amphibious assaults. "Captain Schilling went on a recruiting expedition, looking for large, tough men to carry the heavy machine guns and mortars. The men he found were wonderful soldiers, shining examples of the captain's judgment."

While the 1st Battalion of the 116th encamped at Ivybridge in Devon, a twenty-year-old draftee, Donald McCarthy, sewed on the shoulder patch of the Blue and Gray Division. "I grew up in Belmont, Massachusetts [a suburb of Boston]. Both my parents and my teachers in Catholic school—as well as the history, English, and geography instructors in the Belmont school system—made a point of following events in Europe and the USSR. As the son of a World War I naval officer, I was excited as the 'winds of war' began to stir."

Although McCarthy graduated from New York Military Academy with two years of ROTC in June 1943, he became one more rookie as he received his basic at Fort McClellan, Alabama. Following courses at the radio and wire school and then intelligence and reconnaissance classes, McCarthy received assignment to the I&R squad of Headquarters Company.

Ivybridge presented another problem for the still Virginia-dominated National Guard 116th. Recalls Bob Slaughter, "While we were on an exercise, black troops moved into Ivybridge. The village could not support any more troops. Acrimony led to fighting between newcomers and the battalion. It soon became apparent the troops had to be separated. Every other night town was off-limits for one race or the other. To make matters worse, when the blacks were in town, the whites were the military policemen, and vice versa. A mortar platoon sergeant was caught leaving camp with a submachine gun. He was going to 'clean the place out.'

"I was selected for MP duty and paired with a soldier from one of the rifle companies. After the pubs closed that night, a mob of black soldiers, fortified with stout and bitters, came up the street shouting obscenities and acting belligerent. My partner and I backed into a doorway. One man, a rather large sergeant, was carrying a pistol. I called for him to drop his weapon. He hesitated, and I fired my carbine into the ground at his feet. He dropped the .45 and the crowd dispersed." The internecine hostility around Ivybridge ended when Slaughter's outfit shifted operations to an assembly area near Dorset.

Bill Lewis, the erstwhile Texas National Guardsman and ersatz Nazi soldier in the States, commanded an antitank squad equipped with the 57mm cannon.

"We had very little firing practice—maybe twice we went to the firing range with the weapon. The remainder of the time we drug it around, dug holes, found locations and the best fields of fire. There were ten men on the piece, although three or four could load and fire it. We always had to dig the thing in, because when you fired that son of a gun, it would run a mile backwards.

"At our training on the coast, we would land and never get machine-gunned. The topography was supposed to be like Normandy. Inland, they had hedgerows very similar to, but not as big as, the ones in France; we were never instructed about them, never learned a cockeyed thing about blowing up hedgerows."

George Zenie, as a member of the 1st Division, returned to England in November 1943. By the end of the month the veterans of North Africa and Sicily, their ranks slowly filling with replacements, drilled in street fighting, participated in field exercises, and rebuilt their bodies with conditioning marches while toting full combat equipment.

"The week before Christmas," says Zenie, "I developed malaria, which I had contracted in North Africa. While in the hospital I also got hepatitis. When I finally returned to my company, I found we now had the 57mm guns in place of the 37mms; half-track vehicles pulled the pieces. Mounted on the half-tracks were .50 caliber machine guns. I received specialized training for assault against fortified positions.

"Because we had expected to be sent home after completing our second landing, we old-timers were angry at having to make a third one on enemy soil."

Bill Behlmer added another stripe to become a staff sergeant as his 1st Division antitank section returned to England. "We moved into a small town, had our own billets not far from the pub. We lived with the English people, threw darts with them in the pub at night, and learned to love them.

"We had constant training in every phase of warfare, rifle

marksmanship, street fighting, amphibious landings, which we practiced at Slapton Sands on the Channel. We would pack up everything every two weeks, get in the trucks, board the LSTs, hit the beach, and then back to our small-town billets and the English families.

"We got a new lieutenant, a ninety-day OCS wonder without combat experience, replacements who had no combat background, and half-tracks to pull the guns. We were impressive sights and big targets. Monty—Gen. Montgomery—reviewed us. He stood on the hood of his jeep and asked us to remove our helmets. After we did as ordered, he said, 'I can see why the English girls love you Yanks.'"

Dick Conley, the former national guardsman from Pennsylvania's 28th Division bent on making the army his career, reached Great Britain because "I incurred the wrath of the regimental commander in the 14th Armored Division. He shipped me overseas in December '43, making me an infantry replacement officer.

"When I took over a rifle platoon in Company E of the 18th Infantry Regiment, I felt at a disadvantage because all of the NCOs were combat-experienced while I was not. They instructed us about the German tactics and weapons. And they taught us actions conducive to extending one's life, like every time you stop, dig in. Of course, after you've had an artillery shell in your vicinity once, you don't ever need to be convinced to dig in. It was emphasized to me before the Normandy invasion that we were platoon leaders and we would literally lead our men. After Normandy, the emphasis would change."

Among the replacements who entered the 1st Division during its second stay in Great Britain was former defense-plant welder John Bistrica of Youngstown, Ohio. "I don't think the training in the States was adequate for what I would have to do. While the noncoms were mostly regular army and taught us a lot, some of the officers were ninety-day wonders and knew no more than I did.

"When I came to England at the Lichfield Replacement Depot, about twenty of us were sent to C Company, 16th Regiment, 1st Division. I made good friends with most of the men in the company, as I was a jeep driver.

"I had a lot to learn from the GIs who'd fought in Africa and Sicily," notes Bistrica. "Our training was tough, with night march problems, forced marches, a lot of rifle training and work in demolition. The noncoms in C Company were great; I would follow them anywhere. Fred Erben and Sgt. Nenza took charge of us. They taught us all about mines, bangalores, and special tactics that they learned in Sicily. They wanted us to ask a lot of questions."

As the third of the American infantry divisions nominated for Overlord, the 4th Division, nicknamed "Ivy" by virtue of the Roman-numeral equivalent, crossed the Atlantic in January 1944. Harper Coleman, the draftee originally a member of the 83rd Infantry Division and then a replacement in the Ivy Division, traveled from the debarkation port of Liverpool to the Channel resort town of Torquay.

"There was no letup in the training, mostly amphibious in the English Channel. We would spend two or three days on ships and then land in the Slapton Sands area. We would go over the side of the ship on rope ladders with all equipment. It was quite a task to get into the small LCVP [Landing Craft Vehicles and Personnel] when the water was rough. We would land on the beach and spend two or three days, then back to the barracks before doing it all over again. There was very little leave, except to go to town occasionally."

Nate Fellman, the Omaha draftee who transferred to the 4th Division after a nasty anti-Semitic incident with a training sergeant, encountered hostility to Americans while in England. "Whenever we got to a pub, you could hear the British complaining that the bloody stuff was rationed and we were drinking them dry. One evening, with another fellow, I attended a British dance. We were the only Americans there. We were both bumped several times while dancing. I lost my temper and poked a Brit. A fight started, but things didn't get out of control. The British MPs ejected us promptly. Our dance partners sympathized with us, and we went to a fish-and-chip shop. I believe we were as much to blame as they were for the ill feeling between the British and Americans.

"We did get a pep talk from Gen. Montgomery. One remark sort of roused our outfit. He asked us to take off our 'bonnets.' We wondered what that would prove to him about our combat-readiness. I personally thought he wanted to see how young the men were."

Sam Frackman, a jewelry worker before the draft swept him into the 4th Division, had missed the stateside amphibious training because of special-duty assignment in the personnel office. "I went back to B Company, 22nd Infantry Regiment, as a rifleman in England. But whenever the company went for training, I was left at headquarters to 'watch for spies' and to get in touch with the company if there were messages."

Captain Morgan Adair, the Marietta, Georgia, physician who went on active duty three months before Pearl Harbor, kept a diary as he struggled through the amphibious drills. He wrote of a 1944 exercise, "March 30: We arise at 4:00 A.M., eat breakfast, and wait around to embark. Finally our turn comes and we clamber down cargo nets to a waiting LCVP. It's quite dangerous, because the waves are running about ten feet and the boat pitches and tosses so that jumping into the boat is most difficult.

"Finally, we land just after 9:00 A.M. at Slapton Beach after a rough and hectic ride in which we all get wet and several get sick. I get on the beach and find things buzzing, so I just find a hole and get in it. I'm soaking wet, there is no sun, and it's cold, so I shiver plenty.

"Later Vic [fellow medic Capt. Samuel Victor] and the boys get in and we walk up hill and down dale till I think I'll drop. Finally the sun comes out, but I stay wet all day. Nightfall overtakes us and we have no blankets or bedding rolls. Vic lends me part of his and I try to sleep on a litter.

"March 31: The sun rose about 7:00 A.M. but I've been awake since dawn after shivering all night. There is ice on my raincoat. About 10:00 A.M. the problem ends and we walk about ten miles to an entrucking area." Successive diary entries describe a series of similar exercises.

North Carolinian and former candy salesman Malcolm Williams was among the 4th Division soldiers who participated in an exchange program with the British Army. "It was an outfit that had come back from Dunkirk," says Williams. "We had an Irish sergeant as our guide, and he was very good. He knew the right places to go for Scotch whiskey. While I was with them, they were reviewed by King George VI. He asked about that American in the ranks and then asked me to have tea with him."

A few weeks later, Williams rejoined the division for practice at Slapton Sands. "It was wonderful training for us—and for the German E-boats," recalls Williams. He was referring to a major dress rehearsal for the invasion, Operation Tiger. Some thirty thousand U.S. troops participated in a mock assault on the Slapton beach. But during the night, while the armada was at sea, the E-boats slipped in among the vessels and torpedoed three landing craft, two of which sank. In the confusion, some Americans fired on one another. Unfortunately, many soldiers wore their life jackets incorrectly and when they were thrown into the sea, their heads were forced down into the water. Many drowned. A total of 749 men died during Operation Tiger, yet the exercise was so big and the secrecy so tight that many of those who took part knew nothing of the disaster until years later.

Along with the tens of thousands of American GIs arriving in Britain came ships of the U.S. Navy slated to haul the soldiers to the beaches and support them. Ensign Kenneth Almy had reported for sea duty to LCI 497 berthed at Norfolk, Virginia, in the final days of 1943.

"When I arrived on the quarterdeck I was greeted by an unshaven gentleman in a wrinkled uniform, Texan Theo Pinson, who in spite of his appearance was a likable and capable captain. After receiving my orders, his only words were 'Have you made out your will? We sail January 4.' My basic training was to be on-the-job. I was glad I already knew how to swim.

"We had a regular navy chief assigned to our ship. He was tremendous and respected by all aboard. We had a crew of twenty-five hands, all young, and the chief ran a taut ship. There were at most one or two captain's masts [formal disciplinary proceedings], and those were for minor things.

"The LCI at 150 feet in length, twenty feet at the beam,

was the smallest oceangoing amphibious ship. With a mean draft of three and a half feet—about three at the bow, six at the stern—everything was above the waterline, some thirty feet of freeboard. Designed to land on beaches and then get off, it was a real sucker to turn into the wind. I wonder who figured it could manage an ocean. But we did, in the winter, storms and all. Seen from the conn of an LCI, the ocean is *really big*.

"The captain had me up in the conn when we slipped out of Hampton Roads in the late evening as part of a convoy. We were to the rear as submarine and E-boat protection—with all the firepower of our 20mm cannons. It was a nerve-racking experience. It was black dark, almost blizzardlike, and nothing to see except, from time to time, a little blue light on the stern of the LCI we followed in the column.

"I turned in some time after midnight and then got the 0800–1200 watch. I reported at 0730 to the conn and found the engineering officer had the watch. I expected him to provide some instruction, but I got a rude shock. After a brief good morning and a recitation of the sailing orders, he flipped me a salute and I was left there with a signalman. I'd arrived. Now I was senior officer of the deck.

"I don't know how many practice beach runs my ship had made before I reported, but my first was during the Slapton Sands debacle. In our assault group, three LCIs broached to on the beach, one slapping up against the large seawall of a resort hotel. We couldn't attempt a practice landing. Our after anchor winch, which would be used for pulling us back off the beach, froze up. During this exercise we were the commander's flagship. He was a shaven-headed former merchant marine officer and almost had a stroke when he heard we couldn't beach and then that those ships broached. My captain was only one of the many he was going to trash. But it turned out he never should have continued the exercise in those prevailing seas."

While Almy's ship managed to shape up with fairly minimal difficulties, for apprentice electrician Bill Hughes and his mates aboard LCI 491, with a green lieutenant j.g. as the captain, survival until D-Day appeared doubtful.

Hughes's diary of life aboard LCI 491, starting with the convoy to England, reports a series of breakdowns and collisions.

"Dec. 30, 1943: Lost one engine today, cracked block.

"Jan. 14, 1944: Last night in the Bristol Channel the waves were over the tops of the masts. We would be up on a wave and our bow and our stern and screws would be out of the water.

"Jan. 25: We rammed three ships trying to tie up at a pier. A very inexperienced captain on our ship, as all of us are.

"Jan. 28: Went on the rocks in the River Dart. Hit two barges.

"March 13: Hit two more LCIs, have a hole in our side."

On May 15, Hughes noted a triumph, the downing of a German plane. But two weeks later, during an air raid, four of the crew suffered shrapnel wounds and two of them were hospitalized.

Gil Miller, a third class petty officer, crewed on LCMs, fifty-foot boats, and reached Scotland in December 1943. Designated a signalman, Miller was aboard his LCM in a flotilla practicing beach landings.

"On April 28th, we started out, heading north at 4:00 A.M. in a full column of thirty LCMs. As dawn broke through and the sun was just coming up, we were going through Slapton Sands. We came upon many dead men, floating. We began picking them up, and my boat retrieved twenty sailors. I hooked into one and his belt-type life jacket broke. Down he went, gone forever.

"This had been Operation Tiger. There was no one else around but our thirty boats. It was so quiet; no one spoke, just pulled in the dead. They didn't look as if they had been killed by something; it was the cold water of the Channel. No man could live more than fifteen minutes in that water. When we arrived at Weymouth harbor, no one said anything."

Another resident of boot camp at Sampson when Miller started navy life was Dell Martin, whose mother had emigrated from Hungary when she was nine. "My Uncle

Edward was an officer in the German Army during the First World War and was assumed to be in the second one. My mother worried about her brother and me being on opposite sides. My father had a twenty-footer, which I had handled many times, so when asked if I had experience with small boats, I answered yes. I became a coxswain on the LCM." Like Miller, Martin prepared for the invasion at the various amphibious stations in the United States and then at the Channel ports.

Tip Randolph, snared by an air corps recruiter in the Asheville, North Carolina, post office, reached Great Britain with his fellow glider pilots from the 80th Squadron to find no craft available for training. "While we were waiting for the gliders to be assembled, we attended navigation school to keep us out of trouble. When we finally got the gliders we had two big flights. One was during daylight. The other was at night, and that was the first clue we had that we might be flying in the dark."

Vic Warriner, the power pilot who deliberately washed out, spent the spring of 1944 at the Aldermaston base near Reading. "We were introduced to the English Horsa glider, a plywood behemoth that seemed to dwarf the C-47s that towed it. It carried a much larger load than our CG-4A but was awkward and cumbersome. We all enjoyed flying it, however; its flap system was a delight. With full flaps you could descend almost vertically with little apparent increase in speed.

"Mike Murphy [Lt. Col. Michael Murphy, a former stunt pilot and subsequently specialist in glider flight] arrived at our field and in short order had us landing in small areas over obstacles he installed on runways. He drove us relentlessly.

"A couple of times we went on long cross-country flights that carried us out over the English Channel but usually in sight of land. After one of those trips, we were told we had flown the exact route we would take when the invasion came."

Pete Buckley, then still the youngest glider pilot in the air corps, also remembers the heavy dose of practice during the pre-invasion days. "When we had night landings, it would be with two or three gliders at a time and there were flares to illuminate the fields."

The 507th PR had made its way to Northern Ireland in November 1943. "Belfast with its old sailing ships, horses, and wagons brought us back fifty years," says Raider Nelson of the 507th. "In the daylight, the countryside was green and beautiful, but at night because of the blackout it was dreary and dark. We saw for the first time the hardships of the civilians. Comforts of life we took for granted, like enough food, soap, candy, cigarettes, were in short supply.

"We got along very well and would share our rations whenever we could in Ireland and England. In town we would meet guys from different units, usually in pubs, and I never had any problems. Brawls and race riots? Sure, but not for me. I couldn't see fighting someone wearing the same uniform as mine, but then I was from the North [Chicago].

"When we moved from Northern Ireland to near Nottingham, England, we started intensive training. Near the end of May I noticed a lot of supplies, ammo and medical stuff. On one of our training marches we passed an engineering outfit that were making coffins. Dozens of them were stacked high, and there were lots of wisecracks. The coffin makers might say, 'Don't worry, boys, one size fits all.' We answered, 'Don't worry about our size. You better start thinking about the Kraut size.'

"We listened occasionally to enemy radio programs. It was mostly entertaining, although we were startled to hear mention of our unit and the fact that we had turned in our winter blankets the day before. They also said they had a poppy waiting for each of us in France."

The brother regiment to Nelson's, the 508th, also settled down in the region renowned for Robin Hood. Bill Lord, the Yale dropout, says he avoided brawls in pubs and was aware of racial conflict. "The air force bomb handlers were mostly black troops, and they had been in the area before us. Some guys wanted to clean them out, but the battalion commander put a stop to that."

Lord confesses that although he considered the host people "fairly hateful as a group, I never met an individual

English man or woman I didn't like. The problems were just the tensions of being thrust into close quarters. We owned the world and were not properly respectful of these people who been fighting alone for so long."

He notes some deficiencies in their training. "We had only one night jump in England. There was one tryout for the pathfinders [troopers who would precede the main body and provide guidance for it], and that ran into such lousy weather that the jump was canceled while they were in the air."

Bud Warnecke, another Red Devil, shivered through the dismal winter climate of Northern Ireland. "We trained mostly at night and found out the higher you got into the hills, the wetter it got. We learned what peat bogs were all about. If you lay down on them, you better have a poncho under you.

"There were a lot of poker games and crap shooting. I won about five hundred dollars in a crap game. My platoon leader, Lt. Homer Jones, heard about it and said that was too much money to carry. He told me to give it to him and he would put it into a soldier's savings account, which he did.

"We were in tents on a large estate named Wollington Park. We busted our butts during the day, and at night, if we had a pass, we went into town. Sometimes *without* a pass, since the rock fence around the place was not much of a challenge. I preferred the small towns to the big city of Nottingham, because there were not many soldiers visiting the little places and the chance of a fight with legs or blacks was nil.

"One night I did go to a big pub in Nottingham. There were a bunch of British soldiers and a few troopers drinking. A Brit raised his glass and in a loud voice shouted, 'God save the king!' A dumb trooper raised his voice, yelling, 'Fuck the king!' The damnedest fight broke out. I might have been a little crazy but I wasn't a fool. I did not stick around to see how the brawl turned out."

Bernard McKearney of the 101st Airborne, the New Jersey altar boy who "dumbed his way into the paratroopers," remarks, "My Donegal father would turn over in his grave, but I like the British. Along with three sergeants I was assigned to a Brit paratroop unit in exchange for a similar setup with the 502nd. The sergeants instructed them in our weapons, and I answered questions about our army and our country with company-level troops. They all treated us with courtesy, and the junior officers extended the hands of friendship.

"Early on I discovered Bath and spent more leave time there than in London. I could call a rooming house there and they would hold a room. German bombers on the Bristol run would dump on Bath coming or going. The explosions disclosed that only part of the baths had been exploited. I became friendly with an official and had the experience of going through these eerie caverns before they ever opened them to the public.

"Col. Chappuis [battalion CO] drafted me and three other lieutenants to have Christmas dinner with a 'grande dame' whose husband was a brigadier general in Africa. It was right out of a novel, with her in velvet and an ancient butler in tails so old they were shoddy. But I admired them, and the lady invited me back three other times. I became friendly with a railroad engineer and his wife. They had a son in Southeast Asia, and I suppose I filled a gap. I would chisel some coffee from mess and have breakfast with them some Sundays. Homemade bread, bacon (rashers), and eggs seemed just right in a little cottage with nice people.

"We trained in England much as we did in the U.S. There were one or two practice night jumps. Everything we did was with full equipment, but at the platoon level we never could figure out if the maneuvers were successful. We just put our asses in neutral and let the brass shove them around.

"The division staff could have been on a different planet as far as any personal interaction with us. I never gave a thought to Gen. Taylor [Maxwell Taylor, CO of the 101st] except that he personified the force that was torturing us with the training program. I remember wondering if division staff officers had only one canteen of water a day, as we did when they were enforcing 'water discipline.' I wonder how many men wound up with kidney diseases."

Bill Dunfee, of the 82nd Airborne's 505th, lost his stripes temporarily just before he left Italy for the upper reaches of Ireland. "We had two weeks in Naples waiting on a ship. I took a couple of days unauthorized R&R and was busted. It was fun, though."

He quickly discovered his new hosts congenial. "We liked the kids and the young women, not necessarily in that order, and became used to the perennial request 'Got any gum, chum?' " The only sour note concerned the relative affluence of the paratroopers versus the natives. "I was befriended by Bill Bishop, who owned the Bishop Blaze pub. Each evening he would sell me a case of Pale Ale. I would set it on our table and with my buddies drink it up. The locals resented that, said Bishop, because they wouldn't buy it since it was more expensive than draft. But they didn't want them damn 'Yanks' drinking it either."

Any doubts about what lay ahead for Dunfee and his fellow troopers were settled by a visit from the Supreme Commander of the Allied Forces in Europe. "Within a few weeks after the 505 left Ireland for England, Eisenhower welcomed us. He thanked us for the job we did in Sicily and Italy and said he knew he could count on us in the upcoming invasion of the continent."

# CHAPTER 8

# PLANS AND EXPECTATIONS

FROM THE OUTSET of the war, President Franklin D. Roosevelt had agreed with Prime Minister Winston Churchill that the defeat of Germany was the first priority. Top civilian leaders and most military strategists agreed that Allied soldiers on the road to peace would be required to tramp through Germany itself. The first study of the possibilities for a cross-channel attack began in January 1942, barely a month after the United States entered World War II. From that period until the actual assault, Joseph Stalin, anxious to relieve pressure on the Soviet Union, hectored the Western leaders for a second front.

On their part, Churchill and Roosevelt worried that a Soviet collapse would leave them to confront all of the Nazi might. North Africa, Sicily, and then the slow bloody slog up through Italy were a long way from Berlin and in Stalin's mind did not qualify as second fronts. American leaders, at first impatient to crush the foe, painfully discovered their forces needed further buildup and training before they could expect to overcome Hitler's experienced and well-armed soldiers. Air force brass, especially the British, insisted that bombing could bring the enemy to its knees, or at least weaken him so badly that risk to ground forces would be minimized. That suited vacillating high echelons, including Churchill, fearful of a premature venture and another Dunkirk or Dieppe.

Churchill, whose attitude toward an invasion of France seesawed between wild enthusiasm and brooding despair, had initially thought a 1943 operation feasible. Gen. Dwight D. Eisenhower was not even named as supreme commander for Overlord until December 1943, and by 1944, the blueprints for Overlord had gone back to the drawing boards and conference rooms innumerable times.

The question of where to strike turned on several factors. The beaches needed to be large enough to accommodate huge masses of men and materials. The distance from British airfields had to be within the radius of air cover—all operational aircraft carriers were committed to dealing with the Japanese in the Pacific. A third element was the disposition of enemy forces.

Into the decision-making mix poured a welter of information—intelligence from aerial surveillance, tidbits supplied by Resistance fighters and spies, intercepts of telephone and radio communications on the continent, and even what could be gleaned from postcards, snapshots, and prewar vacationers' memories of the prospective beaches.

Theoretically, the most inviting target was Pas de Calais, the portion of France directly across the Channel from Dover. It was the shortest distance to Germany and highly suitable for the swift passage of armor. But the enemy knew this too. Allied observers detected extremely strong German defenses in that area.

The extreme west coast of France, Brittany, while shortening the sailing distance for supplies from the United States, lay beyond the range of British-based fighter planes. The Cotentin Peninsula lay beneath the umbrella of air cover and boasted the prize harbor of Cherbourg, but troops making a landing there could be pinched off. Furthermore, the terrain was unfavorable to the use of armor. The compromise solution was the beaches of Normandy, between the Pas de Calais and the Cotentin Peninsula. The major drawback lay in the absence of any port for delivery of troops and supplies.

To fool the enemy, Gen. George S. Patton was noisily

named commander of a paper organization called the 1st
U.S. Army Group, whose location in England suggested a
Pas de Calais invasion. Tent camps without soldiers were
erected; trucks drove through the deserted area; dummy
tanks and landing craft added to the deception. German intelligence, although it knew when Raider Nelson turned in
his winter blankets, bought the package, and nineteen enemy divisions battened down to defend Pas de Calais. Adolf
Hitler reportedly intuited Normandy as the site, but he was
swayed by the military logic that favored the more eastern
approach. Furthermore, the Luftwaffe had lost control of
the skies and its aerial reconnaissance failed to penetrate
the shroud cast by the Allies over the deployment of their
forces.

Originally, an overambitious scheme had included not
only Overlord but also Operation Anvil—a simultaneous
thrust from the Mediterranean into southern France. The
strategists realized, however, that they lacked the resources
to pull off both invasions, and Anvil, which would become
Dragoon, occurred in August 1944, eleven weeks after
Overlord began.

Another change widened the front on Normandy from
twenty to fifty miles. Although Sir Trafford Leigh-Mallory,
commander of the Allied Expeditionary Air Force, argued
vehemently against the use of airborne units, prophesying a
minimum of 50 percent casualties and perhaps 90 percent
for paratroopers and glidermen, U.S. officers, including
James Gavin, persuaded Eisenhower they were vital to success.

By 1944, when the major U.S. Army organizations (the
three infantry and two airborne divisions plus the Ranger
battalions) were on hand, the minutely detailed task of
plotting the actual landings busied strategists, tacticians,
and legions of experts.

The British assumed responsibility for the three eastern-
most beaches, designated in code as Gold, Juno, and
Sword, with the last at the extreme left of the Allied line.
Glider-borne soldiers and paratroopers would precede the
dawn landings to cut off German reinforcements and protect the exposed flank of the ground forces.

The Americans would come ashore west of the British, at beaches dubbed Omaha and Utah, the latter as the extreme right flank of the assault. The 1st Division, with two regiments of the 29th Division, the 115th and 116th, attached, was slated for Omaha, and the 4th Division would wade in on Utah. Near the hinge between Omaha and Utah, a hundred-foot precipice, called Pointe du Hoc (denoted on military maps as Pointe du Hoe in a typographical error), towered over the sea. A reported emplacement of a six-gun battery of 155mm cannons there would threaten the invasion fleet and the men pouring ashore. The need to neutralize the guns of Pointe du Hoc explained the Rangers' intensive climbing practices and Sgt. Jack Kuhn's experiments with the ladder-borne machine gun.

The first Americans in France, however, would be troopers from the 82nd and 101st Airborne Divisions, accompanied by glider-borne soldiers. Their drop behind Utah Beach would isolate coastal defenders and block the foe from rushing assistance to them. The British 6th Paratroop Division would provide similar protection behind Sword, Juno, and Gold.

While soldiers, sailors, and airmen prepared for their tasks, sharp argument over features of the plans erupted among the brass, albeit behind the soundproof doors at top-secret conferences. Adm. John L. Hall, Jr., who had responsibility for the transport and support of the Omaha Beach forces, attended a session with Adm. Charles M. Cooke, the chief planning officer under the U.S. Navy chief of staff, Adm. Ernest J. King. Hall remembered, "I banged my fist on the table and said, 'It's a crime to send me on the biggest amphibious attack in history with such inadequate gunfire support.' Roosevelt and Churchill had agreed that England would furnish the naval gunfire support for the Normandy landings. I didn't give a damn what they'd agreed on in conference. I wanted to give my troops the proper support."

When Cooke scolded Hall for his impertinence, Hall refused to back down. He recalled his reply: "All I am asking you to do is detach a couple of squadrons of destroyers from transoceanic convoy, give them to me, [and] give me a chance to train them in gunfire support for the American Army on the Omaha beaches."

Hall obtained his destroyers and also other U.S. warships, including the battleships *Nevada, Texas,* and *Arkansas,* which joined the fleet. Actually, Hall's recollection of the warship disposition was not entirely accurate. Harvey Bennett, the Yalie whose specialty was shore fire control, served on the staff of Rear Adm. Alan G. Kirk, the senior U.S. planner for the Normandy landings and commander of the entire Western Naval Task Force. Bennett was responsible for evaluation of warships engaged in bombardment as well as selection of targets.

Recalls Bennett, "In early February or later January, Adm. King notified our task force of the ships available for Overlord. These were largely the former South Atlantic Fleet cruiser force, which consisted of very old cruisers without modern fire control capability, and some ancient British destroyers. I urged Adm. Kirk to reject this in its entirety and at his direction wrote a letter spelling out the gunfire support required. The letter brought Adm. Cooke to London. There he, Kirk, Hall, and Adm. Donald Moon [Hall's counterpart for Utah Beach] conferred and discussed our requirements. We received *almost* as many vessels as requested.

"Adm. Hall was still correct in saying compared to the Pacific operations, our allocation of firepower was pretty puny. Later, at Okinawa, I was amazed at the number of warships available for short bombardments."

To provide additional firepower for Normandy, the U.S. Navy converted British-made Landing Craft Tanks (LCTs) to rocket launch vessels. The Royal Navy had employed these in the invasion of Sicily. According to official reports, "Prisoners taken during the Sicilian operation were awed by the effectiveness of the projectiles and told Allied military leaders that they had been able to stand up under ordinary shellfire but were not able to bear the fire, explosions, and destruction of the rockets."

Nine of these specially designed LCT(R)s were to blast Omaha, and five would be sent against Utah. The U.S. expert was Larry Carr, who enlisted in the Naval Reserve in July 1941 and won his commission as an ensign in March 1943. As a lieutenant j.g., Carr was appointed group commander in December 1943 and soon had crews learning how to launch the missiles.

Carr describes the seaborne weapons. "Each rocket weighed sixty pounds, was five inches in diameter and thirty-six inches in length. They were mounted in racks at a fixed forty-five-degree angle with a fixed range of 3,500 yards [just under two miles]. Every ship mounted 1,440 rockets, fired in banks of forty. All were to fire in about two minutes. There were no specific targets; the mission was to blanket the beach areas, destroying barbed-wire defenses, pillboxes, etc." The sound, fury, and sight of the rockets added a terrorizing component to their physical destructiveness.

To compensate for the absence of a port, engineers designed artificial replacements known as Mulberries. The structures consisted of hollow, floating concrete caissons, six stories tall, towed across the Channel and then submerged to form piers out into the Channel. Additionally, Gooseberries, obsolete hulls of ships, were to be sunk, providing a breakwater.

Another ingenious piece of design would expedite the transport of fuel through the Pipeline Under the Ocean—PLUTO. Mulberries, Gooseberries, and PLUTO appealed to the imaginations of the likes of Churchill and Franklin Roosevelt and presented seductive challenges to engineers and builders.

The hunt for something special, a stroke of wizardry to employ at a singular moment for a singular purpose, pushed deep into the realm of the bizarre. Karl Sulkis, a pfc drafted into the combat engineers—"I was an art director in advertising and had never handled dynamite, TNT, a jackhammer, rotating rock drill, or land mine"—recalls a damp misty day at a rifle range in England.

"About 150 yards away from us, I saw British troops working with bows and arrows. Upon our dismissal, I walked over and found a young British officer. 'Sir,' I said,

'I noticed from a distance that your men seem to be using bows and arrows, and in the middle of World War II. Why is this?'

" 'Yes, quite right,' he replied. 'You see, when Commandos strike in the black of night they do not want to announce themselves. Now these steel crossbows, used in our medieval times, will knock out a number of German sentries without alerting the whole German Army.' " This fanciful means was apparently discarded, but the experiment indicates the almost unlimited imagination applied to the task ahead.

Meanwhile, the enemy, unaware of the potential menace from twentieth-century bowmen, though expecting the attack at Pas de Calais, continued to prepare the entire coast for the inevitable blow. Field Marshal Erwin Rommel, named by Adolf Hitler as commander of the Army Group for Special Employment, held primary responsibility for the coastal defenses. But Field Marshal Gerd von Rundstedt, as commander in chief in the West, controlled dispositions of the army. To complicate the planning further, Gen. Geyr von Schweppenburg oversaw the panzer forces with their tanks and mobile armored infantry.

Rommel and von Rundstedt differed on a basic principle of the defense. The former believed it imperative to prevent the Allies from gaining a foothold on the continent. His strategy, based on mines, beach obstacles, and gun emplacements, proposed a defense four or five miles in depth. Von Rundstedt considered the coastline much too long to fend off invaders before they established their beachhead. Instead, he posited an approach that would deploy massive, mobile forces that could be rushed to an area under attack. But the panzer leader, von Schweppenburg, acutely aware of the damage done to his armor by offshore naval guns at Gela in Sicily (the use of the USS *Savannah* cited by Bill Behlmer) and Salerno in Italy, insisted on keeping his forces out of warship range. Since Allied bombers and fighter planes ruled the air, and anything that moved by daylight, particularly over roads, was at risk, swift reaction by German reserves was questionable. And Hitler had insisted that some armored divisions could move only under his direct orders.

The differences between Rommel and von Rundstedt were never resolved. Both commanders received some of what they requested but less than they believed essential. The most important asset acquired by Rommel was the movement of some reserves, particularly elements of the veteran 352nd Division, close to the beach. Their presence escaped the notice of Allied intelligence, which described many of the defenders as raw youngsters, overage or wounded vets from Soviet campaigns, and unenthusiastic conscripts from occupied territory.

Rommel invested his energy and tactical brilliance into fortifying the areas where he expected to make his stand. He arranged for a series of deadly barriers to shield the beach. Metal stakes driven into the Channel floor could rip the hull of an unwary landing craft bouncing through the water. He installed iron bars welded into the shapes of giant jackstraws to block access to the beach. Huge metal gates—"Belgian doors"—were anchored offshore to guard the approaches. Rommel's engineers wired mines to all of the obstacles.

Inland he directed his subordinates to plant *Rommel-spargel* ("Rommel's asparagus"), poles garnished with explosives and embedded in open fields to deny landing opportunities to gliders. Shortages of materials hampered but did not entirely halt a frantic program to casemate large-caliber guns overlooking strategic beaches.

From across the Channel, navy reconnaissance patrols delicately probed the target areas. Lt. Comdr. Phil Bucklew, a specialist in amphibious operations who had sneaked ashore in advance of the landings at Sicily and Salerno, was towed by a British torpedo boat to a site off the Normandy coast. He and his crew silently made their way to the beach to collect sand samples. According to Bucklew, "The texture of the sand told what kind of matting to put down to take the weight of tanks and heavy equipment." Bucklew also gathered information on the gradients of the beach.

A four-man team led by Lt. Walter R. Marshall of the Royal Navy went ashore by dinghy at Gold Beach. "Once there, we were to observe and report any unusual troop

movement or obstructions. We were not to engage the enemy. Before leaving the beach, we reported by radio of many
obstructions on the beaches. Our first fright came after
rounding a concrete building, almost running into a sentry.
Luckily, his back was turned, so we made a detour towards a
road about one mile away. On reaching it, all was so quiet
you could hardly believe a war was on. But our peace was
shattered by the rumblings of vehicles. Rounding a bend,
we came almost face to face with a convoy. We scattered into
a ditch like scared rabbits and lay there, hearts pounding.
Fortunately, we weren't seen. We duly reported three trucks
towing field guns, three tanks, and motorcycle escorts. After
that surprise scare, we became more cautious. We spent several more hours scouting the area, reporting on obstacles
and gun emplacements. At 2330 hours, we headed back to
the beach to rendezvous with a submarine."

Even without such missions, the strategists in England
were aware of the beachfront work ordered by Rommel. As
a consequence, the navy people wanted to strike at low
tide, when landing craft could ground before encountering
the obstacles in the water. The army, however, insisted on
high tide because the farther in the troops landed, the less
open beach they would need to cross. A compromise settled on an H-Hour one to three hours after extreme low
water.

To facilitate the nighttime airborne operations, full
moonlight was desired. Less possible to plan for was
weather. High winds would endanger the seaborne movement and the airdrop, which also would suffer from thick
cloud cover.

Based on the readiness of the forces and the conditions
required, the period of June 5–7 became the primary target. The next favorable tidal time thereafter would be June
18–20.

# CHAPTER 9

# FINAL MOMENTS

"ON MAY 20," says Bob Edlin, the lieutenant who had won Rudder's approval as a Ranger recruit by declaring he would surrender if surrounded and out of ammunition, "the 2nd and 5th Ranger Battalions moved into the marshaling area at Weymouth on the English Channel. The weather was beautiful, sunshine; we knew the time was getting close for the invasion.

"The first four days were pretty much carefree. We could go into any nearby town, do just about anything, drink, gamble, or whatever. We had the usual arguments with the paratroopers of the 101st Airborne.

"On May 25, the party was over. We were locked in the marshaling area for a briefing. The area was surrounded by barbed wire. Armed guards, MPs and British, were stationed outside the fence. We were ordered not to communicate with them. We couldn't have any conversation with anybody who wasn't more or less imprisoned in the compound. In fact, we felt more like prisoners than we did invading troops.

"We were briefed by Col. Rudder on the complete invasion, including the roles of the British, Canadians, Americans, paratroopers, 29th Infantry Division, the 4th and 1st Infantry Divisions, and what the Ranger battalions were to do. We were told the date, time, and location of the invasion. I can remember someone saying, 'Hitler would give ten million dollars to know what I know.' "

Behind the barbed wire of the marshaling area Bob Slaughter of the 29th Division realized, "This was serious business. Brand-new equipment was issued and new weapons had to be zeroed in on the firing range. Unlimited amounts of ammo were given for target practice. Bayonets and combat knives were honed to razor sharpness.

"Food not seen since leaving the United States was fed to us, and it was all-you-can-eat. Steak and pork chops with all the trimmings, topped off with lemon meringue pie, were items on a typical menu. One of the wags said, 'They're fattening us up for the kill.' The officers became a bit friendlier, and it seemed that the men were kinder to each other. First-run movies were shown; *Mrs. Miniver* with Greer Garson and Walter Pidgeon was one of my favorites. Touch football, softball, boxing, reading, and letter writing were popular pastimes. Bible verses were must reading for most of us, and prayers were said many times a day.

"New Yorker Francis 'Skeets' Galligan put on a Broadway skit, *Yankee Doodle Dandy*, portraying himself as George M. Cohan. Skeets, agile and a fair tap dancer, concluded the routine by jumping high in the air and clicking his feet together. Seminude hoochie-koochie dancers grinding hips to a beat on a tight canvas cot brought smiles and cheers from a captive audience."

"We knew all those men and equipment in England would be put to a purpose," says Bernard McKearney, the paratroop platoon leader in the 502nd. "But the training just went on. On the day the schedule called for a route march, we had no idea that we were marching to the marshaling area. It gradually dawned on us that the usual ten-minute break had stretched into an hour and that something was afoot. When they began to string the wire around our enclave, we knew, holy moley, show time!"

Lou Merlano, the 101st AB paratrooper who found refuge from the agony of learning to be a medic, accepted a new post when his battalion entered the marshaling area. "I was promoted to corporal and assistant to Sgt. Perko for radio. This would be my first combat experience, but I felt so well trained that I likened myself to a double-edged razor blade.

"I attended church services, continued to study mission plans, kibitzed day in day out, carried on like it was Tennessee maneuvers. One activity was sharpening trench knives, then competing by throwing them at targets.

"During the briefings we received better and better information and aerial photos. They were so clear I could see the faces of cows in some pictures. The sand tables were similar to many exercises we had run. Nobody said much about the nature of our opposition. We were told we'd be up against some of the best, but if we could give it three days without letting up, our mission would be accomplished."

The days before D-Day dwindled, and everybody's drills followed a consistent pattern. As a platoon leader in the 502nd Airborne, the former star Oklahoma State halfback Wallace Swanson recalls, "For those in my position, preparations began with platoon- and squad-size units. Company and battalion officers got their instructions from regimental headquarters. The emphasis for the individual soldier fell on the need to know their special assignments, the roadway, buildings around and along the area we would maneuver in. As a platoon leader I wanted my men to know all the assignments and why each individual's job was so important to the objectives assigned to the platoon. The sand tables were well prepared, showing typical vegetation, the probable roads, trails, buildings, and strongpoints a platoon and company needed to take and hold in order to secure the beach behind us.

"Aerial photos were available, but we had no idea where along the coast of Europe the invasion site was. The area assigned to our unit was small and the pictures never showed enough of the coastline or beach to identify where we would be on the continent."

Swanson apparently was told very little about the overall plan, while Ranger Edlin received a detailed briefing. The differences are partially due to decisions by commanders who decided what information should be communicated.

Policy, based on rank and role, also established what a soldier should know. "Intelligence information was comprehensive," says C. B. McCoid of the 507th PR. "Those of us at the company command level were 'bigoted' [cleared for top secret] according to a very carefully scheduled and controlled briefing plan. All needed maps were on hand, along with a large-scale sand table and day-to-day aerial photography of the objective.

"All German division-size formations were located and identified, or at least we thought they had been. So long as they were not panzer or panzer grenadier, we felt absolutely sure we could handle them. Tanks posed a threat that we could not afford to take lightly.

"Our area was the northernmost of the departure airdromes, so we were spared the inspirational pep talks by the extremely senior and important officials based in London or in the extreme south. Instead we heard from Gens. Ridgway and Gavin. The troops cheered both, but the former scared the hell out of me as he spoke of closing with a 'cruel and brutal enemy.'

"The last-minute instructions, beyond those relating to the scheme of maneuver, involved the sign and password, no firing of weapons before daylight [other troopers claim no order of this nature makes sense], and the requirement for all to jump even if wounded. With respect to prisoners, the plan was to treat them in accordance with the Geneva Convention provisions. If any of our troops had other understandings, there had been no official sanction. Indeed, there was stress on the importance of rapid exploitation of POWs for enemy information."

As a member of the 508th PR, Bill Lord, although only a noncom, had learned of his outfit's mission several days before his fellow GIs. He also heard some unsettling talk. "Two or three days before we left Nottingham for the marshaling area at the airport, I was asked to attend a briefing. I had been in artillery ROTC and then in the 81mm mortar platoon, where I did some special work devising methods for mortars to fire as a battery, something not in the manual for mortars. Because we were expected to do a lot of indirect fire, I was asked to attend the briefing, where we would get some targets, and I could do preliminary work.

"I had mixed feelings. At the first briefing we heard that some people anticipated fifty percent casualties or higher. That was scary, but on the other hand it was good to have finished our training. We were all volunteers, and this was what we had come for. That doesn't mean there wasn't a whole lot of self-questioning. No one knows how he will act in combat."

Bill Dean, another 508th PR trooper, enveloped in a ceaseless series of last-minute rehearsals, experienced many changes in mood—anxiety, uncertainty, fear, even boredom. "The boredom came from spending part of every day during the first week of June in a dry run of packing and unpacking the platoon equipment bundle which would hang under the C-47. It would be electrically released by the first jumper just before he jumped. Each bundle had its own parachute, which opened when the bundle fell from the belly of the plane.

"For us, a bundle was about eight feet long, possibly two feet in diameter, and in it were mortar tubes, mortar ammunition, .30 caliber machine guns, ammunition for them, tripods, and other assorted items like land mines."

"As early as April 12," remembers Dr. Morgan Adair, the Georgia physician serving with the 4th Infantry Division, "Gen. Omar Bradley had spoken to us at Exeter and told us we were going to be the spearhead of the invasion. I had felt dread and relief at the same time then."

Now, six weeks later, behind the fences of the assembly spot, Adair heard some specifics. His March 26 diary declares: "We are to land in France on Cotentin Peninsula on beach Uncle [Utah] about five miles north of le Grand Vey on Seine Bay. I will land thirty minutes after H-Hour and will be in the fourth wave. Vic will land ten minutes later in the fifth wave. The D-Day objective will be Sainte-Marie-du-Mont. Just inland from the beach we will have to cross a flooded area. Looks plenty tough to my jaundiced eye."

A one-sentence entry for May 28: "I brief my boys today and you never saw a more sober group."

A series of small incidents tipped Bob Meyer, the BAR man in the 4th Division, to the imminence of the invasion. "As we moved out of our barracks to a staging area, a couple of things told us it was for real. We had gone out on amphibious drills before, but this time, as we left, construction workers moved in to convert our barracks into a hospital. When we reached the staging area, we had to convert any money we had to French francs. There was a new issue of clothing. I received new shoes with hobnails, great for field work, but when walking on paved areas I sounded like a team of horses.

"We also had religious services which included communion. Chaplain Boice had to improvise—little pieces of bread instead of the usual wafers, cider instead of wine. It was symbolic and no one thought it sacrilegious."

Some in the 29th Division refined the sand-table displays. Bob Slaughter says, "Capt. Schilling briefed us on the big picture and then told us our particular assignment. Lt. William Garner, a West Point graduate and the company exec, rigged up a model of our sector of Omaha Beach, code-named Dog Green. He featured the Vierville draw, Pointe du Hoc, and most importantly, the Vierville church steeple, which we were to guide on. Electric lights simulated shell bursts to enhance the realism of his handiwork."

Slaughter, as well as a number of his buddies, insists, "We were told that during the first three days we were not to take any prisoners. We were going to be too busy to deal with captives."

Bill Lord with the 82nd Airborne's 508th PR does not recall hearing official word on prisoners, but years later a fellow trooper claimed to him that no less a personage than Jim Gavin indicated prisoners could not be accommodated. On the other hand, Wallace Swanson with the 101st AB declares that he was never advised not to accept surrenders and would not have obeyed an order to kill unarmed men. His superior, John Hanlon, also denies any no-prisoners dictum.

While Felix Branham, the tech sergeant in the Virginia-bred 116th Infantry Regiment who enjoyed the hospitality of Lady Astor, professed hatred of the Germans, many men regarded them more dispassionately. "I had no animosity towards the Germans," says Don McCarthy, a replacement with the 116th Infantry's Headquarters Company in England. "And my attitude towards them did not change after D-Day."

In the 1st Division, vets like George Zenie could only swallow their bitterness at being called upon for a third landing after North Africa and Sicily. "Late in May we were told we could not leave our compound because we were going to land in France. Our half-track, which would pull the antitank gun, was waterproofed as much as possible. We would carry antitank mines, bangalore torpedoes, 57mm armor-piercing and antipersonnel rounds, and .50 caliber machine gun ammunition.

"Our platoon leader, Lt. Bizzorti, had been briefed with photos. Since I was his platoon sergeant, he told me the landing would be tough. He was concerned about underwater and beach obstacles, fearing we would have to try and land in water that was too deep for our half-tracks."

Bill Behlmer, now an acting platoon sergeant, had been among those who assumed they would be excused from the invasion because of their previous exposures to combat. But the high command wanted as many experienced GIs as could be mustered. "Finally, we pulled into a staging area and we knew what we were in for. The gnawing feeling returned again. Our objective would be pillboxes and anything moving on the beach. We were to hit the beach, find cover, unhook the 57s, and start firing."

British forces had geared up for Overlord with practice landings and beach assault training. Intelligence specialist Jim Murray with the 8th Battalion of the King's Regiment figured out his outfit's destination very early after an operation that began on Christmas Eve in 1943. "We were issued maps that were called Bogus. They were copies of French ones, but the grids had been altered and the towns had bogus names. Our objective was a place called Haddington on the map. It did not take long for me to puzzle out, with the help of a French map, that it

represented Caen. I discussed this with the intelligence officer and he told me to keep quiet about it and not mention
it to anyone."

Bill Sadler, since his hasty departure from Dunkirk four
years earlier, had served most of his duty driving various vehicles for the Royal Army Medical Corps. During a drill, he
had gone through the ignominious experience of having his
amphibious jeep founder in heavy waves. The higher pow-
ers recognized that seagoing jeeps were too risky and settled for a waterproofing method that would enable them to
wade through the shallows onto the beach.

A few weeks after Sadler had personally waterproofed his
vehicle with a kit, he was in a camp sealed off from the rest
of the world. "On June 3, Saturday, my jeep was taken
away and replaced with a brand-new one which had already
been waterproofed by the Royal Electrical and Mechanical
Engineers. They had taken over the heavier transport main-
tenance for the army. It was real evidence of how well off
we were for equipment when they could do that without
turning a hair.

"The jeep had small red crosses already painted on the
sides and a large one on the bonnet. There was a framework slotted into brackets on the bodywork. With this installed, it was possible to carry three wounded, two above
my head and one alongside. The stretcher framework was
stowed and the back end piled up above the level of my
head with gear of all sorts. In addition I carried, strapped to
the bonnet, a lightweight, two-wheeled trailer normally
used by airborne."

Sadler boarded a U.S. Navy LST (Landing Ship Tank).
Once he arranged for a place to sleep, beneath a water supply bowser (vehicle) tarpaulin, Sadler says, "I went over
what I had been taught at the Combined Ops School for
Wet Landing—the technique and actions for successfully
driving through several feet of water with a vehicle that was
never designed for that purpose. All breathers had to be
blocked. A groundsheet tied to the front axle and brought
up over the bonnet created a bow wave which would direct
water away to the side. It was necessary to select a low gear,
and once in the water, never use the clutch! Once on dry

land, it was mandatory to cut away the groundsheet and clear the breathers. The exhaust was taken up high by the use of metal tubing which came with the kit. As soon as possible, the accelerator and foot brake should be applied at the same time to dry out the brake pads.

"As we moved out during the early evening, the stuff surrounding us was mind-boggling. There were craft of all shapes and sizes, many towing antiaircraft balloons aloft. Whenever we saw aircraft, they all sported black and white stripes under the wings. [Because of the horrible losses from friendly fire during the invasion of Sicily, these markings were decreed for Overlord to indicate Allied aircraft to American and British naval and ground gunners.]

"Also for the first time we saw a strange animal known as a Rhino raft. They consisted of a number of large, airtight tanks bolted together to form a huge square raft. The whole contraption was driven by two large, outboard donkey engines mounted at the rear, where there were also two helms, manned by a crew from the Royal Engineers. But in the convoy while towed behind the larger vessels only one man was aboard."

The glider pilots were locked in at their airfields. Tip Randolph evaluates the intelligence he received. "One thing you learn early in flying is to judge heights of objects on the ground by the shadows thrown at a particular time of day. They presented us with aerial photographs of where we would land, taken around 11:30 A.M. The reconnaissance people said the hedgerows we saw were from six to eight feet high.

"Someone asked the briefing officer how he knew that for sure. It sounded like a wise-ass question, but then he was staying, while we were going. He answered that the people who took the photographs said these were the heights. Two or three days later they showed us another set of pictures taken on a different day but at close to the same hour, around noon. We felt we weren't getting a straight answer. The hedgerows and trees around there turned out to be much much higher than six or eight feet." In fact, the trees in the hedgerows were from thirty to sixty feet in height.

There was a well-publicized ceremony with the glider that Col. Mike Murphy would fly. As the officer in charge of glider training, Murphy could have avoided the mission, but he argued for a role until he was granted the lead spot in the squadron with Buckley and Warriner. Not only was Murphy going to be out in front, but he would carry a prize passenger, Brig. Gen. Don Pratt, the deputy commander of the 101st Airborne. The brigadier had persuaded his boss, Gen. Maxwell Taylor, to let him go in with the gliders rather than come by sea on D plus one.

The glider assigned to Murphy was supposed to be the *Fighting Falcon*, paid for by donations from school kids in Greenville, Michigan. After it had arrived in England, it had been assembled and set aside for use on D-Day. But since its construction, the CG-4A had been modified with the addition of the "Griswold Nose." Composed of a network of curved steel trusses, the Griswold Nose offered more protection to pilots and passengers when a glider collided with small trees, wire barriers, and other small obstacles. To ensure the safety of Gen. Pratt, the original *Fighting Falcon* would be replaced with a model bearing the new nose.

After all of the photographs with Murphy, his copilot, Pratt, and his aide were taken, the *Fighting Falcon* became the ship for a lesser crew while the VIPs were slated for one of the safer models. Into that glider went the general's jeep, the command radio he anticipated using, and some extra cans of gasoline for the vehicle. The weight slightly exceeded the safe load limits of cargo for a CG-4A, but Murphy, an extremely skilled pilot, felt confident he could handle it. However, unknown to him, members of Pratt's staff concerned for the general's survival arranged to install sheet iron plates on the cargo compartment floor to protect against ground fire. The added weight amounted to a gross overload and destroyed the usual flight trim of the glider. Murphy never had an opportunity to test-fly the machine for its performance in the air. He learned of the alterations only when he boarded it, bound for Normandy.

As a number of men noted, both Eisenhower and Montgomery visited the troops shortly before the overture of Overlord. Horace Wright, the former prisoner of war now restored to the post of platoon leader for the Hampshire Regiment, saw both of the top military leaders. "Ike was very impressive," says Wright. "His sincerity was apparent. He spoke freely and clearly as a commander, but there was nothing of the braggart about him. He emphasized the importance of liberating Europe.

"Montgomery turned up with his beret, the two badges on it. He got up on the bonnet of his jeep and surveyed the troops, then beckoned for them to break ranks and surround him. He was a showman and did what was expected of him."

The North Shore Regiment played host to Montgomery, Eisenhower, and George VI. Canadian Everett Gorman appreciated all three. "Montgomery gave us the feeling that he would do everything he could to make it as safe as possible before committing the troops. After he spoke to us standing on his jeep, the men were allowed to swarm around him.

"Eisenhower inspected us, walking through the ranks. He was very nonchalant, shaking hands, stopping here and there to chat. He too seemed to put the seal of approval on us for the invasion."

American paratrooper John Hanlon was somewhat awed by Montgomery. "I don't remember a word he said, but when he opened his greatcoat and we saw all those ribbons from North Africa, it was very impressive. I didn't see Eisenhower but he talked to several of our guys. The questions seemed superficial."

A well-known photograph on the eve of the invasion shows the Supreme Commander with a group of 101st Airborne troopers. In the forefront stands Wallace Strobel, assistant platoon leader to Wallace Swanson. "Strobel was a shy but very conscientious officer," says Swanson. "He told me that Eisenhower asked one soldier where he lived in Kansas, how the fishing was; and another trooper how his folks were doing, how he liked it in the paratroopers. Both Strobel and I felt the questions were ones the soldiers could answer easily, ones that would relax them. Even though he was the Supreme Allied Commander, he had a knack for reaching out to the enlisted man, the mainstay and the real power for our forces."

Bill Dunfee of the 505th PR, confined behind the barbed wire early in June, attended his only briefing. "It was pretty minimal. Take Sainte-Mère-Eglise and set up a perimeter defense. Hold Sainte-Mère-Eglise until contact was made by seaborne forces, then new orders would be issued. I believe we were not told any more than we needed in case we were captured.

"I felt our officers and noncoms were good to excellent. The company commander, Capt. Harold Swingler, was a superior officer in every way. He had been in the hospital for elective knee surgery, and when the invasion became imminent, he signed himself out to rejoin us. Our battalion commander was Lt. Col. 'Cannon Ball' Krause, a character who I believe fancied himself a junior-grade George Patton. I don't question his courage, but his ability to handle people and retain their respect was nonexistent. He ruled by fear.

"Our junior officers were with us, but I didn't see Krause, Gavin, or Ridgway. There was no pep talk as such. The officers were very friendly, as they usually were in combat. They knew we understood what was expected of us. They brought in a swing band that was really great. Even had some of our guys dancing with each other. The band was only there for about an hour. We really appreciated the music."

During the first days of June, with the invasion scheduled to begin on the 5th, the airborne contingents bedded down at the airfields. The men destined to arrive by sea boarded a variety of vessels. Felix Branham's rifle company, like others, increased from roughly 200 to 240 men to compensate for the expected casualties, creating an almost festive atmosphere as the unit left the marshaling camp. "As we marched to the ship, people lined the streets, undoubtedly knowing this would be the great invasion. Military police cordoned off the well-wishers from the troops. We looked very stoic, eyes straight ahead as we marched, loaded down with equipment, through the streets. People threw food, flowers, and kisses, but we had to ignore them as we marched up the gangplank of the USS *Charles Carroll*.

"The food aboard this American Navy ship was super. Nothing was too good for the men who were to beat down the walls of Hitler's fortress. There was steak, white bread, real eggs fixed any way you wanted them, fresh fruit, desserts of all kinds, even ice cream made aboard ship. On Sunday, June 4th, Rome fell. D-Day was scheduled to be the next day.

"That afternoon we assembled on deck with our assault equipment. I had 286 rounds of M-1 ammunition, ten hand grenades, a twenty-pound satchel charge of TNT, a twenty-pound pole charge of TNT, and a half-dozen blasting caps. Everyone was given a quarter-pound block of TNT with a seven-second fuse lighter. It was to be used as an aid to dig a quick foxhole in case of a counterattack, or to blow up a fortification."

"On the 4th of June," recalls Bob Slaughter, "loaded down with sixty pounds of equipment, the 1st Battalion soldiers walked up the gangplank and onto the HMS *Empire Javelin*. A raging storm postponed D-Day for twenty-four hours.

"Capt. Schilling gave us a last pep talk. He was neither universally loved nor hated. George Kobe called him a second father; John B. Sink labeled him a tyrant. We listened, over the roar of the ship's engine, to every word. The mood was solemn and Schilling was subdued. He said, 'This is the real McCoy. The dry runs are over.' He said he was proud to lead this company into battle. The enemy would be well trained and would fight like hell to protect his homeland. He told us that our sector would have twenty-two bunkers protecting it but only one or two of them would be occupied.

"The report on the quality of troops defending our sector was that they were not first-rate soldiers but Polish and Russian volunteers and some overage home guard. Schilling did not expect them to be fanatical defenders. What he and the intelligence experts did not know was that the crack 352nd Division had moved into the area and manned the pillboxes.

"Schilling stressed, 'Cross the beach fast, gain the high ground, and get into a perimeter defense. The enemy has a large reserve force that can counterattack in twenty-four hours. By then the tank and heavy artillery will be in place and you should be able to repel their best effort.' "

Felix Branham with Company K of the 116th prepared to climb into his landing craft, which was a type suspended by davits and then lowered to the water. "We were very tense being cooped up in tight living quarters. I began to gripe to some of my buddies, 'Damn, I sure hope they don't drop us in deep water and I have to swim ashore.'

"Standing behind me was this rather large navy man—he was about six feet four inches—with the collar of his coat turned up, and there was braid on his cap. He said, with authority, 'Soldier, I have put over fifty thousand men ashore and none have ever had to swim!' He was the commander of the ship."

But even as Branham mustered on deck, on the night of June 4–5, the weather adamantly refused to cooperate with the Allied plans. Orders to stand down were issued. Branham and his fellow infantrymen retrieved their equipment from the LCI.

The huge fleet, numbering five thousand vessels, milled about in the Channel waters while the meteorologists consulted their data and formulated a prediction for the following night. Troops who had been aboard the lurching ships for several days coped with seasickness. The airborne forces settled in for another twenty-four hours of waiting.

Ed Jeziorski of the 507th PR says, "Normandy would be my first combat. As foolish as it sounds today, I, among many, felt relief that we would be committed, and excited over the prospect of tangling with Jerry to show what we could do. I felt let down when we were told the invasion was held off for a day.

"While in the hangars, before moving out to the planes, we gathered around a small radio as the 'Berlin Bitch' came on. Her words still live with me. 'Good evening, 82nd Airborne Division. Tomorrow morning, blood from your guts will grease the bogie wheels [weight-bearing wheels of tank tracks] on our tanks.' Then she played tear-jerking songs."

Dave Thomas, the battalion surgeon in the 508th PR,

was among the thousands behind the barbed-wire fences. "I was always an odds player and won a lot of money playing poker. This night I wasn't doing that well at the table, so I thought I might as well go hit a lick with Jesus. I sat down in the last cot; the place was sold out. Chaplain James Elder was really getting the troops in. As I sat down, he said, 'Now, the Lord isn't particularly interested in those who only turn to him in time of want.' I thought, what the hell am I doing here? I got up and went back to the poker game, but still didn't do all that well.

"Some time later back in England after Normandy, I told Chaplain Elder about the incident. He was mortified."

Bill Dunfee recalls, "I was disappointed and let down when the mission was postponed twenty-four hours. I was emotionally ready to go. I did my sweating before a mission. Once airborne I was apprehensive but became very calm and accepted whatever was to come."

Turk Seelye, like Dunfee already a veteran of combat with the 505th, recalls the same uneasiness. "We had spent a couple of days and nights living in barracks close to the landing strip. We spent the time getting our equipment ready, sharpening knives and bayonets, and in general having feelings of apprehension of what was to happen next.

"On the 3rd or 4th of June we had been billeted in the airport hangar itself. Our beds were blankets spread on the concrete floor. We were issued the grenades, ammunition, and other supplies that we would carry. Briefings consisted of studying maps and using sand tables, as well as showing each unit the scope of their particular mission. That's when we had learned that the invasion would take place in Normandy.

"Other activities at the airport included shooting craps and playing poker, using the French invasion currency, watching a movie in the evening, and attending religious services."

In the G-3 section—divisional plans and operations—of the 82nd Airborne, Tom Graham of the 505th PR recalls a frantic, nonstop process. "It was a day-and-night project because of the changes made in where we were supposed to jump. Aerial photos would come in to the war room and things had to be changed. No one knew exactly where we were going to drop until shortly before takeoff."

"We lived under a huge camouflage net at Ramsburg Airfield for about ten days," remembers gliderman Vic Allegretti. "We were all 'gung ho'; this would be our first combat mission by glider after landing in Sicily and Italy by sea."

Medic Frank South with the 2nd Ranger Battalion had entered a marshaling yard near Dorchester. "There was an intelligence tent set up with a detailed sand model of the Pointe du Hoc cliff and the objectives down to gun emplacements, bunkers, tunnel works, and minefields. Stereoscopic slides gave us pictures in 3-D. Each of the noncoms was instructed to copy the layout of Pointe du Hoc on cigarette papers, which could be destroyed easily or swallowed if necessary."

The Ranger assignment was accepted with confidence by Rudder, but viewed in some circles as hopeless. A high-level officer involved in the Overlord planning declared, "Three old women with brooms could knock the Rangers off the cliff."

Battalion surgeon Walter Block wrote in his diary: "This is the last entry to be written before D-Day. If something happens to me, see that my wife Mrs. Alice Block gets this book. Kiddo—I love you."

Frank South and the other Rangers began the first leg of their adventure. "At sea," says South, "I did not go through any religious preparation but I did repeatedly go over the plans and where every item of equipment or supply was in the huge pack I had. I compulsively and repeatedly inspected and cleaned the .45 Colt automatic I buried in the pack, and I sharpened my knife. All the while I chatted with the Combined Operations medic with whom I stayed in the ship's surgery during the night.

"Most of the men and noncoms remained quite sober, reviewing their mission and checking their arms on board the ship. Some did a bit of gambling. Morale was high, and most of us felt confident in our abilities and those of our comrades.

"There was one exception. Our recently appointed battalion commander had been drinking a bit too much. He either originated or supported the opinion that the assault group of the 2nd Rangers were being sent on a suicide mission and that there was no chance we would survive. Communicating this sort of notion would have been devastating. Word of the problem was sent to Rudder, who was on a nearby ship. He immediately transferred over to our *Ben Machree* and assumed direct command of the Pointe du Hoc operation.

"I was aware that something was happening on the *Ben Machree*, since the process of arresting and leading off the former commander of the operation was a noisy one and much of it occurred in the stairwell next to the ship's surgery. I opened the door to find out what was going on, only to see a group of struggling and shouting uniforms, and was immediately ordered back inside by Rudder."

The major in his cups stepped over the line and punched Captain Walter Block, the battalion doctor held in such high esteem. "Block was beloved," says Len Lomell. "Hitting him was like taking a sock at somebody's mother. They held the major down until Rudder came aboard and had him hauled ashore to the stockade."

Ranger sergeant Jack Kuhn, who had experimented with the machine gun mounted atop a firefighter's ladder, was aboard HMS *Amsterdam*. "I could not envision myself going into combat. It seemed so detached from me, as if it were happening to someone else. The one thing I feared was not being able to face the test. I didn't want to coward out. Then everyone else said the same thing, and I was okay. I never had the apprehension that I would be killed or wounded.

"As tension mounted in the hold of the *Amsterdam*, Tom Ruggiero, who had studied acting, and I decided that a skit was needed. We had put on short, crazy ones as gags during training, and with Bill Hoffman and Bob Fruhling we put on a show, and it helped. Sometime after, when I got into my bunk, I lay there and listened to my men talking. They all expressed anxiety at not being able to face the unexpected, and were fearful of running.

"Bill Hoffman remarked, 'I know some of us are going

to get killed. If there is a choice between Kuhn and me being killed, I hope it's me. I am single but Jack has a baby and wife at home.' Bill to this day does not know I heard him. But that was the type of man who formed the Rangers."

While the objective for Rangers Kuhn, Len Lomell, and George Kershner of D Company (aided by E and F from the 2nd Battalion) was Pointe du Hoc, C Company's mission was to land to the right of Omaha Beach's Dog Green sector and advance to Pointe et Raz de la Percée.

When C Company's Sid Salomon, the tall NYU business grad who chose the Rangers after finding his infantry training "a joke," walked up the gangplank of HMS *Prince Charles*, Ranger chief Col. Rudder shook hands with him and with Ralph Goranson, the CO of C Company, and Bill Moody, the other platoon leader. Said Rudder, "You've got the most dangerous mission."

On the British transport, Lt. Salomon became friendly with the vessel's officers. "I roomed with the chief engineer, and they lived an entirely different life from ours. Every morning a steward would knock on the cabin door, with cups of tea for both of us. The men were fed from big pans, the food dealt out like slop to them. But very few of them felt like eating as D-Day approached. There were a lot of seasick Rangers, filling up paper bags. But for the most part, everyone was cheerful. There was great enthusiasm and self-confidence."

On board an American vessel, Bill Sadler was equally nonplussed by the behavior of his hosts. "Over the public address system the Americans were playing the Andrews Sisters singing 'Mr. Five by Five'! Never before or since have I met up with anything as incongruous. Here we were, embarked on the greatest sea invasion of all time, and those Americans were playing a typical pop tune. Strangely enough, my first thought was the Germans would hear it and the gaff would be blown. Stupid—we were miles away.

"Then, with the water bowser driver, I tried to sleep. We didn't have much success. We were excited, and the heaving and swaying of the ship didn't help. Had I known what the dawn held in store, I probably would not even have closed my eyes."

"I was never seasick," says Len Lomell. "But after a couple of days on the ship, I was getting a bit stir-crazy. I am a Protestant but wasn't particularly religious. I never saw anybody praying. We had so much to think about in performing our job, there didn't seem to be time for prayer.

"I had a good relationship with Father Joe Lacy, the Catholic chaplain assigned to the Rangers. I made everyone in D Company attend services, usually. Late on the eve of D-Day, I was in a hot poker game in the mess hall when someone announced a midnight mass by Lacy. Here I was with a good hand and I figured I'm entitled to a few more minutes, so I said I'm staying. Three of the eight guys at the table got up and went. The next morning, all of them died."

The heavy attendance at religious services indicates the high levels of anxiety. Training had hardened the men for their tasks and stripped away some of their naiveté, but nothing could give untested men like Ed Jeziorski or Jack Kuhn a true sense of what they would undergo. The worst worry for many was whether they would look bad in front of their buddies. As mostly young men, only a few years beyond adolescence with its inherent sense of omnipotence, they denied the possibility of their own destruction. On the eve of the invasion, both spirit and flesh were resolute.

PART II

# D-DAY

# CHAPTER 10

# THE AIR DROPS

BOTH THE BRITISH and the American airborne operations were designed to forestall any German deployment of reserves against the soldiers storming onto the beaches. The beneficiaries of the paratroopers from the U.S. 82nd and 101st Airborne Divisions, as well as glidermen, would be the GIs from the 4th Infantry Division on Utah Beach. No airborne forces would be deployed behind Omaha Beach, however. Gavin, among the others involved in the early planning, believed that the flat terrain behind Omaha would expose the paratroopers to the crush of an expected advance by German armor.

The area picked out for the elements of the 82nd straddled the Merderet River five to ten miles behind Utah Beach, forming a rough triangle whose perimeter measured about ten miles. The major objectives included the town of Sainte-Mère-Eglise, which sat astride a crossroads and a rail line that connected Cherbourg in the northwest with Paris.

The 101st Airborne Division under Gen. Maxwell Taylor would form a racetrack-shaped position parallel to Utah only two or three miles behind the beach. The 101st's troopers and their glider component drawn from the 327th Glider Regiment were expected to hold a coastal road that ran toward Carentan, a known stronghold of enemy reserves. The flight plan for all U.S. airborne components carried them on a southwest course toward the Channel Islands of Guernsey and Jersey. There a submarine-borne beacon light would signal the transports to veer east over the Cotentin Peninsula for the final run to the appointed areas.

For recognition purposes, the troopers in the 101st Airborne carried tiny noisemakers, spring-steel crickets of the type usually included in boxes of Cracker Jack caramel popcorn. One click was the challenge and two snaps was the appropriate response. John Hanlon, years later, investigated the origins of the idea and its incorporation into Overlord.

Hanlon asked Gen. Maxwell Taylor, with whom the idea originated, and the former Screaming Eagles commander proudly declared, "It rose out of my experiences earlier in the Mediterranean and from our Eagle exercise in England. There was so much dispersion in Sicily," said Taylor, "that I realized we needed some method of identification behind enemy lines. Eagle convinced me more than ever. We needed a little noisemaker a man could carry in his hand. The cricket seemed just right."

"It was a last-minute thing," says Hanlon. "They were issued literally just a day or so before takeoff. And it was more than a matter of simply sending a supply sergeant or two—the scrounging abilities of that noble breed aside—around to the sweet shops near our English bases and sweeping the shelves clean of Cracker Jack packages."

Somehow, the quartermaster people located the thousands of crickets in the United States and promptly shipped them to England. The tiny gadgets were still being issued even as the troopers moved behind barbed wire in their final staging areas. Hanlon notes, "Each cricket required prepping. A small hole was drilled through its back. Then a length of string was inserted in the hole and tied, after which the contraption was ready to be hung around the neck and tucked inside the jump jacket."

While the 7,500 men of the 101st clicked together in Normandy, the troopers of the 82nd Airborne, according to James Gavin, relied solely on the passwords "Flash" and

"Thunder." Hanlon asked Gavin the rationale. "There was a lot of gadgetry around," Gavin responded, "and a lot of it didn't make much sense. In Normandy, the 82nd used only an oral password. It's always more important to carry more ammunition . . . to stay alive . . . to fight . . . to get there. I even cut the fringes off the many maps I carried so there'd be more room for ammunition. I myself carried 156 rounds of ammo, four grenades, a knife, a rifle, and a pistol, in case I had to fight my way through enemy territory, which once I did."

Of the top U.S. airborne commanders, only Gavin was a fully qualified paratrooper who had earned his wings at jump school. When the 82nd and 101st leaped in Normandy, the most senior commanders, Ridgway and Taylor, had only jumped once or twice in their lives. Taylor's deputy, Gen. Don Pratt, was even less familiar with chutes and could join the division on D-Day only as a glider passenger. Another novice jumper was the commander of the 101st's airborne artillery unit, Gen. Anthony McAuliffe, who would become famous later when he rejected a surrender demand at Bastogne with the one-word reply "Nuts."

For both divisions, pathfinders would jump first to guide in the more than thirteen thousand men. These were specially trained troopers equipped with the Eureka-Rebecca system of homing devices to electronically signal the aircraft and lights with which to illuminate drop zones. Their aircraft roared down the runways and lifted off while the skies were still light, before the midnight prefacing June 6. Because of Double British Summer Time, a gimmick to stretch daylight work hours, darkness arrived very late. The first pathfinders touched down as early as ten minutes into June 6.

Lt. Bob Dickson, as an intelligence officer for the 502nd PR of the 101st, flew in the lead pathfinder plane. His job was not to outline a drop zone for the bulk of the regiment, but to reconnoiter the best route to a major objective, the coastal artillery guns overlooking Utah Beach.

"I looked out and saw the full moon, the searchlights of Jersey and Guernsey islands, blinking the warning of our coming as we flew by them. I remember the cloud cover over France, and finally the apparent quiet of everything.

"There were eighteen men on board. The two reconnaissance specialists with me were to jump sixteen and seventeen and I would be the last out. While I carried a carbine, hand grenades, extra ammunition, rations, water, and a .45 caliber pistol, the pathfinders were heavily loaded with leg bundles. Everyone left the plane, except number fifteen, who had an oversize leg bundle. He somehow tripped in the door and it took a little while to assist him in getting out of the door. By the time it was my turn, the pilot was picking up speed, beginning his turn back to England. The little delay caused the three of us to miss the prescribed DZ. But the pathfinders before us all landed in the proper DZ."

The flak thrown up by the defenders, who thought these were bombing raids, drove most other pathfinder-bearing planes off course. As a consequence less than a third of the 120 troopers assigned to guide in their fellows achieved their targets. Even those who reached the proper place operated on the edge of disaster. German soldiers, alert to the presence of strangers, made the use of illuminating devices suicidal. Radios were damaged or malfunctioned. Right from the beginning of Overlord, plans for a strategically effective airdrop had become imperiled. The enemy, gradually aware of extensive activity overhead, started to fill the skies with exploding shells and bullets. Pilots carrying the airborne units then sought to evade the fire. Simple navigation errors compounded the problem. The intricately plotted first phase of the invasion veered toward total disarray.

Wallace Swanson, the Oklahoma State football star in Company A, 1st Battalion, 502nd PR, describes the ensemble he wore en route to his drop zone. "The parachute jump suit had these baggy pants with large front and rear pockets, two each, plus two more big frontside pockets. One could easily carry twenty-five to fifty pounds of necessary ammunition, K rations, and personal items. The jacket had four pockets, two on the upper chest and two lower that went to hip level. These were also wide enough for more stuff.

"I carried an officer's Colt .45 and a .30 caliber carbine. My favorite was the .45. I was quite accurate with it up to fifty feet. While I used the carbine numerous times, my second choice for combat was the semiautomatic M-1 rifle. It was a deadly weapon for me in numerous situations.

"I had an escape kit with some hacksaw blades, a compass, a map of France, and a knife. Most of the men in my jump stick had a similar kit. There was an inspection before we left to prevent anyone from throwing away necessary items for survival and to get rid of any beer or liquor in canteens.

"There was little conversation during the flight. The leaders checked to see that the individuals for whom they were responsible were ready and alert to what they were to do. Most of the talk was along the lines of 'Are you ready?' and 'This time it's for real.' Maybe among a buddy-buddy group of two or three there was a laugh over a remark from one of the comedians on the plane.

"I dozed off for a while during the flight and saw many others relaxing in similar fashion. My feeling was, get some rest while you can because we might be on the go for many hours through the next day or two. With all that combat equipment on, one snuggled into the most comfortable position possible, sitting up, leaning against others or the fuselage supports. A few stretched out nearly flat in the middle of the aisle and hoped no one would step on them.

"Although I was a platoon leader and second in command of the company, I did not have any info on the flight rendezvous area after takeoff nor the path to our destination. In general I understood we would rendezvous over England, head south in a safe, tight pattern until we would gradually turn east to cross the Cotentin Peninsula well above Sainte-Mère-Eglise, north of Carentan, south of Foucarville, to our drop zone.

"The ground of the Cherbourg or Cotentin Peninsula was in darkness, in contrast to the Channel waters, which reflected the moonlight. I knew we would jump soon. As we crossed the lower portion of the peninsula, we came under antiaircraft flak fire. Visibility was good, with moonlight and scattered clouds. I could see ground fire coming up at our planes. I could hear bullets or pieces of flak hitting the fuselage of the plane, but so far as I know, none pierced it or came into the troop area. Two or three bursts of flak came pretty close; we saw the bright explosion lights from the doorway. Occasionally the blast of a cannon or an artillery battery from below reached our ears, but we could hear very little from the ground because of the roar of wind blowing past the door.

"The pilot took two severe and one slight maneuver to escape the antiaircraft fire. When the green light went on, I heard the crew chief yell, 'Green light! Jump!'

"Our plane was probably at the right airspeed, ninety-five to one hundred miles per hour, when I jumped. But because of the evasive actions we were probably down to five hundred to eight hundred feet. Once outside and dropping, I could see very little because almost everything was dark. The sparse light from the moon and stars scattered, showing only vague outlines. What I could clearly see were tracer bullets coming up from gun positions and flak bursts that exposed things with a blast of light.

"When I jumped I wondered where I would land, since I couldn't affect whether it would be a low area, a rise, hill, bank, or whatever. To manipulate a chute, one needs a reason or a purpose, such as an obstacle. In any case, I had practically no time to try and guide my chute. It was jump, plop open, then me swinging in the air. I had only pushed back my helmet from over my eyes because of the jerk of the chute opening and then checked to see that I had not lost any of my equipment when I hit the ground, probably five seconds after I left the plane.

"Actually, I landed in three or four inches of water covering a grassy area. My chute collapsed; I collected it and hid it. The moonlight enabled me to see the outline of certain terrain features such as higher hills, trees, and bushes. Because the more elevated ground lay on one side, I figured out it was to the west and near the first target for our mission, the big offshore guns that the Germans would use to protect the beaches. When daylight came a few hours later, I saw that we were only a few hundred yards from that objective. Further study of my map indicated it was less than a mile to our second important mission, capture and holding the right flank of Utah Beach at Foucarville.

"I took about fifteen or twenty steps and suddenly felt I had stepped into a bottomless pit. I went down in water over my head. Hanging on to my equipment, I managed to crawl up the bank of what was a drainage ditch by clinging to the tall weeds, grass, and brush."

Shortly after touching down and soaking himself, Swanson began collecting his troopers. With a number of men from his own platoon and the company plus some stragglers from other outfits, he directed a line of march toward the gun emplacements.

Platoon leader Bernard McKearney, with E Company, 2nd Battalion, of "the Deuce," looked out of his C-47. "It was a clear night over the Channel. The invasion fleet below appeared as toy boats. Everything seemed so unreal. I had to keep reminding myself that this was it, the day for which we had waited and sweated so long. The men were very quiet. Some dozed, others were on their knees watching history being made below.

"Then landfall. Fog swirled in. Then the ack-ack started coming up. It didn't look a bit deadly. Strangely enough, I thought of July Fourth. One burst clipped us in the wing. The plane lurched and nearly threw me out of the door. Then the warning red light. Stand up and hook up! No dramatics, no shouting. The men's faces were grim and tight. I tried to relax them by kidding a little. Then the green light, and I shouted, 'Let's go, girls!' and I piled out.

"The air was crisscrossed with tracers. I couldn't see a soul below. I was over an orchard. I slipped frantically to miss the woods under me. Oh God, don't let them catch me in a tree. I hit with a thud. I could hear shouting in German and English. With all of my equipment, I would have been helpless in my chute. I tried to keep cool. I gathered up my chute and ran sixty yards before plunging into some thick undergrowth.

"I placed three hand grenades in front of me and took off my equipment. After some hesitation I started out. Someone challenged me with his cricket. I fumbled for mine. I had lost it! I started swearing at him in good old

Jerseyese. I knew an American GI would recognize it. He did and burst out laughing. It was our company exec, Lt. Ray Hunter, a Carolina boy.

"Finally, we collected a force of about sixty men. All this time we had no idea where we were. We had become hopelessly separated from the rest of the battalion. The men were wonderful. After about an hour we were fired upon by a German machine gun. Someone yelled, 'Stay down, Lt. Mac,' and then I heard an American tommy gun chatter. One of our boys, S/Sgt. Brosseau from Boston, said, 'Come on, I just erased them.' It was the same all through the campaign. The men fought like veterans from the very beginning.

"As it was just getting light, I was looking for someplace to hole up. Remember, we were in German territory. There was sporadic firing going on all around us. I was getting worried. These men trusted my judgment completely. Finally, we came to a little village. As it was surrounded by a stone wall, I decided to move in.

"As we approached, we were challenged in English. Inside the place we found a medic captain from our own battalion and three aidmen. These were the unsung heroes of the paratroopers. Since we had three or four men shot up and in bad shape, I was mighty happy to see the medics. We set up a perimeter defense around the village and remained tight until dawn. With typical Irish luck, I had stopped just short of a battery of eight German field pieces."

John Hanlon, University of New Hampshire halfback and now S-3 for the 1st Battalion of the 502nd, says, "We were issued air-sickness pills. We had never been given them before. They didn't put me to sleep on the plane, but later, after our landing, I just went to sleep in a ditch.

"I was the jumpmaster for my plane, and our mission was the artillery pieces back of Utah Beach. There was supposed to be a ten-to-fifteen-foot wall surrounding the guns, and someone decided we would need grappling hooks to scale the wall. We had practiced with them in England.

"Our three lead planes had the grappling irons carefully

packed in their bundles. During the drop, those planes became separated and we never saw the grappling irons again. As the lead element, we didn't get much flak. After we crossed the Channel Islands we knew we had about five minutes and the red light was supposed to be lit to prepare us. But it did not go on. I looked out at the other planes and saw men jumping. I told my men to hook up, and only then the red light went on. Two seconds later the green light came and we jumped.

"I landed in a field, all by myself. I never saw anyone from my stick. There was no firing around me, only a cow or two. I gave the cricket a click and got an answer. It turned out to be the company cook. I started across a field and picked up thirty to forty men quickly. I was in command and led the troopers towards the objective.

"The only road and the adjacent fields were flooded by a stream. We would have to detour all the way around to avoid the water. I decided to see how deep it was. A little short guy stepped in, and it was up to his neck. I decided we'd cross the stream. It was the dumbest thing I could do. If there were Germans around, we would have been sitting ducks, lights out! When we got halfway across, the short guys had to hold their rifles overhead. The only comforting thing was I later learned that Ridgway and Gavin did the same sort of thing."

"On the night of June 5," says Lou Merlano, elevated to corporal when his Company A of the 502nd had entered the marshaling area, "we marched out to our planes, and there was an eerie silence about us. There seemed to be a smell of death in the air. We were all fully aware of what the twenty-to-thirty-mile-per-hour winds would do to our jump pattern. When word finally came down the jump was canceled, we were all happy about the situation.

"When we got the go signal for June 6, I had my M-1, musette bag full of rations, ammo, and grenades, an infra-ray gun about three feet long to use for Morse code communications, and a map case. Because of my promotion I was moved from the first plane in our flight to second. I expected to jump last, but Sgt. Perko, in charge of the radio and whom I was to help, saw how heavily I was loaded and moved me to second place in the stick. The rest of the guys in the plane were riflemen from the second and third squads.

"The formation of the flight was tremendously impressive. I could look out the window and see the beauty of it. Few of us dozed off. There were conversations about how much we hoped the talk about French gals was true. There was a good feeling about the whole operation.

"During all our briefings in the marshaling area, I clearly remember how this would be like a sneak attack in the pitch of night. However, after we started across the peninsula from west to east, it became like night and day all at one time. For a while we could see planes alongside of us. When the antiaircraft shells and stuff began to come up, the pattern scattered.

"Now I saw no other planes. I know of no shells hitting our ship. The first plane, the one with our CO, Captain Richard Davidson, supposedly was hit and went down in the Channel after only half the men got out. Captain Davidson, the rest of his stick, and the C-47 crew were lost.

"In my plane, only eight of us landed on the ground. I presume the rest, including Sgt. Perko, who had given me his position in the jump, had dropped in the Channel and drowned.

"There were no instructions from the pilot, crew chief, or jumpmaster about what was happening. All I remember is 'Go! Go! Go!' I must have jumped at about three hundred feet because after one and a half oscillations I hit the ground with a thud. I was in Normandy, in a field marked 'Minen.' At the time I did not know it was a dummy mine-field, and I moved very cautiously. I crept through the field towards a little farmhouse I spotted.

"When I got out of the field, I ran towards the house, where I met a man and a woman. They apparently were farmers, who seemed jubilant to see an American. They quickly poured me a glass of calvados. They were anxious to help, and I pulled out my map, asking for directions to Saint-Martin-de-Varreville, where our objective, the German artillery, lay.

"Not speaking French, I couldn't understand what they

said, but they pointed in a direction of an awful lot of firing. I figured I must be about three to five miles from Saint-Martin-de-Varreville. I heard quite a number of planes in the area, so I left the house and headed where I thought was some action. I jumped over a fence, and lo and behold, I was in an area infested with German soldiers running about the courtyard. From a loft a machine gun fired at planes, probably now flying east back to England.

"There was much firing, much commotion everywhere. I would have to say that at this point I was terrified, realizing that I had nowhere to go except into the German hands. I sat quietly and devoured my little code book."

Bill Dunfee, with Company I, 3rd Battalion, of the 505th, remembers his jump. "There was a bright moon, but it was very foggy. As our flight crossed the coastline, all hell broke loose. We were receiving antiaircraft fire in abundance. Machine gun, 20mm cannon, and AA artillery was bouncing us around.

"The pilot took evasive action, adding to our problem of maintaining a stand-up position. It was not a pleasant ride, and it seemed to take forever to arrive over our DZ. I felt machine gun bullets penetrate the aircraft wing. Someone shouted, 'Let's get the hell out of here,' but no one moved. At about 0200 hours, the green light finally came on. It did not take long to empty that airplane.

"Jim Beavers and I were in the middle of the stick, and the equipment bundles were to be released when we jumped. When my chute opened, I figured I had it made. We were still drawing AA fire but I was out of that flying coffin. Looking around, I spotted Jim Beavers next to me and our equipment bundle off to one side.

"When I looked down, I saw C-47s flying *below* us. That scared the hell out of me, and I started cussing those dirty bastards. Those rotten bastards were trying to kill us. They had jumped us at over two thousand feet and now dove down on the deck. I didn't want to be turned into hamburger by our own air force. That had happened during regimental maneuvers in the U.S. when a plane lost flying speed and dropped down, running into three of our guys and killing them.

"While descending, I regained my composure, since it appeared we were going to make it down in one piece. I had told Jim I would meet him at the equipment bundle. He landed on one side of a hedgerow and the bundle and I on the other side. By the time Jim joined me I had the bundle unrolled and the bazooka and ammo out. We loaded up and headed for Sainte-Mère-Eglise. It was easy to locate. That's where most of the firing was coming from."

Jim Irvin, the pre–Pearl Harbor volunteer trooper who chose airborne to escape a vengeful sergeant, had, like Dunfee, been introduced to combat in the 505th at Gela, Sicily. There he had been a platoon leader for B Company. He was now a captain, in command of B Company.

"It was cloudy in spots, foggy. The invasion fleet below us was so thick you thought you could walk across. You slept when you could. The ride was rough and the flak heavy. The pilots were unsure of the patterns and drop zones. Some planes were damaged and some pilots desired to return to England. A night jump in combat is disrupting to everyone involved—pilots, paratroopers, and the enemy. We had done it before, so we always expected the worst and tried to prepare for that. We had no casualties on the jump, but as usual were dropped in the wrong place. Only two planeloads dropped in my area, east of Valognes, about twenty miles from our destination of Sainte-Mère-Eglise."

Turk Seelye, the rifleman and first scout for Company E of the 505th, toted the full load: his M-1, ammunition, grenades, gas mask, a pick-mattock entrenching tool, and some intimate personal items—twenty-four sheets of toilet paper, a French phrase book, tablets to purify water, a billfold with invasion currency, toothbrush and tooth powder, a bar of soap, a spare pair of undershorts, two pairs of socks, a handkerchief, and safety razor with, optimistically, five extra blades.

"The name on our plane was *Miss Carriage*, and no sooner had I sat down on the aluminum bucket-seat benches than I had to urinate. There were no latrines on these flying boxcars. So I had to get up, be helped down the boarding ladder, and then relieve myself under the wing. It is not an easy task when bundled up in parachute straps and equipment. The 'nervous pee' syndrome was shared by almost all. There was a steady file of troopers going up and down the boarding ladder.

"As we neared the Normandy coast, the jumpmaster, seeing the red warning light, issued the order to stand up and hook up. At this point, each trooper attached his own parachute static line to the steel cable that ran the length of the plane. When one jumped out the door of the aircraft, the static line pulled the parachute from the back pack, causing it to be exposed to the propeller blast and open properly. The next order was 'Sound off for equipment check.' Then each trooper checked with his hands the static line and other equipment of the man standing directly in front of him. When my turn came, I shouted, 'Number six, okay!'

"The cruising speed of the aircraft was about 150 miles per hour. I could see very little standing in the aisle, trying to look out the small windows. I did see some tracers whiz by, and also what appeared to be a burning plane on the ground. As we neared the drop zone, the pilot flashed the green light, and the whole stick of sixteen troopers exited in less than thirty seconds. The pilot, no doubt anxious to return to safety and comfort in England, failed to reduce the speed of the aircraft to the normal jump speed of ninety miles an hour.

"After I left the door, the plane nosed downward, and I watched the tail pass a few feet over my head. Then, as the prop blast forced air into my chute, I got the strongest opening shock ever. The chute opened with such a violent jolt that a 7.65 Beretta pistol I took from an Italian naval officer in Sicily was torn loose, along with my new safety razor. Since I reached the ground in no more than half a minute, I estimate the altitude of the plane was no more than 325 feet, very low.

"I was shaken up a bit, nervous and scared, when I hit the ground. I immediately rolled up my parachute, stuck it in under some bushes along with the reserve chute, and then put together the three pieces of my M-1—trigger assembly, barrel, and stock. I put a clip of ammunition into the chamber and fixed my bayonet.

"I heard automatic weapons and saw some tracer and antiaircraft bullets headed skyward. The first human sound was a cry for help from a squad member. Two others from my group also heard the voice and found our friend Maryland J. Golden of Tallahassee, Alabama, lying on the ground, unable to move. His left leg was broken. He received a shot of morphine and we carried him to the protection of a hedgerow to await the arrival of medics.

"We walked in the darkness seeking other Americans. Somehow I became separated from the other two squad members and I was alone in a French farmyard. I used my cricket for identification and happened to run across three Yanks from another airborne unit. We moved about still looking for other Americans and trying to avoid contact with the enemy. We saw none of either. But in the distance we heard the sounds of war.

"At dawn we came across several troopers who seemed to know what was going on. We joined with them and walked the several miles southward to the village of Sainte-Mère-Eglise. This was the site of the C Company command post. The company occupied an open area about the size of a football field. We spent the day setting up a perimeter defense."

James Gavin had elected to jump with the 508th PR. "I was asked to act as his G-3," says Tom Graham.* "William Walton, a *Time* correspondent, had put on an army uniform and was on the plane. Captain Hugo Olson, the general's aide, was also part of our stick.

"We had all been shocked to hear that four men from Headquarters Company of the 1st Battalion had been killed even before takeoff when a grenade one was carrying exploded. All of them had been with us from the Frying Pan days.

"As we crossed over the Channel and into France, the general kept contacting the pilot and copilot, and he went up and down the aisle assuring everyone as he passed that

---

* In his book *On to Berlin*, Gavin notes, "Lt. Thomas Graham and Capt. Willard Harrison [also aboard] were picked for their combat experience and reputation for toughness and courage in combat."

everything was all right. He told us we had run into some fog, but that the flight was going according to plan. When we neared the DZ, I looked out the window and saw the river, but things did not look quite right in terms of where we were supposed to be.

"The green light went on and all went out the door, with Gavin, as the leader in the plane, first. It was a moonlit night and you could see quite a distance once the chute opened. You could see others dropping close by.

"All at once, firing from a chateau on one side of the river streaked toward the bundles, which had lights on them, and then at paratroopers. It was an odd scene when the quiet of the night was broken by the guns.

"As I came close to the ground I thought I was looking at a big pasture. It turned out to be water with grass growing up through it, which broke the shine of water. I had never made a water landing and I didn't know how deep this would be and what it would be like. As my feet came down and struck this grassy water, I pitched forward as my parachute pulled me to my knees in water that was above my waist. I stood up but when I had gone under the water I lost my helmet. I fumbled around for the helmet and found it quickly. My rifle was wet, my map case wet, and my pockets full of water. I was anxious to get to a shore which I could see some distance away.

"Meanwhile, the firing grew heavier with tracers tracking other chutists and gliders now coming down. When I reached the dry ground, there were some other troopers there along with Gen. Gavin."

According to Gavin's recollection, after about seven minutes over the mainland, the clouds broke up and he glimpsed some unfamiliar terrain below. When he gave the signal to exit the C-47, they were more than half a minute beyond their scheduled time to leap. The stick with him, as well as many others, came down several miles east of their drop area.

Not only were the American paratroopers misled by the ineffectiveness of the pathfinder operation and intense anti-aircraft fire that drove the C-47 pilots off course, but they were betrayed by faulty interpretation of reconnaissance

photos. During the spring thaws and rains, the two principal rivers, the Merderet and Douve, had poured over their
banks. The aerial photos indicated the length and breadth
of the flooding, but not the depth. The tall grass that grew
up through the water, as Tom Graham noted, fooled observers into believing the swampy area was at most a few
inches deep. "Ground here probably soft" was the opti-
mistic conclusion of the report. In fact, the water was over
a man's head.

A considerable number of troopers, burdened with
chutes, laden with weapons and extra ammunition, toting
heavy radio bags, with equipment stowed in bags strapped
to their legs, fell into the deep ooze and drowned. Many of
the equipment bundles with precious bazookas, machine
guns, and mortars also disappeared into the marshy depths.

The party that included Gavin and Graham moved away
from the river, while the gunners in the chateau continued
to target the marshes. Graham remembers, "The general
had seen a glider halfway under water. He said there was a
57mm gun in the glider and asked if I would take three or
four troopers to see if we could retrieve the weapon. I
didn't have to ask for volunteers. They were all willing. We
waded out to the glider in the water. We could not raise the
front end. It was wedged into mud and grass. The occupants apparently had gotten out through the side of the
glider.

"Unable to lift the nose, we reported back to Gen.
Gavin. He told us he'd take a group down the road towards
the chateau and take them under fire if we would try again
to remove the 57mm. We started for the glider and the
fire from the chateau became so intense I didn't think we
could even get there. We made it without being hit but we
still could not budge the nose.

"Gavin decided to abandon the effort. Captain Olson
had made a trip across the river, through the grass to a railroad track on the opposite side of the field. He reported
that the other units from the 505 and 508 were on that
side, near the La Fière Bridge.

"Gavin directed us to leave the area, and rightfully so,
because the Germans had begun closing in on us with

heavy fire. We crossed through open water and the river itself; you could not tell when you actually left the flooded field and were in the stream. I looked back while we were partway across and the bullets from the Germans were kicking up water and sometimes you heard them go overhead but you never knew how close.

"When I looked back, I saw Walton taking photographs. It was the start of daylight, and there he was cranking that camera when I thought he should have been moving as fast as he could to save his own life. But I guess he had a mission too.

"I'm sure many of the others like me were both excited and scared. I had cramps in both of my legs. I didn't know whether I could make the next step, and I believe others felt the same. The general was out in front, and when you have someone like that leading, you know you're going to make it. And we all did."

Olson's reconnaissance revealed to Gavin that he had dropped several miles northeast of Drop Zone N, the target plotted for the Red Devils. He quickly surmised he was on the far side of the wide expanse of water sluiced from the Merderet by the Germans to impede invaders. Furthermore, the troopers he collected were not from the 508th but mostly belonged to the 507th.

Gavin led his small force toward the La Fière Causeway across the Merderet, because, he later noted, "It was a terribly important causeway. It was really the only feasible way to get across the Merderet all the way from Montebourg [on the railroad line] down south." Gavin realized that movement in this direction by enemy forces would place them directly behind Utah Beach.

But before Gavin could take command at La Fière, the situation lay in the hands of lesser figures who were much closer to the objective. Among the handful of troopers in the vicinity was the 507th PR's Raider Nelson. Nelson was one of the relatively small number of paratroopers to land near the designated drop zone.

"Our objective was to use the Merderet River, which ran parallel to the beach, as a defense line preventing German reinforcements from reaching the beachheads. Each of us carried an eleven-pound antitank mine below the reserve chute. This was to be buried about fifty feet from the river. We would then dig in along the river. But because of our wide dispersal upon landing in the dark, this plan was not implemented.

"I was separated from my company and in the darkness found other lost troopers. There was no enemy in our area but plenty of small-arms fire around us. We set up a defensive perimeter and by early light had gained several more troopers, but still none from my company. An officer took charge and we started to march single-file, spread out, along a road. The second man in front of me was hit by sniper fire, and from then on, enemy resistance built up."

Trooper Ed Jeziorski of the 507th recalls: "My light machine gun was in a parapack under my plane's belly. I carried eight clips of ammo in my cartridge belt plus two bandoliers draped over my shoulders, one gammon grenade [a British device with a sock into which troopers loaded plastic explosives], two fragmentation grenades, a phosphorus grenade, an antitank mine in my musette bag, a bayonet, a jump knife strapped to my right boot, two antitank rifle grenades, and my trusty M-1 rifle with 'Jean' carved into the stock. When I jumped over the Rhine later, I carried Jean IV.

"It seemed like eternity before we were able to get above treetop level. There was little or no talking. I had a certain amount of tenseness but I know it was not fear. Instead I was apprehensive as to what lay ahead. I did say a prayer, asking God to let me do the job for which I had been trained, and not to let my buddies down. We had been briefed, no lights or smoking, but I had a momentary lapse and lit a cigarette. Parks yelled instantly, 'Put that goddam cigarette out!' Someone else then said, 'Do we really have to go?' That brought some real and some fake laughs and the tension eased.

"As we came over Normandy, the whole sky lit up with sheets of multicolored antiaircraft tracers. Parks had us stand and hook up. We were bouncing and heaving from side to side as our ship tried to dodge the tracers. I lost my balance, went down, and somebody had to help me up.

Our plane was taking violent evasive action and hadn't slowed a bit when the green light flashed. Parks shouted, 'Let's go!'

"We shuffled out as fast as we could behind him. Just as I cleared the door and before my chute popped open, a great ball of red fire and black smoke erupted directly underneath me. Without thought as to how ridiculous it was, I shouted a warning, 'The bastards are waiting for us!' I pulled my knees up to make myself as small a target as possible; the bullets were crackling that close.

"I pulled on my risers to try and slip away from the fire. I landed near the hamlet of Hébert, nowhere near the intended drop zone. As soon as I hit the ground, a machine gun began covering me, very closely. Every time I moved, the gunner opened up on me. I must have been pretty visible because of a burning plane nearby. I pulled my jump knife and cut the leg and chest straps. I rolled over, and as a clip was already in my M-1, I eased off the safety, then squeezed off a couple of shots at the Jerry gunner. I don't think I hit him, but his firing ceased.

"Working my way towards a large hedgerow, I heard a good bit of thrashing about. As the sound came closer, I came close to pulling the trigger. But I called out softly, 'Flash.' Quickly, the response was 'Thunder.' It was my assistant gunner, Grover Boyce. All of a sudden, the world was a lot more friendly.

"Our stick had jumped right on top of a German concentration. Some were immediately surrounded and had no choice but to surrender while still in their harnesses. Lt. Parks was captured but escaped to rejoin the regiment. My squad leader, Greg Howarth, became a POW, as did Jack Kessler and Marshall Griffin. But Boyce and I teamed up with Dante Tonneguzzo, who later was awarded a DSC, and our aidman, Andy Manger.

"We moved on, trying to hook up with other troopers. Germans fired at us and we scrapped back. We took a prisoner and the firefight eased off. As Doc Manger was interrogating the Jerry, the whole left side of his face disappeared. Apparently, one of the Jerries still hidden in a building was not about to let our prisoner give us any helpful information. We stretched the Kraut out on the ground and Doc gave him a heavy dose of morphine. He was turning gray and his eyes were glazing over when we left him.

"We found a pararack, opened it up, and it had a light machine gun with two boxes of ammo. It was just like old home week. Boyce said, 'Here come the Krauts.' About two hundred yards away advanced a small line of Jerries with a machine gun in the center. They spotted us about the same time we saw them. Their gunner went into action fast, and Boyce and I scrambled to get a belt loaded. Most of their bursts went over our heads. I know my fire was a helluva lot more accurate, but damn, that gun of his could throw a bunch of lead in a hurry. They broke off the scrap and we didn't go chasing them."

C. B. McCoid, who saw his first parachutist at a 1928 county fair, was CO of B Company in the 507th's 1st Battalion and was scheduled to lead his unit in the vicinity of Amfreville, a village west of the Merderet.

"One of the skilled armorers of the 507th had devised a modification of the airborne M-1, A-1 folding-stock .30 caliber carbine. By installing a locally procured rod, he made it possible to depress the sear of the trigger mechanism and turn a semiautomatic weapon into a fully automatic shoulder one. The cost was only thirty shillings, or about six dollars. I was delighted to be among the few able to have the modification done prior to the invasion and carry the extra firepower in combat.

"A few men in each company received waterproof escape kits. These contained one thousand French francs, a slim map of Europe, a steel sawblade encased in wax-coated cardboard, and a minute compass. This last was designed to be inserted in a body cavity when capture seemed imminent. It became known to an indelicate few as an 'asshole compass.'

"Our C-47, with sixteen jumpers and six bundles in pararacks mounted on its underside, was heavily laden. It struggled to get into the air. It seemed about to go down at one heart-stopping moment. A couple of men cursed with relief as the plane steadied and resumed climbing.

"I spent much of the flight in the pilots' cabin of the

C-47 leading B Company's part of the formation. As the coast was neared, the pilot ordered the crew chief to open the jump door. I shook the men awake. Attaching my static line to the anchorline cable, I stepped to the open door in time to watch the coastline north of Cap Carteret slip beneath us.

"All was as it should be. We were droning along at about 125 to 130 knots and holding an altitude of some eight hundred feet. The formation was intact. Then the red light came on. The order to stand up and hook up was issued. The heavily burdened men struggled to their feet with difficulty, most receiving and giving pulls and pushes to get in place in line. Meanwhile we were still flying steadily towards our destination, Drop Zone T. The ground was dimly visible below, with tree lines and open fields identifiable without much trouble. I felt we would surely be able to drop on target.

"Suddenly we passed over a bank of white fog or smoke, extending north along the mid-axis of the peninsula, which totally obscured the ground. We may have taken as much as half a minute to cross this surprise—it seemed much longer. But once we did, the action began. Machine gun fire was coming from everywhere. The tracer rounds arced slowly towards us and then flashed by with a sharp, ripping sound that turned into uncountable cracking noises as they came close. This was our first experience with the German MG-42 and its amazingly high rate of fire.

"Now the area was being lit up by fires I associated with crashed aircraft. Just how many I cannot say. At the time I would have said ten, although there may have been as few as five. Sticks of open parachutes started to appear in the illumination, including some that seemed headed into the flaming wreckage.

"A low bang then exploded beneath our ship, as if a 37mm or at least a 20mm antiaircraft round had struck. I felt a sharp pain at the right knee and a sudden loss of my ability to stand. As I fell to the floor, so did the entire stick. We had been battle-damaged and were crashing, or so it seemed. The plane leveled out at 200 to 250 feet. Its speed was so high it was shaking, and we may have reached 150 knots. The sprawled troopers managed to untangle themselves and regain their feet, under the urging of the NCOs and with the help of an attached medic, John Vinski.

"I tried to use the rear bulkhead intercom to reach the pilot and order him to get into drop posture. The system didn't work. The crew chief was useless, or dead. He lay curled up against the bulkhead and didn't respond to prods and shouts. Knowing that the Bay of the Seine was coming up fast and getting the stick out safely would be a near thing, I stepped to the door, salvoed the six parabundles, and shouted, 'Let's go!' I got out, followed quickly by Oneil Boe, the company runner, and the others.

"We seemed to exit the C-47 at treetop level. Our chutes opened so violently that any gear which was not fastened exceptionally firmly on our persons simply tore away and disappeared into the darkness. In my own case, almost every item not encompassed by the T-5 parachute assembly belly band and the reserve parachute was gone. Anything in my jump pants pockets simply burst through the reinforced bottom seams. I lost K rations, canteen, spare magazines of carbine ammunition, three grenades, a folding-handle entrenching tool, and my musette bag along with its contents of a Hawkins mine [a British device against tanks], toilet articles, and spare socks and underwear.

"Fortunately, we carried our individual firearms under the reserve chute, so I had my carbine with its inserted ten-round magazine on landing. The other items I still possessed were maps, escape kit, switchblade jump knife, first-aid packet, and the gammon grenade. I also still had on the Mae West life vest, which I gladly tossed away after I was down.

"I landed on a stony road about one-third mile south of the small village of Saint-Martin-de-Varreville. This after oscillating wildly under my canopy and crashing to the earth on my knees. Stunned initially, I soon was able to check my injuries. I found I had a crushed right kneecap where a wound already existed from the antiaircraft round that hit our plane.

"Meantime, I still had my chute on. It was tough to remove in the darkness. I thought it impossible for me to stand, so I wallowed around in a web of harness, canopy, and suspension lines on the road. Finally the reserve and belly band were off, the snaps unfastened, and I was free.

"More importantly, my automatic carbine was in hand, although with only one magazine. As I took inventory of the few items still with me, a series of low-flying aircraft passed over at very high speeds. Although these seemed to be ours, they were headed on many azimuths and probably lost.

"I wished them well but I had a problem of my own. The sky above was fairly light, so anything higher than one's self tended to be visible in dim outline. The road was a sunken one, placing me in the darkness. A shadowy figure approached from the south. As he came up, I could make out his bayoneted rifle, as well as the shape of his coal-scuttle helmet. By this time he was on the dike, or berm, on the east side of the road. Without any thought beyond 'characteristically shaped helmet,' I thrust up on my good knee and shot him dead.

"There was nothing heroic about the act. We had an intensive series of classes on enemy equipment, and the *Stahlhelm* was easy to remember. My reaction was an example of useful training.

"Now, perhaps because the dead man was not alone, I had to get going, and damn quick. Since there was no way of knowing where I was, any direction seemed as likely as another. By crawling over the dike, I got into a large field with a bunch of curious cows. By now I had found it possible to hobble along by keeping my right leg stiff and swinging it from the hip.

"I made slow progress for about fifty yards before I reached a dense hedgerow, through which it was impossible to pass. Now, with the first light breaking in the east and in considerable pain, I abandoned caution. I returned to the road leading north. Shortly thereafter, two Germans appeared immediately in front of me. Neither bore weapons or wore headgear and they seemed disoriented. Since I had only nine rounds left in my carbine, I decided to bluff them and capture them, if possible.

"About the only useful German phrase I remembered

just then was *Hände hoch*. It had a magical effect. They turned in alarm, with hands raised. I don't know whether they or I were closer to wetting trousers. Certainly they didn't have the look of elite troops. It later turned out they were Russians who had been impressed into German service.

"When we moved forward we came to the outskirts of what I subsequently learned was Saint-Martin-de-Varreville. Now I was really scared. Some desultory fire was coming from several directions; I had no way of knowing the situation. I forced the Krauts to lie down in a ditch, which they were glad to do. I then hobbled forward to the edge of the village and met a group of privates from the 502nd Parachute Infantry. They informed me that the rest of the built-up area was clear and they were checking out the last few houses.

"I was happy to turn my prisoners over to them. Then I slowly made my way through a typical Norman farm village with its stone structures and piles of manure. In one of the large buildings was a battalion-level command post. I reported in."

Pvt. Jim Kurz, a member of B Company's first platoon, says, "When the red light came on, we all stood and hooked up. Cpl. Theis was the last man, and I was right ahead of him. He turned around and I checked his chute and anchorline. Then I yelled, 'Fourteen okay!' He checked my chute and yelled, 'Thirteen okay!' I did the same for Wolfe's chute; he was twelve. As the plane broke out of the clouds, the call 'One okay!' came.

"The green light went on. Jones yelled we were over water. After a few seconds' delay, he shouted, 'Let's go!' All of the troopers left the plane. We had jumped at a very low altitude, maybe 300 to 350 feet. When my chute opened, I hit the trees and hung there. I got my knife out and in less than a minute cut my harness and dropped to the ground. It was pitch-black and I landed in a bunch of stickers. I had only been two feet off the ground.

"I started along the line of flight; planes were still flying overhead, and you could see tracers going up to meet them. I heard a sound in front of me and ran into Pvt.

Wolfe. He had broken his leg. I told him I would return with a medic. When I reached the edge of the field against a hedgerow, I found Lt. Jones and part of the stick. The medic who jumped with us was there. We went back to Wolfe, who told us he had heard others nearby. We discovered Theis and one other man. All three had broken a leg. We put them together in a hedgerow ditch and left them. I realized that the only reason I wasn't hurt was because I had landed in the tree and been saved the shock of hitting the ground."

Mortar squad leader Sgt. Bud Warnecke says that shortly before takeoff "I looked around the hangar at the troopers of Company B who nineteen months ago were mostly recruits. Now they were ready to jump into combat as a family. I knew we were the best trained we could be and capable of beating the Germans in battle. Our morale was high. I thought of my parents, my younger brother Harold, who at seventeen enlisted in the marines and now was in the Pacific, fighting the Japanese.

"We had a meal fit for a king and then went blackface, using soot from the stoves in the kitchens. I waddled out to our plane, carrying a Thompson submachine gun, a magazine loaded with .45 caliber ammo, fragmentation grenades, smoke grenade, a gammon grenade, rations, canteen, shovel, first-aid packets (airborne ones contained five small syringes of morphine), a gas mask, compass, musette bag with clean socks, extra ammo, and a ten-pound antitank mine. I had a Mae West in case we had to jump into the Channel. The reserve chute added extra weight and bulk but it would be useless because of the altitude we jumped at. Every man was loaded down with so much stuff that someone had to help him up the steps into the C-47. My squad loaded into the plane with the company commander, Captain Taylor, who would be jumpmaster.

"A few minutes before takeoff, the battalion commander's runner came to the plane with a bicycle and cargo chute attached. He informed us that Col. Batcheler wanted us to drop the cycle into Normandy so he would have transportation. We had our plate full of bundles, but Captain Taylor said okay.

"As our plane joined the formation before crossing the Channel, I thought about what guys from the 505th had told us about what it would be like jumping into combat. I thought about where and how we were to assemble. I reminded myself of the sign and countersign, 'Flash' and 'Thunder,' and the cricket issued. [Although Gavin would insist no one in the 82nd Airborne used the devices, Warnecke's memory contradicts him.] I reminded Capt. Taylor to release the pararack bundles under the C-47 when the green light came on. There wasn't much talking among the troops but a lot of smoking. I knew all the men prone to airsickness had taken preventive pills before we took off.

"We reached the English Channel and Capt. Taylor had the troops stand up and hook up. In case we were shot down we would have a chance to get out. In the middle of the Channel we looked out the door on a beautiful moonlit night at a sight no one will ever see again. Ships, so many ships it looked as if you could walk from England to France without getting your feet wet.

"About this time, Capt. Taylor or I asked what the hell are we going to do with the damn bicycle. Simultaneously, we kicked it into the Channel without hooking up its chute.

"Flying between the Jersey and Guernsey islands we could see the German antiaircraft gun flashes. The flight was in good formation until we reached the coast of Normandy, where we ran into a thick fog. The formation broke all to hell. It seemed as if they speeded up. We were now under heavy German fire; it seemed as if we were engulfed in red and green tracers. Now, I was scared.

"The red light came on. Capt. Taylor was standing in the door and said something like 'I don't know where the hell we are.' The green light came on, he jumped, and I bailed out right behind him. It took only a second to realize somebody was mad at us. It seemed unbelievable that I would live through this night. We had jumped at four hundred feet or less because it could not have been more than thirty seconds before I'd gone through an apple tree. My canopy had draped around and caught the top. My feet barely touched the ground for the easiest landing I ever had. Using my jump knife, I cut myself out of my harness.

"Using the sign, countersign, and cricket, the first trooper I found was Capt. Taylor. He was lying in a ditch beside a hedgerow and injured from the jump. I saw one of our bundles about fifty yards away and wanted to recover it. Taylor told me to forget it because it was covered by German machine gun fire. Taylor instructed me to roll up the stick, then find Lt. Jones and tell him he was now acting company commander. It tells you something about Jones when you realize he was not the senior lieutenant under Taylor.

"I oriented myself by the aircraft still flying overhead, which gave me the direction our troops should land. It was about 2:30 A.M. when I started moving in and around the hedgerows. We had not been briefed on finding hedgerows as thick or high as these. In about an hour I found most of my stick and by pure luck stumbled upon Lt. Jones and our exec officer with about half of B Company. By now we realized we had jumped several kilometers from our drop zone and our objective.

"We waited and searched for others until Lt. Jones said it was time to go. He organized us into two platoons. He designated me as one platoon leader. Lt. Jones had us ground our heavy musette bags so we could travel faster—I never saw it again—on our way to our objective, the causeway at the Merderet River. On the way, I saw troopers in trees, shot while still in their harnesses. It was dog eat dog, and anger for the Germans turned into hate. There were American and German dead everywhere you looked."

"The three planes with my platoon," says Homer Jones of B Company, 508th PR, "had managed to stay together. In fact, when we came through a break in the clouds over Normandy, they almost ran into one another. After I got out of my chute on the ground it was surprisingly quiet. We used the recognition signals of 'Flash' and 'Thunder.' Later, though, one of my guys told me he heard someone running towards him and called out 'Flash' and the other trooper answered, 'Flash, my ass. They're right behind me.' "

After his superior Royal Taylor assigned command to

him, Jones headed his roughly seventy men in the direction of the Merderet Causeway.

Bill Dean, a member of Jones's B Company, says, "I had one complete K ration consisting of three meals, several D rations, which are nothing more than a real hard chocolate bar, two hand grenades, a smoke grenade, and a British invention, the antitank gammon grenade. Over my jumpsuit I wore a belt supported by suspenders. On the belt hung a full canteen of water, a folded entrenching tool, a first-aid packet, bayonet, and a compass. Strapped to my left leg was a gas mask, and a trench knife was attached to one boot while a second first-aid packet was on my other boot. Over both shoulders were slung two bandoliers of ammunition, forming an X at my breastbone. As the radio operator for our platoon leader, Lt. Homer Jones, I also had under my armpit a small SCR-536 walkie-talkie radio. My normal weight was 160 and when I climbed into the aircraft I was 230 pounds.

"We had jumped about 1:00 A.M. and I landed in a swamp on the east side of the Merderet River, just north of Chef-du-Pont. Our planned drop zone was on the west side of the river, so I was a good piece away from where I was supposed to be. Others landed nearby, and soon a small group of six or seven of us headed north, guiding on the Paris-Cherbourg railroad right-of-way on our left.

"It was past 3:00 A.M. when we got to the La Fière Causeway, leading to one of the two bridges over the Merderet. Here the rigors of the preceding day and night made us first sit down, and not long after, lie down in a ditch and go to sleep. After a two-hour fitful doze, we were joined by Lt. Homer Jones, who was leading another small group of B Company men.

"Lt. Jones had met our regimental commander, Col. Lindquist, who ordered him to attack and take the La Fière Manoir, a group of strongly defended buildings that guarded the approach to the road and bridge over the river."

Assistant rifle squad leader Frank McKee, with Company F of the 508th, remembers a heavy blast shaking his aircraft, which then nosed down as he bailed out. "I landed under heavy small-arms fire in a dry field near a farmhouse. It was a good landing, in spite of about one hundred pounds of equipment and parachute. I cut my way out of my harness and dashed for the nearest hedgerow. I heard someone coming and he identified himself as Lt. Goodale, one of our best officers. More guys, including Lt. Snee, gathered around. Lt. Goodale spied an equipment bundle light on a nearby hill and had us head there. We got off the field in the dark and up that hill without losing a man. What a relief.

"On the hill, Goodale sent some men in different directions to cover our area, pick up more men, and then return to our temporary CP. Lt. Snee had a surprise for me. He had left his musette bag with all his papers in the field we had just left, and he assigned me to return with him to find it. We headed down and soon came to the road bordering the field. There was shooting to the left and right. Snee posted me at the road and disappeared into the field for his bag.

"Down the road, to my left, a group began to form. I couldn't make them out but I could hear some voices. I was tempted to throw a grenade in their midst but I was not sure they were the enemy. While I pondered this, Snee ran up and we scurried up the hill to join Goodale and his gang.

"Lt. Goodale reminded us our mission was the town of Etienville. We didn't know it then, but our small group didn't have a chance in hell of taking this town. It was heavily fortified. We headed west towards Etienville and were soon stopped by small-arms and machine gun fire."

Bill Lord with the 508th PR recalls watching a spy movie about the Germans before boarding his plane. But his departure was delayed when the pilot could not start one engine. The troopers transferred to another aircraft, and over France, Lord saw they were part of a thirty-six-plane vee.

"Our jumpmaster, Lt. Neal Beaver, had us stand, check equipment, the usual routine. All I could see was the back of Beaver; the red light came on, and then the green. I slapped him on the back and shouted 'Go!' as loud as I could. He backed out of the door. I thought at the time he said, 'We're not jumping. There's nothing but water down there. I'm going to talk to the pilots and we'll have to go around again.'

"That meant we'd fly out over the bay, do a 180-degree turn to the left, and come back east to west, well north of the flight path coming in so as not to run into other planes. While Beaver went up and talked to the pilots I stood by the door. I saw us head over the beaches, pass out over Saint-Bains-Louche. As we banked I saw the invasion fleet, called Piccadilly Circus by some, hull down from the beaches. The moon came back out; we could see streaks of moonlight and boats in the sea.

"We hit the beach again, and all hell broke loose with small-arms fire coming up at us. My impression was that the pilot shoved the stick forward and added throttle while diving for the deck. As an afterthought he hit the green light.* I slapped Beaver and out we went. The opening shock was terrific, since we must have been going two hundred miles an hour. I lost my helmet and the aiming circle for the mortar, but because I had strapped the rifle to my body I didn't lose it. I looked down between my feet to see if I recognized any of the road net. As I looked up, I saw the tops of trees level with my eyes. I hit the ground; my chute stayed hung up in a small apple tree. I fell forward but the chute held me at about a forty-five-degree angle.

"Then I heard the damn hobnail boots running down the road. I knew we didn't have hobnail boots. The French civilians didn't have hobnail boots. I was so scared when I tried to spit it felt like I had pebbles in my mouth. It took several minutes to get out of the harness. I put a round in the chamber of the M-1 and began to pull back in the direction from where I thought we could roll up the rest of the stick. The field I was in had barbed wire. As soon as I

---

* Some forty years later, Lord learned that his pilot attempted to turn the ship but discovered his legs did not work. He looked down and saw blood pouring from two bullet wounds. The copilot took the controls, and when the badly damaged plane landed in England, the only member of the crew who had not been wounded was the copilot.

saw it, I knew from all the training there would be booby traps that would blow if I touched the wire. A cow came up, licked my hand, and I realized there couldn't be booby traps in this field.

"Just about that time I heard someone say, 'Flash.' I replied, 'Thunder.' He said, 'Welcome,' and it was Beaver. We hugged each other. He told me he had felt pretty lonely until he saw this big splayfooted hulk that couldn't be anybody but Lord.

"It took us a few hours, but we got almost everybody from our planes together. We dispatched teams to search for our equipment. We had used up most of the night before we were ready to go. At this point I had no idea where we were, except that we were inland a short distance. We had four or five guys hurt or wounded. Suddenly two Germans came walking across the field carrying a wooden case. We blasted them. I went out and opened up the case, which was full of maps of minefields on the peninsula. It seemed important to get this to higher headquarters.

"Just about dawn, in the window of a house bordering the field we saw the head of a little boy, maybe ten years old. Utilizing my best Hotchkiss School French, I said, '*Halloo. Nous son parachutist American. Où est les Alegmanes?*' In the countryside of Normandy, this ten-year-old answered, 'If you speak a little slowly, I think I can understand everything you say in English.' Everybody broke up.

"In the house we asked the farmer who owned it if it was okay to leave our wounded there. He agreed, risking the lives of his family. We had a medic who had a broken leg to stay with the five others. We set them up and the medic. I gathered up our morphine syrettes. He refused to take any for himself, although he was in as much pain as anyone else. It would be two days before anybody would come by and get them back to the beaches and treatment.

"We left them there and started off trying to get close to our regimental assembly area. We were about two miles west of where we should have been, and I knew from our briefing we were in the territory assigned to the 101st.'

The radio to be used by Harold Canyon, the California

son of Finnish immigrants, had been loaded into a parapack bundle under the airplane. He carried the battery along with his other gear. "While we were on our way to France, I had lined my gammon grenade with some loose British coins from my pocket, thereby making a fragmentation grenade out of it. When we went by the island, we seemed out of range. Then things got real hot. Tracers went up all over the place. Our plane was hit hard up front. We got the order to stand up and hook up. Then we started out the door. Just as I approached the door, the top of the plane opened up and the right wing began to dip, the start of the death spiral. It took every bit of strength I could muster to get out that door. Instead of stepping out, I rolled out over the threshold. The cable must have remained intact, because my chute opened.

"Out of force of habit, I checked my chute. Tracers were going through it in disorganized clusters, so there must have been at least several guns contributing to the display. I couldn't tell where I was, but it must have been five hundred feet of elevation or less when I left the plane. I reached for the trench knife but I had taped it to the scabbard so I wouldn't lose it. I oscillated twice and hit the ground.

"Just before I landed, I had heard a gammon explode under me. I hit about thirty feet in front of a German bunker that had just been knocked out by that exploding grenade. I never knew the trooper who did the job. I lay there for a moment, fully expecting a German to stick me with a bayonet. Then I took hold of the handle of my trench knife and from the strength of sheer desperation, tore it loose, destroying the scabbard. I cut the straps, even the ones on my personal musette bag, took the carbine out of its case, and with grenades and carbine in one hand, a trench knife in the other, I ran for the nearest hedgerow and dove over. Immediately, two Germans came towards me from the other side of the hedgerow. I prepared my gammon grenade and when they reached the opposite side I threw it just as one fired. The muzzle blast from his rifle knocked me out. When I came to, my face was in the dirt with my mouth open, saliva and blood drooling into the sand. I still couldn't move, but I had regained my senses and could hear the two Germans moaning. I could taste gunpowder in my mouth. Later I found a bullet hole through the crotch of the outer pair of pants.

"I thought I was dead and that when people died, their senses went later. I wondered if I would feel the dirt in my face when they buried me or the maggots later.

"I regained movement just as someone approached on my side of the hedgerow. I challenged with 'Flash' and he responded with the correct 'Thunder.' Almost immediately, someone else came along and I challenged him with 'Flash' and he said 'Thunder.' But somehow he seemed confused, because he opened fire. The first bullet hit my helmet and glanced off. The second one struck my hip pocket and went through the first pair of pants and one of the paper maps in the second pair of pants. After the first shot I swore quite profusely, which he finally heard and he realized that I was American, so he quit.

"Two more shapes emerged, and we scattered before they saw us. I unfortunately rolled over in some dry brush. They heard me and it was too late to move so I played dead. The two Germans stood over me looking down. I had to potty real bad, so I did. I guess the Germans thought they were looking at a bleeding corpse and walked on. I moved into a brushy area and slept from sheer exhaustion.

"As daylight approached, another trooper walked up and I challenged him. He took another step and I saw his boot, then the perplexed look on his face. He couldn't remember what he was supposed to say. I said, 'It's okay, Malcolm. I know who you are.' We jumped up and down embracing each other.

"We met three other troopers. One of them said a German battalion had gone up the road and would be coming back. They had left a truck with two Germans. One of our guys threw a grenade that hit the truck windshield dead center. The two Germans jumped out and ran while we kept shooting. Talk about divine luck. They escaped in spite of all we threw at them."

Battalion surgeon Dave Thomas, still smarting from indifferent success at the poker table, enjoyed a brief moment of optimism in the sky. "In the nice bright moonlight, as far as I could see behind were echelon of C-47s upon echelon of C-47s, each filled with a bunch of troopers. I thought, boy, this is going to be a piece of cake. We are really organized.

"We turned to the coast and hit a cloudbank. When we came out of it, the airplane I was in was the only one I could see in the sky. When the flight hit those clouds they just split up like a bunch of ducks being shot at.

"Trying to find out where we were, I kept looking down, and finally I saw a stream. I was jumping number two, behind the battalion commander, Col. Harrison, and I said, 'That has to be the Merderet. Let's get the hell out of here.'

"We jumped, and I landed in a field. As I got out of my chute, I saw something white. I crept up to it—a cow chewing its cud. The first guy I ran into was Bill Ekman, who'd been the exec in the 508 but when Gavin was promoted to a brigadier they made Ekman CO of the 505 [the regiment of Bill Dunfee].

"Ekman wanted me to come with him and one of his battalions, which was moving on Sainte-Mère-Eglise. I said no, I would follow the railroad line, which was west of where I came down near Beuzeville-la-Bastille. I picked up about nine or ten troopers and then bumped into a group with Col. Harrison and a redheaded major from the 507 with thirty or forty men. Soon, we were fighting on the edge of the Merderet, which was flooded, and on our other three sides were hedgerows. These guys had been kicking a little ass before I got there, because they had a lot of German prisoners. But there was no place for us to go and the enemy was all around.

"We took positions manning the ditches and hedgerows and threw the captured Krauts some entrenching tools. We told them to get out in the orchard and dig in. They had the dirt flying soon.

"I had one patient, a trooper in a ditch with his leg almost blown off, except for his patellar tendon. I had very little to work with, a small kit, a few instruments, a bit of morphine, but no way to anesthetize him. I said, 'Son, it's like the days in the Wild West. You're going to have to bite the bullet and I am going to have to separate the leg.' I cut the patellar tendon and put a dressing on it. He never whimpered.

"We put the wounded in a little farmhouse. It had a thatched roof. There wasn't much we could do for them. We didn't have a one of our equipment bundles, only what we carried."

Like their subordinates, Gens. Maxwell Taylor and Matthew Ridgway plunged into a miasma of confusion far from their objectives. Taylor, CO of the 101st, said, "I dropped halfway between Sainte-Marie-du-Mont and Vierville, just west of the highway connecting the two villages. I landed alone in a field surrounded by the usual high hedges and trees with a few cows as witnesses. The rest of my stick went into an adjacent field, and it took me about twenty minutes to find anyone. The area into which I wandered was covered with field fortifications, newly constructed, but fortunately I encountered no Germans. Later I found it to be a new antiaircraft battery emplacement for which trenches had been dug but the guns not yet installed. Gradually, I picked up a few men of the 501st and later contacted Gen. McAuliffe, who had a group of artillery personnel with him.

"Still under the cover of darkness, we worked our way eastward for about a quarter of a mile and finally halted in an enclosed field, where we began to gather stragglers. It was here that I first ran into Col. Ewell [Julian, CO of the 3rd Battalion, 501st PR]. We outposted the field and sent out patrols in all directions. They, however, learned very little in the darkness and were driven back by enemy fire, which seemed to be on all sides. Col. Higgins [Gerald, Taylor's chief of staff] soon turned up with Lt. Col. Pappas, the division engineer."

The concentration of big brass and the paltry number of enlisted men caused Taylor to remark, "Never in the history of military operations have so few been commanded by so many."

Burrowing in a ditch, the crew of chiefs studied an aerial photograph by flashlight, trying to decide in the darkness just where they were. Said Taylor, "In spite of the attempts to patrol and to identify terrain features in the vicinity, we did not know exactly where we were until the first light. Looking through the tree line which protected our field, I spotted the church tower of Sainte-Marie-du-Mont. I had studied this so many times on the air photograph that I recognized it at once."

Taylor now realized that his 506th PR, assigned the task of securing the two southernmost causeways over the Douve, "had received a bad drop." He did not recall seeing a single trooper from the 506th, although there were many from other regiments.

His opposite number with the 82nd Airborne, Gen. Matthew Ridgway, fared no better. "About forty-eight hours before D-Day, they told us what they had just discovered. I think it was the 92nd German Division [actually it was the 91st] had just been moved into our drop zone. Bradley asked, what will you do? It was too late to change things on the plans. My chief worry was enemy air interference. I was confident there would be no planes or night fighters, but we might come over unlocated and unneutralized concentrated flak. We would be down so low, we would be just sitting ducks with our slow planes.

"The kids that were flying the troop carrier C-47s hadn't had much flying training. They had done the minimum numbers of hours in the air. The glider pilots still less." In spite of his fears and the gloomy talk, Ridgway professes a calm state of mind on the eve of his departure. "My soul was at peace, my heart was light, my spirits almost gay."

Once over the continent, he said, "Normandy looked like a Fourth of July celebration on the Mall in Washington. The sky was covered with stuff, rockets and tracers were streaking through the air and big explosions were going off everywhere."

His parachute carried him into a pasture bordered by the ubiquitous hedgerows. "I felt a great exhilaration at being here alone in the dark on this greatest of adventures." After challenging a shape in the dark that proved to be a cow, Ridgway spotted another figure. "We had these little crickets, and I had one in my hand but I didn't use it. I used the challenge of 'Flash.'" The respondent was company commander Willard Follmer, by some lottery-size long shot the same man Ridgway had first encountered when he jumped in Sicily. Ridgway was no lucky talisman for Follmer, however, for the captain had fractured his right ankle in Sicily and now in Normandy he had broken his right hip.

Ridgway was in no better position than Taylor or Gavin to exercise true command and control. Instead of conducting precise, well-planned maneuvers, the troopers initially performed like gangs of desperadoes, marauding through the countryside. The dispersion of the air drop sowed great confusion among the enemy, as the invaders seemed all over the place and difficult to pin down. During the darkness the parachutists ravaged communications by blowing telephone wires, to add to the disorder among the Germans. The defenders themselves had also lost much of their command and control, particularly since Erwin Rommel was back in Germany on a joint venture to visit his family and plead with the Führer for more resources.

Paratrooper training had included exercises in which the men operated as isolated bands, using individual initiative. Because of the dislocation during the drops, the initial phase of Overlord would require the utmost in small-unit tactics. Until the daylight assault on the beaches, the airborne forces would be on their own.

# CHAPTER 11

# GLIDER-BORNE

THE OTHER COMPONENT of the airborne operations was the glider-borne soldiers—antitank crews, light artillerymen, riflemen, medics, engineers, and their equipment.

At 12:19 A.M, pilots of the towplanes at Aldermaston Airbase throttled up, and the glider-borne troops in the mission dubbed Chicago began their trip toward Normandy. "Lt. Col. Mike Murphy was in the lead glider to my immediate left," remembers Vic Warriner, "and to my right in the four-ship echelon was Capt. Jack Willoughby, CO of the 434th Group. The takeoff was uneventful, except that it seemed to take much longer than normal for Murphy's glider to become airborne." Warriner, at the time, knew nothing of the installation in Murphy's CG-4A of the metal plates which were to protect his passenger Gen. Pratt but seriously compromised its flight dynamics.

"Our takeoff," continues Warriner, "was smooth, and we quickly pulled into formation on the leader's wing. My copilot was Robert V. 'Bob' Kaufman. He was more than qualified to pilot a glider himself but agreed to sacrifice that spot so that we would be assured of having a competent replacement if something happened to me. My glider was important, because we carried part of a top medical team from the 101st Airborne who would immediately set up a field hospital upon landing. Capts. Charles O. Van Gorder and Albert J. Crandall and several medical technicians were in my CG-4A. In addition we carried a two-wheeled trailer loaded with medical supplies that was to be towed by the jeep carried in Gen. Pratt's ship.

"The flight proceeded as envisioned, but the night was so dark we never knew when we left England and headed southwest, out to sea. The weather wasn't really that bad but occasionally rain would splatter against the Plexiglas windshield. Bob and I alternated flying, for it was rather a long haul for one pilot, considering the stress.*

"We knew when we made the rendezvous with the submarine stationed in the Channel, for we made a ninety-degree left turn to head east-southeast towards the coast of France. And sometime later we made another slight turn to the left that lined us up directly with the Normandy area.

"As we approached land we could see several fires burning that we thought had been ignited by the pathfinder crews for the paratroops. Wrong! They were bonfires built by the Germans on top of flak towers to help them stay warm on a chilly night. We encountered heavy machine gun fire, but it was mostly inaccurate and caused very little deviation in our planned route. At one time I thought we had been hit, for the controls suddenly were very stiff and unresponsive. I glanced over at Bob, and he was flying the glider too. He grinned sheepishly and let go of the wheel.

"When we were at about five hundred feet, the light in the dome of the towplane signaled for us to release. I could see the one from the plane towing Mike Murphy flash at the same time. Even though it was still dark, there was enough light for me to see Murphy release and immediately turn left in a steep climb, using the velocity of the tow to gain enough altitude that he disappeared into the black sky.

* Contrary to some published accounts, all of the gliders invading Normandy included a qualified copilot in the crew. Subsequently, in the much larger glider operations for the September 1944 airborne assault in Holland, the shortage of personnel did require some troopers with only rudimentary instruction to serve as copilots.

His actions puzzled me, because during all our training and briefing it was stressed that we were to maintain level flight when released until the glider slowed enough to reach its normal gliding speed.

"With Bob calling out the speed and altitude, we descended into darkness. Finally, we could see the vague outline of a row of trees, and I put the glider into a slip to kill off excess altitude. We actually brushed the tops of the trees as we went in. We touched down almost immediately, and I put the glider up on its skids and applied full brakes. It seemed that instead of slowing down, we were gaining speed. As we hurtled through a herd of terrorized dairy cattle, I could see through the darkness the end of the field coming fast. Luckily, we slowed up enough so the crash was only minimal. We hit a large poplar tree on my side of the cockpit only hard enough for me to end up with my chin against the trunk of the tree.

"Even before the Plexiglas stopped falling, Capt. Van Gorder asked if everyone was okay. We were, and all I got out of the experience was skinned knees from the bark of the poplar.

"We had been on the ground for an interval of perhaps only fifteen seconds when we heard a tremendous crash close to our left side as a glider smashed into another huge poplar at deadly speed. The impact actually shook the ground. At the very same moment, we spotted the blackout lights of vehicles traveling along a little dirt road just beyond the nose of our glider. We knew they were Germans; the briefing had stressed that no Allied vehicles would move before dawn. The convoy of three vehicles halted by the glider that had crashed nearby. A couple of soldiers emerged and entered what remained of the glider. We could see their flashlight beams as they poked around the wreckage. Soon they left and got back into the vehicles and disappeared down the road.

"We all were greatly relieved, because in the confusion of landing and the subsequent crash, Bob and I had no idea where our rifles were. I was still entangled in the remains of our glider's nose, so we couldn't have offered much resistance if they had come into our area. I have always felt that they had no idea of what they had discovered. Since the night was filled with the roar of towplane engines and the occasional noises of a glider crashing, they must have decided to get the heck out of there and report to someone with more authority.

"As soon as they left, Capt. Van Gorder said he was going to the smashed glider to see if he could help anyone, although he doubted anyone could have lived through such a crash. He had no more than stated his intentions when we heard another glider thump down in the field and rumble towards us. As it got closer we noticed it was up on its skids and gradually slowing down. I then realized that the field we picked sloped downhill severely and was covered in lush, wet pasture grass. The incoming ship hit the tail of our glider but with little speed. It did minimum damage and injured no one. Meanwhile, Capt. Van Gorder ran towards the first stricken glider.

"The rest of us started to pull away from our tail the latest arrival so we could move it from the tree and raise the nose to remove the trailer load of medical supplies. Our efforts were to no avail. Van Gorder returned and told us the crashed ship was Mike Murphy's glider. Two of the people aboard, Gen. Pratt and copilot Butler, were dead. Murphy was seriously injured and Van Gorder doubted he would survive. Only Gen. Pratt's aide came through relatively uninjured." Pratt died apparently of a broken neck, either from the impact of the glider against the tree or as a result of his jeep shifting forward to crush him.

"I learned later," says Warriner, "about the sheet iron on the cargo-compartment floor. It completely upset the balance of the glider and constituted a gross overload. That's why Murphy had used so much runway to get airborne. Years afterwards, Murphy told Van Gorder, 'It was like trying to fly a freight train.' He and his copilot fought that glider for three and a half hours, somehow staying on tow till the designated time for release. And that's why Murphy utilized every bit of speed from the tow to gain as much altitude as possible; he had no idea how the glider would behave in free flight, except that the glide ratio would be like that of a flat rock. To keep from stalling into a crash, he had

to fly at speeds much above normal. Consequently, he hit
the landing field like a meteor. Combine that with the
downhill slope of a wet, grassy field and they had no
chance. It's a wonder anyone survived. As far as I know,
Murphy never complained publicly about a disaster for
which he was not to blame."

In the dark pasture, Warriner and the other able-bodied
crews pitched in to unload their cargo. "After that we
were on our own and took off trying to establish contact
with the rest of our glider pilots. We had all been issued
the clickers. The whole Normandy peninsula that night
sounded as if it had been hit by the greatest cricket infesta-
tion in history. It wasn't unusual to hear someone shout in
the eerie darkness, 'Don't shoot! I lost my goddam
clicker!' "

The youngest man to earn his pilot wings, Pete Buckley
flew Glider 49 in the same serial (fifty-two CG-4As altogether) as Warriner. "Thirty minutes before takeoff the engines of the tow ships started up. The muffled noise and
throbbing from their motors spread around the field like a
distant, approaching thunderstorm, and contributed to our
uneasiness. We all climbed aboard trying not to show our
true feelings. My own were that in roughly three and a half
hours I might be dead. It was a very sobering moment, and
I wondered why I had been so foolish as to volunteer for
this job. When I first went into the glider program, nobody
had ever explained to me how gliders were going to be
used.

"My copilot was F/O Bill Bruner. Our passengers were
Pfc Paul Nagelbush, Pfc Stanley Milewiski, and Pfc Russel
Kamp, antitank crewmen from the 101st AB. The cargo included their 57mm gun, ammunition, entrenching tools, a
camouflage net, rations, and some supplies.

"Our tow ship gunned its engines and started down the
runway through a light rain shower and into the black of
night. As the wheels of the glider left the ground, someone
in the back yelled, 'Look out, Hitler, here we come!' This
helped break the ice for a moment, after which no one said
a word as I trimmed the glider for the long flight ahead.

"For the next three and one half hours, we would be

alone with our thoughts and fears. It wasn't too bad for me, because I was busy flying the glider. But the airborne men in back and Bill Bruner, with nothing to do, must have been going through hell with their thoughts.

"We settled into position behind the C-47, keeping the faint blue formation lights on the top of the plane centered up in line between the glow from the towplane's engine flame dampeners. This is not the easiest job in the world at night. The longer you stare at them, the more your eyes start playing tricks. I turned the controls over to Bruner occasionally so I could look away and refocus my eyes again. An added problem was the extreme turbulence from the prop-wash of the forty-eight planes ahead of us.

"Shortly after we crossed the coast of France, small arms fire and heavier flak started coming up at the planes in the front of the formation. These intensified as we came closer to our landing zone. It looked like fluid streams of tracers zigzagging and hosing across the sky, mixed in with heavier explosions of flak. You wondered how anything could fly through that and come out in one piece.

"The lead ships of the formation had passed over the Kraut positions and woke them all up. We, at the tail end of the line, began to be hit by a heavier volume of small-arms fire. When it went through our glider it sounded like corn popping, or typewriter keys banging on loose paper.

"I tried to pull my head down into my chest to make myself as small as possible. I tucked my elbows in close to my body, pulled my knees together to protect vital parts of my manhood, and even was tempted to take my feet off the rudder pedals so they wouldn't stick out so far. I really started to sweat it out.

"A few minutes after crossing the coast, and before we reached the glider release point near Hiesville, the group plunged into some low-lying clouds and fog banks. All the planes started to spread out to avoid collisions. This caused many of us to land wide, short, or beyond our objective when we got to the cutoff point.

"In a very short time, too soon for me, the moment I dreaded arrived. The green light came on in the astrodome of the towplane, indicating we were over the LZ and it was

time to release. At this moment, I had a very strong urge
not to cut loose. I'm sure I wasn't the only one who felt
this way on that night. It was dark; everything but the
kitchen sink was coming up at us from the Germans below,
and that towrope, as long as it was hooked up, was my um-
bilical cord. The steady pull signified safety, and a nice ride
back to England out of this mess, if I hung on. I quickly
put this thought out of my mind and waited about ten seconds before I released the towrope.

"As soon as the rope disconnected from our glider, I
made a 360-degree turn to the left, feeling my way down
through the darkness. I held the glider as close to stall
speed as I could. It is almost impossible to describe my feelings. I knew the ground was down there but I couldn't see
it. I didn't know if I was going to hit trees, ditches, barns,
houses, or what. And all the time, the flak and tracers are
still coming up. The only thing for sure was that Krauts
were shooting at me and they were going to be right there
waiting for me when I climbed out of the glider.

"Finally, out of the corner of my eye, I noticed a faint
light patch that looked like an open field outlined by trees.
By this time we were so low that we had no choice in the
matter. There would be no chance for a go-around. With a
prayer on my lips, and a very tight pucker string, I straightened out my glide path and headed in while Bruner held on
full spoilers. We flared out for a landing, just above the
stalling speed, and touched down as smooth as glass. I
couldn't believe it. How lucky can you get?

"Just as we thought we had it made, there was a tremendous, bone-jarring crash. We hit one of those damn ditches
that the Germans had dug across the fields. This ditch was
ten to twelve feet across, five to six feet deep, with water at
the bottom. The main purpose was to prevent gliders from
landing in one piece, and it sure worked with us. We
plunged down into the ditch, and when the nose slammed
into the other side, the glider's back broke as it slid up over
the opposite bank. The floor split open and we skidded to a
halt in the field on the other side.

"For a split second we sat in stunned silence, and then I
breathed a sigh of relief because none of us seemed injured.

We bailed out fast, because there was rifle and machine gun fire going off in the fields around us. Fortunately, none seemed aimed at our area at the moment. It took us almost thirty minutes to dig the nose of the glider out of the dirt so we could open it up and roll out the 57mm antitank gun. Midway through this task, the Germans set off a flare right over our heads. Lo and behold, we saw Glider No. 50, piloted by F/Os Calvani and Ryan, sitting on the other side of the ditch without a scratch on it. They were carrying the jeep to tow our antitank gun. Calvani must have stuck right on my tail in the dark in order to land so close. I don't know how he managed to do it.

"You're supposed to trust the tow pilot, but I did hesitate for a few seconds, and it was a good thing, because I still landed about half a mile short of the LZ. If I had let go at the first signal from the towplane I would have come down in the swampy area that the Germans had flooded, where many paratroopers and glidermen drowned in the dark."

Just ahead of Buckley, in Glider No. 42, Native American Irwin Morales and his copilot, Lt. Thomas Ahmad, were far less fortunate. "Right before the takeoff, at 12:21 A.M.," says Morales, "Ahmad and I made a pact. If I got killed, he would visit my folks, and if he were, I'd go to his parents' home. The enemy fire turned heavy once we entered onto the continent. Jesus! The flak and tracers became so thick that I don't know how the hell we walked through it. The tow ship turned right down the coastline, made a left, and came back in near the La Grange area."

In fact, the glider with Morales and Ahmad at the controls missed the LZ by twelve miles, plopping into a swamp only seven miles south of Carentan, deep in enemy territory. Both pilots soon found themselves in the role of foot soldiers, members of an embattled band of paratroopers dropped equally far from their objective.

One of the happier landings of a glider brought to earth Vic Allegretti, five others in the crew, and their 57mm gun with its jeep. "I carried a .30 caliber carbine, an M-1, bandoliers of ammunition, and hand grenades. On the floor of the glider was the ammo for the 57 and some TNT blocks.

"About 1:00 A.M. we came out of the cloudbank into heavy ground fire. We were all quiet and sweating. Coming down, there was plenty of gunfire and a lot of fires. We just missed a large bridge over the Merderet River. The pilot did his very best as he made a complete circle to slow down and land wherever he could. There was no such thing as the right place. When daybreak came the next day we could see we had been very lucky. The next field over was marked with a skull-and-crossbones sign on a tree; it was mined.

"Germans were all around us, but none of us were injured. We took the gun and jeep out immediately and set up at a crossroads. Around us lay a lot of dead cows, very smelly, plenty of mortar and machine gun fire. Also there were some bodies of paratroopers and glidermen who crashed into trees and hedgerows. The medics were very busy.

"Gen. Gavin came along and was very happy to see us with the 57 in position. It was a delight to see him with our boys. He had a pistol in hand and there was no saluting or standing up. We all stayed on our bellies or crouched."

The American gliders had aimed for a landing zone of perhaps two square miles. Operations by the British invaders demanded a much more precise touchdown. Protection of the British troops landing on Gold, Juno, and particularly Sword beaches required shutting off mobilization of strong German armor quartered around Caen. The routes from inland to the Channel crossed a trio of almost parallel waterways, the Caen Canal, the River Orne, and the River Dives.

To hamper any invaders, the defenders had arranged for the Dives to overflow its banks, transforming a meadowy valley into an impenetrable marsh. But the tactic also restricted the German armor and infantry. To advance on any beachhead, the reserve forces—the mighty 12th SS Panzer and 21st Panzer Divisions, each with twenty thousand troops—would need to cross five bridges over the Dives and one each over the Orne and the Caen Canal.

To forestall the foe and to enable their forces to advance, the Allied strategists planned to destroy all five spans over the Dives and to capture the pair crossing the Caen Canal and the River Orne, which would give passage for their own troops. Only a quarter mile separated the latter two bridges, which were to be seized intact.

The missions depended upon a finely meshed schedule of glider landings and paratroop drops. Because a parachute assault inevitably meant a delay until the scattered sticks assembled, the critical operations focusing on the Caen Canal and River Orne bridges became the responsibility of soldiers from the Oxford and Buckinghamshire Light Infantry aboard six wooden-frame Horsa gliders. If the Horsas landed near the targets, they could disgorge immediately a fighting force sufficient to overcome the bridge garrisons and capture the canal and Orne spans.

There were no convenient fields close to the objectives, and furthermore, reconnaissance photos showed the positions surrounded by barbed wire, pillboxes, and machine gun emplacements. It was decided that the gliders could crash-land right by the bridges without killing or seriously injuring their cargo of "Ox and Bucks." The plan required a prodigious feat of navigation and flying in the dark.

The timetable specified an arrival a few minutes after midnight. Maj. John Howard, a thirty-one-year-old professional soldier and D Company CO, rode in the lead Horsa in a flight of three ships towed by British Halifax bombers that aimed for the Caen Canal bridge. A second trio of Horsas left the ground shortly after, aiming for the River Orne target.

After studying the aerial surveillance pictures, Howard had charged his two pilots, S/Sgt. Jim Wallwork and S/Sgt. Jim Ainsworth, not only to set down at the Caen Canal bridge but to use the glider as a kind of battering ram and mash the barbed wire shielding the main defensive positions.

A few minutes after midnight, the Horsa swooped toward the earth, touching down at about ninety miles an hour. A parachute deployed by the copilot slowed the glider to sixty miles an hour as it plowed into the tangle of barbed wire, careening along before an abrupt halt. The two pilots, still strapped in their seats, hurtled forward and out of the cockpit to the ground, probably the first men in the invasion to set foot on French soil.

Astonishingly, a sentry heard the tremendous crash but failed to sound an alarm. Stricken aircraft from raids over the continent slammed into the ground frequently enough to make such noises common. The men of the Ox and Bucks, having recovered their wits, dashed forward, tossing grenades and spewing fire from automatic weapons. The firefight lasted only a few minutes as the glider-borne forces overwhelmed the small garrison, composed of some veteran German NCOs and ill-trained, poorly motivated conscripts. Sappers quickly disarmed the explosives that could have been employed to blow the bridge.

Even less of a fight ensued at the other objective, on the Orne. A mortar round fired by a British sergeant blasted a machine gun nest, and the remainder of the defenders fled. The costs of the entire operation to the Ox and Bucks, for the moment, were light.

The most important bridge, the one at the small town of Troarn, lay seven miles away from where the dismayed group of troopers assigned to blow it landed. Furthermore, the gliders carrying jeeps to haul the explosives failed to show. Maj. J.C.A. Roseveare resolutely started toward the target with a small party of men who pulled handcarts packed with demolition materials. By sheer luck, they happened upon a jeep with a trailer that belonged to the Royal Army Medical Corps. Roseveare commandeered the vehicle, replacing the medical supplies with the explosives. Roseveare himself took the wheel. There was room only for one more officer and seven enlisted men.

The jeep and trailer with the raiders aboard smashed through barriers and overcame an occasional sentry but made enough noise to alert the enemy. At Troarn, the main street ran straight toward the bridge, but Germans concealed in houses poured intense fire on them. The passengers responded with Sten guns and a heavier Bren. One man disappeared as they bucketed downhill, accelerating until they outran the gauntlet. In five minutes of quick work, they blasted the center span at Troarn into the river.

Roseveare and the survivors of the mad dash melted away on foot, wading and swimming through the inundated area until they reached the safety of the paratrooper perimeter.

The remaining bridges were soon destroyed by small bands of invaders. But elsewhere, losses for the troopers in the British sector were heavy. During the parachute drop, 192 men of the 750 in the 9th Parachute Battalion disappeared, never to be located again. Many undoubtedly drowned in the bogs and flooded streams.

The 9th, detailed for a battalion-size assault on a big gun emplacement at Merville that threatened Sword Beach, could muster only 150 troopers to attack a well-entrenched and alerted enemy. When the battle ended, half of the Brits lay dead or wounded. Only twenty-two of two hundred Germans survived for the formal surrender.

The British airborne operations had encountered problems similar to those that plagued the Americans. But they too achieved positions from which they could resist deployment of forces summoned to bolster the beachfront defenders.

# CHAPTER 12

# MAKING THE POINTES

FOR ALL OF the fury of the night, the enemy still seemed uncertain whether this was a full-scale invasion. The bad weather masked movement of the huge fleet from the few German planes that sought to pierce the all-encompassing curtain drawn by Allied fighters. Some sources within the German intelligence network had predicted Normandy as the target in the first week of June, but these reports conflicted with others that insisted the strike would come elsewhere.

The sea landings were scheduled for "nautical dawn," an astronomical designation based on the position of the sun when it is two and a half degrees below the horizon. With Double British Summer Time in effect, the first faint streaks of light appeared at 3:00 A.M. But those ashore could not have seen the vast armada more than nine miles away, nor could those on board pick out the coastline.

The exact time at which the naval bombardment began is unknown. Adm. Alan Kirk, the U.S. fleet commander, said his ships opened up at 6:00 A.M., but vessels smashing at the British beaches commenced firing as much as half an hour earlier. By the time the first shells from the navy guns crashed down among the German installations defending the American sectors, landing craft packed with the first assault waves had rendezvoused at sea and were racing for the shore.

About the same hour, huge flocks of warplanes began opening bomb bay doors to unload their devastating cargos. Thick overcast obscured ground targets. Fearful of a deadly deluge of friendly fire from the planes working at high altitudes, the U.S. Eighth Air Force obtained permission from Eisenhower for a deliberate delay in the release of its bombs. As a consequence, while aiming at Omaha Beach, 329 B-24 heavy bombers dumped thirteen thousand bombs, all of which missed both the beach and the enemy defenses behind it. The tons of high explosives fell as much as three miles inland. At Utah Beach, the medium bombers relying on visual sightings had only slightly better results.

One site already had been struck previously. Pointe du Hoc, where the intelligence experts believed the Germans had installed guns that could threaten both the fleet and the beaches, had been visited by bombers on several occasions. Because concentrated efforts might tip the Nazis to the area chosen for Overlord, these attacks were infrequent and were intended merely to delay full operation of the battery rather than to destroy it.

Now, as dawn crept over the coast and the 2nd Ranger Battalion bounced in the choppy Channel seas, a sustained barrage broke over Pointe du Hoc. Naval salvos and aerial ordnance blasted the target. The bombardment was to begin twenty minutes before H-Hour, at 0630, and end with the arrival on Beach Charley of the 2nd Battalion Rangers. Naval guns would remain available for support as requested through communications from a shore fire control party accompanying the Rangers.

The 2nd and 5th Ranger Battalions were under the overall command of Col. James Rudder, with the 5th's CO, Lt. Col. Max Schneider, serving as his deputy. From his 2nd Battalion, Rudder deployed boats bearing men from E and F Companies for landings on the eastern, or left, side of the precipice, while D Company struck from the other direction. Meanwhile, Schneider would hold his 5th Battalion Rangers just offshore watching for a rocket signal that would declare a successful ascent before coming ashore

on Beach Charley. In the event Rudder advised that his at-
tack had failed, the 5th Rangers, reinforced by A and B
Companies of the 2nd Battalion, would try to neutralize
Pointe du Hoc with a flanking attack.

"We put on a show of confidence boarding our assault
crafts, ready to be lowered into the water," says D
Company's Jack Kuhn, who had turned over his fire-
department-ladder job to another Ranger. "We tried to impress the British sailors with our seeming disregard for what
was coming. They kept calling out, 'Give them what for,
Yanks.' I shook hands with one sailor whom I didn't ever
know and he simply said, 'Good luck.'

"Our departure from the *Amsterdam* went smoothly,
proof of our training. But the moment we hit the water it
was apparent this was to be a most hazardous trip. The seas
were high and rough. The swells were big and the winds
whipped the water into a mass of rollers, tossing our crafts
severely. These were the smallest boats I had ever seen
used. When you stood up, the upper part of your body was
exposed to the enemy and the elements. There was very little room in the craft, and it was heavily loaded. Men who
had never suffered seasickness before did so that day."

The boats were roughly twelve feet wide and thirty feet
long, with seating along the sides. In the middle was a place
for the boat team leader, a second in command, and a radioman. D Company traveled on three craft—one commanded by Duke Slater, a second boat under Lt. George
Kerchner, and the third led by 1st Sgt. Len Lomell.
Battalion CO Rudder and his staff were in another group.

Kuhn remembers, "Almost as soon as we left the mother
ship, the men became apprehensive about the boats sinking. Len Lomell and I, at the rear of the boat, discussed this
possibility. Well aware that we were already shipping water,
we instructed the men to start bailing, using their helmets.

"Nobody had much, if any, sleep the night before. The
guys were sick and cold; they turned apathetic. Lomell and
I verbally forced them to their feet to keep bailing water. I
noticed that Captain Slater's boat was very low in the water, in danger of foundering. It was losing speed and dropping back from the formation.

"As soon as I mentioned it to Len, we saw the boat start to go down. We didn't want our men to see it, so we pretended to spot the Pointe and told them to keep watch. I don't know if anyone else was aware that the Duke was now out of the invasion. I wondered whether we should try to rescue him, but the time lost would have made us late. Len and I agreed the mission came first. It was his decision to make; personally I felt I was deserting our commander.

"We spotted our fighter planes overhead and saw the navy ships blasting the shoreline and inland. We saw the rockets projected. We had never seen these before. I realized now that we were taking part in the greatest battle in history and felt proud to be in it.

"As we got closer, it became my job to arm all six rockets on our boat, No. 668, which would carry our ropes up the cliff. When I armed them I saw that everything was under water or very damp from being exposed. I doubted they would fire at all.

"Still trying to see Pointe du Hoc, I noticed the boat was taking on less water and realized we must be much closer to the shore. The swells subsided slightly.

"When I armed the rockets, I had leaned my Thompson submachine gun against the bulkhead. Now I couldn't find it. I yelled to Sheldon Bare, a young man from my hometown who was bailing water, if he could find it. Bare groped around in the knee-deep water of the boat, found my weapon, and handed it to me. I fired into the air and it worked fine. Later in the day, Sheldon Bare would suffer a bullet wound in the neck, then return to the company only to be hit again.

"About this time, we spotted a cliff jutting out into the Channel, and it looked just like the pictures of Pointe du Hoc. But the lead boat with Rudder turned right and started a course parallel to the cliff and the shoreline. We surmised we had come toward the wrong site—Pointe et Raz de la Percée." Rudder, in the lead landing craft, had discovered the error and directed the flotilla toward Pointe du Hoc.

"Now we realized we would land late," says Kuhn. "The enemy would have time to regroup after the bombing attacks. The landing would be contested more heavily than expected. To save time, instead of our boat rounding Pointe du Hoc to land on the right side of the cliff, we went in to the left of the Pointe. It was time to fire our rockets, and I prayed for success. I pushed the switches and all of them fired. I couldn't watch where my ropes landed, because I was busy under the cover of the boat sides, firing the rockets. Later, I learned that three of the six made the cliffs.

"Our boat pilot was a corporal from the Canadian Army who had been with me when we checked out the DUKWs in London. He was extremely brave, and I heard our army gave him the Silver Star."

Len Lomell, in the same boat with Kuhn, remembers that as the flotilla maneuvered for its run toward the shore, "It was cloudy, foggy, dawn breaking. When we got within a mile, I could see a little dark line across the horizon. Then our rocket barges lit up the whole sky, the biggest display of fireworks you would ever see. Boom! Boom! Thousands. As you got closer, the louder the booms.

"I said to the men, 'Guys, look on this as a big football game, hit them fast and hard and keep moving faster. Never stop, because that's when they're going to pinwheel you.'"

Along with Kuhn, Lomell had watched the craft with Duke Slater go down. According to the former first sergeant, he and Kuhn were not alone in observing the ill fortune of their companions. "But no one seemed sympathetic. We had bet hundreds of bucks on who would get there first and destroy the guns. We never thought four guys would drown." Other landing craft rescued the remainder from Slater's boat.

"The ramp was dropped presumably where you could stand. But there was a bomb crater eight to ten feet deep; I stepped into it and got soaked." As he emerged with help from others, Lomell swiveled about to take stock of his boat team. "I felt a burning sensation in my right side. I spun around and didn't know where the shot came from. I didn't see anyone shoot me. But behind me was a Ranger, Harry Fate, with whom I had a nasty confrontation a few days earlier. It was decided to break him from the rank of sergeant because I didn't think he was hacking it the way he should. He had been angry ever since.

"At the time of his demotion Harry had said, 'You know, Top, what they do with first sergeants in combat.' I made light of it then, but now I was the first guy shot. Fate was about fifty feet away and in position where he could have fired the bullet. I yelled at him, 'You son of a bitch.' But he protested, 'Honestly, Len, I didn't do it.' Our medic, Bill Geitz, grabbed me and assured me it wasn't Harry.

"We couldn't waste time to sort this out—later Fate got his stripes back and we became very good friends. Our second platoon headed hell-for-leather up the cliff. The Germans held up some of the guys behind us with their intense firepower. One of the first guys up, Lt. Baugh [Gilbert] from E Company, took a bullet that went through the back of his hand and into his pistol grip. He was hurt badly and said to me, 'Send me a medic. Keep going, Lomell, keep going!' I think either Sgt. Robey [Hayward] of E Company or Bill Vaughn from D actually were the first to get all the way up and brush the Germans back with their BARs."

Lou Lisko, assigned to Headquarters Company and responsible for communications, breakfasted on a single pancake and a cup of coffee before embarking. "Seventy yards from the cliff, a Ranger who was sitting across from me was hit by a bullet in the upper left chest. He lost a considerable amount of blood and started groaning and moaning from the pain. Bullets from machine guns and rifles were flying from the top of the Hoc, and nobody dared move to help him. Another Ranger sitting by my side got sick. Though we all had paper bags under our field jackets near the throat in case of vomiting, this man did not have time to reach it. He threw up all over my left leg, my carbine and radio equipment. That made me sick too. I vomited into my paper bag and threw it overboard.

"When our LCA 722 came close to the beach, the Rangers began disembarking. I watched and saw some of them jumping neck-deep and unable to walk. The two Rangers ahead of me jumped and disappeared, so I decided to go to the left. I fell chest-deep with all my equipment, radio, ammunition, carbine. At the same time bullets were hitting the seawater around us. I struggled towards the base of the cliffs, not far away but so difficult to reach."

Lisko managed to get beneath the precipice and set up the radio. "After being so scared about this terrible ordeal, we were so emotional that we lost all our saliva. My tongue was stuck to the roof of my mouth. My friend Steven gave me a stick of chewing gum, and we chewed until we had some saliva and were able to talk. We could see Rangers climbing the cliffs, pulling themselves up on ropes and aluminum ladders. The Germans were throwing hand grenades, the 'potato mashers' that were shaped like that kind of cooking tool. It had a wooden handle and a canlike container with explosives.

"We looked back at the sea. Our LCA 722 was stuck on the sand and couldn't return to the transport. Then we saw two British sailors come out of it and start running towards an LCA moving out. Steven and I yelled as loud as we could that there was an injured Ranger in 722. They heard us and although they had almost reached the outgoing LCA went back to ours to bring the Ranger out. While a machine gun fired at them, they carried him, one by the knees and the other by the arms. Later we learned the Ranger was wounded two more times en route to safety but the sailors escaped any injury.

"Although our radio was set up, we couldn't contact anybody. I went to inform our communications officer, Lt. Ike [James] Eikner. As I started to move to find him, a machine gun and a rifleman on the left flank fired at me. First I thought I saw pebbles; then I realized they were bullets. I ran fast and jumped into a crevasse. Eikner was there where he couldn't be seen and he had twelve German prisoners. One of the prisoners stood up, as if he wanted to escape. The lieutenant and I grabbed our carbines and said, 'Halt!' When we stood, we exposed ourselves and drew fire again. Eikner shouted, 'Down!' but I was already down. One bullet struck the cliff between our heads. That's the way it would be for two and a half days, with German soldiers everywhere. You never knew when you would be fired on by a German who was in a position a Ranger had not reached."

All along the narrow ground beneath the towering promontory, Rangers struggled to make their way up. In some cases, climbers ascended thirty or forty feet on a rocket-launched rope only to fall to the beach as their grapnel gave way or a rope slipped—or was cut.

The Rangers from LCA 668 tried to exploit the success of the three rockets fired by Jack Kuhn that had carried two smooth ropes and one with toggles to the heights. To expedite the ascent, Lomell ordered sections of extension ladders put in play. They reached high enough for agile Rangers to scramble the last yards by free-climbing over the debris created by the bombardment. "We were shot at as we climbed," says Kuhn, "but it was possible to get some cover by climbing behind chunks of cliff dislodged by the shelling." The innovation of a machine gun elevated on a fire ladder never played a role. Only one DUKW bearing the gear could get far enough onto the beach to deploy the weapon. For the most part, individual Rangers, using their rifles, submachine guns, and BARs, doggedly exchanged fire with an enemy who showed himself while shooting or flinging grenades.

In spite of the loss of boats at sea, the small-arms fire and grenades from the defenders, and the rigors of the climb, a number of Rangers completed the frantic race up the cliff in less than fifteen minutes. Immediately, the bulk of Rudder's task force moved out in search of their objective, the casemated big guns. (According to Lomell, of the 225 Rangers assigned to assault Pointe du Hoc, about 175 actually reached the summit.) To their surprise and chagrin, they found the battered emplacements on Pointe du Hoc empty of the expected coastal artillery.

"Upon topping the cliff," says Kuhn, "I was shocked to find nothing that resembled the mock-ups and overlays we had studied prior to D-Day. The terrain was in complete disarray. Since there were no guns, we headed towards D Company's second objective, to fight through to the highway three-quarters of a mile directly ahead and set up roadblocks against the German troops.

"I was at this time alone, trying to contact my men. As I neared the exit road from Pointe du Hoc, I spotted John Conaboy. We were running from a shell hole to the exit road when a sniper hit Conaboy. We reached a communications ditch and I checked Conaboy. He insisted he was okay and I should go on. I could tell his wound wasn't serious, and not seeing any blood, I asked him where he was hit. He laughed, and said in his canteen. Actually he'd been hit in the right cheek of his behind.

"About ten yards further, I spotted a column of second platoon D Company Rangers, where I made contact with our platoon leader, Len Lomell. We split into two groups to make our way to the road. Heading for the main highway, Len and I walked up the road, scanning it and the hedgerows to our sides. Just as we came abreast of the battered remains of a small French farm building, Lomell grabbed me and threw both of us through the doorway.

" 'Didn't you see that Jerry kneeling in the road aiming at us?' I had not, and went to check him out. I took a quick peek and the German was still kneeling. He was combat-wise and had figured one of us would probably do this. He fired twice and a slug hit the doorframe above my head. Len went through a window or a door to cut the Jerry off. I looked again a few seconds later and the German was running away. I stepped out to cut him down, but the tommy gun would not fire. When I checked it, I found my clip had been hit right where it inserts into the gun.

"I yelled to Len I was going back to the communication trench, where I retrieved another tommy gun which had been left after a sergeant had been captured. I found Lomell setting up the men in the hedgerows to block the coast road. Larry Johnson and I settled down in a very shallow rain ditch which was pretty well hidden by hedge and high grass. We had excellent vision over the three sites we were to guard. Lomell took a position across from us covering the same area. We felt the Germans would probably use an opening in a stone wall across the way.

"We heard movement from behind the stone fence. A German soldier appeared at the opening, looking up and down the highway. Seeing it apparently clear, he came through the wall and ran across the road right up to me. I saw a German burp gun slung across his chest. I jumped up and fired point-blank, hitting him in the chest. My slugs must have cut the strap on his weapon, for it fell to the ground about three feet in front of me. The German ran a few steps, then dropped.

"Larry Johnson said, 'Hey, Jack, get me his gun.' I leaned out and picked up the weapon. As I did, I noticed movement and saw another German soldier standing in the opening of the stone fence aiming at me. I had no way to protect myself and felt I was about to be shot. Len saw it all and gunned the German just as he shot at me. His bullet struck the road near me. For the second time on D-Day, Lomell had saved my life. I learned the hard way to observe and proceed with caution."

"Because we couldn't stop until we reached the coast road, we had to move fast," recalls Lomell, "with the wounded men dropping behind to help one another. After we set up our roadblocks—there were maybe thirteen of us—Jack and I made up a two-man patrol going in one direction while another two Rangers went the opposite way. I saw some wheel tracks in a sunken road between two high hedgerows. We followed them, and about two hundred yards from the highway, I found five 155mm guns in a draw or vale of an orchard. They were all in place, pointed and ready to fire toward Utah Beach, but with not a soul around them, not a single guard that we could see near the position.

"It was about eight-thirty in the morning and maybe they hadn't realized that there was anyone landing on Utah Beach. But another hundred yards off, in a field, were a bunch of Germans forming up, putting on their jackets, starting their vehicles. I think they were the gun crews getting organized. They certainly never dreamt that a couple of American soldiers would be in their gun positions or even within miles.

" 'Jack,' I instructed Kuhn, 'keep your eyes on them and if one starts towards here, get him.' While he watched the Germans, I took his thermite grenade and the one I carried. I put them in the traversing and elevation mechanisms of two of the guns. They made a light popping noise that couldn't be heard by the enemy but destroyed the gears and breechblock. Then we ran back to the rest of the guys, got their thermite grenades, and did the same to the remaining guns. For good measure, I busted out the sights of all five guns with the butt of my weapon. We had rendered the battery inoperable in ten or fifteen minutes by 8:30 A.M. We couldn't do anything to the gun barrels; they were too high. In fact, even if the Germans had been firing the pieces they could not have depressed the barrels enough to fire on the Rangers climbing the cliff.

"Just as we returned to our hedgerow, there was a tremendous roar, like the whole world had blown up. There was a shower of dirt, metal, ramrods. I figured that a round from the *Texas* or some other warship had hit the ammunition dump for the artillery, or maybe it was a short round from the enemy. Jack and I scurried back to our roadblock like scared rabbits. [Actually, another band of Rangers had exploded the munitions stores.]

"When we had first come over the top of the Pointe, we were a lot of disappointed guys upon finding no guns there. But now, just by a piece of luck, we had found them and were able to destroy the pieces, a case of being at the right place at the right time."

Lt. George Kerchner recalls leaving the *Amsterdam* at 4:30 A.M. He noted in his diary, "Heavy seas, began bailing immediately. Motor launch led us to wrong point. Sailed along under machine gun fire, bailing all the time." Later, Kerchner amplified his terse first recollections. "We passed not far from the large warships. About five o'clock, the battleship *Texas* started to fire. It was a terrifying sound. The 14-inch guns shot far over our heads, but still close enough for us to hear and feel some of the muzzle blast.

"When we were a little better than halfway in, the rocket craft fired their barrages, salvos of ten or fifteen rockets at a time. It too was terrifying, one continuous sheet of flame going up. How could anybody live on the beaches with all this fire landing there from the warships and the rocket-firing boats? Our air force bombers were overhead. We couldn't see them, because there was a low overcast in a dull gray sky with clouds down to one or two thousand feet. But we could hear the bombs dropping and see them exploding as we came closer to the shore.

"We had been told these landing craft were unsinkable. They had large air tanks along both sides, supposedly to support the craft even if holed by a shell. At first we did not worry about shipping water. The heavy seas hit the ramp in the front and washed right over the top, and shortly we had six to twelve inches of water in the bottom of the boat. I saw one boat from D Company [Duke Slater's], carrying a group of men with whom I was very friendly, sink because of shipping water. That convinced me our landing craft were not unsinkable. We immediately began bailing with our helmets and managed to keep us afloat, even though we were taking on a lot of water as the boat speeded up."

The coxswain had accelerated to compensate for the mistake of being directed to the wrong landing spot. To Kerchner, the change in course seemed "a catastrophe. We were due to land at six-thirty on the dot. In the forty minutes before that time, the heavy bombers would drop their sticks on the Pointe and the *Texas* would deliver several hundred rounds. Then medium bombers would plaster the area, and only three minutes before six-thirty, fighters would strafe the Pointe. The attacks were designed to keep the defenders pinned down, so they wouldn't see us approach the Pointe. They would be kept from the edge of the cliff. Otherwise they could cut our ropes before we even managed to get halfway up the cliff.

"Although we were about half a mile offshore and sailing parallel for half an hour under fire by German anti-aircraft guns, 20 and 40mm, none of the men in my boat were wounded. I believe several other craft were struck, one sunk.

"As we neared Pointe du Hoc I looked at my watch and saw it was 7:00 A.M. We were far behind schedule. All of the preparatory fire on the Pointe had been lifted by half an hour. The Germans were now coming out of their underground shelters and starting to look about to see what was happening. As we turned to make our approach, I looked up and saw Germans standing atop the cliff. I thought, this whole thing is a big mistake. None of us will ever get up that cliff because we are so vulnerable. The Germans could just stay back from the edge and cut the ropes.

"When we were about twenty to twenty-five yards off-shore, I gave the order to fire our rockets. All of them fired, and five actually cleared the cliff. Some other landing craft had a great deal of trouble, firing too soon. In other cases, the seas had wet the ropes and made them too heavy to reach the cliff.

"The ramp was lowered immediately after the rockets fired. It was our hope and desire to run right up on the beach for a dry landing, not because we were afraid of getting wet but because if we were soaked it would be added weight to carry while climbing. The British Navy man had promised to put us down dry, but suddenly we ran aground with the ramp dropped. The officer said, 'Everybody out.' Looking ahead, I could see fifteen or twenty feet of water, a muddy, dirty gray stretch. The entire area was marked by craters, shell holes from the guns on the *Texas* and the bombers.

"We had run up on the edge of one of these shell craters, as I discovered almost immediately. I figured the water was only a foot or two deep, because the landing craft drew only about that much, and that we could run through it. So I yelled, 'Come on, let's go!' I rushed ahead, first one off, and fell into eight feet of water. It had to be at least that deep because I couldn't touch bottom.

"My first impulse was anger at the boat crew because they'd made us get off saying it was shallow there. When I came to the surface, I started to doggie-paddle, keeping my head above water while I tried to reach the beach. The men behind me realized what had happened when I went under, and they went off both sides of the crater, getting nothing more than their feet wet. Instead of being the first ashore, I was one of the last. I looked around for someone to help me cuss out the British Navy for dumping me in eight feet of water, but there was nobody to sympathize with me. They were all busily engaged.

"I tried my SCR-536 hand radio. It wouldn't work, and I threw it down on the beach. Then I realized we were being fired upon by a machine gun off to the left at the top of the cliff, several hundred yards away. Sgt. Francis Pacyga, William Cruz, and Lester Harris were all hit. I don't know how they missed me, since I was right next to the ones who were wounded. I felt rather helpless with my .45 pistol. I picked up the rifle dropped by Harris.

"My first impulse was to go after the machine gun, but I realized this was stupid. Our mission was to get to the top of the cliff and destroy the guns up there. The men all knew what they had to do. They had their ropes and the order in which they were to climb, and they were all starting up. There was no need to tell one man to do this or another to do that. The only command I gave was for the platoon messenger to stay with the wounded after we got them in as close to the cliff, protected as much as possible.

"I thought I had better inform Col. Rudder that the boat with our company commander and a number of men had sunk. I located him about twenty-five or fifty yards down the beach as he was beginning to climb one of the rope ladders. He had his hands and his mind full and did not seem particularly interested in my information that I was assuming command of the company. He told me to get out of there and climb my rope.

"Getting up the cliff was very easy after all the training we had in England. The shells from the warships and the bomb damage at the edge of the cliff caused dirt and large chunks of clay and shale to fall. You could almost walk up the first twenty-five feet. Using a smooth rope, I had no trouble getting all the way up."

Medic Frank South was one of the few Rangers whose primary responsibility was something other than climbing Pointe du Hoc. "During the planning stage, the medics realized they had a problem. It would be impractical for us to carry all the equipment and supplies we would need in our aid kits or simple packs, and we did not know when we would be able to retrieve the rest of our materials from a supply boat. We decided each of us would carry an enlarged kit.

"Since I was the biggest and presumably strong—as well as the youngest and perhaps the most naive—Block asked me to work with him putting together a *very* large pack of medical gear and supplies to be carried on a mountain packboard. On its horns I coiled about fifty feet of three-eighths-inch line in case I had to ditch it in the surf and pull it to shore. The pack contained plasma, sulfa-based antibiotics—there was no penicillin yet—drugs, additional instruments, bandages, suture material, and whatever else I could think of. God knows how much it weighed, perhaps sixty-five or seventy pounds. It was a walking aid station, and I don't recall any other medic making or carrying such a pack. In addition, I carried my regular aid kit, side arm, knife, canteen, an Argus C-3 camera which I lost in the surf, and a D-ration bar.

"As a medic on the LCA, I was to be the last one off. There was not much conversation around me, a little black humor maybe—'Now if the lieutenant and I get hit, you know who to take care of first, Doc.' Then someone lamented that the army had never issued bulletproof jockstraps. 'After all, I got married just before we left. Could you requisition one for me, Doc?' I suggested he borrow someone's helmet for comfort and protection.

"Approaching the beach, our LCA was able to fire its grapnel-bearing rockets in good order, and most men got off in about two or three feet of water while under almost continuous MG fire from the cliff. Expectably, as the boat load lightened, the LCA rose and shifted its position. When my turn came, I jumped off the ramp with my pack into an underwater bomb or shell crater that was over my head. Before either the pack or I became waterlogged, I scrambled out and crawled into a drier crater ashore, where I was able to shuck my burden.

"Immediately, there was the first call of 'Medic!' My regular aid kit was still attached to my pistol belt. Opening it, as I dodged the fire from the cliff, I reached the fallen Ranger with a chest wound. I was able to drag him to an indentation in the cliff face and begin to help him. The call 'Medic!' was now repeated time after time. For a while it seemed as if I was the only one retrieving and working on the wounded. Block and another medic had worked their way up to the cliff base and were beginning to treat men as fast as they could, but it was not possible to set up a proper aid station on the beach. The highest priority went to scaling and securing the cliff, and the wounded were too scattered. I worked along the entire beach, covering all three companies. Block devoted most of his attention to the most critically wounded.

"Although the LCA I was on got its grapnel rockets off effectively, the one with the first platoon was in the wrong position to launch theirs. The rockets were designed so they could be removed and fired by hand, a risky procedure. Sgt. John Cripps took four rockets off the LCA and, while exposed to machine gun fire from above, mounted them on the beach. He hot-wired and fired one, receiving a blast in the face. With terrific determination, he fired the rest, just as successfully.

"Nearly blinded, almost fainting, Cripps stumbled over to Block and me. His face, neck, and hands were covered with powder burns and embedded with black unburned explosives. He said to me, 'Jesus, South, didn't you ever stand too close to a big firecracker?' All we could do was blot his face and neck with water from our canteens and pat on, as gently as possible, some burn ointment I found in the bottom of my aid kit. He immediately left to rejoin his platoon and the attack. For all that courage, willpower, and determination that Cripps displayed while under direct fire, he never was cited or decorated.

"Very early on, while I was finishing working on someone near our left flank, Sgt. Bill 'L Rod' Petty, his BAR slung across his shoulders, was struggling with a straight rope. It was slippery with wet clay, and he was having a terrible time getting a purchase on it and ascending the cliff. During a pause, while he was trying to dry his hands and catch his breath, Block appeared and said in a loud, commanding voice, 'Soldier, get hold of that rope and up the cliff!'

"Petty, face flushed both by anger and his efforts, replied something like, 'What the hell, if you think you can do any better, you can fucking well try!' Short-tempered Capt. Block was stymied by the equally short-tempered Sgt. Petty, one of our most effective noncoms. Somehow Block controlled his temper and realized his charge was unjust. He looked at Petty, turned, stared at me for an instant, and then stalked down to the beach where he was needed."

Lost in the waterborne assault were rockets intended to inform Schneider of the storming of Pointe du Hoc. A radio message also failed to advise the 5th Battalion commander. Furthermore, the delay due to the mistake in locating Pointe du Hoc forced Schneider to choose the alternate plan, to go in alongside the 29th Infantry Division's 116th Regiment.

The Rangers under Rudder were listed as Force A, while Schneider's men were designated Force C. The 2nd Battalion's Company C, sixty-five enlisted men and three officers including platoon leader Sid Salomon, received a separate mission. About two miles east of Pointe du Hoc rose another sheer wall known as Pointe et Raz de la Percée, the landmark mistaken by Rudder's helmsman for Pointe du Hoc. Working with the 116th Infantry's A Company, the Rangers were to neutralize a series of defensive positions which had a clear field of fire upon any invaders along the Vierville beach area.

Says Salomon, "There had been detailed planning. We had looked at postcards, travel material on what before the war was a resort area, and we had sand tables. But we never met with anyone from the 29th to go over the mission.

"In all our training, we had never gotten on a landing craft with all of the weapons, ammo, food, and other supplies required for the actual invasion. Suddenly, we found ourselves so jammed in that I couldn't sit down. I stood behind the steel doors in the bow. Our two landing craft looked forlorn and lonesome as they splashed forward towards the shoreline.

"I was looking ahead when suddenly I heard pings on the side of the boat. It was machine gun fire from the shore. There were splashes around the craft, white water cascades, then concentric circles as shells landed in our vicinity. I saw a barge with rockets. They made a tremendous amount of noise, a huge whoosh, and then the shells burst like fireworks. But every one of them fell short, splashing down right at the water's edge. I saw no flashes erupting on the cliffs.

"The British sublieutenant nodded to his helmsman, who opened the throttle a notch. The intensity of the pings against the outside of the steel hull increased. Everyone kept his head down. When the words 'Get ready' were passed, everyone inched forward a little. All were tense. The sublieutenant had his hands on the ropes that would release the catch for the steel ramp.

" 'Now!' he called out, and the ramp flopped down into the water. I immediately jumped off the landing craft, the men following one to the right, the next left. I knew first off was the safest, since the guys aiming didn't know when the ramp would go down and it takes a second or two before they squeeze off a shot. My section sergeant, Oliver Reed, right behind me, was hit in the stomach. I was in water up to my chest, and I pulled Reed out from under the ramp to keep him from being crushed.

"I told Reed, 'You've got to go on your own from here.' I was running across the sand, with the mortar section behind me, when a mortar shell exploded. It wiped out those around me, killing or wounding them. Some pieces of shrapnel hit me in the back and knocked me flat. I thought I was finished. My platoon sergeant ran up to me. I was about to turn over my maps to him when bullets kicked up sand in my face. I jumped up and ran to the base of the cliff, which gave some cover against the machine guns.

"In the shelter there, I took off my shirt and jacket. An aidman sprinkled on sulfa powder and said, 'That's all I can do now, lieutenant.'

"So we started up Pointe et Raz de la Percée. The Germans threw grenades down while the Rangers returned small-arms fire. First two men inched up, using ropes and hand- and footholds. Then another pair followed them while the men at the bottom continued firing at the top, taking off some of the pressure and direct attacks on the climbers."

Turning his gaze to the beach for a moment, Salomon beheld bodies strewn about, blood in the sand. He saw some wounded crawling toward shelter with looks of despair upon their faces. Others who tried to get back on their feet went down again from enemy bullets. At the water's edge, bodies rolled back and forth in the ebb and flow of the Channel.

The second boat, with Goranson, Moody, and the remainder of C Company, took a direct hit in the bow as it reached the beach. A number of Rangers were killed or wounded from the blast, but the two officers at the rear of the craft remained sound.

Observing the carnage and the enormous casualties among C Company until noon of June 6, Salomon thought the invasion had failed.

Atop the Pointe, he counted only nine able-bodied Rangers, the remnants of thirty-nine jammed into the landing craft only minutes earlier. Nevertheless, the Rangers doggedly advanced. Moody led an assault that cleaned out a battered stone building housing some enemy gunners.

In a shell hole, Salomon and Moody met to surveil the battleground and determine their next moves. "We were shoulder to shoulder," says Salomon. "I was pointing towards a series of trenches when suddenly he rolled to one side. A bullet struck him directly between his eyes. I told Ralph [Goranson] I was going ahead. Stooping down and with two men, I walked through a series of trenches. We worked our way to a dugout. A white phosphorus grenade was tossed in, and when the Germans came out, the Rangers turned their tommy guns and rifles on them. Further down the line we silenced a mortar crew. Then we withdrew back to the rest of the platoon. C Company now held Pointe et Raz de la Percée."

On Pointe du Hoc, Rudder dispatched Rangers to capture other troublesome bastions in enemy hands. One was a command post, presumably for the big guns which Lomell and Kuhn found elsewhere. The other was an antiaircraft battery emplacement that was inflicting considerable damage on the invaders. In both instances the defenders were too numerous and strongly entrenched to be overrun by the limited number of men Rudder could muster. The German command post, which included a series of underground tunnels, troubled the invaders for hours as enemy soldiers disappeared in its warrens only to surface at some protected place and fire.

The gun battery, however, yielded to the U.S. Navy. The destroyer *Satterlee*, which earlier took under fire Germans atop the Pointe and helped drive them off, under the guidance of a shore fire control officer, blasted the antiaircraft guns. Gun crew members who survived the volley fled.

When Rudder and his headquarters party achieved the heights of the Pointe, they set up their command post in the revetments of that AA post. Unfortunately, a round from enemy artillery smashed into their position, wounding Rudder in the arm—down on the beach a bullet had passed through the fleshy part of his leg. The same explosion killed the naval observer. Lou Lisko assumed the responsibility for contacting the warships to enlist their aid.

"I had a signal lamp," says Lisko. "I was able to get in touch with the *Satterlee*, but the navy guys were much too fast with their lights for me. Finally, they told me the wavelength to use and we began to communicate by radio. When the *Satterlee* expended all its ammunition, the destroyer *Harding* took over. Their fire support saved our necks, breaking up counterattacks."

With limited numbers prescribed by their table of organization, the Rangers regarded everyone, including even the company clerk, as a combat soldier. "Joe Devoli, our company clerk," says Lomell, "was the worst-looking Ranger I ever saw, bad posture, balding, his uniform never fitted him well. But he insisted, 'I'll be the best company clerk the Rangers ever had.' He rescued a man when Slater's boat sank and he made every payroll throughout the war, even if he had to forge signatures to do it. He was a brave soldier." An appalled Sid Salomon, however, watched his company clerk, carrying a typewriter in one hand and his rifle in the other, cut down on the beach, a senseless loss in Salomon's view.

The Rangers and all of the soldiers assaulting the beaches received virtually no tactical aid from the air. U.S. fighters either flew air cover for the bombers or devoted themselves to sanitizing the inland highways of any would-be reinforcements. There was no system for air-to-ground or air-to-ship communications. The absence of coordination sharply contrasted with naval operations in the Pacific, where U.S. Navy warships worked closely with their air arm. Protection for the five thousand vessels from any Luftwaffe marauders depended upon RAF Spitfires.

Like the airborne forces who had arrived before them, the Rangers were taught to operate as small units. Unfortunately for Rudder's people, their mission called for a union with the infantrymen coming ashore on Omaha Beach. What happened there would leave the Rangers in desperate circumstances.

# CHAPTER 13

# DOG GREEN AND EASY RED, OMAHA BEACH

THE CHOREOGRAPHY FOR conquest of Omaha Beach called for the 1st and 29th Infantry Divisions, abetted by amphibious tanks and with the aid of some Ranger companies, to head for the shore at H-Hour, 6:30 A.M. The naval and aerial barrage on the defenders would commence forty minutes earlier. Amphibious tanks would lead the parade towards the seven-thousand-yard-long, crescent-shaped strand. These Sherman tanks would be followed by more armor deposited close in by landing craft; then the initial wave of 1,450 infantrymen would come ashore.

Those first soldiers were expected to provide adequate protection for demolition task forces assigned to clear and mark lanes for the main body of troops, ferried onto the beach through the offshore obstacles and mines.

Bob Slaughter of the 29th Division, with his fellow GIs from the 116th Regiment, heard the steady drone of bombers in the darkness overhead. "We saw bomb explosions causing fires that illuminated clouds in the otherwise dark sky. We were twelve miles offshore as we climbed into our seat assignments on the LCAs and were lowered into the heavy sea from davits. The navy hadn't begun its firing because it was still dark. We couldn't see the armada but we knew it was there.

"Prior to loading, friends said their so longs and good lucks. I remember finding Sgt. Jack Ingram, an old friend from Roanoke. He had suffered a back injury during training and I asked him how he felt. 'I'm okay. Good luck, I'll see you on the beach.' Another Roanoker, a neighbor and classmate, George D. Johnson, who'd joined the army with me, asked, 'Are your men ready?' I couldn't imagine why he asked, but I answered yes.

"Sgt. Robert Bixler of Shamokin, Pennsylvania, joked, 'I'm going to land with a comb in one hand'—running his hand through his blond hair—'and a pass to Paris in the other.' The feeling among most of the men was that the landing would be a 'walk-in affair' but later we could expect a stiff counterattack. That didn't worry us too much, since by then the tanks, heavy artillery, and air support should bolster our defense until the beachhead grew strong enough for a breakout.

"All of us had a letter signed by the Supreme Commander, Gen. Eisenhower, saying that we were about to embark upon a great crusade. A few of my cohorts autographed it and I carried it in my wallet throughout the war.

"The Channel was extremely rough, and it wasn't long before we had to help the craft's pumps by bailing with our helmets. The cold spray blew in and soon we were soaking wet. I used a gas cape [a plastic sack for protection against skin irritants] as shelter. Lack of oxygen under the sack brought seasickness.

"As the sky lightened, the armada became visible. The smoking and burning French shoreline also became more defined. At 0600, the huge guns of the Allied navies opened up with what must have been one of the greatest artillery barrages ever. The diesels on board our craft failed to muffle the tornadic blasting. I could see the *Texas* firing broadside into the coastline. Boom-ba-ba-boom-ba-ba-boom! Within minutes, giant swells from the recoil of those guns nearly swamped us and added to the seasickness and misery. But one could also actually see the two-thousand-pound missiles tumbling on their targets. Twin-fuselaged P-38 fighter-bombers were also overhead protecting us from the Luftwaffe and giving us a false sense of security. This should be a piece of cake.

"A few thousand yards from shore we rescued three or four survivors from a craft that had been swamped and sunk. Other men were left in the water bobbing in their Mae Wests, because we did not have room for them.

"About two or three hundred yards from shore we encountered artillery fire. Near misses sent water skyward and then it rained back on us. The British coxswain said he had to lower the ramp and for us to quickly disembark. Back in Weymouth these sailors had bragged they had been on several invasions and we were in capable hands. I heard Sgt. Willard Norfleet say, 'These men have heavy equipment. You *will* take them all the way in.'

"The coxswain pleaded, 'But we'll all be killed!' Norfleet unholstered his .45 Colt, put it to the sailor's head, and ordered, '*All the way in!*' The craft kept going, plowing through the choppy water.

"I thought, if this boat doesn't hurry and get us in, I'll die from seasickness. Thinking I was immune to this malady, I had given my puke bag to a buddy who already had filled his. Minus the paper bag, I used my steel helmet.

"About 150 yards from shore, I raised my head despite the warning 'Keep your head down.' I saw the boat on our right taking a terrific licking from small arms. Tracer bullets were bouncing and skipping off the ramp and sides as the enemy zeroed in on the boat which had beached a few minutes before us. Had we not delayed a few minutes to pick up the survivors of the sunken craft, we might have taken that concentration of fire.

"Great plumes of water from enemy artillery and mortars sprouted close by. We knew then this was not going to be a walk-in. No one thought the enemy would give us this kind of opposition at the water's edge. We expected A and B Companies to have the beach secured by the time we landed. In reality no one had set foot in our sector. The coxswain had missed the Vierville church steeple, our point to guide on, and the tides also helped pull us two hundred yards east.

"The location didn't make much difference. We could hear the 'p-r-r-r-r, p-r-r-r-r' of enemy machine guns to our right, towards the west. It was obvious someone down there was catching that hell, getting chewed up where we had been supposed to come in."

The "someone catching hell" on Dog Green was Company A; more than half of the dead from Bedford, Virginia, were slain there. GIs from battalion headquarters following A Company were shocked to see their beach empty of living men.

"The ramp went down while shells exploded on land and in the water. Unseen snipers were shooting down from the cliffs, but the most havoc came from automatic weapons. I was at the left side of the craft, about fifth from the front. Norfleet led the right side. The ramp was in the surf, and the front of the steel boat bucked violently up and down. Only two at a time could exit.

"When my turn came, I sat on the edge of the bucking ramp, trying to time my leap on the down cycle. I sat there way too long, causing a bottleneck and endangering myself and the men to follow. But the ramp was bouncing six or seven feet, and I was afraid it would slam me in the head. One man was crushed and killed instantly.

"When I did get out, I was in the water. It was very difficult to shed the sixty pounds of equipment, and if one were a weak swimmer he could drown before he inflated his Mae West. Many were hit in the water and drowned, good swimmers or not. There were dead men floating in the water and live men acting dead, letting the tide take them in. Initially, I tried to take cover behind one of the heavy timbers and then noticed an innocent-looking Teller mine tied to the top. I crouched down to chin deep in the water as shells fell at the water's edge. Small-arms fire kicked up sand. I noticed a GI running, trying to get across the beach. He was weighted down with equipment and having difficulty moving. An enemy gunner shot him. He screamed for a medic. An aidman moved quickly to help him and he was also shot. I'll never forget seeing that medic lying next to that wounded soldier, both of them screaming. They died in minutes.

"Boys were turned into men. Some would be very brave men; others would soon be dead men, but any who survived would be frightened men. Some wet their pants, others cried unashamedly. Many just had to find within themselves the strength to get the job done. Discipline and training took over.

"For me, it was time to get the hell away from the killing zone and across the beach. Getting across the beach became an obsession. I told Pfc Walfred Williams, my number one gunner, to follow. He still had his fifty-one-pound machine gun tripod. He once told me he developed his strength by cradling an old iron cookstove in his arms and walking around with it, daily. I felt secure with Williams on the gun. A Chicago boy of nineteen, he was dependable and loyal. He loved the army and didn't believe a German weapon could kill him. I didn't think so either. (We were both wrong. Enemy shrapnel killed him six weeks after D-Day. Part of me would die with him.)

"Our rifles were encased in a plastic bag to shield them from salt water. Before disembarking, because I wanted to be ready, I had removed the covering and fixed the bayonet. I gathered my courage and started running as fast as my long legs would carry me. I ran as low as I could to lessen the target, but since I am six-foot-five, I presented a good one. It was a long way to go, one hundred yards or more. We were loaded with gear, our shoes full of water, our impregnated woolen clothes soaked. I tripped in a tidal pool of a few inches of water, began to stumble, and accidentally fired my rifle, barely missing my foot. But I made it to the seawall.

"I was joined by Pvt. Sal Augeri, and Pvt. Ernest McCanless and Williams. Augeri lost the machine gun receiver in the water. We still had one box of MG ammo and the tripod. I had gotten sand in my rifle, so I don't believe we had a weapon that would fire. I felt like a naked morsel on a giant sandy platter.

"I took off my assault jacket and spread out my raincoat so I could clean my rifle. It was then I saw bullet holes in my jacket and raincoat. I lit my first cigarette; I had to rest and compose myself because I became weak in the knees."

Already dead were many of Slaughter's childhood play-mates and brothers-in-arms in the 116th. In the pre-invasion hours, his D Company commander, Capt. Walter Schilling, had confided to a fellow officer, "I don't believe I will make it." He was right. A German 88 slammed into his landing craft, killing him instantly. In fact, the COs from three of the four 1st Battalion companies, along with six-teen other junior officers, perished without ever setting foot on dry land. Dead too were Sgt. Russell Ingram, who had shrugged off a back injury in order to participate; Cpl. Jack Simms, who had stuffed himself with bananas in order to achieve the minimum weight; 1st Sgt. Obenshein; and Slaughter's fellow Roanoker George Johnson. Also killed were the Hoback brothers and T/Sgt. Ray Stevens from Bedford. Ray Stevens's twin brother, Roy, had waved off a handshake as the two walked up the gangplank on the eve of the invasion. "I'll see you at Vierville-sur-Mer," Roy had said, but he would never again lay eyes on his twin.

Bob Sales, who had donned the 29th's National Guard uniform at fifteen, had, upon his return from Ranger train-ing with Bob Slaughter, been assigned as radio operator and bodyguard for B Company's leader, Capt. Ettore Zappacosta. "About one hundred yards from shore, the English coxswain said he couldn't get us in closer. As the ramp lowered, enemy machine guns opened up, firing di-rectly into our boat. Capt. Zappacosta, a great leader, was first off and the first hit. S/Sgt. Dick Wright was second, and he also was hit as he left the boat, falling into the water. A medic was third, and I didn't see what happened to him.

"I was fourth, caught my heel in the ramp, and fell side-ways, out of the path of that MG-42, and this undoubtedly saved my life. All of the men who followed were either killed by the Germans or drowned. So far as I know, no one else from my craft was ever found alive."

Sales dumped his heavy radio in the water. A log bearing an unexploded Teller mine drifted by, and Sales clung to it as the tide carried him to the shoreline. On the beach he saw the badly wounded Sgt. Wright succumb to a sniper bullet in his head and then the battalion surgeon cut down by a machine gun.

"I crawled on my belly, using the dead and wounded as a shield." But when he saw some other B Company men sheltering themselves by the seawall he started to administer help to the wounded. "I kept crawling back to the water's edge, dragging out the still-living men. You can't imagine how helpless it was to be lying on that beach and those snipers shooting everything that moved."

Felix Branham, with Company K of the 116th, climbed into a landing craft at 0420. Like Slaughter, he and his mates quickly found the Channel rough. Rain and spray soaked them, and the swells turned many men ill. "Each time a boat hit the water, it joined a circle that became larger and larger. We circled around until finally we headed for Normandy. We weren't within machine gun or rifle range and there was only an occasional artillery shell that would splash down. We were getting near enough and the sky lightening enough to see the contour of the bluffs and skyline. They looked just like Slapton Sands. One guy in my boat raised up and looked over the side. He was disgusted and said, 'Goddam, another dry run. I thought this was the real thing.'

"At 0600, the navy began firing. The noise made by shells going over, bombs being dropped by medium bombers and fighter-bombers, and the return fire from the German shore batteries and heavy mortars was deafening. As our LCVP got closer, machine gun bullets beat a tattoo on the ramp and sides.

"About fifty yards from the beach, we hit a sandbar parallel to the shore. Back at the marshaling area, we had been told there was a sandbar there and we were not to let anyone stop there and lower the ramp to let us off. We were to make them close it up. The two fellows from the navy moved to let down the ramp, but Lt. Lucas, our boat team commander, hollered, 'No, no!' He ordered the coxswain to go over the sandbar sideways, as we had been instructed. Unfortunately, some of the guys in my company in another boat team didn't remember their homework and left the landing craft when it reached the sandbar. With all of the heavy equipment they had, with the waves coming and the tide rising a foot every ten minutes, they drowned. Other boats stopped at the sandbar and were demolished; seasick men who'd stayed on board were blasted to smithereens.

"I got out in water up to the top of my boots. People were yelling, screaming, dying, running on the beach, equipment was flying everywhere, men were bleeding to death, crawling, lying everywhere, firing coming from all directions. We dropped down behind anything that was the size of a golf ball.

"Col. Canham [Charles, CO of the regiment], Lt. Cooper, and Sgt. Crawford were screaming at us to get off the beach. I turned to say to Gino Ferrari, 'Let's move up, Gino,' but before I could finish the sentence, something spattered all over the side of my face. He'd been hit in the face and his brains splattered all over my face and my stuff. I moved forward and the tide came on so fast it covered him and I no longer could see him.

"Canham previously had a BAR shot out of his hand. The bullet went through his right wrist and he wore a makeshift sling. His bodyguard, Pfc Nami, followed closely behind, keeping the colonel's .45 loaded. Canham would fire a clip and hand the gun back to Nami, who would inject another into the weapon. Back in training we used to call Col. Canham everything not fit to print. When he took command of the 116th, he made life miserable for us. We thought he would be another rear-echelon commander. After seeing him in action, I sure had to eat a mess of crow."

As a member of the intelligence and reconnaissance squad of the 116th's 1st Battalion, Don McCarthy expected to set foot at the juncture of the two sections known as Dog Green and Easy Green. "The LCA," says McCarthy, "would have touched the beach approximately fifteen hundred yards east of the Vierville draw [one of several key exits through the bluffs overlooking Omaha Beach]. The British coxswain handled the boat well, but the sea and tidal effect, as well as the close proximity of the other LCAs, created turbulent waves that broke over the relatively low coaming [a deck barrier intended to prevent water from running below].

"It became obvious that the LCA had taken on considerable water, that the center of gravity had been altered and the boat might broach. We drifted east under full throttle and she finally broached about seven hundred yards from the shore. I managed to stay afloat after it capsized. The flood stage of the tide helped carry me toward the shore, and I worked myself to the beach during what seemed an eternity.

"There was an officer yelling at people in the water to get up and run for cover. I crawled to a point where while still in the water, I could stand up and run. I have no idea who the officer was but I will always be grateful for his leadership and inspiration."

Antitank squad leader Bill Lewis was twelve miles offshore on an LST when he, his crew, and their weapon were loaded aboard a DUKW for the trip to the beach. "We had never trained on a DUKW," said Lewis. "The DUKW was like a truck, and we had a big load on. The guy driving it was busy trying to keep it heading in. If we got into a trough, we were going to turn over. He let the waves coming from behind push it along.

"When we got to the metal obstacles there was a man hanging on one. He hollered for help. We couldn't control the DUKW very good, and when we got close to him, Lt. Van de Voort yelled, 'We're out here to kill people, not save lives. Jump if you want on this damn thing.' He leaped and came on board.

"Then we sheared a pin and lost power. We were adrift in the Teller-mine area and going right into them, sideways. They were sticking out two or three inches above the water. We hit one mine more than once, kept bumping it, but I guess the salt water had deteriorated it. It didn't explode.

"It was about thirty minutes after the first wave and they started to machine-gun the DUKW. We jumped out, and down went the DUKW with the AT gun and everything else. When I jumped out, I could stand on my toes except when a wave crashed over me. The natural assumption was, the closer you went towards the shore, the more solid it would get. That wasn't true, because sand had built up around some obstacles, and I stepped off into a hole.

"I kept paddling. I wasn't about to go back the other

way but just kept coming in. The water around me was dancing to that damn machine gun fire." Lewis and another managed to run to the seawall, where, cold and scared, they lay until a third man piled in on top of them. "He said, 'Is that you shaking, sarge?' I said, 'Yeah, damn right!' He answered, 'My God, I thought it was *me*!' I could see him and he was shaking all right. Both of us were.

"We huddled there, just trying to stay alive. There was nothing we could do except keep our butts down. There was no place to go, and the automatic fire became heavier. Everyone coming up could see that seawall, so they got on top of us, piling up and trying to get below the damn thing."

Sharing the horror of Omaha Beach with the GIs of the 29th were men from the 1st Division slated for the adjoining section, called Easy Red. The LCT with Bill Behlmer and his antitank platoon had never returned to port after the one-day postponement on June 5. "We rode out the weather. It was so bad you had to look up to see the water. Everybody, including the navy crew, was seasick. My halftrack, *Hitler's Hearse*, was at the front of the LCT. We were to be first off and I was to lead my platoon on Omaha Beach. My driver, Stan Stypulkowski, who had come all the way through North Africa and Sicily, sat and talked with me all night. We knew this was it for us.

"Our navy CO told us to hit the beach when the ramp dropped. On the way in, another LCT, not far from us, just disappeared, went to the bottom. An LCI on the other side with red crosses on the side took a couple of hits. Medics were hanging on to the ramp and in the water.

"As far as the eye could see was wall-to-wall boats headed for Easy Red near the small town of Colleville-sur-Mer. That morning, some of Easy Red would be my red blood.

"We neared the beach and the ramp dropped. Small arms, machine guns, mortars, artillery raked across the ramp. The navy CO said we were pulling out to try again. We came back in, and when the ramp dropped, I told Stan to gun the half-track. We hit the ground, turned right, and headed down the beach, a big turkey at a turkey shoot.

Every gun covering that beach zeroed in on us. We didn't stand a chance.

"I stood up and turned to the back, told the guys to get out. Stan and I jumped from the hood to the ground. On the way down, it felt like someone jabbed me in the legs with a red-hot poker. Stan, with his arms across his chest, oozed blood. I must have gone into shock, because I drifted in and out. Shells were falling everywhere. But for me the war seemed to have gone away.

"Much later, I heard voices. Sailors were on the beach. One of them rolled me over and said I was still alive. He took me out to the troopship, the *Samuel Chase*, which was now a hospital ship. It was around noon, I later learned. That probably saved my life. The war was over for me. The next morning I was in a hospital in England, where they amputated my right leg above the knee due to gangrene. No one was at fault or could have done more for me." Stypulkowski also recovered from his bullet wounds.

Fred Erben, the Brooklyn youth who joined the 1st Division as a seventeen-year-old with his parents' blessing almost a year before Pearl Harbor, was a member of C Company, 16th Regiment, for the initial assault on Omaha's Easy Red.

"As luck would have it," says Erben, "we were in the first wave and hit the beaches at low tide. We were fortunate because we could see the underwater obstacles and skirt them. However, we hit a sandbar and had to unload. Beyond the sandbar there were obstacles we did not see. Our craft made it out of there in a hurry, but some boats that got over the bar struck the mines and blew up. It was horrible seeing men blown all over the place. Some, still alive, were swimming ashore. The ones not so lucky floated ashore.

"We had to wade in with all of our equipment, a pair of twenty-pound TNT Bangalore torpedoes, and ammo. Our flotation devices helped. My squad made it intact, but the beach was rocky and there was no chance to dig in. Many men were hit all around us by the intense crossfire from two pillboxes on either side of us. That's when Omaha Easy Red became known as Bloody Red.

"We got the word to advance and get the hell off the beach. We had barbed wire in front of us and land mines to contend with. One of my scouts, Pvt. Tripoletti, set his ammunition down on a mine and was killed.

"This is where the Bangalores—we called them stove-pipes—came in. They were assembled under fire, one by one, with three-foot lengths of tubing pressed into one another until they formed a long pole that could be passed through the barbed wire. The pipes were loaded with high explosives and an ignition cap placed in the last one. A man would lie directly behind the tube and pull the cap, setting off an explosion that caused the tubes to burst sideways, cutting the wires. It also blew up any buried mines. We kept passing these things forward and the tubes made a large enough hole for us to pass through.

"This was about twenty minutes after we landed. We inched our way up the hill toward one pillbox. I and another man put a charge attached to a wooden pole into the aperture of the pillbox. It sounds crazy but it worked.

"We moved into a wooded area and went on a recon mission, moving forward to a hedgerow. Peering over it, we saw a group of men on our left flank. Thinking they were another patrol, we waved to them. They waved back; then we motioned for them to come over. They must have realized we were Americans, because they dropped down behind their hedge and opened fire. No one was hit at the moment.

"Then they started to drop in mortars on us. We opened up with rifle grenades fired from an adapter on our M-1s. I told my squad to withdraw when a mortar shell struck near us. A piece of shrapnel hit me and knocked me out. I came to and heard German voices nearby. They must have thought I was dead, and they left.

"Now I heard Americans, but I didn't move. Someone said, 'That's Erben. Is he dead?' Gene Greco came over and bandaged my head. After he patched me up, I headed back towards the beach. It was devastation, littered with bodies and wounded being tended to. Sunken boats lay on their sides. More troops were coming ashore. Finally one of the medics directed me to a ship, where I saw more men being put in body bags."

John Bistrica, the infantry replacement assigned to C Company in the 16th Regiment when he arrived in England, did not get seasick as his landing craft took off for the Easy Red Beach. "My heart must have been going a mile a minute, and I was sort of dizzy from seeing everything happening. You could see the hedgehogs [the tetrahedral steel barriers] and bodies up against them. They were the combat engineers who had tried to blow up these obstacles. You could see rockets firing off the ships, see shells from German guns hitting the water. You could see American fighter planes crossing over the beaches. You could hear what sounded like roaring lions—the German six-barrel mortars.

"The sailor steering our craft was good. We came in and stuck on a sandbar. He backed off, started forward again, and moved closer. He was stopped again and we were hung up on a sandbar, unable to go further. The ramp came down and we got off in knee-deep water. But we kept heading into ever deeper water. We had hit a false beach and went in up to our heads. I inflated the life preserver around my waist and the assault gas mask [an inflatable device] under my chin to keep me afloat. As I came up to the shale of the beach, I saw more GIs, up against the hedgehogs. Along with others I lay down on the beach. While I was there, another man came down beside me. He said, 'I'm hit!' He wasn't; the bullet had only skimmed his helmet. But his preserver was on too tight and he couldn't breathe. I took my knife and punched a hole in his preserver. He was fine. Those GIs who were hit simply lay there. There was no way you could get out and back to the landing craft.

"Our regimental CO, Col. George Taylor, came on the beach [about 8:15 A.M.], and he started to get the officers and noncoms organized, getting us going. He said, 'There are two kinds of people on this beach. Those that are dead and those that are about to die. Let's get out of here.'"

Fred Erben and his squad had been among the very few

Americans to blast an opening for themselves fairly quickly and actually get off the beach. Most of the men, whether from the 116th like Slaughter and Branham, the 1st Division, or the Rangers detailed for Omaha, endured a prolonged and savage rain of destruction before they managed to get beyond the shoreline.

Lawrence Zieckler, combat-savvy after North Africa and Sicily, never succumbed to the optimism voiced by Bob Slaughter and his fellows who thought it would be a "walk-in." "We knew the German soldier was a fighter. Especially when we heard Rommel was in charge of the beach, we knew it wasn't going to be a picnic. There is always a sense of fear when you go into combat, particularly before you hit the beaches. Anyone who said he wasn't scared isn't kidding anyone who knows. You should be scared when someone is shooting at you, hoping to hit you.

"The one nice thing about this invasion was we didn't have to climb down the side of the ship. We in the first wave were lowered over the side in our LST without using a cargo net. When we looked over the sides of the landing craft as we started in towards the beach, we could see tanks, some of them still afloat with rafts around them holding them up. It was weird to see a tank in the water and floating. Others had gone down; the crews were sitting in their little dinghies after the tanks swamped.

"When we reached the beach, things were not busted up as we expected. The tide was out, and we could see obstacles. The air support had missed the beach, falling inland, and the rockets fell short.

"I got out of the landing craft, but I must have hit a hole at the end of the sandbar, because I sank down into the water. My helmet flew on the back of my head and was pulling on my neck. As I started down in the water, I thought, what the hell, North Africa, Sicily—it seems like there's nothing to look forward to but being killed. I thought I'd give up as I went deeper and deeper.

"Suddenly, it came to my mind someone saying that drowning is a helluva way to die. I started to tread water, and I finally got my equipment loose and could shed it. I was a fairly good swimmer and made it to shore. My objective was to go to the left with my squad across the beach. I saw men taking cover behind the underwater obstacles. But the tide was coming in now, and to stay there was sure death. We started kicking butts to get 'em out, up on shore. Those who were wounded we drug up behind. It happened that right off the beach where high tide came was a pile of rocks that looked like a stone fence, and we could get down behind it and try to figure out where the hell to go from there.

"When I set my helmet back on my head and put my hand beneath it, there was dried blood. A bullet or piece of shrapnel had strafed the top of my head; another half inch and I wouldn't be here.

"Right to the front was a German gun bunker that was supposed to be blown to smithereens—but the air force wasn't able to do it. All this time, the navy is coming in, bringing more men and stuff piling up on the beach. I found Pvt. Ratti from my squad, and we headed up the beach trying to find the others from our group. We found some medics and they told us the rest of the company had gone up a nearby wadi.

"The man who had broken the barrier to an exit from the beach was a sergeant from our company, Philip Streczyk. Almost everyone followed him through." (Streczyk belonged to a section led by Lt. John Spaulding. Their efforts on D-Day earned five men, including Streczyk and Spaulding, the Distinguished Service Cross.)

Bill Lewis from the 29th Division credits someone, perhaps Streczyk, with preparing the way for his departure from the killing ground. "This 1st Division boy who had been in combat said, 'I see what they're doing—from the big bunker by the exit. Get some fire on that baby.' A shore control man got on his radio, but the shells didn't even touch it. He [the 1st Division GI] said everybody get up and start firing on the embrasures and get them back away from that hole. They are running back up there. He knew what he was doing. We started firing on the embrasure. He took some men and went up there. They put some

Bangalore torpedoes under that baby. It stopped that fire. That was the thing that was murdering us, an 88 or 75mm gun."

There were four such exits from Omaha Beach through which the assault companies had been expected to thrust inland. The Allied high command had anticipated that even if the big ships and sky fleets failed to demolish the barriers and fortifications defending these openings, the Duplex Drive Sherman tanks would overwhelm the enemy. But the rough water ripped away the fragile canvas flotation devices. The seaborne armor, launched thousands of yards offshore, sank almost instantly. Of thirty-two tanks the U.S. forces expected to float to the beach, twenty-seven quickly disappeared below the waves, many of the crews unable to escape entombment. Only two with the wraparound flotation device actually gained the shore under their own power. Three others made it to land solely because an accident aboard their LCT prevented them from trundling down the ramp into the water. Their boat was forced to deposit them on the shore.

The small number of tanks that clanked up onto the sand and shale of Omaha consisted of those DD tanks that scuttled across the sea bottom rather than plowing through the waves on canvas "bloomers." Eddie Ireland, the Calumet City high school grad who chose armor because he didn't care to walk to war, drove one of the wading-type DD tanks.

"We started out sitting on top of the vehicles. But when we came close to the shore, we were told to get inside the tank. They let us off in water that was about turret-high. I had a camera and I wanted to take a picture of the beach. So I cracked the hatch open, and just then we hit a shell hole. Water poured in and I got soaked.

"The tide was in, and we rode through the water for quite a bit. The engineers had made a path for us [through the obstacles]. When we did come ashore, the infantry guys had to move the bodies lying at the edge so we wouldn't run over them.

"The troops were still hugging the shoreline, and there wasn't much land between the hill and the water. There was a lot of mortar fire coming down, not so much small arms. We didn't have much trouble there on the beach. But once we got over the hill, we started to catch artillery fire."

The mission for the 1st Engineer Combat Battalion Company A troops lay in the Easy Red sector. The responsibilities included knocking out beach barriers and construction of a road able to support tanks and trucks bound for an assembly area inland. Perhaps a half hour before noon, two platoons from the outfit arrived. Using bulldozers, they began cutting a path through an antitank ditch. They then put down rolls of metal track to support the weight of the traffic expected off the beach.

William Carter, a member of the 18th Regiment's Intelligence and Reconnaissance platoon, could barely climb down the cargo net into the landing craft. He, a sometime drinking buddy, Carleton Barrett, and a lieutenant made up a three-man team assigned to guide in the waves of riflemen from their regiment.

"I had come down with tonsillitis," says Carter, "and hadn't been able to eat anything but soup. I was so fucking sick; I got into the boat, crouched between some radios in the back, and put my head between my knees. I didn't see anything but I heard the bullets bouncing off us. I didn't look up until I felt the boat run aground. I saw everyone was off, and I didn't want a repeat of the landing in Sicily, where I nearly drowned. I ran as hard as I could and jumped as far as I could.

"I came down in a few inches of water and damn near drove my knees up into my shoulders. We got up on the beach; Barrett was on one side of me and the lieutenant on the other. Mortar shells were falling all around. Shrapnel nicked Barrett on the arm and scratched the lieutenant's face. But I wasn't touched.

"We moved up the beach, past a halftrack. I saw a pair of coveralls with hands coming out of the sleeves but there was no head. Bodies were all over the place. The 16th Infantry had gotten off the beach, and the lieutenant told us to stay and direct the 18th to the path that was cleared of mines.

"There was no hardware, tanks, or halftracks moving

anywhere. Barrett and I started pulling guys out of the water, moving bodies so that boats could come in without running over them. We dragged as many as we could out of the way, while the Germans kept shelling the beach, hitting first one end and then the other. We'd wait and move to the area they'd just finished pounding.

"This went on until about four in the afternoon and we still hadn't seen our guys. Barrett and I split up to look for them, agreeing to meet at a spot in twenty minutes. When I got there, I couldn't find him and I looked all over the beach for him. Later, I learned he'd been wounded and some guys threw him on a boat taking out men.

"Finally, the 18th landed and the lieutenant told me to join my platoon. I started up the path. We moved very slowly, single-file. I was right behind a big tall guy when there was a huge explosion right in front of us. He turned around and his eyeglasses were all white, shattered by the explosion. The GI in front of him had stepped on a mine and blown off his foot. We couldn't do anything for him, except to tell him to stay put until help came."

By the time Dick Conley, an officer replacement with the 18th Infantry Regiment of the 1st Division, arrived in the second wave of infantry, Easy Red was less lethal. "We climbed down rope cargo nets from the sides of the Liberty ships around 0700. The waves were so high, the LCVPs going up and down, many feet, you had to time the moment you let go of the net to drop into the boat. If you hit it while it was going down, that was okay. But if you dropped while it was coming up, that was not good. Altogether, we had about thirty soldiers.

"We spent four and a half hours in the LCVP. We were supposed to keep our heads down, but everybody had to stand up to take a look at what we were facing, what was waiting. When we looked at the beach, all we could see was a haze of smoke. As we closed in on it, the place was so crowded with debris, wrecked craft, and vehicles that we had a great deal of difficulty finding a place to get in. But we had a good crew that dropped us in fairly shallow water.

"It was about eleven-thirty, an hour and a quarter later than our schedule called for. As the leader I charged off first. It was knee-deep, and when I hit it, my feet didn't keep up with the rest of me. I went down flat. But I didn't get any wetter than I already was.

"As soon as we got ashore, we stripped off the plastic covering from our rifles and carbines and I assembled my platoon. We dropped our life belts, and also I directed that pole charges, satchel charges, and Bangalore torpedoes be discarded, since I could see the beach had been breached and we wouldn't need them. I saw my first dead American soldiers as soon as I got ashore. Most were in the water at the shoreline."

George Zenie, another 1st Division vet from North Africa and Sicily, was aboard an LCT with three half-tracks, three 57mm antitank guns, and the crews to man them. They were to come in on Easy Red. "As we approached the beach, we had to wait until the LCIs and LCTs which were in front of us discharged their troops and equipment and headed to open sea. Our section was crowded with men trying to move. On the right was a landing craft that had taken a direct hit, and next to it was an antiaircraft balloon sticking out of the water. I discovered later that the truck to which it was attached lay under eight feet of water. To our left were underwater obstacles, so we couldn't land there. Two destroyers were moving as close to the beach as they could, firing their guns at the top of the bluff and at any puff of artillery fire coming at us. Overhead we could hear the shells from the big guns on the battleships and cruisers. They sounded like a freight train rumbling over our heads.

"I don't recall being afraid. I was excited and anxious to land. I was surprised that the equipment on the shore in front of us—tanks, bulldozers, trucks, and other vehicles—hadn't moved forward. They were getting hit and we wondered why they did not clear the beach.

"Finally, our LCT landed, dropped the ramp, and we disembarked. It was around noon and we had been scheduled to land between ten and ten-thirty. We followed the two other half-tracks onto Easy Red. Artillery and mortar fire was falling around us. A piece of shrapnel flew through the driver's slit and cut the side of his face. He screamed and stopped the half-track. I put my first-aid gauze against his face, told him to hold it there, moved him over, and drove the half-track down the beach as planned.

"When the whole line halted, I got the driver out and told one of the other men to drive, to follow the other vehicles. I helped the driver to an aid station where they took the wounded aboard an LCI. The scene around me depicted the real horror of war. Dead bodies floated in the water and were scattered about the beach. Wounded lay everywhere. All types of equipment were broken and abandoned. A gasoline truck ahead of us was in flames.

"The entire beach was under constant fire from small arms, mortar, and artillery. The guns of destroyers, cruisers, and battleships were still battering heavily fortified beach emplacements and pillboxes which blocked the important exits from the beach. A bulldozer trying to clear our exit was a target for enemy fire. Two drivers had been wounded; a third soldier tried to restart the machine. Our line was still contained.

"The army and navy medics showed great courage. The men who drove the bulldozers to clear the beach were also heroes. They knew they were targets, but they had to open a road to get the heavy equipment from the beach. They stuck to their jobs. Three bulldozers were put out of action. Two men working on another one were wounded, but there was always someone to replace them and continue opening the road.

"When I returned to the half-track, another of my men had been wounded, hit in the buttocks by shrapnel. Pappy Henderson, a sergeant in our platoon, and a very close friend of mine, came along. He was called Pappy because he was a little older than most of us—earlier thirties—and sought after for all kinds of advice. He and I put the wounded man in a blanket and carried him close to the bluff, where a first-aid unit was set up in a gully. We left the wounded man there. I told the rest of the men to get into the gully, where they were better protected. Pappy and I carried another soldier with chest and arm wounds to the aid station in the gully.

"Pappy said he was going to see if we could move forward. When he left, I maneuvered the half-track close to

Allied Supreme Commander Gen. Dwight D. Eisenhower visited
the 502nd Parachute Infantry Regiment in the marshaling area
shortly before it took off for France. *(U.S. Military History Institute)*

Trucks, cargo, and men load aboard U.S. landing craft in England in preparation for D-Day. *(Imperial War Museum)*

Visible at low tide, slanted poles designed to rip the bottoms from landing craft protected the beaches near Grandcamp-les-Bains. *(Signal Corps, U.S. National Archives)*

USS *Nevada* fired broadsides from its 14-inch guns at defenses along Utah Beach. *(U.S. National Archives)*

Seemingly unaware of what lies ahead, the troops relaxed as they prepared to shove off. *(U.S. National Archives)*

Heavy seas whipped up by strong winds buffeted the landing boats racing toward the beaches. *(U.S. National Archives)*

Rope lines were stretched to men floundering in the Channel after their landing craft sank. *(Signal Corps, U.S. National Archives)*

Stunned soldiers, shorn of helmets and weapons, were rescued from the water with an inflated rubber dinghy. The samaritan at the right himself needed to be saved soon after, and other troops pulled him onto the pebbly beach. *(Signal Corps, U.S. National Archives and Imperial War Museum)*

While some huddled beneath the low stone wall on Utah Beach, other U.S. soldiers climbed over and headed inland.
*(Imperial War Museum)*

An American machine gun section—note the barrel shouldered by the third man and the ammunition toted by the last soldier—trekked past dead and wounded comrades near Colleville-sur-Mer.
*(Signal Corps, U.S. National Archives)*

On less strongly defended Utah Beach, GIs poured ashore in good order. *(Signal Corps, U.S. National Archives)*

Horsa gliders carrying British soldiers and equipment littered a field. The rear of the fuselages detached readily to allow easier unloading.

*(Imperial War Museum)*

British glidermen dug positions a few yards away from where they landed. *(Imperial War Museum)*

A dead American lay amid the wreckage of his glider, which crashed into a tree. *(Signal Corps, U.S. National Archives)*

Soldiers hunkered down at Utah Beach and watched gliders with reinforcements and supplies fly overhead.
*(Signal Corps, U.S. National Archives)*

British commandos, wearing their berets rather than steel helmets, waded ashore where tanks had already landed.
*(Imperial War Museum)*

British infantrymen, some equipped with folding bicycles, landed at a waterside resort. *(Imperial War Museum)*

At the water's edge, aidmen applied artificial respiration to an exhausted victim of the Channel. *(Signal Corps, U.S. National Archives)*

On Utah Beach, enemy shelling continued to wound or kill, and medics worked frantically to save lives. *(Signal Corps, U.S. National Archives)*

A battalion surgeon from the 82nd Airborne Division offered a cigarette to a fallen trooper. An aide, wearing a trench knife on his boot, handled the paperwork. *(Signal Corps, U.S. National Archives)*

An American doctor, his insignia blotted out by censors at the time, treated a wounded German soldier. Other defenders received less mercy. *(Signal Corps, U.S. National Archives)*

Wounded GIs, brought out from the beaches on litters by landing craft, were winched up a gangway to a hospital ship. *(U.S. National Archives)*

German prisoners assisted their own wounded after surrendering
near Utah Beach. *(U.S. National Archives)*

British tanks near Hermanville-sur-Mer trundled through fields
in search of the enemy. *(Imperial War Museum)*

A British 3rd Division sergeant inspected a German "beetle" or "doodlebug" miniature tank loaded with explosives and radio-controlled. *(Imperial War Museum)*

American combat Military Police investigated a shell-smashed enemy pillbox overlooking the beach.
*(Signal Corps, U.S. National Archives)*

Huge artificial docks, called "Mulberries," were towed across the English Channel and anchored off the beaches. For ten days an avalanche of men and equipment swept across a causeway floating on reinforced concrete pontoons. Then, overnight, a savage storm destroyed the Mulberry system. *(Signal Corps, U.S. National Archives)*

With Omaha Beach secured, and barrage balloons aloft in the event of an enemy air attack, an armada of ships unloaded tons of cargo and thousands of troops. *(U.S. National Archives)*

Troopers from the 101st Airborne Division fraternized with French citizens in a freshly liberated town.

*(Signal Corps, U.S. National Archives)*

the gully. I never saw Pappy Henderson again. To this day he is listed as MIA."

Dick Biehl, who joined B Company of the 26th Infantry Regiment for combat in Sicily, did not feel particularly reassured with his outfit's assignment to follow the two other 1st Division regiments to Omaha Beach. "I cannot recall if I was more sick than scared. I was very seasick and frightened. Mentally, I knew I had to accept where I was and what was expected of me. On the way in I could see smoke, some fire, hear shells exploding. Lots of friendly aircraft passed overhead with the black and white stripes on the wings and fuselage as we were told they would be. Those planes were something of a comfort.

"About one hundred yards from the edge of the water we ran aground. The young officer commanding the vessel wanted us off the ship as soon as possible, so he could back off the sandbar and proceed away from the artillery fire that was hitting the water around the craft. I don't think he was chicken. From his vantage point he could tell wounded were being brought out to his ship to be taken back to England or hospital ships, and he needed to lighten his load and so ordered us off.

"I am six foot one half inch, and as the first one off the ladder on the port side I stepped into water neck-deep. I do not understand how the fellows shorter than I made it. Some things I saw remain quite vivid. I recall two medics dragging out to the ship we had just vacated a wounded GI with a hole in his forehead I could have laid my fist in. I saw burning landing craft, a jeep bobbing on the water like a cork . . . a lone sailor who I suppose survived a damaged or sunken landing craft, appearing very confused . . . one of our guys wandering into a mine area but being retrieved okay by two engineers with mine detectors . . . a dead engineer still in a kneeling position with his shovel in his hands, trying to dig into some cover.

"We had a few wounded on the beach, but training paid off as reactions became automatic in given situations. Assigned missions were scrubbed. The resistance was greater than anticipated because the German 352nd Infantry Division had arrived just prior to the landings.

Those guys were scattered, but pockets of resistance were numerous."

Incurring horrific losses, the U.S. forces, during the few hours after the first waves hit Dog Green and Easy Red on Omaha Beach, claimed little more than a toehold in Normandy. Unless the defenses could be penetrated in greater depth, operations based on Omaha Beach were in jeopardy.

# CHAPTER 14

# "RANGERS, LEAD THE WAY"

RATHER THAN JOINING the frontal assault of Pointe du Hoc, the A and B Company Rangers from the 2nd Battalion were assigned to the force under Lt. Col. Max Schneider of the 5th Rangers. In the event the attack directed by Rudder, using D, E, and F Companies, failed, these remaining Rangers were to come from the east and capture the big guns. Their route led through Omaha's Dog Green, the sector assigned to the 116th Regiment with Bob Slaughter and others from the 29th Division.

When Schneider failed to receive a signal of triumph from Rudder, gloom enveloped the Rangers. The small parade of landing craft, in accordance with the contingency plan, chugged toward Dog Green. But instead of coming ashore there as prescribed, the boats suddenly detoured toward an adjacent sector known as Dog White.

Lt. Charles Parker, CO of A Company in the 5th Ranger Battalion, says, "We were delayed maybe thirty minutes, and it was about 8:00 A.M. This is where Max Schneider's leadership and experience paid off. He saw what had happened to the 116th on Dog Green, where they were cut to pieces, disorganized, the support elements like tanks, transport, artillery, and supply smashed together in a jumble. The enemy fire from casemated guns, pillboxes, and fortifications was just butchering them. Schneider swung the entire group further east, from Dog Green to Dog White."

Some of the Ranger landing craft, driving for the beach at the edge of Dog Green, came under intense fire. The boat with Bob Edlin, the Ranger platoon leader in the 2nd Battalion's Company A, struck a sandbar. "I looked over the ramp and we were at least seventy-five yards from the shore, and we had hoped for a dry landing. I told the coxswain, 'Try to get in further.' He screamed he couldn't. That British seaman had all the guts in the world but couldn't get off the sandbar. I told him to drop the ramp or we were going to die right there.

"We had been trained for years not to go off the front of the ramp, because the boat might get rocked by a wave and run over you. So we went off the sides. I looked to my right and saw a B Company boat next to us with Lt. Bob Fitzsimmons, a good friend, take a direct hit on the ramp from a mortar or mine. I thought, there goes half of B Company.

"It was cold, miserably cold, even though it was June. The water temperature was probably forty-five or fifty degrees. It was up to my shoulders when I went in, and I saw men sinking all about me. I tried to grab a couple, but my job was to get on in and get to the guns. There were bodies from the 116th floating everywhere. They were facedown in the water with packs still on their backs. They had inflated their life jackets. Fortunately, most of the Rangers did not inflate theirs or they also might have turned over and drowned.

"I began to run with my rifle in front of me. I went directly across the beach to try to get to the seawall. In front of me was part of the 116th Infantry, pinned down and lying behind beach obstacles. They hadn't made it to the seawall. I kept screaming at them, 'You have to get up and go! You gotta get up and go!' But they didn't. They were worn out and defeated completely. There wasn't any time to help them.

"I continued across the beach. There were mines and obstacles all up and down the beach. The air corps had missed it entirely. There were no shell holes in which to take cover. The mines had not been detonated. Absolutely nothing that had been planned for that part of the beach had worked. I knew that Vierville-sur-Mer was going to be a hellhole, and it was.

"When I was about twenty yards from the seawall, I was hit by what I assume was a sniper bullet. It shattered and broke my right leg. I thought, well, I've got a Purple Heart. I fell, and as I did, it was like a searing hot poker rammed into my leg. My rifle fell ten feet or so in front of me. I crawled forward to get to it, picked it up, and as I rose on my left leg, another burst of I think machine gun fire tore the muscles out of that leg, knocking me down again.

"I lay there for seconds, looked ahead, and saw several Rangers lying there. One was Butch Bladorn from Wisconsin. I screamed at Butch, 'Get up and run!' Butch, a big, power-ful man, just looked back and said, 'I can't.' I got up and hobbled towards him. I was going to kick him in the ass and get him off the beach. He was lying on his stomach, his face in the sand. Then I saw the blood coming out of his back. I realized he had been hit in the stomach and the bullet had come out his spine and he was completely immobilized. Even then I was sorry for screaming at him but I didn't have time to stop and help him. I thought, well, that's the end of Butch. Fortunately, it wasn't. He became a farmer in Wisconsin.

"As I moved forward, I hobbled. After you've been hit by gunfire, your legs stiffen up, not all at once but slowly. The pain was indescribable. I fell to my hands and knees and tried to crawl forwards. I managed a few yards, then blacked out for several minutes. When I came to, I saw Sgt. Bill Klaus. He was up to the seawall. When he saw my predicament, he crawled back to me under heavy rifle and mortar fire and dragged me up to the cover of the wall.

"Klaus had also been wounded in one leg, and a medic gave him a shot of morphine. The medic did the same for me. My mental state was such that I told him to shoot it di-rectly into my left leg, as that was the one hurting the most. He reminded me that if I took it in the ass or the arm it would get to the leg. I told him to give me a second shot because I was hit in the other leg. He didn't.

"There were some Rangers gathered at the seawall—Sgt. William Courtney, Pvt. William Dreher, Garfield Ray, Gabby Hart, Sgt. Charles Berg. I yelled at them, 'You have to get off of here! You have to get up and get the guns!' They were gone immediately.

"My platoon sergeant, Bill White, an ex-jockey whom we called Whitey, took charge. He was small, very active, and very courageous. He led what few men were left of the first platoon and started up the cliffs. I crawled and staggered forward as far as I could to some cover in the bushes behind a villa. There was a round stone well with a bucket and handle that turned the rope. It was so inviting. I was alone and I wanted that water so bad. But years of training told me it was booby-trapped.

"I looked up at the top of the cliffs and thought, I can't make it on this leg. Where was everyone? Had they all quit? Then I heard Dreher yelling, 'Come on up. These trenches are empty.' Then Kraut burp guns cut loose. I thought, oh God, I can't get there! I heard an American tommy gun, and Courtney shouted, 'Damn it, Dreher! They're empty *now*.'

"There was more German small-arms fire and German grenades popping. I could hear Whitey yelling, 'Cover me!' I heard Garfield Ray's BAR talking American. Then there was silence.

"Now, I thought, where are the 5th Rangers? I turned and I couldn't walk or even hobble anymore. I crawled back to the beach. I saw 5th Rangers coming through the smoke of a burning LST that had been hit by artillery fire. Col. Schneider had seen the slaughter on the beaches and used his experience with the Rangers in Africa, Sicily, and Anzio. He used the smoke as a screen and moved in behind it, saving the 5th Ranger Battalion many casualties.

"My years of training told me there would be a counter-attack. I gathered the wounded by the seawall and told them to arm themselves as well as possible. I said if the Germans come we are either going to be captured or die on the beach, but we might as well take the Germans with us. I know it sounds ridiculous, but ten or fifteen Rangers lay there, facing up to the cliffs, praying that Sgt. White, Courtney, Dreher, and the 5th Ranger Battalion would get to the guns. Our fight was over unless the Germans coun-terattacked.

"I looked back to the sea. There was nothing. There were no reinforcements. I thought the invasion had been abandoned. We would be dead or prisoners soon. Everyone had withdrawn and left us. Well, we had tried. Some guy crawled over and told me he was a colonel from the 29th Infantry Division. He said for us to relax, we were going to be okay. D, E, and F Companies were on the Pointe. The guns had destroyed. A and B Companies and the 5th Rangers were inland. The 29th and 1st Divisions were getting off the beaches.

"This colonel looked at me and said, 'You've done your job.' I answered, 'How? By using up two rounds of German ammo on my legs?' Despite the awful pain, I hoped to catch up with the platoon the next day. Someone gave me another shot of morphine."

Charles Parker and the Rangers with him touched down farther away from the carnage on Dog Green. "We had fewer casualties and the command group was intact. We were the only cohesive force in that vital invasion area. The coxswain of our boat put us off in waist-deep water. He then held his boat in and used his machine gun, trying to suppress enemy fire to give us a better opportunity for crossing the beach. I don't think it did much good, because the Germans were all shooting from massively prepared positions. Still, it was an incredibly brave thing for him to do.

"We had to get across what seemed an endless expanse of sand and then an area of shingle, small rocks with bad footing. Behind us, boats were being blown up and burning, artillery and mortar shells were exploding, machine gun bullets ricocheting around. The water looked dimpled from the shrapnel and bullets.

"By the seawall the first thing was to get the company under control. The damage reports showed I had virtually no losses. In addition to Schneider picking Dog White, we got another break. The grass and low bushes that grew on the flat portion of the land behind the beach and up the sides of the bluffs themselves were on fire. Smoke covered the whole area, and the Germans couldn't put much observed fire on us. The fire also revealed the mines when the grass burned off. Later I heard the engineers removed about 150 of them from the area.

"There was concertina wire behind the seawall, and we had to blow that with Bangalore torpedoes. The assistant division commander of the 29th, Gen. Cota, came strolling up the beach to where Schneider was. He asked who was in command and then supposedly made his famous line, 'Rangers, lead the way.' Schneider gave the word to us, 'Tallyho,' our planned signal to move out and assemble at the rally point south and west of Vierville."

Ranger lieutenant Frank Dawson, a platoon leader in D Company of the 5th Battalion, occupied a ringside seat during the drive for Dog White beach. "I saw several large ships moving towards the beach. One fired a volley of rockets, and I noticed a destroyer had cut across our front between us and the beach and was firing at gun positions as it moved along.

"Finally, the signal came for us to move out. The LCAs formed a skirmish line parallel to the beach. I could not make out the shore through the haze and smoke. I began to notice the obstacles. Just ahead were four posts set at an angle with mines attached to the tops. We were just about on them, and in the boat no one was talking.

"We were very lucky. The landing craft was heading straight toward one of the pole obstacles leaning seaward with a large mine attached to the top. The skipper on the LCA steered sharply left, and the breaking waves just lifted our craft over it. We came to a halt in knee-deep water.

"I could see my immediate destination, a seawall about fifty to seventy-five yards across a flat beach. I was completely pooped by the dash. I had wet boots and equipment with an ammo bag of .45 caliber magazines for my Thompson, gas mask, light pack, and entrenching tool. I kept running but still noticed machine gun rounds hitting near. The ones who stopped to take shelter behind obstacles and stayed at the water's edge were unlucky.

"I saw disabled tanks; one was burning. The noise of gunfire was everywhere, incoming and outgoing. Mortar rounds were falling between the seawall and the water's edge. At the seawall there were other men besides Rangers. You had to push in to get to the wall. I wanted to see what was on the other side. No effort was being made in my sector to get off the beach.

"I was busy getting my platoon head count and then sending my runner off to contact the company commander, telling him where we were and finding out any order he might have for me. My runner, Pfc Robert Stein, who was later killed by an American tank which mistook us for Germans, returned, and then we broke out.

"I would not have known Gen. Cota from anyone else," says Dawson, the man who did lead. "I never heard him if he said 'Rangers, lead the way!' The confusion was enormous. When the word 'Go' was given, my two Bangalore torpedo men, Dorman [Elwood] and Reed [Ellis], set off the charge. Before the dust cleared, I stepped into the cupped hands of my company first sergeant and platoon sergeant and was lifted over the wall through the area just blown. I began my run for the high ground. The ground was very flat, grassy, and in full view of the enemy.

"Knowing I was being fired on, I twice hit the ground, rolled over, sprang up, and continued. I chose to go to my right about fifty yards and then picked a route to climb. The bluff was steep but it wasn't a cliff. I knew there were mines in the area, but I took a chance.

"I was alone while climbing the bluff, having outdistanced my platoon following in single file. I hadn't looked back because I was too busy looking forward, right, and left. I knew they were coming behind me; I just had that feeling.

"Beyond the top lay a battery of German rockets, which were firing. As I neared the crest, smoke started to drift towards me, but not enough to block my sight. So far, I had not seen any Germans, and I continued to climb, using my hands on the ground to help me.

"Suddenly I reached the top and traversed to the right, where there were trenches and German soldiers. One in particular, a huge man, came straight at me. He was my first kill. Having a Thompson sub, I kept it hot. Several prisoners came out of a trench, and I got them spread-eagled on the ground. By then, members of my platoon took over. One young German emerged with a hand blown off. We were not instructed regarding prisoners. It is rather difficult to go into an assault and use your men to guard prisoners. But we were attacking in a narrow column, so we passed the prisoners back, hoping they got to the rear.

"As I continued along the crest I saw, below, active machine gun positions still firing on the beach. These Germans had not seen my platoon. My BAR man was near, and I pointed out the positions to him. But he exposed himself too much and a German crew killed him. I retrieved the BAR and killed that crew. Others in the area were making a hasty retreat towards Vierville."

Later, Dawson received a Distinguished Service Cross for his efforts and the two Bangalore torpedo men, Dorman and Ellis, were awarded Silver Stars.

A Company, led by Lt. Charles Parker, doggedly advanced on the bluffs described by Dawson as the eastern anchor of the Ranger line. In the turmoil of the battle, communications broke down, and Parker, with his runner William Fox and a lieutenant from E Company, halted to investigate a field with trees on the side opposite them.

"We didn't know it at first," says Parker, "but there were snipers in those trees. One of them got us in his sights and we all went down. Fox squatted while the lieutenant and I went prone. A bullet hit Fox in the shoulder, leaving a small blue hole, and then angled down. Another one struck the lieutenant in the right side of his head, blowing out a piece of his skull, leaving his brains partly exposed.

"I kept trying to wriggle out from under my pack while lying flat. It was a huge one, with enough in it for me to survive for a month. I finally got my pistol out and unbuckled the pack, although meanwhile that sniper put several bullets in it. I rolled over into a ditch and we roped the legs of the two wounded and pulled them into the ditch also.

"We stayed in that ditch for about three and a half hours before we could get to the rallying point, a chateau. Every man behind Fox had to crawl over him in that ditch. He waved to everyone and smiled. We gave him a canteen of water and went on our way, on our bellies. There wasn't anything we could do for them. Later, they picked up the lieutenant, who somehow survived, hospitalized him, and he eventually regained his ability to speak and function. We didn't know, on the other hand, that the bullet which hit Fox had ranged down and cut his spine. He died in that ditch."

At the chateau, Parker counted his troops and discovered he had only twenty-three left from his normal complement of nearly seventy. The rest were casualties or had become separated during the breakout from the beach. Parker reasoned that the remainder of the 5th Battalion must already be ahead on their way to Pointe du Hoc. He led his troops through a series of hedgerows and secondary roads, hoping to catch up with the main body.

Meanwhile, reinforcements and support troops arrived to strengthen the beleaguered of Omaha Beach. Leo Des Champs, another member of the 1st Engineer Combat Battalion, was assigned to a thirty-man assault team. Even though it was H plus five hours when his group arrived, the enemy resistance continued.

"As the landing craft neared the beach, a shell hit the lowering mechanism and the gate fell down. The navy man told us this was it; he couldn't get any closer. We stepped off three hundred yards offshore. As I entered the water, DeLuca stepped into a shell hole. I grabbed him by his Mae West and squeezed the belt to activate the air unit. He bounced back up and treaded water until his feet touched ground. Dave Perlis went to the left up a ravine; his body was found three days later. The others went right. The beach itself was a madhouse; bodies lay where they fell and shouts for medics were in the air. Some corpses were half in and half out of the water, and as the waves rolled in the bodies would sway back and forth like dolls.

"There was a depression in the beach, a tank trap, and we had to go through the water a second time to get to the beach proper. A sergeant directed us to go right, and we assembled at the battalion command post. We were sitting eating our rations by 1:00 or 1:30 P.M. I am not ashamed to say I prayed all the way in, and I prayed also till the next day whenever I had free time."

Bill Wills, squad leader with B Company of the 1st Engineers, was responsible for two mine detection teams, a machine gun crew, and a small truck fitted with a .50 caliber machine gun. Every soldier had qualified with the M-1.

"We reached the beach about five or six hours after H-Hour," recalls Wills. "The beachmaster waved us off four or five times because the LCT had too much equipment and they didn't want it destroyed. The info we received about the beach and inland was not very good. The air force didn't do much damage and most of the obstacles were still in place.

"When we did come in, we were in three feet of $H_2O$ with mortar and artillery fire on us. Wounded and dead men were lying all over the beach, and it seemed as if every piece of equipment was burning. We got off the beach to a point where there was some cover. The squad carried the equipment ashore, mine detectors and TNT.

"We went over the dunes, and to our surprise there was more water, a marsh and a canal. We crossed the canal, which was waist-deep, and entered a minefield. A path had been cleared through it by someone else and marked with tracing tape. Off to the side of the path were two men, each with a foot blown off. They were still conscious and directed us through the field. We all had morphine syrettes in our first-aid kits and these men had used them to kill their pain. I will always remember them and their bravery."

Scattered elements of the invasion force had now broken through the outer defenses. But success demanded more than mere survival or a few extra yards of French soil.

# CHAPTER 15

# VIEW FROM THE SEA

TWENTY-FOUR HOURS before the first paratroopers left for France, Supreme Commander Gen. Dwight D. Eisenhower had drafted in longhand a brief handwritten statement which he then stuffed in his wallet. The terse announcement declared: "Our landings in the Cherbourg-Havre area have failed to gain a satisfactory foothold and I have withdrawn the troops. My decision to attack at this time and place was based upon the best information available. The troops, the air, and the navy did all that bravery and devotion to duty could do. If any blame or fault attaches to the attempt, it is mine alone."

In his 1948 memoir *Crusade in Europe*, Eisenhower claims that once the invasion began he never felt he would need to release the message. In his book, he wrote, "As the morning wore on, it became apparent that the landing was going fairly well." The statement does not square with the facts or the reactions of those of his own high command.

Aboard the flagship of the American naval forces, the USS *Augusta*, Gen. Omar Bradley, commander of the U.S. First Army, anxiously awaited word on the invasion's progress. In his autobiography he says, "As the morning lengthened, my worries deepened over the alarming and fragmentary reports we picked up on the navy net. From these messages we could piece together only an incoherent account of sinkings, swampings, heavy enemy fire, and chaos on the beaches."

Bradley's timetable expected the two assault regiments—the 116th from the 29th Division and one from the 1st Division augmented by the Rangers and the waterborne tanks—to have broken through to a mile inland by 8:30 A.M. But at 10:00, the first report from Gen. Leonard Gerow, commander of V Corps, charged with the conquest of Omaha Beach, brought gloom and fear. Gerow advised, "Obstacles mined, progress slow . . . DD tanks for Fox Green [the eastern end of Omaha] swamped."

Adm. Kirk and Bradley dispatched Rear Adm. Charles "Savvy" Cooke and Brig. Gen. Thomas Handy for a first-hand look. The latter remembers an appalled Cooke exclaiming, "My God, this is carnage!" Handy was equally dismayed. "It was terrible along that damned beach, because they were not only under mortar fire but they were under small-arms fire. The amphibious tanks were all sinking and the beach obstacles blocked access."

To V Corps commander Gerow, Handy reported, "It isn't very good." When Gerow pressed for advice on what to do, Handy says he responded, "The only thing you can do, and you've got to do, regardless of the losses, you've got to push your doughboys* in far enough to get that damned beach out from under small-arms fire and if possible mortar fire because it's just terrible."

The anxious brass at sea, concerned with Omaha Beach, heard only a series of discouraging words about troops pinned down at the seawall, a beach swept by deadly enemy fire, assault and supply craft milling offshore because of the failure to open more than six pathways through the honeycomb of mined obstacles. Navy underwater demolition teams and army engineers trying to blast lanes for the invaders suffered devastating losses. Not only were the demolition teams forced to contend with what the foe threw at them but they were frustrated by GIs who clung to the mined obstacles. Detonation by the experts would kill the

---

* Handy dated from World War I and used that war's term for GIs.

hapless soldiers. The sole good news was the report that Pointe du Hoc had fallen. Handy remarked, "At Omaha, we just hung on by our eyelashes for several hours. I don't believe they ever realized how close that thing was."

As noon approached, V Corps reported the situation "still critical" at all four of the avenues to a breakout from Omaha. Bradley admitted, "I reluctantly contemplated the diversion of Omaha follow-up forces to Utah and the British beaches. Scanty reports from both those sectors indicated the landings there had gone according to plan."

Lt. Harvey Bennett, serving as assistant gunnery officer for Adm. Kirk aboard the *Augusta*, insists he saw no evidence of any wavering by Bradley. "I sat very close to him and at no time do I recall his intent to pull troops off the beaches."

According to Bennett, the responsibility for carrying out bombardment on the beaches, rather than to the dugouts, pillboxes, and emplacements guarding the approaches, lay with the U.S. Army Air Corps. "AAC decided on D-Day that visibility was not suitable. As far as I know, no other command was notified of this omission." Because of this apparent failure to communicate, the shoreline at Omaha Beach remained an almost pristinely smooth surface without abundant shell holes that might have preserved the lives of those in the first waves.

Bennett also emphasizes the serious flaw that marked combined assaults by Allied forces in Europe. "It would have taken more than a joint command to provide the same sort of air support the navy had for the marines in the Pacific. The AAC and the RAF were basically concerned about their own war against German industry. In no operation in which I have been concerned has there ever been any liaison with the AAC."

Whereas there was no tactical partnership between aircraft and ground forces, the navy dispatched sailors equipped with radios to serve as shore fire control parties. These teams acted as forward observers for the ships and accompanied the earliest invaders, including the Rangers attempting to scale Pointe du Hoc. As soon as minesweepers cleared the seas nearest land, destroyers moved in so close as to risk grounding in order to hammer targets named by the shore fire control parties. In some instances where the navy personnel were killed or wounded, GIs such as Ranger Lou Lisko assumed the role of liaison with the seaborne gunners.

One of the first sailors to navigate the treacherous Channel waters to Omaha Beach was Dell Martin, the coxswain aboard the last of thirteen LCMs bearing the spearhead forces around 6:00 A.M. "We circled around waiting to form into a line. I passed alongside a large French ship as she fired some very big guns. As the coxswain, I was in an enclosure by myself. When those shells went over my head, it felt like someone had socked me in the jaw. My ears started ringing and have ever since. I get a ten percent pension as a result, and the VA also gives me hearing aids.

"It was low tide and the men on our ship got off in knee-deep water after we hit a sandbar. All the obstacles were high and dry. Each boat carried fifty men, half army and half navy. Their job was to blow hundred-yard gaps at fifty-yard intervals to open lanes for succeeding boats. The army men were responsible for the landward obstacles and the navy the ones in the sea. We ran into very heavy opposition. I understand losses went as high as eighty-five percent.

"We left the beach and went to a hospital ship to put off a man we had picked up on our way in. He was from one of the amphibious tanks that sank. From there we returned to a rendezvous area, circling about until called to shuttle 1st Division and Rangers in to the beach."

Aboard the 150-foot LCI on which Kenneth Almy served as a junior officer, three hundred soldiers embarked in full battle gear. "I learned from these soldiers," says Almy, "the proper use of condoms. They used them by the gross, waterproofing wallets, watches, ammunition, and even fitted them over their rifle muzzles. One joker even tried to fit them over his shoes and helmet.

"We were scheduled to land with the fourth or fifth waves. All seemed to be going normally as we reached the line of departure and started our run for the beach. The battlewagons were blasting away, and I was glad I was wearing earphones. My battle station was in the conn with the captain, and my job was landing officer. The earphones on my large 'turtle' helmet connected me with the officer in charge of the bow ramps and the guys handling the anchor winch. I would relay any and all orders from the captain to these stations. Standing there, in the open of the conn, exposed to the world and enemy, generated a great sense of vulnerability.

"When we were ordered in and still a mile or so from our landing area, we found ourselves in the gridlock caused by the stiff resistance of the Germans perched up on the hillside behind the beach. We milled about and at one moment had come about to run parallel to the beach. We were bracketed by three shells from what I suppose were 88s. The captain ordered hard about and we cranked up all of our ten knots and moved temporarily out of danger.

"The approach to the beach was a shambles. Several small craft drifted about showing all manner of destruction. Some unlucky soldiers floated around. Other vessels, unable to land, also shuffled about, seemingly aimless. As we closed near our group's flagship, their loud hailer bellowed, 'Proceed to beach immediately!' We came about, called for standard speed, and headed in.

"At the appropriate distance offshore, we dropped our stern anchor. It dug in, the cable spooled out. The bow ramp crews were alert at their stations. The bow ramp winches chugged noisily. The troops, fully loaded for war, were lined up and out of their quarters.

"The next ten minutes were relatively quiet aboard ship. I was so busy, so interested in what was going on, anticipation of the landing, the smoke billowing about the beach, and absolutely no one else but us heading into Easy Red Omaha Beach.

"As we neared the beach, a sizable black object suddenly appeared close abeam. I recall shouting to the captain, 'What in the hell is that?' Then, WHAM! The whole ship shuddered. WHAM! again. A mine had exploded against the side of our ship.

"The captain shouted into the pilot house, 'Full speed

ahead!' The ship was slowly going down at the bow. We traveled only a short distance before we ground to a halt. We had hit the runnel which we had been told ran parallel to the beach. That left a good thirty to fifty yards of armpit-deep water to wade through before reaching the beach.

"Fortunately, there was no serious wave action, but we extended lines from the ramps and anchored them on the beach. The troops sped off in great fashion. We started to collect damage-control reports. Three or four soldiers had been killed; they were down in the forward troop quarters where nobody was supposed to be at the time. Four GIs were injured. No navy personnel were hurt, since we were all high, above decks. LCI 491 had made its first and last invasion landing.

"Once the troops were all debarked, the captain gathered us together to take stock. We were in no danger of sinking at the moment, but the ship was finished. It was dangerous to stay with it, because every time someone went out on deck, the Germans sent a round at us. Happily, the German accuracy was poor. Twice I attempted to burn material that had to be destroyed, but each time I appeared on the fantail to get a blaze going, a couple of scary rounds whistled in. It was decided we would wait until nightfall and then deep-six the items in the surrounding waters. All of the invasion material was designed to destruct in water.

"Abandon ship was ordered. I, along with another officer, the radioman, and the pharmacist's mate, opted to stay with the ship and help attend to the wounded. I held a battle lamp while the pharmacist's mate tended to a soldier's wounded arm. The explosion had taken the limb off just above the elbow. The other casualties were also seriously injured but not quite as bloody.

"After the wounded were put aright, the captain told us to leave the ship. He would remain until the army medics could be summoned to remove the soldiers. There was no danger of the ship sinking or capsizing. Whether the tide was high or low, it was solidly planted in the shore.

"We took off down the ramp. The Channel water, up to our chests, was frigid. But I didn't feel any chill. The [anti-]gas impregnated clothes issued to all amphibious personnel for the invasion were something like overalls. Whatever substance they used on the clothing, it sure stank. We also had some goo we put on our hands and faces to protect further against possible gas attack. The impregnated clothing, including my boots, shed the water and the cold.

"Arrival on the beach was not an inspiring moment. My first view was of two dead GIs who had been down for some time. I was not encouraged when one of my companions reported we had been fired on while we waded through the water. I saw absolutely no activity around us. Later I learned this beach had been closed and there was talk of abandoning the sector. Army losses had been quite heavy in the waves immediately preceding us.

"A couple of gun emplacements up on the bluff were still very active. Indeed, one of our destroyers drew practically up on the beach and had a great, good gun duel with the emplacements. The destroyer finally silenced it, but not before shot and shell whistled for some time over our heads.

"Without soldiers around, we all felt lonely and 'naked' there. During our basic training, nowhere was there ever a topic headed 'What to do when stranded on a hostile beach.' We were in effect marooned. There was absolutely no place to go, save back to the ship or to join the badly beat-up and beleaguered troops inland. The latter alternative only briefly, very briefly, occurred to me. Except for side arms the other officers and I had, we had nothing to fight with.

"We huddled together on the beach, near a knocked-out tank. But it was smoking, so we moved away. Shortly thereafter it erupted in flames. We found a hollow in the shaley beach—you couldn't blast a foxhole in the stuff. The hollow, in which we felt somewhat more secure, actually was located where a German could not only see all of us but if he had a real good arm, he could practically have hit us with rocks. That is an exaggeration, but in fact our shelter was no protection at all. None existed on our expanse of beach.

"I have no idea how long we were there. Periodically, rounds would explode on the beach without seeming to do much damage. Once I felt something slap against my leg and picked up a small, marble-size spent piece of shell casing. I wish I had saved it for my grandchildren, evidence of my heroic near miss.

"Finally, an LCT braved a small clearing amid the obstacles. Men were going out to board her, and we decided to follow suit. We must have run two hundred yards or more across the open beach, through obstacles with mean-looking mines attached. I felt like a great hurdler as I leaped over wires and dodged around the obstacles with the rest of our group following almost in my footsteps.

"We made the LCI and joined other navy survivors and some wounded. It wasn't until I sat down on the deck that I realized how hard my heart was pounding. For I believe the first time in my life, I realized fear."

Gil Miller crewed on one of five boats that made up LCM (fifty-footers) Amphibious Force 88 and traveled under its own power from its British port at about six miles an hour.

"Our job would be salvage, and we were to go in at Omaha Beach one hour after H-Hour with the mission of keeping the lanes to the beach open. Six waves were to precede us, and they would do any fighting that was necessary. We had a twenty-ton bulldozer which, once dropped off, would push aside anything that blocked the movement of troops or vehicles.

"The obstructions to the beach, crossed steel beams embedded deep in the sand and with mines on top, were eerie-looking and sinister. I didn't have time to take notice of what was happening on the beach. Once we unloaded the bulldozer, we backed off with a load of wounded. Our starboard engine shut down. The shaft became caught in camouflage netting and bent in an S shape.

"It wasn't a critical problem—one big engine could do the work of two. I happened to look up for a moment and lost my helmet. I then went down into the well of the LCM and talked to the wounded, passing out cigarettes. An officer called me over and offered me his helmet, saying, 'Here, you need this more than I.' He was badly wounded; his right hindquarter was gone. I went down between the engines and got out of our kit a clean undershirt to patch him up the best we could. I put on his helmet and it had the bars of a lieutenant or captain on the front. Every time I passed any of our crew, they saluted. With my knife I scraped off the markings. After we transferred the wounded, an LSD repair ship pulled us up out of the water and in half an hour we had a new screw and shaft."

Aboard the mishap-prone LCI 491, Bill Hughes, the ship's electrician who learned his duties on the job, watched about one hundred good-humored soldiers settle in on his vessel for the ride to Omaha Beach. "One June 5th we fed them all their last hot meal. We were told to destroy all letters, mail, any papers we carried with us. By 0200 of the 6th we were off the coast of France. The word from the beach all morning was bad. Until noon, the rumor was they were all going to come off the beach, and that's why we didn't go in. We were held back and did not land our troops until 1400 hours. It was high tide, and none of the obstacles were visible. On the way back, we saw all of them sticking out of the water with bodies, missing their shoes, floating among them. A British LCT broke in half; we pulled out the survivors."

As the engineering officer, Richard Willstatter, a lieutenant j.g. on LST 133, was belowdecks as his ship proceeded toward its position two or three miles off Omaha Beach to await instructions. The invasion plans slated LST 133 for triple duty. On board were men from the 1st Division with an attached unit of five DUKWs each packed with seven tons of munitions as well as trucks, jeeps, ammunition, and weapons carriers. In addition, the vessel's personnel included a hospital unit with a pair of navy physicians and roughly twenty pharmacist's mates to assist them. An army doctor and his two assistants rounded out the team designated to treat wounded taken off the beach. In its third role, LST 133 had towed a Rhino ferry bearing a navy construction battalion (CB), more commonly known as Sea Bees, and its personal tug to the outer anchorage off Omaha Beach.

"When we reached our position and stopped while awaiting further instructions, it was realized that the situation on the beach was far from 'proceeding according to plan.' A great many ships had been set afire and sunk in the region of the beach which itself was badly infested with obstacles and mines and still was under heavy 88mm and machine gun fire. Most of the LCTs and LCIs that had hit the beach that morning were casualties and blocked the further approach of other landing craft. As we learned later, the first soldiers had sustained heavy losses and hardly any reinforcements had been able to land.

"Sometime during the day, we received orders to beach at utmost speed—'your cargo urgently needed.' We could see that the beach and nearby water were still very much under 88 fire. However, we weighed anchor and proceeded in toward Dog Red. We were stationed at general quarters, and in the engine room we received the command, "All engines ahead flank!'

"On our ship, the 'captain's talker' [an enlisted man with a set of sound-powered phones, who stands alongside the captain where he can instantly communicate with any section of the ship] was a married yeoman who when ashore indulged himself extraordinarily and was not an admirable person. On the way to the beach he was very loudly praying to God to protect us, to save him and us. Everyone on the phone system was deluged with this outpouring of begging. Then there was a loud voice from some unknown quarter, 'Oh, Allen, shut the hell up!'

"About the time we figured we should be hitting the beach came the orders, 'All engines stop!' Then immediately, 'All engines back emergency!' Later, I learned we had been approached by a control boat who gave us contrary orders and commanded we retire from the beach at once. We were so close in that it would have been impossible for us to turn, normally, without going on the beach sidewise. We returned to our anchorage area close off the beach.

"Very shortly thereafter, various small boats and DUKWs came to us, carrying wounded from the beach. Because we were an auxiliary hospital ship, we accepted all casualties brought to us. Since all the troops and cargo still remained aboard, our crew vacated their aft quarters for use as bunks for wounded. A makeshift operating room with operating lights was installed on a raised platform on the aft end of the tank deck. A second site for surgeons was a starboard table in the wardroom.

"Somewhere around eighty patients, all on stretchers in the small craft and DUKWs, were lifted through a sling arrangement that raised litters by electric power. Once aboard, stretcher bearers took the litters through a hatch from the galley passageway, passed them through the window over the galley steam tables, and then down the ladder into the crew's quarters. Patients so badly injured that they probably could not survive this treatment went immediately into the wardroom for attention.

"During the afternoon, two Rhino barges tied up alongside. One had a complete unit of doctors with all its equipment and personnel and had made three unsuccessful attempts to beach. Both Rhinos remained until the following dawn, with their men sleeping in any place they could find.

"One nasty incident occurred. A reporter from the Associated Press came aboard, wanting to know how soon we were leaving for England. When he found we hadn't beached yet and momentarily expected orders to go in, he created a great fuss, conjured up an injury, had his arm put in a sling, and finally managed to grab one of our small boats bound for another ship.

"Shortly before dark, the DUKW officer on our LST decided his loads of ammunition must be badly needed and he would try to get through. The captain gave permission for the attempt. The bow doors opened and the ramp lowered. The lieutenant and his five ducks rolled out and headed for the beach. They made it."

Although Willstatter indicates that the correspondent for the Associated Press connived his way to safety, the anecdote indicates the presence of reporters during Overlord. Secrecy was maintained by sequestering the journalists on the same basis as the troops. Several newsmen, including Phil Bucknell for the army's *Stars and Stripes* and William Walton of *Time*, qualified as parachutists and had jumped with the airborne forces. Photographer Robert Capa captured memorable scenes of the fury at Omaha Beach, although much of his film was ruined by an accident while being processed in London. Hanson Baldwin of the *New York Times* occupied a berth on the *Augusta*, where the naval and army commanders, Kirk and Bradley, shared information on the progress of the invasion. On another ship, Don Whitehead, writing for a wire service, was also a close-in spectator.

On Sword Beach, in the British zone, Commando Arnold Wheeldon noticed an unnamed U.S. war correspondent nearby. "He was only about five foot three inches tall and almost out of his depth as he struggled ashore. He carried a typewriter in his rucksack and in reality he was an overweight civilian. Yet, he acted like a war-experienced Commando."

Leo Des Champs, a member of the 1st Engineers Combat Battalion, noticed shortly before leaving for Omaha Beach, "Standing two or three guys away from me was Ernest Hemingway, whom I recognized from photos on books of his that I read." Hemingway rode in on an LCVP to what was the Fox Green Sector after the first six assault waves. He remained aboard the landing craft while it disgorged its infantrymen and then left the area.

In spite of the presence of the press, word of the desperate situation along Omaha Beach and the disarray of the air drop never reached the public. Official confusion, uncertain communications, the swiftly changing status of the battles, and censorship prevented dissemination of more than minimal news.

# CHAPTER 16

# UTAH BEACH

ADJACENT AND WEST of Omaha Beach lay the nine-mile-long shelf of yellow sand code-named Utah Beach. At low tide it was three to four hundred yards wide, with a low concrete wall inland. Beyond the beach lay the heavily inundated areas into which the troopers from the 82nd and 101st had dropped. Ordinarily eleven causeways led toward the heart of France, but the flooding meant only three were dry. Once off the beach, the infantrymen with tank and artillery support would advance over these causeways, secured by the paratroopers against any attempt by German reserves to push the 4th Infantry Division back into the sea.

Separated from Omaha by an incursion of the Bay of the Seine, Utah was less heavily defended. Two casemated positions overlooked the shoreline, but only one actually held big guns. The Germans had not yet gotten around to full installation of the barriers, and there were fewer mines. Underwater demolition teams blew up much of what posed a threat to landing craft. Furthermore, the naval bombardment, in contrast to what happened off Omaha, pounded the shoreline, not only punishing the existing German positions but also providing convenient shell holes in which foot soldiers could take refuge.

Although Bradley spoke of the assault on Utah going

"according to plan," in fact, Utah, assigned to the 4th Infantry Division, did not follow the script any more closely than the airborne operations or the assault on Pointe du Hoc. The deviation at Utah, however, had much to do with the success enjoyed there. Yet it was not a "walk-in."

Lt. Col. Arthur S. Teague commanded the 22nd Regiment's 3rd Battalion, and he described the initial wave. "Just as we were coming in to shore, we saw a shell fired from up the beach, and I knew some of us were going to be hit. I saw spurts of water coming up. I saw one small landing craft hit, and thinking the same might happen to us, I told the navy man to ram the beach as hard as possible. He said he would, and after holding it wide open for about two hundred yards, we hit the beach and stepped off on dry soil. A couple of boats behind us—about seventy-five yards back in the water—were hit, and then I saw a number of casualties. Many were killed and quite a few wounded.

"I started up by the seawall on the sand dunes and stopped for a moment. It was then I heard someone call me. It was Gen. Roosevelt. He called me over and told me we had landed way to the left of where we were supposed to have been and he wanted us to get this part of the beach cleared as soon as possible. He wanted action from my men immediately after landing and asked me to get them down the beach as soon as I could. This was about 0930."

Roosevelt, who had been with the 1st Division in Tunisia and Sicily, was an extra brigadier general placed with the 4th Division. He volunteered to accompany the first GIs onto Utah. He quickly realized that the landing vessel's helmsman had erred and delivered the initial wave some two thousand yards south of the prescribed location. Instead of seeking to correct the mistake and moving his forces laterally, Roosevelt, observing the relative success of the landing and deeming a hookup with the airborne troopers the paramount objective, ordered the troops to advance inland.

Following Roosevelt's instructions, Teague tried to move the men out. As he rallied the GIs on the beach, Teague says, "I passed a number of enemy baby tanks which had electrical wiring [remote-control systems] and were loaded with TNT. Some troops wanted to fire into one, and I told them to stop that action and I posted guards on it." What Teague described was a remote-controlled child-sized version of a tank devised by German engineers to career about the beach demolishing the positions of invaders. The "doodlebugs," as some GIs labeled them, were totally ineffective; their sole value lay in the ability to distract some American soldiers.

The first U.S. DD tanks had come ashore and began knocking off enemy fortifications. Barriers to prevent an exit from Utah fell under the onslaught of the tankers. A flamethrower drove twenty-five defenders from their pillbox, as well as two American paratroopers being held prisoners. The Germans could not pin down elements of the 4th Division in a beach killing zone as they had on Omaha.

W. H. Boies, a former Illinois grain dealer and now a platoon leader in G Company of the 22nd Infantry Regiment, led an assault team bearing Bangalore torpedoes and a flamethrower. "We were so heavily loaded we could barely climb into the landing craft," recalls Boies. "We were going to go in right about H-Hour and exploit any weak spot. There was a pillbox we were supposed to knock out. The boat brought us close to the place chosen. But when we came ashore, about a dozen Polish men, forced into German uniforms after they were captured, were sitting in front of the pillbox. They were dazed from the naval bombardment that had hit the emplacement, and when their German officers ran off, the Poles all cried '*Kamerad!*'

"We got rid of all of our heavy stuff and became a rifle platoon again. There was a route that had been used to supply the pillbox right behind it. We started up that pathway as an exit from the beach."

Harper Coleman, a member of the heavy weapons H Company in the 8th Infantry Regiment, stepped into an LCVP while aboard a larger ship. "Being with the first waves had some advantage. We were not required to go over the sides of the ship. As the small craft were in the water, they began to gather and form groups. Our circle was under one of the larger battleships. It was firing the big guns, I guess as fast as could be done. You could actually see the projectile going through the air.

"As we started to move toward the beach in lines, we passed rocket launcher ships, and they were releasing salvos on the beach, still some distance ahead. It was almost hidden from view by smoke and shell bursts.

"I saw the craft in front of ours going up with some sort of direct hit, which left us first. Before we reached the shore, something came through the side of our craft and tore quite a hole, in one side and out the other. It also ripped a good-size piece from my back pack. I saw a navy ship lying on its side with many people hanging on. We did not stop to render assistance.

"The history books say we landed some distance to the left of where we were supposed to be, and they claim this made it one of the easier landings. It did not seem good at the time. We went into water more than waist-deep. Our first casualty was just behind me with a serious wound to the stomach. A second man, in front of me, stepped on a land mine. After this we found out that the mines were all marked with a wooden stick. It seems they did not have time to remove the markers or else didn't expect a landing could take place. Those wooden sticks saved many.

"When we came ashore, we had a greeter. How he got there I do not know, other than he was in one of the first landing craft. But Brig. Gen. Theodore Roosevelt was standing there waving his cane and giving out instructions as only he could. If we were afraid of the enemy, we were more afraid of him and could not have stopped on the beach had we wanted.

"Our squad of six was down to four very early—one person was killed on the beach and one when we came to a higher ridge, just beyond the sandy area. We made a left turn as we came over the top of the beach onto what seemed to be a path. Moving as fast as we could, we reached a road that led toward the beach, and this took us through the swamps which had been flooded by the Germans. We came up on the small town of Pouppeville. This was where we began to see the results of our work, our first dead enemies. Shortly beyond the town, we began to meet some of the air-drop people."

John Beck, the sergeant with the 87th Chemical Mortar Battalion, had boarded the coast guard's *Joseph Dickman* at Torquay, the British resort town. "On the way down we had passed through long lines of the English people. There was total silence on their part and on ours. It was like a death march. Both the people and we knew that soon some of the men going to the boats would be killed or wounded.

"As we paused before entering the ship, an officer with stars on his shoulders came along and spoke to each one of us. To me he said, 'How are you, son?' 'Okay, sir,' I replied. Later, I found out he was Gen. Theodore Roosevelt.

"At about five-thirty we descended from the *Joseph Dickman* via large nets hanging down from the side of the ship to an LCVP. It was about eighteen feet long, with a sailor in front to steer and one at the rear for the engine. We drew an English boat from the pool. We had twenty men crammed into the boat with our mortars and ammunition.

"Our boat was only about a foot above the top of the water. I was up front, next to the English sailor, as we began a journey of fifteen miles which lasted two hours. We had all been issued seasick pills and vomit bags. I took a pill and crouched down underneath the gunwale of the boat. We passed larger landing craft which were sinking, and there was no way to help them. We also passed our navy, which was shelling the French coast.

"The seasick pill made me feel better, and I dozed off, only to awake with a start. We had reached the shore. There were about twenty yards of beach and then a levee about twenty-five feet high. The crew brought us right in; we got out in water about waist-deep. The cold water helped bring us back to reality. We unloaded and set up the mortars right on the beach.

"Right at that moment, paratroopers from the 82nd Airborne herded about a hundred German prisoners over the levee. They were placed in boats and taken off to be interrogated.

"All of our battalion boats made it to the beach, and we fired our mortars from there through the morning and afternoon. Occasionally, I would go up and look over the levee. I saw my first American dead there; a chaplain knelt by him giving the last rites. On another peek I saw one of our jeeps run over a mine, setting off a tremendous explosion. I thought of the driver—'Oh my God, he's dead.' But when the smoke cleared, the GI calmly climbed out of the wreckage, jotted down the serial number of the vehicle, and walked off. I couldn't help but laugh."

Bob Meyer, the BAR man with G Company, 2nd Battalion of the 22nd Infantry Regiment, believes he stepped from his boat directly onto the sand. "Wet feet, though, were the least of our worries. The beach was being shelled by artillery, and it was a very serious reminder that someone would like to kill us.

"As we were moving forward, a shell exploded near us and Kinser hit the ground. But if the shell has exploded and you're still going, there's little point of hitting the ground, even though it is one's first instinct. I grabbed his shoulder strap and helped him to his feet so we could continue running.

"In one of our early engagements we ran out of ammunition for our BAR. Fortunately, a machine gun crew gave us some to keep going. The BAR had a crew of three. One is the gunner, who carries the weapon, ten magazines with twenty rounds each, and some bandoliers of ammunition. The assistant gunner, who has an M-1 rifle and bullets for it, plus bandoliers for the BAR, takes over the weapon if the gunner is hit. The third man is designated ammunition carrier, and he also has an M-1 with its ammo plus bandoliers for the BAR.

"We started out with something like two hundred rounds each in addition to what I had in my ten magazines. But after we ran out of ammunition once, we increased our load to all we could carry. I would take about six hundred rounds, plus the magazines to add up to eight hundred rounds. That means about forty pounds to carry plus the BAR, which was around twenty-one pounds. Then there were things like hand grenades, an entrenching tool, canteen, and other stuff. I was so heavy that when I stepped down from a little curbing or the like, I often just fell in a heap and had to pick myself up.

"Shortly after we landed we came upon the weapon the GIs named the screaming meemie because of the soul-wrenching sounds they made when launched. It was a kind of rocket that could be fired right out of the crate, and originally they fired them from six barrels. We saw individual ones, about the size of a five-gallon can. When they were fired from their six-barrel mortar, everything in the circular strike zone could be killed by the concussion alone. If you happened to be where one landed, there would be nothing left to indicate you'd ever been there. We had a scout hit and all we found of him was his shoes.

"We had a person in our company named W—— who was more animallike than anyone I had ever seen before. When he stood, his arms and hands stretched down past his knees. I never heard him speak. If he had to respond, a sort of grunt was all you would get. It took several trips for him to qualify with an M-1, and I wondered if he really did qualify or whether they tired of taking him out to the range. He would sit in the mess hall and with those long arms just reach for what he wanted. Once he reached across Sgt. Garner's plate and Garner stabbed him in the back of his hand with a fork. He didn't even say 'Ouch.' Just became a little more careful where he put his hand.

"There'd been several attempts to get him out of the army on a Section 8 [discharge because of mental problems], but our captain was convinced he was faking. During our early confrontation with the Germans, W—— was still with us. Bullets were flying everywhere, and we were all keeping as low as possible. Suddenly, he stood up and said the only thing I ever heard from him. It was something like 'To hell with this.' He walked to the rear.

"We watched him disappear over the little hill behind us as he walked back to the beach. Bullets were everywhere, but W—— didn't get hit. God must have been watching over him. We were sure that back on the beach he was seen for what he was, a Section 8, and sent home.

"I think it was at the end of this firefight when we

routed the Germans that a German SS officer hid in ambush and opened fire with a machine gun, cutting our captain, Robert Russell, a VMI graduate, practically in half. Then he dropped his weapon, threw up his hands. This might have gotten him captured, except as he put up his hands, he was laughing. It was his last laugh. Our executive officer, Joe Jackson, who weighed 240 pounds with no fat, stuck him with a bayonet and pitched him like a bundle of grain.

"We weren't too fond of our captain, but he was one of us. We were certainly motivated by his death, which we thought cruel and unnecessary. We went through the rest of that German group like a hot knife through butter."

Reed Jensen, a litter bearer in a medical unit, was aboard an LST that came "within a mile of the appointed site. The sailors were good but they were in a hurry. They opened it wide open and ran in until they hit a sandbar and hollered at us to get out. When they hit the sandbar so hard it knocked most of us off our feet. We were only in a foot or two of water before we got onto the beach.

"We started up the road, didn't go very far before we dug foxholes. A rifleman captured a German soldier who had part of his shoulder blown away. He stood there, straight and tall, as if nothing was wrong with him. One of the guys said, 'Let's kill him.' The captain said, 'Look, men, he's never even shaved.' So they fixed his shoulder so he could be productive after the war."

The 8th Infantry Regiment's 2nd Battalion surgeon, Marion Adair, clambered into an LCVP at 2:30 A.M. In his diary he wrote: "We churn around about 22,000 yards offshore and for a while I think we are lost. Eventually our wave forms and we started towards the beach about dawn. It is terribly rough. We are all drenched and all but another and myself get terribly seasick.

"We pass Iles de Marcourf [an offshore spit of land seized just before the invaders struck the mainland], past battleships and cruisers firing, past rocket LSTs which loose a deafening barrage. There is so much smoke and dust that we can hardly see. Finally, soaked to the skin, we brace and our boat touches land. We jump off into three feet of muddy water and wade to the beach, which is extremely wide at this time (the tide is just past ebb and coming in).

"We hear shells whining in and think at first it's our own navy. But it isn't. The time is 7:00 A.M., thirty minutes after H-Hour. I see my first casualty, gunshot wound of the mouth. We keep working to the seawall, diving into shell holes every time a shell whines. I get very muddy and my pack weighs a ton. We see the engineers blowing up the beach obstacles, and logs are sailing through the air.

"Finally, I make contact with Vic and Chaplain Ellenberg and we set up a temporary aid station on the beach. Our next patient that comes was blown up by a mine and dies. After about two hours, the engineers have blown a path through the seawall and opened a path through the minefield.

"We clear off the beach and work inland. We set up an aid station just off a little road, eat our ration, and begin to treat some casualties, including a Jerry. We move south, and I'm glad, because the Jerries are shelling the beach quite vigorously. I see my first dead German and we have a few casualties, including Stark, who lost his foot due to stepping on a mine.

"We cross the flooded area into Pouppeville, where we run into some wounded from the 101st Airborne and some Jerry wounded. After this we keep walking to Sainte-Marie-du-Mont, pass through that town, and follow the highway toward the Carentan–Cherbourg highway."

The progress made by Adair indicates the success of the Utah landings. Three hours or so after the surgeon set foot on Utah Beach, Sgt. Charles Mastro (who had guarded a railroad trestle in Tennessee as the 4th Division's first response to Pearl Harbor and was now aide to the operations officer for the 3rd Battalion of the 22nd Infantry Regiment) encountered no problems initially.

"During the two thousand yards traveling aboard the LCI, the water was rough, but we were not bothered by the beach obstacles. We didn't have life vests but an inflatable belt, which we were instructed to retain, because beyond the beach we would have to inflate them in order to cross an inundated area.

"Some of the fellows from Brooklyn tried to wear these belts very low. When they got off a boat in deep water and then inflated them, they'd wind up head down with two legs sticking up out of the water.

"I wore these [anti-]gas impregnated fatigues, and shoes that buckled at the ankle. The fatigues were stiff as a board, and when water trickled down your open collar, you got wet underneath. We all had on either ODs or long underwear underneath and it took days for the water to dry out.

"But we got off the beach quickly and then paused for a few minutes. We didn't run into stiff opposition until much further inland, where we met up with German Tiger tanks."

When Mastro set foot on Utah he too saw Gen. Ted Roosevelt, wearing his trademark wool sweater and waving his cane as he directed the traffic off the beach. So did Malcolm Williams as a member of the 12th Infantry Regiment, a later arrival. Recalls Williams, "Roosevelt said to us, 'How do you boys like the beach?' After we got off the beach, the trouble started. The heavy equipment on the only open causeway was drawing enemy fire. So we decided to cross the flooded area. We'd been told it was about three to five feet deep and if we stepped in over our heads to swim for about six feet and we would be back where we could walk. We did that until we reached the other side. We could hear machine gun fire in the distance but it was on the causeway.

"Our first wounded was a major, but it wasn't serious. Sgt. Noe, whom I always paired off with when digging a hole, had a bullet hit the stock of his rifle, clipping off a piece of wood that struck him in the face. Boy, that got the attention of all of us. The worst thing I saw on D-Day was some men from the 82nd or 101st, tied by their feet, hung up a tree, and then cut all the way down their bodies with a knife. I also saw where wounded had been tied to a bed and then the house burned down around them."

Jeep driver Ollie Clark expected to drive his vehicle towing a trailer loaded with a heavy machine gun and munitions up onto the beach. "As we came in," says Clark, "the shelling seemed continuous. The sailor steering our landing craft told us he could only take us up so far and that would be it. I saw several men go down after stepping in shell holes in the water. One man in my company had a nervous breakdown after falling into one.

"I kept hoping that I would be able to get the jeep off the boat and out of the water without it drowning out. As I went through the water in the jeep, I hit a shell hole. Then I had to stand up and continued to drive towards the beach. Fortunately, I made it without stalling. After I was on dry land, I had to uncover the motor or else it would burn up. As I was doing this, a sniper took a shot at me. A fellow GI shot him and remarked that the German wouldn't bother me anymore."

Sam Frackman, who manufactured jewelry before being swept up in the draft, says of his voyage to the Normandy shore, "We were crouched low and did not see anything except some planes, and we heard the sounds of the big guns from our ships. We were let off in deep water bearing heavy loads of mortar and machine gun ammunition we were supposed to deposit on the beach. We had life preservers, but why I don't know. If you fell over, the preserver didn't help. There were many bodies floating by and a lot of shots being fired.

"On the beach, lines had been marked for the mines. One of my best friends was killed when he ignored the markers. When I had gone about a hundred yards inland, I heard crying coming from a crater. I went over to investigate and one of the men from my company lay there with blood spurting from his hip or thigh area. I had no first-aid experience and we had orders to move up. I couldn't get a tourniquet around his leg, so I called for a medic and went looking for my platoon. Later, I found out he had died and was the first casualty from B Company.

"Most men just did their job. Some prayed for a 'million-dollar wound' and others were too scared to move. As far as our training was concerned, you can shove it. It amounted to a zero. We had on-the-job training and we learned quickly. We learned when to hit the dirt, when to run, where to cross, when to lie still."

Nathan Fellman, who transferred to B Company of the

12th Regiment in the 4th Division after a superior focused his anti-Semitism on him, was an ammunition sergeant responsible for three jeeps with trailers. For his ride to Utah, Fellman separated from his usual companions and rode in a boatload of GIs from C Company.

"There were LCIs to the right and left of us, and we got off in water that was up to my waist. I am six feet tall, and while wading quite a distance to the beach, two of us taller men put our rifles across to pull in a very short GI until we got to shallower water. We did not suffer any casualties on the landing.

"I quickly separated from C Company and began studying my map. I wanted to get to my own unit. I looked up and saw some sand fly in the air. A lieutenant started to give me hell for not taking cover from those 88s. I informed him that I didn't know the sound of 88s. But I decided to get off that sand beach.

"I found myself joining up with some 101st Airborne men. That brought my first combat experience. A sniper fired on us. The paratroopers quickly took cover, but before I realized what was happening, three or four more shots came at me. The paratroop sergeant asked me where I thought they were coming from. I pointed out a tree. We all turned our weapons on that tree and fired many rounds. Then the sergeant sent one of his troopers up the tree. He cut down two German soldiers. They were very much dead.

"Shortly thereafter, the sergeant was taking us up a trail when he gave the signal to disperse and take cover. We did while he and his second in command pointed to a barn. The pair of them quickly ran to the barn and threw a hand grenade inside. Before it could explode, five German soldiers rushed out with their hands up and yelling 'Kamerad.'

"The young sergeant lined up the prisoners while we covered them. He asked his assistant what he thought they should do with the Germans. Without hesitation, the paratrooper answered, 'Kill them!' A GI with a small machine gun mowed them down in Chicago gangster style. We promptly resumed our march.

"On our first rest, I sat down next to the sergeant and

asked him how he knew there were any Germans in that barn. He grinned at me and said he could smell them. [Many veterans claim they could detect the odor of the enemy from their diet or their uniforms when damp.]

"I voiced an opinion about shooting prisoners, that if they knew they would get shot, none would ever surrender. He said his landing instructions were to kill all enemy and he merely followed his orders. There were no provisions for taking captives. And none of his commanders had changed these instructions. I shook my head, but he told me not to worry. However, I did. In his mind he did the right thing. But even though I had no love for the Germans I would rather not have had this experience. I never talked about this incident either with my officers or the men in my company."

Gen. Handy credits the ordinary GIs for much of the success at Utah Beach. "The performance of the 4th Division was remarkable. It was a new division that had never been blooded. We all thought Utah was going to be more of a problem than Omaha—the damned terrain, swampy, with causeways [on which a crew with one gun] could stop tanks from coming through."

But luck of the draw and a spontaneous stroke of strategic genius played significant roles. The relatively weak German defenses along that area enabled substantial numbers of troops and equipment to debark. With his on-site snap decision, Gen. Roosevelt transformed the lemon of a navigation mistake into a welcome refreshment for the hard-pressed American strategists as the GIs moved inland quickly, to establish a firmer foothold than that gained at Omaha Beach. Behind the shoreline, the parachutists and glider troopers squeezed the waterfront defenders as they sought to merge their forces with elements of the 4th Division.

# CHAPTER 17

# LINKUPS

ONE OF THE first GIs to encounter the 4th Division soldiers was paratrooper Lou Merlano, whose C-47 had dodged flak so vigorously that Merlano almost dropped into the Channel. During his nocturnal wanderings, Merlano had blundered into a German compound. He had hidden himself until he could chew up the pages for his radio code book, and now, in the last hour of darkness, he gathered his wits sufficiently to creep away through the shrubbery.

"From what the French farmer told me, I figured I was anywhere from three to five miles away from our primary objective, the guns at Saint-Martin-de-Vierville. I could see planes still coming across, occasional tracers in the air, and I moved in the direction of the most activity.

"Around the crack of dawn, I ran into Eddie Stiles and Danny Steinbach. The three of us cautiously searched for others. We finally teamed up with Bob Barnes [a pfc in the same company] and Sgt. George Barner with a bunch of people. We now had a complement of a dozen or so troopers. We were still considering our next objectives, such as a crossroads, when we were caught in the middle of an attack by a flight of U.S. bombers intent on softening up the beaches for the landing forces. A number of us jumped in a creek for no purpose except we were scared to death.

"After the bombers left, we headed out to the road near us. It was just behind the beach, and we could see quite a bit of ocean. Something was going on south of us, and we started to destroy whatever lines of communication were still standing. We used hand grenades to blow telephone poles and any wiring around.

"We split the group in an effort to find the rest of our company and to secure crossroads. Stiles, Steinbach, and I took one of them. We brought out carts and anything else we could find that would serve as an obstacle, then took positions in a farmhouse right at one corner.

"In no time at all, the Jerries found us. From inland we received heavy fire, mortars and machine guns. In hopes of confusing the Germans, not letting them know how many people were at this crossroads, two of us went upstairs while one stayed down below. We would run from window to window, firing our M-1s. More and more shells hit the house, practically obliterating it. We took positions in the courtyard, using the craters made by the bombers. Every so often, one of us would sneak out to the highway just to keep them off guard.

"We felt an ambush was coming and decided I should cross the road, go through the hedgerow to the Channel side while they held the ends of the yard. There was an eerie quiet, and we felt something was abrew.

"Danny Steinbach first noticed someone coming up the road from the south. Crouched down, we couldn't determine whether friend or foe. I motioned to Danny I would move to the Channel side to attack as the person came up. Much to our surprise, he was from the 4th Division, proceeding in a crouched position with his rifle at port arms, just as a first scout should. When I surprised him, I screamed and hollered, 'What took you so long?' I said we had expected them at six in the morning and here it was eleven or twelve.

"We were jubilant, and I wanted to arrange to speak with his CO to let him know what was up ahead. I explained to a major that since he had a battalion he should be able to move on and take over completely. The officer asked us to act as point men for him, but we felt we should get back to our own units. Eddie Stiles and Danny Steinbach were two great soldiers to have with you in a situation like this. Eddie became a regular army man, eventually retiring as a captain. Danny, unfortunately, was KIA at Bastogne.

"The three of us decided to ride some vehicles which had just come in, and I jumped on a tank. I thought we were all together, but I soon found myself alone with the tankers while looking for A Company. The first real gathering of paratroopers I came across was F Company of the 501. I jumped off the tank and joined them. It didn't take long to get into firefights and sniper chases around the hedgerows. During this period, I saw many of our troopers, snagged in the trees, butchered.

"At no time in the marshaling area, where all aspects of combat were covered, was it ever said we should take no prisoners. However, on the scene with so many troopers so brutally killed, without question we had no intention to take prisoners. That happened in numerous skirmishes over the next two days I was with F Company in the hedgerows."

Bernard McKearney, as a platoon leader for E Company in the same 502nd AB Regiment, was similarly struck by the savagery visited upon invaders. During the night, after the drop, he gathered some sixty men and staked out a small village with a stone wall surrounding it as his group's redoubt. Dawn had displayed a nearby enemy artillery position, and for several hours, the opposing forces exchanged small-arms fire.

"About ten that morning, a considerable force of paratroopers passed through us and the Jerries retired. We were assigned the mission of destroying the field pieces. I took a demolition squad to carry out the detail. What a scene of carnage! This was my first intimate association with violent death. A man at one hundred yards seemed so impersonal. About ten paratroopers had landed amid the gun emplacements. We had expected sudden death or capture. But not this! Mutilation! Horrible, terrible, vicious mutilation of dead soldiers. Most of the men were slashed about the face and body. One man was wrapped in a chute, a thermite grenade applied to this unholy shroud.

"The men said nothing. Words are so useless at a time like this. We removed the bodies from the trees and covered them with their chutes. Your mind functions oddly under stress. I tried to think of a suitable prayer. All I could think of was my mass prayers in Latin. So, very slowly, I said, '*Requiesce in pace.*' A solemn Italian boy standing by responded, '*Deo gratias.*' That broke the tension. We moved on to complete our mission and returned to the village.

"All during the day, snipers harassed us. One was especially dangerous, wounding three men during the morning. We could pick out his approximate location by the sound of his rifle and the thud of the bullet as it hit. Finally, Sgt. Richard Willburn, a lanky Texan, decided to go after him. He spotted the Jerry up in a tree, wrapped in one of our camouflaged chutes. Willburn's first shot tumbled the sniper from his perch. But before Willburn could reach him, he disappeared. A little French boy, no more than seven years old, took Willburn by the arm and pulled him into a barn. Inside the sniper cowered and trembled. This Nazi superman presented a very sorry picture. For us, D-Day night passed uneventful."

For Wallace Swanson with A Company of the 1st Battalion under Lt. Col. Pat Cassidy, June 6 presented a hectic series of encounters. Following his landing, Swanson had engaged in exchanges of small-arms fire, mostly from a distance, with enemy forces. In some instances the foe were Germans pulling back from the Utah Beach area.

"I had started with about sixty-five men and was moving north towards Foucarville, a tiny village of maybe eight to ten houses surrounded by farms. I was collecting men and combat gear on the way, but as we continued towards the objective some troopers withdrew to go to their own units. My number dropped about twenty men. Foucarville was our main assignment after the coastal batteries. I suppose the French underground had given the Allied command a

pretty good description of what was at and around
Foucarville. It was heavily guarded."

Unknown to Swanson, elements of Baker Company had
already battled with the Germans at Foucarville before
being forced to withdraw because of the enemy's vastly
superior numbers and fortified positions on a knoll overlooking the village. Before backing off, Lt. Harold
Hoggard, who took charge of the Americans there after his
CO was felled, captured several prisoners. Upon interroga-
tion they revealed the deployment of the Germans.

"I could never countenance killing unarmed men," says
Swanson, "and prisoners can be a valuable source of information, as Hoggard found. He obtained information that
enabled us to maneuver our platoons and company-size
forces. Later, when a group of Germans surrendered to
troopers from C Company and someone said, 'Let's shoot
these bastards now,' their CO, Captain Fred Hancock,
squelched them with 'Don't you think we've had enough
shooting for one day?' That shows how a good dedicated
officer can put a stop to the consequences of bitter feelings.

"When I got to Foucarville, I met Hoggard, who'd been
there since the early dawn hours. Most of the Germans had
retreated to their fortified spots in the nearby hills. But a
wasp's nest of snipers occupied well-protected positions in
the village church steeple. Any trooper who tried to cross
open areas to get at the snipers was cut down by withering
fire from the hillside venues—concrete pillboxes, dugouts,
and machine gun platforms erected up in the trees with
deadly sight lines into Foucarville.

"Hoggard's actions," says Swanson, "placing riflemen
and setting up machine gun positions, provided us with
strong security. What followed at Foucarville was Company
A's first organized confrontation with the enemy. Until
then, the Germans we encountered were scattered or in
flight. Here we needed to be organized into effective fighting forces as squads or platoons. The Germans were always
famous for counterattacks, and our men had to be ready for
that kind of action. Some of our people attached their bayonets, prepared for close contact.

"We had been told that jumping behind enemy lines we

would be in situations where an individual or small force would find enemy on all sides of him, and up against rifle and machine gun fire. We had trained to meet this kind of engagement. Furthermore, we had some very fine soldiers among us.

"Sgt. Cecil Thelan, our company communications non-com, who had a strong knowledge of explosives and demolition, was in charge of a roadblock to the north. In midafternoon, Germans tried to outflank Thelan's block, but with two machine guns and a dozen riflemen, Thelan's group drove them off. But then the enemy turned a small cannon concealed in dugouts on the slope towards Thelan's group. On his own, Pvt. John Lyell crawled up the slope through the brush until he spotted the gun. Holding a grenade in his hand, Lyell yelled for the Germans to surrender, and three of them emerged from the dugouts. Behind them came a fourth soldier, and Lyell saw him starting to pitch a potato masher. Lyell tossed his grenade, which killed the Germans, but the one thrown at him badly wounded him in the shoulder. He went down.

"For a while we couldn't get to him. Finally, two troopers, Pvts. Richard Feeney and James Goodyear, covered by fire from Sgt. Thomas Wright, tried to drag Lyell away. Feeney eventually managed to pull the wounded man back while Goodyear and Wright pinned down the enemy. But it took too long to get effective cover fire, and by the time we reached Lyell he had lost a lot of blood. He died of his wounds several hours later. He had stopped one spot of enemy fire on us. But they were able to replace men and weapons, and we couldn't silence that machine gun position.

"During this free-for-all, trying to capture, kill, or drive the enemy off, I never saw any wounded or dead enemy. But after I continued to reconnoiter I spotted three to five Germans headed away from Foucarville along a hedge fenceline. They were trotting, single-file. I took several pot-shots at them with my carbine, which was not effective at a distance of a hundred yards or so. Shots came from one of our roadblocks, indicating some of our guys were also trying to hit them."

Snipers in the church tower winged a bunch of troopers at one roadblock. Swanson's people tried to suppress the threat with their own assortment of weapons, and apparently the Germans holed up in the steeple decided to slip away by a side door. Unfortunately for them, a misdropped soldier from the 82nd Airborne lay quietly opposite the exit. He killed them all with several bursts from his tommy gun.

A German artillery column racing to reinforce Foucarville headed for one of Swanson's roadblocks. A well-placed charge blasted the lead vehicle into a pile of flaming wreckage. Two machine guns sprayed the artillerymen in the trucks behind, and a pair of bazookas destroyed the remainder of the convoy. But the German soldiers who survived sought to shoot their way through the small group of paratroopers.

Dispatched to reinforce the Americans were five men under Lt. Delmar Idol, "a quiet, low-key individual, always there when needed," according to Swanson. The added help stopped the efforts of the enemy to get around the roadblock.

The positions held by Swanson stood firm, and rather than assuming a defensive stance, he began to pound the remnants of the enemy still hunkered down on the fortified hill looking down on Foucarville. "Pvt. Charles Charles, an American Indian," says Swanson, "was an outstanding 60mm mortar man, and he hammered the works. I also had several machine guns working the area over. Just before ten o'clock at night, the enemy stopped firing. A white flag was raised. Eighty-seven Germans came out with their hands up. There was a French woman, widow of a soldier killed that day."

As the enemy surrendered, Swanson and his companions were startled by an eruption of gunfire. Suddenly, seventeen U.S. paratroopers emerged from the now abandoned stronghold blasting away at some Germans who chose to flee. These troopers had been parachuted directly into the enemy redoubts during the early hours of the invasion and had been captured.

Sgt. Charles Ryan, an A Company operations noncom

and one of the just-freed prisoners, had had a series of conversations with the captors. The Germans' confidence in their capacity to resist had eroded steadily. Ryan had informed them that his fellow invaders planned to unleash a huge artillery barrage on the hill at 10:30 P.M. As the alleged zero hour approached and the Americans continued to talk up the tale, the garrison became increasingly apprehensive until finally most decided to yield.

But not all of the enemy were prepared to give up. The GIs learned that a considerable number hoped to run off to fight another day. When the main group quit their positions, dropping their weapons behind them, the paratroopers snatched them up and opened fire upon the fugitive Germans. Other paratroopers also turned their sights on the retreating foe. About fifty Germans died while on the run.

Foucarville, strategically important to the western end of Utah Beach, now belonged to the 101st Airborne and soon the advancing infantrymen from the 4th Division.

Bazooka man Sgt. Bill Dunfee, Company I of the 505th PR, 82nd Airborne, had regained his composure after a brief outburst at the C-47 pilots whose props threatened to chew him up. He had found his buddy Jim Beavers, retrieved their equipment bundle, loaded up, and headed for Sainte-Mère-Eglise.

"Jim and I joined a group on the outskirts of the town. Our battalion CO, Lt. Col. 'Cannonball' Krause, ordered all bazooka teams forward. I was shocked by the sight of the men hanging in the trees. It became apparent they had suffered more than jump injuries. They were cut down immediately. I'm sure each of us said a silent prayer, 'There but for the grace of God am I.' My hatred of the enemy ratcheted up several notches to the point of shoot first and discuss it later. I accepted the enemy as another man fighting his country's war but never lost sight that we were there for one purpose, to kill each other.

"Prior to my first day in combat I had accepted the possibility of my early demise. But then, on D-Day, a close friend of mine was killed, and that changed my feeling from the possibility I would die to a sense that it was probable.

My acceptance of my fate was because of what had happened to this friend. I had seen him become emotionally unstable. He had changed from an anything-for-a-laugh extrovert into a subdued and withdrawn shell. He seemed to have a premonition of his death. This was the same man who had exhibited great strength and courage in Sicily and Italy. I assumed that each of us had a breaking point and I prayed I could die like a man and be spared the horror of coming unglued. Personal vanity took over.

"I have no idea of any context in which 'Take no prisoners' was issued, but it sounds like bullshit to me. We were instructed in the Geneva Convention rules of our rights as a POW, and how we were to treat enemy POWs. No responsible officer or noncom would issue such an order. You would most certainly be court-martialed and spend the rest of the war in Leavenworth. Gen. Maxwell Taylor, who was the 101st AB commander in Normandy, was formerly the 82nd's artillery commander and then assistant division commander. I don't believe he would tolerate the suggestion of such an order. Most of our field-grade officers and all senior officers were West Pointers. To be a party to such a thing would have ended their careers.

"At Sainte-Mère-Eglise, we established a perimeter defense, then dug in to await the counterattack that came all too swiftly. The enemy really socked it to us with 88s and screaming meemies. The 88s must have used timed fuses, because we were getting airbursts. The *Nebelwerfers* [screaming meemies] were so erratic you couldn't tell where the rockets would land.

"We learned in a hurry to cut laterally into the side of your foxhole for a safe place to hide the family jewels. My bazooka became a casualty when shrapnel penetrated the tube, blowing away the firing mechanism. My musette bag was hit, and a gammon grenade destroyed the composition C it contained but without setting it off. I acquired a BAR; my .45 seemed inadequate.

"We also found that the safest place to relieve one's bladder was in the bottom of your foxhole. If Mother Nature required further relief you were in serious trouble. We were being shelled almost constantly. During a brief letup, I yelled to Louis DiGiralamo, who was dug in nearby, 'Are you okay, Dee Gee?' His response was 'If blood smells like shit, I'm bleeding to death.' [DiGiralamo survived Normandy only to die six months later during the German offensive in the Ardennes, the Battle of the Bulge.]

"We suffered a number of casualties during these bombardments. The most gruesome came when a rocket landed among three men in a mortar squad. They were all killed, but the explosion must have detonated a gammon grenade in the leg pocket of one man. The secondary explosion blew him to bits. His head, chest, and right arm were all that remained intact. One of our men remarked, 'That's what you call going to hell in a hurry.' He wasn't being callous or unfeeling; his statement seemed appropriate at the time.

"By midafternoon of D-Day, I Company was ordered to move south towards Fauville. We didn't actually know where we were going or why. But not too far along the way, fire on the point killed four men—our CO, Capt. Harold Swingler; Sgt. Sandefur; and Pvts. Irvin and Vanich. Edwin Jones, the lone survivor in the group, crawled back to us under our covering fire and reported the news of those KIA.

"I was really close with both Sam Vanich and George Irvin. Sam and I shared a pup tent in Oujda, French North Africa. He was mischievous, always good for a laugh. George was the strong silent type, the kind you wanted with you when the going got tough. Their deaths were a deep personal loss. I couldn't help but think of my mortality. Swingler was an excellent leader and could have remained safe in a hospital for his knee operation.

"I don't think Swingler anticipated running into enemy between Sainte-Mère-Eglise and Fauville, because our 1st Battalion supposedly held the bridge at La Fière. There must have been a corridor between our forces that enabled a German battalion to move between. The entire situation was in flux during those first few days in Normandy. On the platoon level we were pretty much in the dark. At times you got the feeling that nobody knew what the hell was going on."

The 505th's B Company CO, Capt. James Irvin, who actually served briefly under Swingler with I Company, had been jumpmaster for his stick. His pilot and one other had flown far off course, dropping Irvin's two sticks some twenty miles from Sainte-Mère-Eglise and in the vicinity of a large town, Valognes.

With this tiny group of paratroopers, Irvin attempted to slip through the concentrations of enemy forces and reach Sainte-Mère-Eglise, in the hands of the 82nd AB but itself the target of the German counterattacks. The Americans made little progress and soon became besieged by forces many times larger and with much heavier firepower.

"About five o'clock in the afternoon, I was wounded in the head. We were surrounded by at least a company-size unit and tanks. One of our men stood up, exposing our position. I gave the order to stop fighting, and we surrendered. I was taken to a French hospital in Valognes."

Battalion surgeon Dave Thomas, with a band of troopers hemmed in by the flooded Merderet and ducked down beneath the hedgerows or in ditches, tried to reach friendly forces. "Using anything we could, blankets, barn doors, tree limbs tied together, we carried the wounded into our aid station. We had German prisoners carrying some wounded who couldn't walk.

"A machine gunner brought in his buddy who'd been shot. There was a German prisoner who wasn't badly hurt making a lot of racket. The trooper kept telling him to shut up, but he wouldn't. The GI said, 'To hell with it!' He stuck his bayonet in the German's guts, threw him over his shoulder, and carried him outside the aid station, dumped him in a ditch, and went back to his machine gun. However, we weren't going anywhere. We were surrounded."

Bill Lord, as a member of an 81mm mortar platoon in the 3rd Battalion of the 508th, figured out he had come to earth south and east of his assigned drop zone and in the area assigned to the 101st. "Lt. Beaver [the platoon leader] led us through some typical Norman sunken roads, the back ways alongside of fields. Around midmorning we came to a big tree with a glider that had crashed against it.

We investigated and found the body of a one-star general in it. Later we were told it was Gen. Pratt, the 101st artillery commander.

"Near dusk, we encountered a small group of Germans with a machine gun. Our people managed to quiet them down. We ended up at an old farmhouse or chateau being used as a hospital by some medics from the 101st. They had nobody to defend them, and we agreed to stay there, setting up a perimeter to protect the place.

"The hospital was a mess. The medics had little if any morphine and other stuff with them. There were a lot of American wounded and some Germans who were very badly hurt who spent the night screaming and moaning. It was like a scene out of the Atlanta siege in *Gone with the Wind*."

Critical to keeping Sainte-Mère-Eglise in Allied hands was the bridge across the overflowing Merderet at La Fière. Once he had determined his location, Gavin deployed a patchwork assortment of troopers to seize both ends of the La Fière span. In the peculiar circumstances of the dispersed airborne drop, the opposing forces in effect surrounded each other. Gavin had maneuvered into a position on the Channel side of the river. Behind him, however, enemy still defended against the incoming 4th Division. Across the Merderet, elements of the 507th and 508th AB Regiments would attack their end of the bridge, while to their rear marched a regiment of German reserves intent on hurling all of the Americans back into the sea. The battle for this bridge would last several days and inflict heavy casualties on both sides.

Frank McKee, assistant leader of a rifle squad in F Company of the 508th, had dropped fairly close to the mark. With a platoon-size band of other troopers led by Lt. Hoyt Goodale, he had started at daybreak from near Picauville toward their objective, Etienville, the location of a crossing over the Douve River. "In a courtyard, we came across a dead GI surrounded by four or five dead Germans. I thought if we could keep that ratio we ought to win the war. We passed the farmhouse we had seen during the night. There was now a shot-up German staff car near it.

There were also two or three high-ranking German officers strewn about. I picked up a Luger, but later discarded it when I found the pistol had been badly damaged."

The bullet-battered automobile, the corpses, and the broken pistol testified to a brief encounter of a quartet of 508th troopers, led by Lt. Malcolm Brannen, with German Maj. Gen. Wilhelm Halley, commanding general of the 91st Airlanding Division. The Americans were trying to discover their own whereabouts when they intercepted Halley as he rushed back to his unit.

When the German car, flying a black-white-and-red pennant, failed to heed the shouts of the GIs to halt, a cascade of machine gun and rifle fire smashed through the windshield. The bullets snuffed out the life of an aide in the front seat, and the driver lost control. The vehicle careened into a wall, spilling out its occupants. The injured Halley landed on the road. Calling out in English, "Don't kill, don't kill!" he nevertheless crept toward his Luger, which lay a few yards off.

Brannen shot him. Later the American lieutenant said, "I can still remember the way the blood gushed from his forehead. At first it stood three feet in the air, and then it started to subside—just like turning off a fountain." Aware from the uniform that the dead man might be someone important, Brannen ripped the lining with its owner's name out of Halley's cap, confirming identification.

McKee and his companions only knew that a high-ranker had been killed. "We couldn't get to Etienville because of heavy resistance. The town wasn't taken until D plus thirteen. We only had maybe twenty or thirty men. We fought a series of hit-and-run engagements. At one point we were trapped in a swamp. The Germans in front of us were trying to mount some small tanks as we picked them off. Our squad served as a rearguard holding force while the balance of the men under Lt. Goodale escaped across the swamp. Once they were out of sight, we were to withdraw any way possible.

"We held and then broke contact, making a dash for the swamp, running like hell. I passed one of our men still sitting in his foxhole, staring straight ahead like in a trance. I yelled to him, 'Get going!' He didn't move, and if I stopped, I was dead. The water and weeds in the swamp were only about knee-high. I half ran, half crawled through the water and low grass. I don't know why I wasn't hit, as bullets were snapping all around me. For some dumb reason, I stopped and made a gesture with my hand that they couldn't hit the side of a barn, then dropped into a crawling position in the swamp grass. Quite a few men, including Lt. Snee, were killed in that swamp.

"Somehow, I reached the river, crossed it, came to a railroad bed, and finally was on dry land. Along with the others who made it, I continued a short way north, where we came upon a large number of troopers who were assembling on the east side of the Merderet at La Fière.

"I saw Gen. Gavin and Col. Lindquist there. Lindquist sorted out all 508 men and was given the mission of moving south to force a cross of the Merderet at Chef-du-Pont. We came under fire most of the way down. There was a cheese factory in the town, and freight cars from it had evidently been bombed, because there were cartwheels of cheese scattered around. I cut a large wedge with my bayonet and feasted.

"During that first day and night we learned the difference between the sounds of German weapons and the American ones. But some men picked up the German ones and used them. When GIs fired them, they drew friendly fire. Particularly at night there were several instances of U.S. forces thinking they were dealing with the enemy and firing upon their own men. No German weapons were used after that, as far as I can remember.

"In our briefing in England, we were ordered to take no prisoners until we hooked up with U.S. troops coming from the beach. We really had no place for them, no real lines. We were in the middle of everything and couldn't afford prisoners. They just had to fight until the end, I guess."

The briefly held bridgehead across the Merderet mentioned by McKee also belonged to a group of B Company troopers. The 508th's Sgt. Bud Warnecke, whose B Company CO, Capt. Royal Taylor, hurt his leg in the landing, was designated a platoon leader by Lt. Homer Jones, now commanding the eighty troopers collected. "Our objective," says Warnecke, "was on the west side of the Merderet. But we had landed north of Sainte-Mère-Eglise and the river. We passed through Sainte-Mère-Eglise sometime after daybreak when the American flag was flying over the first town on the continent to be liberated. Chills went down my spine.

"The assault on the beach had been going on for some time. I could hear the 16-inch shells from the USS *Texas* rumbling through the air like boxcars and the terrific explosions on impact. Shortly after noon, we ran into a strong German roadblock at the La Fière Manoir [a clump of stone buildings], controlling the causeway and bridge, our objective across the Merderet. We got into our first real firefight. The Germans were holed up in a house and several barns. We had more firepower, and after what seemed like an hour, the Germans who were not killed waved a white flag, came out, and surrendered. We would have liked to shoot them, but didn't. We treated them as prisoners of war.

"We started through the marshes near the causeway. When the water became too deep we used the bridge to cross the Merderet. Then, back in the water, we got concealment and cover from the edge of the causeway. We reached the other side of the marshes. There Lt. Jones had the company, numbering about sixty men, strung out along a hedgerow with instructions to dig in. We heard tanks coming down the road. All we had were light weapons, really no defense against armor. The order to withdraw came.

"The only route to retreat was by way of the marshes back towards the Merderet. It was an unorganized rout; control over my platoon was impossible. I kept contact with as many men as I could while the Germans fired at random into the reeds. I finally reached the Merderet with about half of my platoon. I didn't think there was a chance to swim the river, even if we were good swimmers. It wasn't very wide, nor was there much current, but the banks were very steep. I ordered my men into the river and to move along the bank, using their hands, with only their heads out of the water. I was scared, fearful of us drowning but hoping to find safety.

"The next thing I heard was machine gun fire coming from a long way off, from a small French Renault tank on the causeway. Like in the movies, the bullets were dancing off the water near our heads. When the tank machine guns opened fire, Lefty Brewer and I dove under the water. Brewer had been one of the original cadre when I came to Camp Blanding in October 1942. I had been assigned to his platoon almost immediately after I arrived. We all admired and respected him, since he had already been through Fort Benning and wore the wings. The Lefty tag remained from his stint with a Double A baseball team, the Charlotte Hornets.

"For some reason, Lefty had memorized every verse of Rudyard Kipling's 'Gunga Din,' and at night in the barracks he would recite them with such enthusiasm that I was prompted to visit the library at Camp Mackall to learn the poem.

"Now, an instant after we plunged into the water, Lefty Brewer lay facedown in the water, dead! I swam the river back to the east shore, like a porpoise going down and up, down and up, because they were firing on me the whole way over and even beyond, since I had to climb a ten-foot-high bank in order to leave the river.

"I lost my rifle, ammunition, and all my gear during the frightful swim. After my breathing returned to normal, I headed north along the river until I came upon a makeshift aid station where twenty or more troopers were being attended to by several medics. The weapons and gear of the wounded had been stacked in a corner of the room, so I went to the pile and reequipped myself. Out of nowhere, a 57mm antitank gun had blown the tank away. I traveled north again to the La Fière Bridge and recrossed to the west during the night.

"I took a head count and there were at least two men missing. One of them was Tooley, the squad comedian, who had entertained us once by smoking five cigarettes at one time. He had been concerned about going into combat and had asked me to promise him I would take care of him.

The promise has haunted me for years. The other fellow
who was gone was Brewer."

Bill Dean, radioman for Homer Jones, was among those
engaged in the firefight at the La Fière Manoir and the La
Fière Causeway. "The Manoir was a typical Norman house-
and-barn combination of stone and concrete, and rather
large. The Germans considered it important enough to defend it with a full platoon armed with many automatic
weapons. Our equipment bundles with our machine guns
and mortars were scattered and lost; our heaviest artillery
consisted of the two hand grenades each of us hung from
our rifle belt suspenders. There was one hell of a firefight.
Point scout John McGuire, who was beside my right elbow,
was shot through the head and killed. I just stared down at
him, not wanting to believe what I saw. My shock was
short-lived when several more volleys whizzed by my head.

"It was about 2:00 P.M. when Lt. Jones led an inspired
attack on the place. By 2:30 P.M., the remaining fifteen or
so German troops surrendered. After hastily eating a K ration in the presence of eight or ten dead Germans we
crossed the bridge that we had just captured. When we got
to the west side of the river, we turned south towards Hill
30 and at that instant came under heavy fire from tanks,
mortars, and machine guns from our right rear. They had
us in a pocket. We couldn't go back across the bridge.
Straight ahead or to the right put us in their gunsights. To
our left was the flooded river. At this point, Lt. Jones yelled
for us to pull back."

Jim Kurz, another trooper with B Company, recalled the
daylight trek toward La Fière beginning with sights of
crashed gliders, including the one with Gen. Pratt's body.
He too saw the dead troopers still hanging by their chutes
in the trees and then four officers, shot either through the
head or heart, on the ground.

"We went to the south side of the Manoir. From against
an outer wall we were firing at the windows. Pvt. Green,
the boy next to me, died instantly. Lt. Frigo crawled into
the cellar of the building and spoke in French to the civilians held there. They left the cellar, and now Lt. Jones with
Lt. Frigo took a group of B Company paratroopers inside

the cellar. They started shooting up through the wooden floor. The Germans surrendered in short order.

"Jones now told us we would head for the river to see if we could cross the swamp and then join the regiment. I was head scout, staring out into the marsh and then the Merderet River. It wasn't very wide but it was flowing pretty fast. I tried to see how deep it was, but it was over my head. I could see a bridge to my right. Lt. Jones called us back and said we could use the bridge. We thought we were the first ones over it. There was no firing as we crossed. After six hundred or so yards of open ground we went to our left and were about to dig in when the tanks, rifles, mortars, and machine guns opened up. We only had rifles. We were caught on top of the ground but behind a hedgerow. Lt. Jones said, 'Every man for himself.'

"We reached the marsh, and I found a ditch that led back to the river. A boy from the 506th [101st AB Division] was nearest to me as we crawled down the ditch several hundred yards. Machine guns, cannons from the tank, mortars, and rifle fire went over our heads and hit in the marsh. The boy from the 506th said he wanted to surrender. I told him this was combat and the Germans were shooting real bullets. He fixed something white to his rifle and stood up with his hands raised. He lasted about a minute. Several bullets hit him and he was dead when he hit the ground.

"I continued to the river, and there were about ten men there, most of them from B Company. I said I was going to swim across and went in, rifle, helmet, and all. I dropped my rifle and helmet but made it to the other side. One fellow behind me started to go under, so I went back and got him. Three of us were on the east side of the river, the others still on the west. We cut the lines from a parachute, made a rope, and strung it across. The others used the rope to get to our side.

"We headed for our lines. With less than one hundred yards to travel, we were so tired we just stood up and walked. None of us were hit. Out of the seventy or eighty troopers who crossed the causeway together, ten of us returned this way. Up on the bank after we had crossed, a paratrooper with a mortar squad from the 505th Regiment told us he wanted to fire smoke shells to cover us. But the officer in charge refused because he didn't want to give their position away. We said, thanks a lot for nothing. It was now around 7:00 P.M.

"We stayed with the mortar squad that night. After they set up, I found a parachute, rolled up in it, and went to sleep about 11:00 P.M., June 6, 1944. This ended my first day in combat."

Homer Jones, who led the attack on the La Fière Manoir, offers his own details on the firefight there and the subsequent withdrawal dictated by the confrontation of superior numbers and heavier weapons.

"Lee Frigo was with the support group on a hill close by the Manoir. I had already worked my way into the basement, and the Germans and I had been exchanging fire through the ceiling.

"Someone, I believe it was Lee, shouted to me that everyone should cease fire in order to let the civilians in the building get out. He spoke fluent French, and he arranged the cease-fire. Once the French had left, the firing from the hill and within the house started again, including the exchanges through the floor.

"Lee dashed into the basement, a most welcome sight. There were no other troopers there. The two of us continued to fire up and watch the bullet holes appear above us. We decided they had organized a line and were advancing in an orderly fashion. Since the Germans had bolt-action rifles, there was a pause between volleys. Lee and I figured that during one of those pauses, we could skip to the half of the cellar already covered by the German fire. I may be giving them too much credit for a methodical procedure, but in any event they never hit us.

"There was another small room in the cellar; a light machine gun fired on us, cutting my trousers and bruising my leg. I tossed a grenade in there and it killed three Germans. When we looked inside there were some barrels spouting what I presume was calvados from the holes made by the grenades and bullets fired.

"Frigo and I started up a narrow flight of stairs, and just

as he was about to toss another grenade through an inside window without glass, we heard shouts that the Germans had surrendered. We escorted seventeen prisoners, leaving eight dead or badly wounded in the house. A couple of the prisoners had been hit in the testicles by our fire coming up from beneath them."

After the two groups led by Jones and Goodale pushed across the bridge and causeway, Jones quickly realized they lacked the strength to maintain their toehold. "I discovered that Goodale and his people had left. Our right flank was totally exposed. I didn't say 'Every man for himself,' " demurs Jones. "I simply told everyone to get out and get back. Frigo, Bill Dean, and I were the last ones to leave. I swam across while hearing the crackle of small arms in the bullrushes."

For his valor, Jones earned a Silver Star, while several others, including Jim Kurz, received Bronze Stars. But the bridge and causeway at La Fière continued to witness a murderous series of punches and counterattacks between the two armies for four bloody days.

For glider pilots Vic Warriner and Pete Buckley, the remainder of the hours of darkness and the day meant a tense waiting game. Although schooled in combat, they were expected to rejoin air transport operations.

Vic Warriner, who had brought his CG-4A down safely near the crash that killed Gen. Pratt and badly-injured pilot Mike Murphy, recalls, "By daylight, we joined up with about a dozen glider pilots. We kept busy unloading gliders and doing messenger work for the airborne. We all realized that the next flight of gliders coming in that evening was going to have great difficulty landing the huge Horsas in the small fields that had destroyed our small CG-4As. We borrowed some plastic explosives from the airborne and blew down the larger trees dividing the pastures so the Horsas could have a longer glide area. That was partially successful, but many of them still crashed that afternoon with severe losses for pilots and passengers.

"The airborne command had taken over a chateau for headquarters. We glider pilots gathered there to act as a perimeter guard for as long as was needed. A field nearby

served as the area for casualties who were brought in for
identification and burial. It seemed like acres of dead, row
on row, covered with blankets or tarps where available. It
took away the excitement and enthusiasm I had been feeling and made me realize that this was a pretty rough game
we were playing.

"From the field hospital we heard that Mike Murphy
was going to survive, but his would be a long and painful
recovery. He was smashed up so badly that our surgeon,
Capt. Charles Van Gorder, told me, 'It looked like Murphy
had undergone an explosion inside his body.'"

Pete Buckley, whose glider brought in an antitank cannon, left the gun crew shortly after daylight with the
sounds of the naval bombardment off Utah Beach fresh in
his memory. "I started on foot to find the 101st Division
CP at Hiesville. On my way I stopped a jeep driven by a
paratrooper headed in what we hoped was the right direction to the CP. I hopped on the hood and we went up a
narrow path between the hedgerows. About five minutes
later, some Krauts opened up on us with machine pistol and
rifle fire. I fell off and the jeep almost ran over me.

"I got up and began walking on my own. While still going up this narrow lane I glanced to my left and saw a rec-
tangular opening with a rifle barrel sticking out, pointing at
me. I froze in midstep, waiting for the bullet I thought had
my name on it. Nothing happened. The gun didn't move. I
crawled over the hedge and looked in. It was a complete
German bunker, big enough for five or six soldiers. Its sole
occupant was a dead German, his rifle poking through the
slot. Thank God for the paratroopers who had taken care of
him earlier and then left him probably to scare some of
their buddies. They succeeded in scaring the hell out of me.
It also made me more cautious. I started to walk in a
crouch, keeping my head on a swivel.

"The next German I ran across lay at a crossroads in a
pool of blood. He had just been hit by a mortar or shell
fragment and was still alive. But his gut was ripped open,
his intestines spilling out onto the road. I felt horrible while
I stood there watching him die, knowing I could do nothing for him. I had not yet developed the hate for the enemy

that would come to me as the day progressed and I saw and heard of what they had done to some of our airborne. This particular German dying on the ground in front of me was a young kid and sure didn't look like a Nazi superman.

"I passed an opening in the hedgerows and saw a lone paratrooper in the center of a large meadow. Being a little on the lonesome side and a little curious why he was out there by himself, I walked out to see what the scoop was. As I approached him, I noticed he wore an air force flak vest. I introduced myself and he thanked me for coming out to help him, but suggested I find a flak vest. Being a little naive or just plain stupid, I asked him why. He informed me there were German snipers in the woods on the edge of the field and he was trying to draw their fire so his buddies could nail them. At this moment something buzzed by my head and I dropped to the ground.

"Still standing, the trooper remarked, 'There's that son of a bitch now.' I wished him luck, picked myself up, and beat a hasty retreat in search of a flak vest. I had no luck in finding one from the wreckage of all of the gliders in the area. The paratroopers had grabbed them all for their own protection. I began to realize that by walking around alone, I was asking to be knocked off by a sniper.

"In late afternoon, I arrived at the CP and was assigned with other glider pilots to guard the perimeter in case the Germans tried to infiltrate back into what we thought was a secure area. We didn't know it, but they were all through the area, playing possum. Some snipers were still in the trees around us.

"At eight-thirty that evening, some of us were asked to go back into the fields to meet and cover the landing of the second serial of gliders. A large force of Horsa gliders were expected to arrive by nine o'clock. They came right on time, and all hell broke loose. The Germans in the fields around us, who had been playing possum, opened up on the gliders with everything they had. Their heavy AA guns outside the perimeters were firing airbursts over and into the fields while the gliders landed.

"The fields around Hiesville were much too small for these big British gliders, and those that weren't shot down crashed head-on into the hedgerows. Some were fortunate, making it down in one piece. Others came under heavy small-arms fire after they landed. Many glidermen and pilots were killed or captured while climbing out of their Horsas. For an hour or so, it was a godawful mess. The casualties in men and equipment were heavy before the situation stabilized."

Glider pilot Tip Randolph had not been a party to the Chicago mission in the early, dark hours of the morning. Instead, he was assigned to Elmira, the evening operation employing Horsas to tote supplies and added weaponry. "I had a jeep, a 75mm pack howitzer, twenty-two rounds of ammunition for it, and five men from the 82nd Airborne. Our squadron carried a battery of these guns, six in all, with their jeeps, crews, and ammunition. My copilot was Joe Bickett.

"We were all excited. We were going off to win the war. The trip was uneventful until we came to Normandy. Over the Channel—it was dusk, and with Double British Summer Time, visibility was unimpaired—it looked like if you landed in the water, you could take a step either way and put your foot on a boat. They were all headed the same way, towards France. I saw the battleships firing, a lot of stuff was being poured in.

"There had been some dark and light clouds, but just after we turned over the beaches the sky turned black. I could see ahead of me the first echelon of Elmira, and about five minutes in I started to see tow ships catch fire where they shot up an engine. We also saw fires on the ground, tracers flying up.

"It was seven or eight miles inland to our LZ, and when we got the green light it was off we go into the blackness. I thought, there's no way I'm going to make it into the field. I couldn't see anything. All you could do is a 270-degree landing—count five and then turn to make two-seven-zero, which should line you up. The most important thing now was the altitude. The Horsa had flaps that looked like billboards and could almost put the thing down on its nose, like letting you down in an elevator.

"We kept watching the altimeter. Flying in the dark, there's no sense of where you are until you come level with the horizon. Tracers crossed in front of us, some coming up to indicate ground fire. We were eighty feet in the air when we finally saw the horizon. We made the decision to drop her on her nose when we were at sixty feet and we felt ourselves brushing the tops of trees in the hedgerows. As we came down further, we could see streams of light from tracers, people were firing across the field. We set down in the field and went past one glider but didn't hit it. We rolled further and now could see we were near the end of a field, with less than eight hundred feet while we were traveling eighty miles per hour. Bullets hit the Horsa; the sounds were like thuds; in a CG-4A the noise was like a snare drum.

"We came to a stop and got out as quick as we could. One man, the radio operator sitting in the jeep, had been hit in the arm. When everyone was out and on the ground, I got behind a glider wheel, because there was a lot of firing going on. We didn't know who was doing what but figured if they were on our side, they'd stop. We were sprawled there for ten minutes to half an hour when all the shooting stopped. We started to hear the sound of those crickets. Someone put a patch on the wounded man. He was okay, having been hit in the fat part of the shoulder.

"We figured we were near Sainte-Mère-Eglise. We didn't know a division of Germans who weren't supposed to be in that area occupied positions between us and our objective. The men kept setting up the 75s, then moving to another quadrant, but they never received any firing orders. Meanwhile, a bunch of paratroopers came along and captured the Germans who had been firing at the gliders coming down in this field. Things were so mixed up that Germans had moved down the road not realizing where the GIs were.

"In theory, if you could get to an evacuation point and return to the base you could make a second trip and bring in more supplies. We always had backup stuff, ammo, food, medical items, loaded and ready. But I couldn't get out at

this point. I reached the CP and about nine that night we
saw the first people who'd come ashore with the 4th
Infantry Division.

"The next day, they sent all the glider pilots back to the
beach to check in with the beachmaster for an LCI which
had landed supplies to take us back in a kind of shuttle. On
our way out, I saw one load blow up and disappear. It hit a
mine. We got on a troopship to Portsmouth. At the pier
there, a fifteen-piece band was playing their heads off for
us. We waited until the wounded left the ship and then
went to an airfield, where a plane from our base picked up
about twenty-five or thirty pilots."

While some paratrooper elements and infantry units
from the 4th Division had broken through enemy lines to
consolidate the Utah Beach landings, other American
forces remained isolated and in danger of annihilation.
Even though the assault upon Utah Beach was successful,
large numbers of airborne GIs remained at risk inland, and
neither linkups nor deep penetrations had been achieved in
the area of Omaha Beach.

# CHAPTER 18

# SWORD, JUNO, AND GOLD BEACHES

BRITISH AND CANADIAN troops, aided by a smattering of men from the free forces of occupied nations, targeted a trio of beaches designated as Sword, Juno, and Gold, reading from east to west. The twenty-mile stretch of shoreline assigned to United Kingdom forces sloped gently down to the sea. There were no elevated bluffs from which defenders could shoot down on invaders while enjoying natural protection.

The appalling results at Dieppe had taught the British planners that stealth was no substitute for a sustained barrage by heavy guns. Furthermore, the schedule for the actual landings dispatched the landing craft to the beaches anywhere from thirty to sixty minutes later than the American forces to the west. The extra time enabled the offshore bombardment to continue substantially longer than that supporting the GIs.

The order of battle for Sword Beach led with a formation of DD tanks. Like the Americans, the British could deploy both fully amphibious versions and ones waterproofed enough to creep along the seafloor up onto the actual beach. As the time to launch the seagoing tanks approached, those in command realized the turbulent waters of the Channel were far too hostile for the fragile flotation gear. In a critical decision, the landing craft bearing the seagoing tanks were directed not to dispatch their cargo but to ferry it to the beach.

At approximately 7:25 A.M., tanks from the 22nd Dragoon Guards lumbered onto the sands of Sword. Some of the Shermans were flail tanks. These specially modified tanks bore a rotating drum with chains on the front end. The chains, flung ahead, beat the ground to detonate mines. Other tanks dubbed Crocodiles mounted flame-throwing gear. The American command had disdained both of these British innovations, which now quickly demonstrated their worth. German machine gun fire hammered engineers and the first infantrymen accompanying the tankers, but within minutes, the first Shermans had advanced across the dunes to engage the defensive gun emplacements. The tankers poured 75mm cannon fire at the resisters. The Crocodiles incinerated holdouts.

Although some armor pushed clear of Sword swiftly, Bill Bidmead from A Troop, No. 4 Commando, who had volunteered to avenge his brother's death in the merchant marine, was greeted by a downpour of enemy fire. "While we were in the LCA, men who had been on the Dieppe raid said that this landing was going to be a lot worse because the landing area seemed like a holocaust. The navy had prepared a first-class breakfast, but I was soon feeding mine to the fishes. Even the torpedoing of a destroyer [a Norwegian-crewed vessel sunk by a German E-boat] a few hundred yards away failed to have much effect. I just wanted to die.

"We were taken to the right place, but the LCA struck an explosive, and that caused mayhem. We were practically vertical. I found myself under a pile of chaps and also held down by my ninety-pound rucksack. As we crashed down, the ramp was kicked open. The first chap out was practically ripped in half by bursts of machine gun fire.

"Still on my back, jammed in between seat and boat and weak with seasickness, I had visions of drowning, because the boat was now sinking. A comrade, seeing my plight, turned back and pulled me free.

"As I jumped out of the boat, the sea nearly covered my

head; the boat had been drifting out. I could see wounded men being drowned in the shallow water, pulled under by the weight of their rucksacks."

Arnold Wheeldon, serving with No. 6 Commando, carried a Sten, the lightweight handheld British version of a tommy gun. He knew the mission for his unit was to reinforce the tiny band led by John Howard at Pegasus Bridge.

"We came in right on time at 7:30 A.M. behind the East Yorks. We had been promised a dry landing, but I never believed that. We got off in water up to our chests. Because we were assigned to the Pegasus Bridge position, we were supposed to get off the beach quickly, avoiding combat. What surprised me was the lack of any carnage on our beach. In our particular sector, there was not a lot of ground shelling from gun emplacements. There was a mass of iron barricades and barbed wire. I followed right in the tracks of a flail tank as far as the sand hills."

Derrick Cakebread, a member of the 45th Royal Marine Commando, toted a sniper's Lee Enfield rifle with telescopic sights. "Our objective was to advance to the bridges on the River Orne and link up with the 6th Airborne under Maj. Howard. From there we would go to silence the Merville Battery and continue to Franceville Plage to clear that town of the enemy." The Merville Battery was on the books because the strategists were uncertain whether the paratroop drop earlier would succeed.

"As we made our run in, we recognized landmarks from the sand tables used at briefings. When the sailor put our ramps down it was necessary to wade ashore. There were lots of dead boys floating on the water and lots of wounded men dying on the sand. The noise was indescribable. The LCI next to ours, the one carrying B Troop, was hit several times, and there were a lot of dead and wounded.

"The beachmaster in control was shouting at the top of his voice for us to get off the beach and away from the small-arms fire and shelling. There was no panic."

Vincent Osborne, who had been with No. 3 Commando during the crushing defeat at Dieppe, brought a dash of panache to Sword. Peter Young, the CO of Osborne's unit, later wrote: "No. 3 Troop comes ashore in grand style and

almost unscathed. In the bows, Troopers Osborne and
Jennings make mock of the German gunners: 'Put your
sights up, Jerry!' 'Down a little!' 'Give her more wind
gauge!' "

They could afford to be somewhat cavalier, since the
only damage to their boat was a decapitated radio aerial.
Others in No. 3 Commando were not so lucky. A hit detonated ammunition aboard one landing craft, killing or
wounding most of one section.

As his troop from No. 3 Commando sped toward the
beach, Osborne says, "I wore an assault jacket with a couple of phosphorus grenades, two days' rations, socks, a
shirt, and a bright-colored scarf I could pull out for aircraft
to identify. I had a Bren gun but no gas mask—no one expected the Germans to use gas. [Again the British high
command differed with the Americans.] My entire troop
had been issued folding bikes. We got off the beach in
good order."

In the invasion line, the five-mile stretch of beach adjacent to Sword was known as Juno. It had been assigned to
the 3rd Canadian Infantry Division, a kind of conglomerate
augmented with several armored regiments to go along
with the foot soldiers. As at Sword and all the other sections of the shore picked for debarkation of Allied troops, a
substantial fleet of warships preceded the landing with a furious bombardment.

John Keegan in *Six Armies in Normandy* calculated that
the weight of naval support was twelve times greater than
that which prepared the way for the-ill fated Canadian raid
on Dieppe. Apart from the tonnage of explosives fired by
battleships, cruisers, and destroyers, waves of gun-wielding
landing craft and amphibious armor targeted the defensive
positions. These latter weapons included vessels bearing
ninety-six 105mm field pieces mounted on tank chassis and
the DD tanks. The purely amphibious armor plowing the
Channel at four miles an hour would have to hold their fire
until they climbed ashore. The canvas flotation gear for
the armor could not survive the explosion and recoil from
the tanks' own guns.

The Canadians enjoyed another great advantage over

Dieppe in that neither the number nor the quality of the defenders matched that of the 1942 expedition. Where earlier the attackers held only a slightly better than two-to-one advantage in soldiers, the figures for Juno made it nine Canadians to every German. And at that, the thin line manning the fortifications consisted largely of soldiers under eighteen or over thirty-five with two battalions of "volunteers" from the Soviet Union as a second line of defense. On the other hand, the Wehrmacht infantrymen, in well-separated concrete emplacements, enjoyed adequate protection against all but direct hits. At Juno, Rommel's hastily implemented program for enhancing coastline defenses had as yet not provided more than minimal bunkers for most of the artillery.

Demolition teams had managed to blow only a few open lanes through the barriers. Some landing craft rushed through these breaches; others were forced to maneuver among the murderous web of obstacles. Perhaps 25 percent of the assault fleet failed to make it to the beach.

Much of the seagoing army artillery failed to contribute. Some vessels bearing cannons or howitzers foundered, while others broke away from their tows. The four-foot waves whipped up by a fifteen-knot wind convinced commanders that a voyage of the amphibious tanks from the planned distance would be suicidal. Some of the tanks scheduled to reach Juno under their own power were instead disgorged right at the beach by landing craft. That meant the armor arrived not in advance of the foot soldiers but simultaneously or even after they went ashore. Furthermore, the obstreperous Channel waters delayed everyone sufficiently for the tide to recede, making the shallow-draft landing craft vulnerable to the bands of deadly obstacles.

All was not well for the defenders either. The naval guns either neutralized coastal batteries or at least cowed their crews sufficiently to keep them from striking at the waves of boats bearing down on the shore. All seaward-facing guns were rendered temporarily ineffective by smoke and haze. The beach emplacement soldiers huddled for cover. Their smaller-caliber pieces were of no use against those still at sea, since the design of the gun ports prevented them from firing at anything unless it was actually on the beach.

James Dixon, a twenty-year-old U.S. sailor, had been involved in several Mediterranean landings as the coxswain of an LCVP, a thirty-six-footer able to carry thirty-six soldiers or one jeep and eighteen soldiers. An LST would carry six LCVP craft and their crews and passengers until close enough to the shore for a launch. "Around June 1 we learned that Gen. Montgomery wanted our flotilla of LSTs to land his British troops, because our ships were experienced. We were all disheartened, for we would much rather land with our countrymen.

"When the troops started boarding, our spirits rose considerably when we saw a little shoulder patch on the soldiers which read CANADA. Right from the start we got along fine trading yarns about Canada and the U.S.

"It was light enough to see the church steeple at Bernières-sur-Mer, which I was to guide on. The smoke and fire from the big naval guns and noise in general were awesome. Soon we formed a line abreast, about one hundred feet apart. Our engines were up to full speed. I was looking over the ramp of the boat and under the bill of my helmet, saying, 'Hail Mary, full of grace!' A soldier who could see nothing ashore asked, 'What are you saying, Cox?' 'I'm saying Hail Marys, for if you could see what I see, you'd be saying a novena.' Some of the boys kind of ducked under hard hats.

"Soon the boat hit the first sandbar and the engine was cut to zero in order to let the boat's backwash push it over the bar; then it was full speed again. We passed over a second sandbar and onto the beach. The ramp dropped, and my Canadian troops ran like hell to their objective, hardly getting their feet wet. Some waved to me. It was a good landing, and I was proud of the Canadians. They were some of the best soldiers I ever landed with, and I'd been with the American 1st, 3rd, 36th, and 45th Divisions."

Everett Gorman, the North Shore Regiment D Company platoon leader, says Overlord began "as if it were just another scheme [training exercise]. We were so well trained that as we got into the LCIs and were let down in the water the only difference from a beach in southern England was the great armada crossing the Channel."

As their vessel jounced over the choppy water, the enemy greeted them with mortar and artillery shells. Gorman along with the other thirty-nine in his boat coped with the physical forms of fear, the roiling stomach and accelerated heartbeat. He says he thought of home, his wife, and a son born three weeks after he disembarked in England.

"I looked at the church steeple in the town, wondering how long it would last, since it was probably an observation post. The naval guns were firing, and there were our aircraft bombing the shore. It was kind of scary. I was glad I was an officer. My mind filled up with the things I had to think about.

"Able and Baker Companies were to land first with Charlie and Dog, my company, to follow. Our assault landing craft struck rocks near the shore, forcing us to get out in water so deep I had to carry my rifle over my head. The officers had removed their pips and everyone had rifles, so the Germans could not tell an enlisted man from an officer.

"I saw one of my boys floating in the water, our first casualty. There was an 88 in the center of the village [Saint-Aubin-sur-Mer] firing right down the street at us, as well as small arms, and we had to get to the shelter of a wall on the beach. Our objective at Saint-Aubin was a radar station, but it was so well dug in that we had to bypass it."

Tank gunner Earl Kitching, with the Fort Garry Horse, was in the first wave. "We had been prepared to launch from six miles out, but the navy figured that was too risky. We started from about a mile offshore, and it took us about an hour to get onto the beach. This was our first time in battle, and while we had confidence in our machines, we did not know what we might be walking into. We had never lost an amphibious tank in training, but here we ran into complications, the rough water, mines, and obstacles. Of the twenty in our troop, seven were lost, probably swamped. One tank was disabled on the beach but repaired the following day. Twelve of us made it to shore and moved inland."

Fred Rogers, with the 16th Battery of the 12th Field

Regiment, a unit in the 3rd Canadian Division, handled ammunition for the M-7 Priest, which mounted a 105mm gun. They commenced firing while still offshore. "I had the job of handing the shells over the side of the gun to a member of the gun crew. The ammunition was piled at the back of the landing craft in cardboard containers. They became wet and slippery during the crossing and it was hard to cut the containers open and remove the shells.

"All our vehicles were waterproofed and had extra sides, so that when the ramp went down, the vehicles could float until the tracks touched the bottom. All the vehicles in our craft landed on the beach safely, but we had a few sinkings among the other boats.

"When we were ashore, and started down the beach, an officer, a gunner, and I walked alongside to move anybody out of the way to avoid running over them. Because of the high sand dunes, we couldn't get off the beach. Our guns lined up, side by side, and fired on targets given from observation posts with the infantry."

Intelligence specialist Jim Murray of the Liverpool-based King's Regiment was part of a contingent attached to a brigade that included the Winnipeg Rifles, the Regina Rifles, and the Canadian Scottish. "They had the same comradery amongst themselves as we did, a by-product of raising regiments in cities and areas. They also seemed to have a good relationship with their officers. The old 'pukka sahib' of two classes had eroded since I first joined. Our officers were mostly Territorial Army from before the war, and local to Liverpool. We relied on them and they on us.

"We left our transport, the MV *Ulster Monarch*, scrambling down nets into the LCI. The weather was atrocious. As we started in toward the shore the waves were so high that one minute we were looking up at the sky and the next we were staring miles into the countryside.

"The bad weather had delayed the program half an hour, and that meant the tide was turning. We had a wet landing, waist-deep. The weight we carried was enormous. In front of me was a stretcher bearer with a large rucksack of supplies for the field dressing station, his own gear, and half a stretcher. As he jumped from the ramp, he fell backwards into the water, and couldn't get up. We grabbed him and dragged him to dry land. This happened to dozens because of being overloaded.

"At one spot, there was a large concrete structure, thirty or so feet high with gun slits. It had been hit by naval shells but was still in action when the first troops got ashore. A Royal Engineer tank put the emplacement out of action with a Blacker Bombard, which penetrated the concrete and then exploded.

"The first German we saw was hanging head down from the top of the bunker. Then we started to pick up prisoners. In the first few hours they kept arriving at the beach with suitcases and packs as if they were going on vacation. On examining them, we found they were Ukrainians and Poles. The Germans were mostly signalmen and gunners."

Bill Sadler, the Briton whose infatuation with automobiles was consummated after he enlisted just before the invasion, had chauffeured some Canadian officers. "They were both very friendly types and we got on first-name basis. After I finished my stint they gave me a Canadian beret and a pair of super Canadian goggles." With everyone's attention devoted to preparations for the big event, officers and noncoms "did not go around nit-picking over dress." Sadler says he garbed himself for this special occasion in a one-piece tank suit "full of zips, pockets, and special panels" with an inflatable life belt atop, a parachute silk scarf, his newly won beret, and the goggles slung about his neck. "Quite the kiddy, I thought; pity there was nobody around I could impress!

"Came the dawn. First the sight of all those vessels around us, then the sound of our bombers going in, unseen because of a mist. Another noise, like that of an Underground train passing over our heads, turned out to be the battleship *Warspite* throwing 16-inch shells at the Germans. What about the Germans? In my imagination they were lined up against us in the thousands, machine guns at the ready and set to hurl us back into the water—I still couldn't really swim.

"The thin line of the enemy coast showed ahead, and I could see flashes of gunfire or bombing—it was difficult to

tell. We were ordered to our vehicles, which we had un-
shackled early on, although there was still quite a swell.
Down on the lift, and then I got a nasty surprise. The bow
doors opened and there in front was the wretched Rhino
raft! The rise and fall of the waves created a gap of four to
five feet at worst and one to two feet at best. We were going to make a mad dash for the raft as it was in the act of
rising to the level of the ship's ramp and hope for the best.

"Then I got another shock. Some U.S. naval officer
hitched my jeep up to a full-size jeep trailer *containing ammunition!* What about the red crosses on the jeep? What
about the Geneva Convention? There was no time for acting the righteous rule-keeper. I just had to get on with it,
but it would make the transfer to the Rhino that much
more difficult.

"I nipped round to the front and untied the bow-wave
groundsheet. I dare not risk the engine overheating during
the maneuver. The first three vehicles made it onto the raft
without mishap. However, immediately in front of me, a
small scout car almost misjudged it, but his rear wheels
climbed about six inches on the upswing and he was on.

"I couldn't help thinking of all that training with landing craft, but of this caper? Not a snit! I decided to go like
clappers as the raft was above the level of the ship's ramp,
so that if worse came to worse, I would be taking jeep and
trailer into a dropping situation rather than risk getting
hung up. It worked. I was on, albeit with a mighty thump.

"The mist had thickened, and then I realized it must
have been a smoke screen. A Coastal Command aircraft
came low through a gap in the screen, and some idiot on
board fired at it. Then some machine gun bullets pinged
into the tanks around us, perhaps from a German aircraft
we could not see. The driver of the armored scout car
yelled to me he'd made a mess of his trousers.

"As we pressed on towards the beach, I refastened the
groundsheet ready for wading. All this time, of course, the
Canadian assault troops had gone into the attack on Juno
Beach. And the Duplex Drive tanks and the armored recovery vehicles to remove any lame tank that might impede the
assault were gone ahead.

"Because of the smoke screen we couldn't see anything until almost at the point of the ramp being lowered. Then I saw the infantry had made it over the seawall. But our touchdown and unloading depended on our Royal Engineer crew getting the all clear from the beachmaster, an officer of the Royal Navy responsible for keeping the traffic flowing. We were rather behind schedule, and I supposed the initial assault must have met with fiercer opposition than expected. I knew I was to make for the beach dressing station, purely an offshoot of the forward dressing station. That was expected to be at the back of the village, a mile and a half or so away. My main job would be to take casualties from BDS to FDS and bring them to the former wherever they were struck down.

"Finally we went in and our ramp went down. The first vehicle in the water was a truck, and he entered quite gingerly—and stayed there, or, in our jargon, drowned. The width of the raft allowed the rest of us to steer around him. I began to wonder about the depth of water in comparison to the low profile of the jeep, but not for long; my turn came. All the way to the beach, perhaps two hundred yards, my mind was filled with admiration for Willys, who built the jeep, and the Royal Engineers, who waterproofed it. We went through about four feet of water, which meant the vehicle was completely submerged and I was up to my neck in it. But the training paid off and there was never a falter.

"On the beach, I removed the groundsheet, which had been making a lovely bow wave, unblocked the breathers, and unhitched that wretched ammo trailer. Someone directed me to our BDS, which was atop the seawall and flying the Red Cross flag and a black banner with 'BDS' in white lettering.

"Before I met any of our crowd, however, I was struck by the sight of four deck chairs ranged along the top of the seawall. They were occupied by German soldiers, who looked for all the world like day trippers sunning themselves on the front at Margate. When I got closer, I saw their faces were covered in the treated gauze which the medics use for burns. The lads told me their very first task had been to get these men out of the pillbox from which

they had been firing on the French Canadian Régiment de
la Chaudières. The Canadians, having reached the base of
the seawall almost directly beneath the pillbox, had simply
poked their flamethrowers through the aperture and let fly.
There was nothing more that could be done for the
Germans, and they were literally put out to die! Our people
also dealt with Germans who had been bayoneted right up
their backsides. Those French Canadians were fearsome."

The third and westernmost landing zone for the British
was Gold Beach. Lt. Walter Marshall, who had scouted the
Gold Beach area earlier, was aboard a small coastal destroyer. "We had collected what we could in the way of
cigs, chocolate, and the like. We passed these to the troops
as we slid past. They were grateful and muttered their
thanks. One or two asked, 'When's this bloody show going
to start?' Some had been cramped in their barges for days.
They were seasick, cold, and damp.

"My job was to keep in radio contact with the beachmaster and also signal the landing craft into their allotted
slots on the beach. Sadly, mistakes were still made. One
landing craft stopped in deep water. As the troops, with
their heavy packs, came off they sank. Quite a few were
drowned. One or two were picked up and brought to our
ship. I saw another LCT halt short, and what looked like a
Sherman tank sank with the loss of life. Watching these
things happen made you feel so inadequate at not being
able to help. But at the beach we had our troubles with
landing craft being damaged or breaking down, making it
necessary to tow them out of the way."

Committed to Gold Beach was the British 50th Infantry
Division and 8th Armored Brigade, supplemented by a
Royal Marine Commando unit. Horace Wright, the platoon commander who'd endured nine months as a POW
after the North African battle of Tébourba, went in as a
member of the second wave of the Royal Hampshire
Regiment.

"Our LCA was on a mother ship, and we loaded aboard
while it was hoisted on davits. It was a seven-mile run in,
and they don't ride very well in a very bumpy sea. It took

about fifty minutes, and I was seasick. I could see a bit of the coast by looking over the top ramp.

"It was seven forty-five, H-Hour plus twenty minutes, when I debarked in knee-high water, carrying a Sten gun, standard issue for someone in my position. The beach was very wide at this point, about 350 yards. The only firing coming in was mortars. We just ran like hell. There was no shirking. The entire platoon rushed forward. Two chaps were killed in the process. I saw one of them go down, but the orders were don't stop.

"It's largely a matter of luck that one does not get hit. You can have a situation going according to plan, but luck determines whether an individual is hit. Of course, in the worst situation, where things go wrong and no one knows what the hell to do, luck becomes even more critical. An officer such as myself is perhaps in a better position, because although he may be more exposed, he may have a better chance by knowing more about the situation.

"I didn't realize at the time that the air attack had dropped its loads too far forward. Nor was I aware that the DD tanks were not on hand because of the weather and the conditions in the Channel. I knew that the heavy opposition meant something had not gone as planned. But we never expected it to be a walkover."

E. H. Gibbs, as a member of the 2nd Battalion of the Hertfordshire Regiment, embarked on a U.S. Liberty ship, *Empire Mace*, one of a number of such vessels constructed at the Kaiser shipyards in the United States and manned by British tars. "The different regiments," notes Gibbs, "were spread throughout a number of ships so if one went down, a whole unit was not lost. On the *Empire Mace*, we had men from the Durham Light Infantry, the Green Howards, the East Yorks, and several more.

"We missed our appointed beach and the H-Hour target and were greeted by the beachmaster with some flowery language. He was a large, bewhiskered navy commander and he constantly urged men to get clear of the beach. He made himself heard above the incredible din and seemed impervious to any of the damage around him."

Once ashore, the U.K. troops encountered formidable opposition, if not at the water's edge then a short distance inland. On Sword, the 1st Special Service Brigade under Brigadier the Lord Lovat, consisting of Nos. 3, 4, 6, and 45 Commando (the last a Royal Marine unit), had followed the initial waves. Two of these, Nos. 4 and 6, would arrive within minutes of H-Hour, while the other pair were scheduled for H plus ninety.

In the British military establishment, the status of the Commando outfits had fallen. With Allied forces engaged in direct, heavyweight confrontations with the enemy, the time for Commando jabs, morale-lifting raids against the enemy, had passed. Once the mainland invasion began, the Commandos would become no more than highly trained infantrymen.

Bill Bidmead of No. 4 Commando discovered that the earlier arrivals at his beach sector had been pinned down. "A company of infantry given the task of clearing the beach [units from the South Lancashire and East Yorkshire Regiments] and laying white tapes to show a clear passage had tried to dig in at the water's edge. They did not move ten yards off the beach before they started to be cut down. Some idiot also gave them the order to dig in, which made the carnage greater. The sandy beach seemed littered with dead and wounded. Some tanks could not avoid running over them. It was horrible but unavoidable. The fire was continuous, artillery shells and mortars mainly. I could see two of the tanks brewing up [afire]. No. 4 Commando lost two hundred men during the landing.

"The whole of our unit showed extraordinary valor by not hesitating and going up the beach in practically extended order. I stepped over an officer from the East Yorks with his stomach hanging out. Minefields were ignored and beach defenses quickly overcome. The strongpoints were dealt with in quite an efficient manner. Many different acts of murder were carried out.

"I found myself at the foot of one of the strongpoints waiting for someone to come and cut the barbed wire at its base. A German soldier was busy throwing hand grenades over the top. I tried firing at his arm every time it appeared, but my bolt jammed owing to a mixture of sand and seawater that covered it. I commenced cleaning it there and then with a shaving brush.

"Meanwhile, the wire was cut and the unfortunate German disposed of. Our colonel, whose eye was pouring blood, told us to dump our rucksacks and pick them up on our way back. This was a relief. Running along the coast road towards the battery, we were not only shelled by oil bombs, we were being sniped at, apparently by women married to German soldiers! One old Frenchman greeted us, waving a big French flag. It seemed he had cut the cable leading from the Merville Battery that would have set the whole beach alight.

"We said goodbye to the French troops who had landed with us as they branched off to attack the casino. They had a terrific battle but achieved their object, though not without loss. Some were captured, murdered, and buried in a front garden. These Frenchmen stayed with 4 Commando until VE Day. Magnificent men they were."

For other Commandos, the arrival on the European continent was less traumatic. Bob Cubitt, with No. 3 Commando, got off Sword Beach in good order. "I was a sniper and it was my job to get out there in no-man's-land and stay out there as an observer for six hours, looking for their snipers. Everyone did what he had to do, because if you slacked off, you were a dead one."

Geoffrey Wilson, who had been among the British troops that gave a good account of themselves seeking to halt the German steamroller through France in 1940, then lost a thumb in North Africa, came ashore with No. 3 Commando as a lieutenant with a thirty-man section.

"We were held up by a sign that said, '*Achtung! Minen!*' Then Lord Lovat comes along with his bloody piper and goes right through it, saying, 'Come on, follow me!' We didn't know it was a dummy minefield.

"Then we started to follow the tanks. They would raise, then lower their flails, once, twice, thrice. We came to a crossroads and saw our first Germans, putting on their equipment. We shot the lot up and took only one casualty.

"Then we're at the bridge over the river where the

gliders came in, Pegasus Bridge. Suddenly, out of a field, here's Lovat again, and his piper starts to play. Some men break into tears. Behind Lovat came a groan, from a wounded Jerry."

Getting off Sword in good order, Vincent Osborne and others in his Commando troop cleaned their bikes of any herbage and then rode toward the enemy positions. They were halted by nearly impassable bogs and enemy fire. "Up came Lord Lovat to put some ginger into the assault." Lovat changed the troop's mission, charging them to aid the embattled airborne elements that, having neutralized the guns, were retreating from the Merville Battery position.

"We literally went straight up the road into the village of Amfreville and almost immediately got into a heavy firefight. I could see the weapon giving us trouble. It was a Russian-made machine gun. I knocked it off and then discovered the rest of the troop had withdrawn, so I did also."

Using his machine gun to good advantage, Osborne worked with his mates to gain control of the village. "We dug in along a hedgerow. And then, dear to my heart, I brewed a cup of tea."

After the first hour or so, there was never any question of the British control over Sword, even though the intricate schedule for arrivals fell apart and troops, tanks, supplies, and landing craft vied for space on the sand. From inland, German gunners continued to lob explosives on those still at the shoreline. The first defenders proved to be mostly second-line soldiers, middle-aged men with some experienced noncoms to guide them. But as the infantrymen, including the Commandos and the airborne forces, pushed to the interior, they were hard pressed by powerful, skilled enemy reserve forces.

At Juno Beach, the defenders resisted just as strongly. Everett Gorman, with the North Shore Regiment, says, "We lost six men quite quickly, and I thought that maybe this would be just a raid, and that then they'd take us off and we'd go for another beach. By noon of that first day, I didn't know whether we would be able to stay or not. By nightfall our bridgehead had so little depth of penetration we were sitting ducks, getting bombed and strafed. We figured there was an armored division probably coming at us. The word was that the colonel, in what must have been a joke, had said, 'Where's the white flag?' However, when we realized what a huge force there was behind us, the reinforcements that were coming, we knew we were there to stay."

Equally uncertain of their success was tanker Earl Kitching. "Our troop officer was wounded by a grenade on the beach. The crew commander of my tank was hit by a sniper, and when the lance corporal took over, the sniper got him also. I became the tank commander.

"We rolled through the village of Saint-Aubin-sur-Mer and did not see a sign of any enemy other than the mines. We did not have flail tanks with us but didn't have any losses from mines after we left the beach. By the afternoon we secured our first objective, a small village about two kilometers south of Saint-Aubin. We supported the North Shore New Brunswick Regiment, with whom we worked off and on during training. They were in action constantly from the moment they arrived.

"When night fell, we held a narrow strip, just two miles wide. The men had been on the go for seventy-two hours, and if a counterattack hit us there was considerable doubt as to whether we could withstand it."

Fred Rogers, as a member of a field artillery battery in the 3rd Canadian Division, could not move off Juno until hours after his unit reached the shore. "The engineers finally brought armored bulldozers in and cleared a road through the dunes to enable us to move inland during the afternoon."

The enemy, recovering from the shock of the heavy guns at sea, resisted sporadically and sometimes ferociously. One Canadian Infantry company of close to 175 soldiers attacked a sector virtually untouched by the offshore bombardment. By the time these men managed to drive beyond Juno, only twenty-six of their number could still function. In contrast, some other units met little opposition until they pushed inland.

Bill Sadler, the British ambulance driver attached to the

Canadians at Juno, remembers, "The medical unit had taken over a largish house set back a bit from the promenade, and by the beach was a German bunker. There I met a medic from the Wehrmacht who had stayed behind to look after his charges, but ended up helping to look after the British wounded as well. He was a mild-mannered person, not a bit like the arrogant Nazi type we had been expecting and did indeed meet in due course.

"When I needed to transfer some wounded and made my way through the village, we were fired upon by a sniper hiding in the church tower. Obviously red crosses meant nothing to him. He gave me some of my worst moments, because with my load of wounded men I was forced to keep my speed down. I also kept my head down and swerved a lot. I had to make about three such journeys before the sniper was removed by tank fire.

"On my first arrival it had become a sunny, warm day. I was rather shocked to see rows of wounded lying on stretchers out in the open as the ward marquees overflowed. Another sight was that of heavily bloodstained surgeons coming out for some air and maybe a smoke between operations. In that first day I was literally blooded: from then on I quickly began to get used to handling cases bearing the most terrible wounds. Above all there was this great feeling that I was doing good and not harm."

Two hours after the first Canadians set foot on Juno, the beach was clean of defenders, if not of mines that continued to kill. Those who remained near the water were contained only by minefields and mortars falling on the inshore dunes. With the beachhead secured, the Canadians advanced through the thin and dispirited ranks of the enemy. Losses on Juno, expected to reach as high as two thousand, totaled half that number, with 335 dead and the remainder wounded or missing.

On Gold Beach, Horace Wright and his platoon from the Royal Hampshire Regiment advanced beyond the shoreline relatively unscathed. "Our platoon objective was the capture of a complex of machine gun emplacements overlooking Le Hamel near Arromanches." The reception there was far more lethal. Wright and his companions began the slow, methodical, and dangerous task of destroying the enemy.

The 2nd Battalion of the Hertfordshire Regiment with E. H. Gibbs reached its objective early on. "We organized a line of defensive positions at Ver-sur-Mer to protect succeeding waves of incoming troops. By noon we had dug in with orders to hold on at all costs."

In contrast to the Americans, the United Kingdom forces occupied well-defined chunks of real estate several miles inland by the time June 6 drew to a close. The invaders along Gold and Juno had merged, and only a narrow corridor separated them from those who came ashore at Sword. The British were now back in France. But after five years of war, the costly defeat that culminated at Dunkirk, heavy casualties suffered in North Africa, and losses to the Japanese in the Pacific, they were starting to run short on manpower.

# CHAPTER 19

# HANGING ON

PERHAPS THE MOST isolated outfit among the invaders was the Rangers clinging to their small piece of turf atop Pointe du Hoc. Lt. George Kerchner, having scaled the heights, remembers, "When I headed toward the portion of the Pointe where the guns were supposed to be, the Germans began shelling us from inland. This was my first time under artillery fire, and it was a terrifying experience. I kept going in the direction of the emplacements, because most of the shells were falling near the cliff edge, and I figured inland I could be away from shell bursts.

"I began picking up men. Some were from my own company and others from different ones. You would jump into these craters twenty-five feet wide and there might be one or two Rangers there. As soon as a shell had landed, you would get out of your hole, run, and jump in the next one. The faster you moved, the safer you felt.

"I couldn't see any Jerries but saw Branley, Long, and Hefflebower trying to locate mortar targets. At times I saw Spleen, Clifton, Carty, McLaughlin, Rubin, Fate, Huff, Webb. About two hundred yards inland, I saw a Jerry in a 40mm gun emplacement, the first live one I'd seen. I told Huff to fire at him, but he missed five times. The rest of the men set out for the road. I stayed behind to get the Jerry, but I couldn't get a shot at him and left when he turned the AA gun on me.

"I crawled through a communications trench to a house. As I went through it, a shell hit it and a sniper fired at me. I found some E Company men pinned down and asked them where D Company was. They said some of my men were up ahead. I set out up the road as two Jerries came in with hands up. A sergeant reported that the guns were not in the casemates, which eliminated our initial mission. I decided to set off for our second objective, a roadblock along the coastal road running from Grandcamp-les-Bains to Vierville-sur-Mer behind Omaha Beach.

"The men took off in small groups. I followed, and as I crossed Pointe du Hoc I dropped into a communications ditch two feet wide and eight feet deep. My first impression was, I'm safe from artillery fire. But the trench zigzagged every twenty-five yards. You couldn't see any further ahead, and as you went around a corner you never knew whether you would come face to face with a German. I never felt so lonesome before or after. I became all the more anxious and started to think in terms of my being captured. I hurried to reach the coastal road and the other men.

"Pointe du Hoc was a self-contained fort. On the land side it was surrounded by minefields, barbed wire, and machine gun emplacements, all to protect it from a land attack. I don't think the Germans really believed anyone would come from the sea and scale the cliffs. Now we began running into the German defenders along the perimeter of the fortified area.

"As I came on, I saw one of my Rangers, Bill Vaughn, a machine gunner and a real fine boy. As soon as I saw him, I realized he was dying. He had practically been stitched across by a machine gun. He wasn't in any pain. He knew he was dying. All I could do was tell him, 'Bill, we'll send a medic up to take care of you.' There was no point in my staying with him, since I could do nothing for him.

"Now I saw more and more of our casualties. The Germans were defending their positions more strongly, coming out of their holes and moving back and forth across the Pointe. I'm certain they were as confused as we were, maybe more so. There were a series of little engagements; two or three Rangers would run into a couple of Germans. It was all at close range, and usually who got the first shot off or threw the first grenade won the small battle.

"However, I myself did not run into any Germans and did not fire a shot. I finally made contact with the two sergeants next in command of my boat team and also 1st Sgt. Lomell, who headed the team in the other boat from our company that reached the beach. At this point we felt disappointed that for all of our efforts the guns were gone. Apparently, the Germans had stuck some large logs in the emplacements, which fooled the people looking at the aerial photographs. [Lomell remembers seeing at least one telephone pole sticking up in the bunkers.]

"When we had started the day, there were sixty-eight men and two officers. After we lost the one boat, we were down to forty-five, and up on the road there were about twenty left. The remaining twenty-five were mostly casualties or prisoners. A few were with Col. Rudder at the edge of the cliff, where he established his CP.

"We were not in a position to do a whole lot of fighting. We'd gone in with very light equipment, very little ammunition, traveling light to make it easier to climb. We had no mortars, we had one bazooka, a couple of BARs; these were our only heavy weapons. The remainder consisted of submachine guns and rifles.

"Other Ranger companies were doing the same as us, infiltrating to the coastal highway in small groups. Two other officers, Lt. Ted Lapres from E Company and Lt. Robert Arman from F, met with me, and we agreed upon a perimeter defense, holding the road until, according to the D-Day schedule, elements of the 116th would fight their way up to relieve us, probably towards noon. It was now eight or eight-thirty, and we figured we had only a few hours to wait before those fellows showed up.

"Sgt. Lomell and Sgt. Kuhn took ten or twelve men down the road. I headed back on the Pointe to see if I could find more Rangers. That's when Lomell, Kuhn, and a couple of others on a patrol found and destroyed the five 155mm guns. I knew something had happened, because the ammunition went up with a tremendous explosion, smoke and a huge sheet of flame. We felt pretty good now, having accomplished the primary mission."

With morale at least temporarily buoyed, Kerchner now busied himself with devising a defense of the roadblock. "While I hunted for more men, I met someone who informed me a sniper had zeroed in on this area and already killed perhaps half a dozen soldiers going back and forth. I saw some of the bodies. The sniper had gotten Long and Hefflebower. I realized I was not doing the smartest thing to walk along looking for people when I didn't even know if they were about. I headed back to the roadblock."

The "cavalry" Kerchner expected in the form of the 116th Regiment never arrived during the day, nor that evening, as Bob Slaughter and the others in the Blue and Gray Division barely survived their day at the beach. On the Pointe, Kerchner and his companions played out a desperate cat-and-mouse affair with vastly superior numbers of enemy.

"About six o'clock," says Kerchner, "we realized we were not going to be relieved by the 116th. The hours had passed so fast that what some call 'the longest day' was to me the shortest. For a while, we weren't even sure that the Americans had not pulled everyone out, gone back to England, and left us alone. We only knew of a group of Rangers at the CP with Col. Rudder, where they were also treating the wounded, and that a naval shore fire control party and a couple of guys from the 29th Division Recon were on hand. Meanwhile, we were about three-quarters of a mile inland and there were a tremendous amount of Germans around, several hundred at least. They had the advantage of knowing the terrain, and of having underground rooms and passageways.

"A little later, however, a platoon from the 5th Ranger Battalion with Lt. [Charles] Parker in command broke through and joined us. We were so happy to see them, the first men from Omaha Beach. Now we realized the invasion was here to stay and that other men would come forward. Parker and his troops helped contribute to our perimeter."

Diary entries by Kerchner telescope the night hours after Parker and his platoon augmented the band at the road:

"About an hour later, three Jerries including an officer ran across the rd. towards us but we got them all. 15 min. later we saw approx. 40 or 50 Jerries behind wall about 50 yds from our pos. We were well hidden but had no field of fire in that direction. I told my men to withdraw inland approx 300 yds & join up with E and F Cos. We got away unseen."

Kerchner describes a heavier attack. "At around eleven-thirty at night, it had been quiet for several hours. I felt the war was maybe almost over for us, that we would go back to England as soon as the friendly troops came up. Suddenly—blowing of whistles, a lot of yelling, a flare fired, and then a series of grenade explosions. The Germans knew we were there and planned a well-coordinated night attack, creeping within fifty to seventy-five yards.

"It was the most frightening moment of my entire life. From all quiet and silent to this tremendous outbreak of firing, exploding grenades, furious yelling—and it seemed there were hundreds and hundreds of Germans running towards us. From their firing, we began to see their outlines; it was not real dark. We started firing, and although they did not break our lines, we suffered casualties.

"[Harry] Fate and I went up the line trying to get enough men for a counterattack. I could only find ten, and before we could organize, Jerry hit us again on our left flank, using 75mms, mortars, machine guns, and grenades. He had us in direct enfilading fire, and he captured my CP, which I had just left, killing Johnson and killing or capturing Jones, Stecki, and McLaughlin. After this attack, F and E Companies withdrew without my knowledge to Pointe du Hoc, leaving us completely surrounded and cut off."

Kerchner later admitted that he was "quite rattled" when he jumped into the hole occupied by Bud Lomell to share the notion of a counterattack. "He calmed me down and said, 'Now, George. What do you expect to accomplish by this? First, you don't know how many there are. Second, you don't know where they are. Let's talk it over.' I settled down and we decided the best thing was just to hold our positions.

"We were well hidden in a hedgerow, and were widely

separated and from time to time out of communication with each other. Down the line were Sgts. Lomell, Kuhn, Arthur, and Huff; further down were Hoover and Fate. Next were Flanagan, Austin, Sweany; and nearest the enemy, wounded and unarmed, was Branley in an outpost with Carty. Jerry tried to get to us, but not knowing our strength and losing a lot of men to our grenades, he gave up."

Len Lomell confirms Kerchner's description of the reception for the Rangers as they advanced across Pointe du Hoc. "The Germans seemed surprised to see us. But as the fighting developed, more and more of them appeared. They weren't paratroopers; most of them struck me as older men. They had an elaborate set of living quarters connected by subterranean tunnels, and they would surface behind and in front of us. Then the enemy troops inland, advancing under their own artillery, started to come at us also. We had already set up our roadblocks to control the highway."

Jack Kuhn remembers, "We stayed at the roadblock the remainder of the day. As it began to get dark, a defense by all men of all companies was set up. Along with several others I was assigned to the right flank. Harry Fate and I shared a position. Len was in command, and my orders were to repel any attacks to our right flank.

"Harry and Gordon Luning had volunteered to return to the Pointe to inform Col. Rudder that the guns had been found and put out of action. They had returned with orders that the D Company Rangers were to hold their positions and under no circumstances were they to leave these positions until officially relieved. Harry and I shook hands and swore to hold without question until relieved and that we would not surrender for any reason. We were in a trench dug along the hedgerows, which towered about eight to ten feet in our area. To observe, you had to get out of your trench and climb the hedgerow. When the German counterattack came, I could see their muzzle blasts as they charged point-blank into our front, yelling and blowing whistles for control and to create confusion. I had a large tree to cover me from their frontal fire.

"I got off a complete clip of thirty rounds from my tommy gun and was almost immediately aware that the enemy was aiming at my muzzle blasts, as I could hear bullets clipping the branches all around me."

Kerchner mentioned the welcome sight of the platoon led by Lt. Charles Parker from Company A of the 5th Battalion. With his platoon separated from the rest of the company and determined to reach the Pointe, Parker had chosen a route that exploited secondary roads. "We kept switching directions in the hedgerows," says Parker, "and as we did we would meet up with small numbers of Germans, killing some, accepting others' surrender, although we did not want prisoners.

"About three-quarters of the way to the Pointe, we reached a small village. Germans began crawling along each side of the road on the other side of the hedgerows. We could hear them and then they began to get behind us. We turned all of the prisoners loose and retreated, double-time, until we got well beyond where the Germans were. We cut off into a field towards the beach and about nine at night made contact with the outposted people of the 2nd Battalion.

"There were three officers there, and since they knew the positions, our men were integrated into the line. When the German counterattacks came and finally broke right into our ranks, some of the 2nd Battalion people began pulling out, without giving us notice. It was extremely difficult to get our men out, since they were scattered along the line, but we managed."

Among those in the 5th Battalion battling to augment the survivors atop Pointe du Hoc was Frank Dawson, the D Company platoon leader who led the way up an Omaha Beach bluff. His line of march along the Vierville road, the one on which Kerchner, Lomell, and Kuhn installed their roadblock, was abruptly halted by machine gun fire.

"We failed to eliminate this gun, because they moved it back through the hedgerows when we attacked," says Dawson. "We withdrew, and then sought to skirt the enemy and strike out for Pointe du Hoc. But as night fell, we were not too far from Vierville. We dug in and, reinforced by some elements of the 116th Infantry and other scattered remnants, formed a perimeter for the beachhead south of the town. I had lost only one killed and several wounded, but an eighteen-man Ranger platoon can't afford to lose a single soldier. The only action my platoon had for the night of the 6th was several stray cows that caused alarms. That night at Vierville, I heard a rumor of the possibility of a pullout, but it was only a rumor."

Meanwhile, down on the beach itself, Robert Edlin from A Company, after being knocked down by two bullets and receiving a second morphine shot, had fallen asleep. "When I awoke it was late afternoon. The sun was shining and there was a lot of incoming artillery fire. The tide was going out, taking bodies and debris. It kept reaching back to pick up another body, but they didn't want to go. They had earned this part of the beach with their lives.

"Other troops were coming ashore. I couldn't walk, but as a light tank came by, a wounded sergeant and I got on. They were going up the Vierville exit. If we went that far, maybe we could find out something about the rest of the battalion. Then the tank stopped. A motionless tank in front of a Kraut pillbox is not a healthy place to be.

"We bailed off the tank and crawled away a few yards. It got popped. Now we were in a hell of a fix. A burning tank a few yards away and we couldn't get to the seawall. Artillery, mortar, and rockets are still pounding away inland.

"I looked at the exit again. The large pillbox was still there, a big stone dinosaur. Because of the heavy artillery fire, people were taking cover under the seawall. They wouldn't come and help us. Finally, two black soldiers, part of an engineer battalion, came out under heavy fire and dragged us to cover. They would have made good Rangers.

"Things began to loosen up as it got toward four or five in the evening. There was still artillery, mortar, and rocket fire on the beach, but it was obvious that we had established a beachhead. As it got toward dark, a boat came in to evacuate the wounded. I was immobilized by this time. A full colonel said they would only take the walking wounded out to the ship. Two or three of the Rangers had put me on a stretcher, and they informed the colonel I was the one man on a stretcher who was going to leave. He agreed.

"It was almost dark when we reached the small landing craft. The American air force had finished their job and moved back. There weren't any landing strips for them in France, yet. The Germans took over. Fighter planes and light bombers began to attack the beachhead. We went out on the landing craft, coming up beside a ship. Sgt. Ted James of B Company had lost some or all of the fingers from one of his hands. It was impossible for him to climb the ladder. I was lying in the bottom of the boat and just about everyone had gone up except James and me.

"A German fighter came in, strafing the living hell out of the boat. I saw Sgt. James go up the ladder with no problem. His hand got better in a hurry. Now I was the only one left. The strafing and bombing around the ship became so heavy I thought they would leave me.

"I looked up. It seemed a long distance. There was a redheaded, heavyset American sailor. He said, 'I'll get that son of a bitch!' He dropped a big net, climbed down the ladder, and put me, stretcher and all, into the net, almost single-handedly forcing the navy to take me. I'll never know who he was, but he was a good man.

"We began to feel more secure, like we were going to make it. But all night long the Germans continued to strafe and bomb. It seemed unfair.

"They took me down into the hospital section of the ship. I was given more morphine, and as I lay there on the operating table, I heard a conversation between an army and a navy doctor. One said, 'We're going to have to take his leg off.' The other answered, 'It's not going to get any worse. Why don't we just leave it alone? We don't have time to fool with him anyway. Let's get to the seriously wounded people first. Let's get this man back to England and they can decide what should be done.' Thank God they were busy, because that leg still works."

Sid Salomon, the platoon leader for C Company atop Pointe et Raz de la Percée, found the heights a lonely place after the German defenders were ousted. "There was nobody around. We had so many killed. We were supposed to go after Isigny that night, but we had only nine men left from the thirty-one in our boat. The other platoon had ten men. We didn't have a sufficient force for an effective fire-fight.

"I took Sgt. Otto Stevens through the German communications trench. It was like a big sewer, and on the wall they had painted beach positions marked by stakes. The mortars were zeroed in on these stakes, and gunners could fire by preregistration as soon as troops reached the areas of the stakes.

"It wasn't until sometime in the afternoon that I felt the tide of the invasion seemed to change. Until then, it had seemed a failure, but I could look down on the beach and see wave after wave of manpower come in with tanks firing from the beach. We spent the remainder of the day there on the Pointe."

Frank South, the Ranger medic under Captain Block, remained on the beach for a period of an hour or so after Pointe du Hoc fell. "Block ordered most of the medics to the top, but I was to tend any new casualties on the beach and protect those that couldn't be moved until we had a place for them—which turned out to be the bunker above."

Fire on the beach diminished to an occasional outburst as patrols sought out defenders. After helping to move the wounded up to the aid station run by Block, South joined his companions on the Pointe. The medics used flashlights until gas lanterns were received. As ammunition ran low, Rudder assigned Block to ration the supply, and the doctor delegated the job to South.

"By then," says South, "many of our men had resorted to using German arms, because we were so short of ammunition. One supply LCA had foundered while another pulled out too soon.

"I was still working in the aid station bunker at midnight. I do not remember where or if I slept. I doubt that I was thinking any profundity at the moment but instead tended to my job. I did have a sense of wonderment that all this was actually taking place and that we had made it to the top and appeared to be holding on at that time."

While the situation of the Rangers atop Pointe du Hoc was desperate, things were improving for much of the invading forces. Utah Beach was secure. The airborne forces that remained isolated repulsed counterattacks. There was no reason, as Bradley feared, to pull the troops off Omaha Beach, even though they were still struggling to widen their turf. And to the east, the landings by the United Kingdom forces were going reasonably well.

# CHAPTER 20

# GETTING OFF THE
# U.S. BEACHES

THE RANGERS HAD expected relief from the 116th Infantry Regiment, but the dreadful hammering absorbed by the 116th at Dog Green, Dog White, Dog Red, and Easy Green, the four westernmost sections of Omaha Beach, shattered it during those first hours.

At the seawall, Bob Slaughter, still dazed from the appalling losses among men with whom he had grown up, huddled with a handful from his D Company as 1st Sgt. Bill Presley of B Company arrived with eight or nine men. "A dead naval officer lay at the bottom of the bluffs, head pointing downhill. Strapped to his back was a huge radio. He had been observing a battery of *Nebelwerfers*—screaming meemies—firing from a few hundred yards away. The rocket shells were playing havoc with later waves coming into the beach.

"Presley remembered the radio, retrieved it from the dead officer, and made contact with a destroyer out in the channel. He radioed the ship he had a target and to fire at a certain coordinate on the map. We heard the report of the 5-inch gun and then followed where the shell landed. Getting the pattern closer to the target, he fired for effect.

"We heard the salvo. 'Boom-b-b-boom-ba-ba-boom!' Soon the large shells screamed overhead on the way to the target. Kerwhoom-kerwhoom-kerwhoom! The ground trembled beneath us. The exploding shells saturated the area to our right front, some landing too close for comfort. But that action put the gun emplacement out of action and earned Presley the DSC.

"Later, that afternoon, we still hadn't gotten farther than the top of the hill. German bicycle troops appeared down the road parallel to the beach, pedaling along as if on a Sunday outing. We surprised them with some well-placed rifle fire.

"That night—it was almost eleven before darkness due to Double British Summer Time—we got into our perimeter of defense, close to a copse of trees. I had never been so tired in my life. We dug shallow foxholes in the hard shale, because we didn't have energy to dig deeper. I thought we were lost. I couldn't see us hanging in there. I didn't know what had happened to the whole division. I had heard the 116th had lost a thousand men. The number was actually around eight hundred. That scared me, and we didn't have much ammunition.

"As dawn's early light on June 7th broke over the Normandy coastline, the second squad of the first platoon of D Company awoke from a sound sleep less than twenty-five yards from enemy soldiers. We had heard Germans talking, the rattling of their cooking utensils, the night before.

"The day and night of June 6th, 1944, was not like any other day of my life. Yet, at the time, I failed to realize its significance. Later, the bad news about casualties would sicken me, and for days I labored in shocked disbelief."

Felix Branham, the I Company, 116th Regiment, sergeant, counted twenty left from the thirty in his boat team when they reached their assembly area. "We dug two-man foxholes, hoping all the boat teams would join us, that they would sift in. In the morning, we regrouped, 150 guys, and went back to the beach. I never saw so many dead and wounded in my life. The tide had come in and washed bodies up on the beach. Before it could take them out, they were retrieved."

Branham had grown up with a profound dislike for Germans after hearing tales from his father and uncles about World War I. D-Day intensified his feelings. "I hated the Germans, those bastards. I was there to destroy them for the misery, for the buddies killed, the guys I grew up with. When I saw any fallen American, my bitterness against the Germans grew stronger. We had a couple of wounded left along the road. We found the Germans came back and killed them with their own weapons, shot them in their faces. One man who played dead got to the medical station and told us what happened.

"We had orders, first three days to kill and destroy, not to take prisoners. I came within an ace of taking an old lady's life near Vierville. I heard a noise, whirled around, ready to fire my M-1. It was an old lady picking glass from a broken window. A chaplain from the 5th Rangers pushed my rifle down. 'No, son. Not her.' "

Bob Sales of B Company, loaded down with an SCR-300 radio, had been the sole survivor from his boat team, saved because he tripped and fell sideways out of the line of fire from a machine gun.

"Lying on the beach, we were not sure the invasion would succeed. Our company was shot up so badly that there was no organization, and we didn't know what the other sectors were doing. We felt helpless and alone. It was touch and go until we finally did secure a beachhead in our sector.

"That night, I was really mad. I'd been together with these boys since I was fifteen. I felt I had to go back and find out who was still there."

Bill Lewis, the antitank squad leader in the 116th, left Omaha Beach via the Vierville draw after a courageous 1st Division sergeant charged the bunker guarding the exit and placed some Bangalore torpedoes. "We turned towards Pointe du Hoc," says Lewis, "with a ragtag bunch, some Rangers, some sailors, some assault craft drivers, some boys from the 29th and 1st Divisions.

"We got past Vierville and then everybody was digging like hell alongside of the hedgerows that night. When I got up on top and could see that damn fleet, I felt the Germans must have had the same feeling I did. 'Look at all those sons of bitches. How can we ever stop 'em?' "

Like Branham and Lewis, Don McCarthy, the intelligence and reconnaissance squad member whose landing craft capsized as much as seven hundred yards from the shore, escaped the downpour of destruction through the Vierville draw.

"When I was thrown in the water, I dropped the combat vest, rifle, and gas mask in order to stay afloat. Prior to entering the draw, we began to smell what we thought was gas. We all scrambled in some panic to remove gas masks from the dead and dying. Someone yelled that the smell came from gunpowder. I found a mask and put it on, just in case. I also found an M-1, but it was full of sand. Later, I picked up a Springfield '03.

"We experienced some small-arms fire and stayed put until we could determine where it came from. Within a short time, we watched a dozen German prisoners led by some 29ers coming down towards the beach. This was encouraging.

"Many LCs were landing, drawing fire as they approached the beach. The large German gun emplacement just to the west of the draw that had caused so much havoc earlier had been silenced. A tech sergeant from the 29th led five or six of us up the draw.

"As we approached the top of the hill, we met several groups of men from the 29th. We found ourselves under bombardment from the navy in the Channel. I was instructed to go back to the beach, find the beachmaster, and request the naval shore fire be lifted. While I was trying to locate the beachmaster, I caught shrapnel in my leg. A Canadian corpsman treated the wound and pulled me to a safer place with protection from an overhang. Before I could do anything about it, I was evacuated to England for treatment of my wounds. I had been in France for just a handful of hours.

"Thirty years after the invasion I met an officer from the 116th I&R unit who told me the majority of men with him were hit by our naval bombardment. It has always bothered me that I was unable to find the beachmaster and have the fire lifted."

Behind the 116th Infantry assault on Omaha Beach landed the GIs from the 115th Regiment, the second component of the 29th Division committed to the invasion. Four hours after the initial waves, Frank Wawrynovic in C Company waded through neck-deep water.

"I dropped down for just a few seconds with the row of battered men from the 116th to let some of the water drain from my clothes. The survivors and I looked at each other but did not speak. Then, like a deer when the hunters are shooting at it, as the shells exploded and the machine gun bullets zipped by, I ran across the open sand into the grassy area back of the beach. I got so caught up in the action that nothing else seemed to matter—keep low, move fast, get away from the crossfire on the beach, move inland. When something hit me on the left thigh and almost knocked me down, my feeling was one of surprise, not fear—keep moving, get away from the beach. In the confusion, with shells still exploding all around, it was every man for himself. Move inland or die on the beach.

"I was all alone. I found a shell-torn opening in a barbed-wire entanglement, ran through what was supposed to be a minefield, and stopped only when I reached the high ground back of the beach. I had survived the massacre on Omaha Beach with only a heavy, painful bruise on my left thigh from either a piece of spent shrapnel or flying debris.

"At the end of this first day, I felt I was involved in something big and that somehow I was destined to be there. However, at that time and in the days that followed I felt much greater battles lay ahead when the Germans got better organized."

Alongside the two regiments from the 29th Division, the battle-tested 1st Division, after crashing into the same withering wall of death-dealing beach barriers, mines, artillery, mortar, and small-arms fire, drove inland.

Lawrence Zieckler, a veteran of North Africa and Sicily with E Company of the 16th Regiment, started to look for others in his unit as soon as he got beyond the crescent of sand and shale. "Up the wadi, I finally found what was left of my company. By five or six at night, we still couldn't muster more than a platoon. The others were killed, wounded, or missing. And we had been overstrength, carrying extra people to serve as replacements for expected casualties. This was the first time in combat for a lot of men, and it was not the best of circumstances for newcomers. A lot of them didn't make it."

One who did come through was John Bistrica, a replacement assigned to C Company as a rifleman in the third platoon. "I saw that my platoon's BAR man got it. He was up against a hedgerow and I came around his right side. I asked, 'Schur, where are the other C Company guys?' He didn't answer. Then I saw he was dead, with a bullet through his head. He was a replacement with me.

"I didn't know it at the time, but I lost many of my third platoon and C Company buddies. I didn't find out about most of them until later in the day when we started to get organized as a company after lunch. It didn't look then like things were going to get better.

"That first night off the beach, we dug in as they taught us, because there might be a counterattack with tanks. I dug a hole about four feet deep. I was tired, wet, with nothing to eat but a D bar. That night, I was called to go on a patrol. The lieutenant told the sergeant, 'See where the Germans are.' We found nothing. The next morning, we got up and heard noises on the other side of the hedgerows. You guessed it! Germans were just getting up, and we captured them."

Dick Conley, a replacement like Bistrica, was an officer in command of a platoon in E Company of the 18th Regiment and had been part of the second wave to hit the Easy Red sector around 10:00 A.M. Conley was in a column advancing inland through the Colleville exit, a few miles east of the Vierville draw.

"We began to move slowly up the slope. We were receiving fire constantly from screaming meemies. It was very frightening to hear, and artillery came in quite regularly. We advanced in single file between engineer tape strung by some brave soldiers who preceded us. We were alerted for shu mines, small wooden antipersonnel mines designed to blow off half of your foot. Sure enough, partway up the hill, a GI lay just off the trail with the front half of one foot gone. But he was smiling. He knew he'd be going home.

"We were so close together in this file that when incoming shells came close, we couldn't even lie down. All we could do was squat. I had a fearful urge to hurry up and get away from the beach and find some cover somewhere. We were all fully exposed.

"When we finally got on the high ground, we stopped while the company assembled. I was shivering, shaking uncontrollably, and I was ashamed of it, until I noticed that all of the combat veterans of North Africa and Sicily were shaking just as much as I was. I immediately felt better, seeing evidence that we all shared the same fear.

"The regimental plan called for E Company to move to a battalion assembly area at Colleville-sur-Mer and then move four miles to our objective, Mosles. En route, we were engaged in small-arms firefights and I began seeing the first dead German soldiers. The result of their resistance was that we only reached the assembly area by evening. Orders were issued to secure that area and dig in.

"Checking my men, I learned that nine in my platoon had been wounded but no one killed in action. That would happen the next day. One of the most welcome sounds I ever heard in my life was firing by the 32nd Field Artillery—105mm howitzers, our direct support—before midnight. With that music and with local security established, I finally fell asleep."

Platoon sergeant George Zenie, in the antitank company of the 18th, and his gun crews waited until 5:00 P.M.

"When our turn to move came, the lieutenant and I attempted to gather our men. Half were missing. We took whatever men we had and drove up the valley about one half mile from the beach. This was our specific mission area, to cover the road against a counterattack. We set up our antitank and .50 caliber machine guns in selected defensive positions.

"Since we were able to find so few men, we assumed they must be on the beach. The lieutenant sent me to

search for them. I grabbed my M-1 and went back. It was
about 7:00 P.M. and artillery and mortar fire had eased.
Snipers were still shooting. Once in a while I heard the
blast of a mine as it blew sand in the air. There was a
tremendous litter of wreckage on the shore. The wounded
had been removed; some of the dead lay in rows covered
with blankets. Others were scattered about.

"I started back with the only three men I could find. On
the way, I heard someone yell, 'Hey, sarge, what the hell
happened to our half-tracks and guns?' It seems four of our
people had followed a rifle company up the bluff. One
stepped on a mine and the medics took him away. The
other three had waited by the road until I came along.

"I brought back the six men, and we prepared for the
night. As darkness fell, the enemy air force flew over and
bombed the beach we had just left. The sky filled with all
kinds of our missiles. About 3:00 A.M. one of our .50 caliber guns began shooting at the road. The men had seen
shapes ahead. After that it was quiet until daylight, when
again we had to move forward."

Tom McCann, with the main group from the 18th
Regiment's I&R platoon, had been gratified by the skill
and determination of his landing craft's coxswain, who
achieved a near-dry landing. "On the beaches is where we
saw most of the casualties. After leaving there, we saw very
few wounded or dead GIs. A wounded American was evacuated immediately, while the dead were taken away as soon
as possible. It was depressing to see either, and American
dead on the field were reason enough for an officer to chew
someone out."

The last infantry organization from the 1st Division to
land was the 26th Regiment, whose ranks included Dick
Biehl, the B Company corporal. His most vivid memory of
his first moments ashore is of medics dragging out to his
LCI a badly wounded GI. "During the first twenty-four
hours, I remember being very cold, tired, and hungry. Fear
also was with me, as I'm sure it gnawed at everyone. Our
first night ashore was sort of confused. I recall going over
the bluff, being fired on by a machine gun. I lost my gas
mask while crawling beneath that fire and felt somewhat

'naked,' because every GI had one in the event of gas against us. A few days later, I removed one from a dead GI and I again felt 'complete.'

"The first night, as soon as darkness fell, the Luftwaffe must have made an appearance. Every ship out there opened up with every weapon—all sizes, and orange, white, red tracers and exploding shells streamed towards the darkened sky. A Fourth of July celebration on June 6. Small pieces of metal, particles of exploding shells, fell on our helmets, making a sort of clattering noise."

As a member of the 1st Combat Engineer Battalion, Leo Des Champs drew perimeter defense for the CP in the afternoon. "We were receiving small-arms fire but nothing of big caliber. About 9:00 P.M. a 29th Division officer came up from the beach and did not give the password. I halted him and he said he was a lieutenant from the 29th Division. I told him if he persisted in these tactics he would be a dead lieutenant. A colonel came up and quieted us down with the admonition that if we were ordered off the beach, to be sure we had our rifles, because no one would be allowed on evacuation vessels without a rifle. It would not be a repeat of Dunkirk.

"I asked him how precarious was our position, and he said, 'We are holding on by the thickness of hen's teeth. By 0600 hours of the 7th, we should know for sure.' "

Pfc Karl Sulkis, the advertising man who had been dumbfounded at the sight of crossbows being tested by the British, recalls the final hours of June 6. "In the late afternoon, we wangled our way single-file up muddy little goat trails to the top of these cliffs. As night fell, we dug in. We had only what we could carry, M-1s, bazookas, grenades, and machine guns. We were all soaked and pretty well done in. We dug holes immediately, wondering what in the hell might be next.

"Way off in the distant night, we could see little pin-points of light going straight up to a great height. None of us knew it, but these were German V-2s being shot off to hit London.

"We could look backwards and see our great navy lying out there in the Atlantic, tracers and cannons going hard and hot, while the Luftwaffe tore over our heads to attack the fleet. If von Rundstedt had gotten his way that night and won out over Rommel and Hitler and attacked us full force with panzers, Wehrmacht, and Luftwaffe, we'd have been thrown back into the sea before dawn."

Sulkis's hindsight conclusion is debatable. The hedge-row countryside or *bocage*, the flooded areas that limited access toward the beaches, and the seizure of strategic crossings all severely limited the ability of the Germans to launch a full-scale armored counterattack, particularly at night. Movement during the day exposed defensive rein-forcements to Allied air power, which dominated the sky, and to the offshore naval gunners.

Bill Wills, the combat engineer squad leader, passed through a minefield with the aid of two GI victims of the explosives and set up a roadblock for the night. "I sent out a patrol. They were not gone for more than ten minutes when one hell of a firefight developed. It lasted about five minutes and then all was quiet. The patrol then returned with no one wounded. They had run into a German patrol, and they were on one side of the hedgerow and the enemy on the other. Both kept shooting but neither side seemed to be hit.

"Before we got off the beach, I thought we might be driven into the sea. But once we were inland, I didn't think we could lose."

Particularly on Omaha Beach, infantrymen remarked on the absence of tanks during the first hours. In the 741st Tank Battalion, B and C Companies operated the DD vari-ety, supposedly able to propel themselves through the wa-ter like landing craft. John Barner, as a driver with A Company's waterproofed-only tanks, which were designed to crawl through the shallows while partially submerged, says, "I don't think any from B or C made it."

Barner's Sherman, *Adeline*, weathered hits that blew off the left front fender and smashed into the air ducts for the air-cooled engine twice. A fourth shell struck the left rear side, missing the gas tank by about an inch. *Adeline* lost one man, its gunner. "He wasn't hit," says Barner, "but he went into shock. We got him out of the tank and replaced him with a man from another tank.

"In midafternoon, a path up the cliff was cleared and we drove up until we moved a little ways beyond the edge and stopped. We gave fire support to the infantry as needed. About 10:00 P.M., an officer asked for some help with a machine gun that was in a difficult place. Under Lt. Barcellona's direction, we fired two rounds, followed by a burst from our coaxial machine gun, and there was no further fire coming from that spot."

Eddie Ireland, making the landing at high tide, navigated his Sherman over a path hewn by engineers until he crested the slope. "There were not many troops there, just some tanks and a few lookouts. We started to catch artillery there, and we had to watch out for the giant shell holes made by our ships. The hedgerows, which were six to eight feet high, were too steep to climb. They could turn a tank over, or at least expose the underside to enemy fire. We had to hunt for openings. For the next two or three days, we never left our tanks."

While tanks contributed relatively little to the opening of Omaha Beach, they at least made a showing. The artillery assigned to support the infantrymen never became a factor. All but one of the 105mm howitzers from the 111th Field Artillery Battalion were sunk. Six 105s from the 7th FA Battalion also foundered. The 16th Infantry's Cannon Company lost five of its six pieces to the Channel.

Relatively lightly damaged at Utah Beach, the troops from the 4th Infantry Division remained on the alert. Malcolm Williams, with Headquarters Company, 2nd Battalion, 22nd Regiment, was among those who'd come across the sands of Utah after being greeted by Gen. Roosevelt. "That first night, glider troops came in, and it was a pitiful, bloody thing to see and hear. We spent most of the night helping them back to an aid station. I had landed with a carbine, but I exchanged it with one of the glidermen for his M-1, and I carried that weapon through the rest of the war.

"We didn't get much sleep that night. We figured we

were all lucky to get ashore safe. Now we felt we had a chance to live a little longer."

Harper Coleman, a machine gunner in Company H, 8th Infantry Regiment, had carried his thirty-three-pound weapon across the sand and along a path inland to Pouppeville. "We started to meet up with air-drop people. They were rather glad to see us and joined up with us for several days. We advanced approximately three miles on that first day, for the most part accomplishing our objectives. [This is in stark contrast to footholds measured in yards beyond Omaha Beach.]

"We dug in for the night on a dirt road with high hedgerows on either side. There were a number of enemy dead lying in this roadway near us. One of the common remarks was 'These ones won't hurt you.' "

The LST ferrying ashore Fred Tannery, assigned to 4th Division headquarters, halted close enough so that Tannery, a messenger, and his driver, Pappy Sloane, did not even wet their shoes. Tannery's first hours ashore suggest little of the fury that enveloped Normandy.

"We drove on up through the sand dunes, continued on a little road until we topped, and started to dig our foxholes. While I was resting, I noticed two signal corpsmen take out a cage with a pair of homing pigeons. They attached the messages to be sent back to England. Then they took one of the birds and gently nudged him into the air. He circled around very nicely, then disappeared into the distance.

"Later, they did the same with the second pigeon. They gently boosted him into the air, but for some ungodly reason, this pigeon had a mind of his own. He just wouldn't go anywhere. He hopped from tree to tree, from mound to mound. He jumped on the jeep, jumped on top of a crate. We had a hell of a time persuading this pigeon he had a duty to perform. Finally, we scared him somehow and he seemed to make up his mind—'All right, this is it'—and he disappeared. Later, I understand, one of those two pigeons had been shot down. It's lucky there were two of them.

"As I looked around the area after I dug my foxhole,

there was a little mist lying along the ground at a distance, and it looked so beautiful. Then I spotted these magnificent red poppies, the famous French red poppies you get when you donate money to the American Legion. The haze, though, began to bother me. Suddenly rumors were this might be a gas attack. We all donned our masks, and I remembered very strongly my father telling me about gas attacks while he was in World War I. It shook me up a bit, until it was realized the rumor was false.

"That night, a plane came over and I saw such a barrage, a curtain of fire, as if every other projectile that came out of the guns was a tracer making a solid wall of fire going up towards this German plane. Whether he was hit I don't know.

"I have never seen a sight like that in my life. All these thousands of ships on the coastline were incredible to behold. It was the most beautiful, spectacular thing I've ever laid eyes on."

For 8th Regiment battalion surgeon Captain M. C. Adair, the demand for his services continued at a steady pace. After setting up a facility close to the beach, he and others on the medical team moved south, a shift welcomed by Adair, because enemy guns continued to flog the beach zone vigorously.

Adair's diary laconically lists the afternoon and evening events:

"I run into the first dead German and we have a few casualties, including Stark [T/5 Tilmon, a medical technician], who lost his foot due to stepping on a mine. Then we cross over the flooded area into Pouppeville, where we run into some casualties from the 101st AB and some Jerry wounded.

"We treated them. After this we keep walking to Sainte-Marie-du-Mont, pass through that town, and follow along the highway towards the Carentan-Cherbourg highway. Major [George] Ambrecht [regimental surgeon] contacts us in the late afternoon. He has a jeep but I have none. Fortunately, the casualties are not too heavy. About this time, the gliders begin landing (6:00 P.M.) and several have severe crashes, killing and injuring many. After helping here, we finally contact the battalion and dig in for the night. We can hear artillery through the night."

After firing their heavy mortars from the beach during the morning and into the afternoon, the squad that included John Beck packed up and headed inland. "We used a road across the flooded area. We were about a mile from where we had been supposed to land, and luckily this road had been, for some reason, left unguarded by the Germans. In addition, the 82nd Airborne drop to the rear of where we were attacking had broken German resistance, making our lot easier.

"Our outfit, with the 8th Infantry Regiment, was involved in the fighting around Sainte-Mère-Eglise, the first French town to fall to the Americans. The Germans had requisitioned all the French farmhouses along the coast to house their invasion-repelling troops. We took over one of these as our ammunition dump. In the back of the place, which had been cut in two by a bomb, were foxholes dug by the Germans.

"Down the road about fifty yards lay a German soldier, facedown, stripped to the waist, with shaving cream still on his face. You could see the scenario. He had been in the kitchen, shaving before going on duty, when our paratroopers burst in early in the morning. He ran out the front of the house and was killed when he got about twenty-five yards down the road.

"Also on the road was an overturned German field kitchen, the horses and driver dead. The Germans used these wagons to bring food to their men up and down the road. This one had run into an ambush by our paratroopers.

"As night fell, my companion in charge of the ammunition and I flopped in the German foxholes."

# CHAPTER 21

# GETTING OFF THE BRITISH BEACHES

THE AMERICAN AIRBORNE force would spend several days coping with counterattacks and trying to wipe out the enemy between them and those fighting to break through beach defenses to the interior. At the eastern end of the Allied front, the British operations initially presented a more tidy map of conquest. The strategic points on the Cæn Canal and the Orne and Dives rivers had all fallen. From Sword Beach, the Commandos, complete with Lord Lovat and his piper, had linked up by early afternoon, and the salient into that sector extended five miles.

For many, the path had been a brutal stretch. Stout and deadly resistance plagued Commandos like Bill Bidmead, whose colonel, one eye "pouring blood," had urged them off the beach and onward to rendezvous with the airborne forces. Following separation from the Free French who had accompanied them for a short period after pushing beyond the beach, Bidmead's No. 4 Commando advanced upon the Merville Battery area, the artillery position overrun earlier by British paratroopers under Lt. Col. Terence Otway. Having eliminated the garrison, Otway's troop had abandoned the position because of the threat of encirclement. Germans returned to the emplacements, and once again guns from Merville threatened the offshore fleet.

Behind the battery stood a four-story building. The plan of attack called for Bidmead's A Troop to use that structure to pour machine gun fire into the defenses. "The only entrance," said Bidmead, "was a huge gate that appeared locked from the inside. We began to climb over the wall, but we must have been observed, because immediately machine gun fire came at us. Rather confused, I lay in the gutter and commenced firing into the house, believing the fire was coming from that direction.

" 'Bloody fool,' said our troop sergeant major. 'We're being fired at from a pillbox one hundred yards to our right.' Luckily, at that moment, a supporting tank rumbled up. We drew the attention of the tank commander and explained our plight. Right as we were talking, the German machine gunner hit the flaps of the cupola atop the tank. We all thought he had had it until we saw the gun turret traverse in the direction of the pillbox. One round of HE [high explosive] was fired.

"The flaps of the turret opened, the tank commander's head appeared. 'Okay, chaps, you can go over now.' He had destroyed the pillbox with one shot.

"We were soon in the house, up the stairs to the top rooms. What a marvelous view we had of the battery. But in its midst was a sixty-foot observation tower, which we had been told would be a pile of white rubble. Germans were throwing hundreds of hand grenades off the top at the troops getting into position for the assault. All hell was let loose as a dozen K guns [Vickers machine guns capable of nine hundred rounds per minute] let loose. The fire was kept up until a Very light was fired by the assaulting troops to let us know they were ready for the attack. We stopped firing into the battery and looked for targets among the outer defenses.

"I was leaning out of the top window shooting at everything that moved with my rifle. Didn't sink in, in my excitement, what a grand target I made. 'Just hit one of them,' I said to a comrade, and moved my head to one side to reload my rifle. Bang! A bullet missed my head by a fraction and struck a Commando standing on the top of a few stairs leading into our room. He was hit in the stomach, practically blowing his back out.

"Our job finished, we started to make our way back to our rendezvous point in Ouistreham. Four of us were carrying one wounded chap on a makeshift stretcher, a door, when a shell or mortar bomb fell behind us, blowing us all on the deck. Two were killed; the chap on my right had his arm cut off with shrapnel. I was not touched. God was being very good to me.

"On our way again for a few yards, a lone Messerschmitt reared out of the sky, machine-gunning us. We all ended up in a big heap in the doorway of a bank with two wounded chaps under the lot of us. The horror we came across on the way back was indescribable. Dead Commandos piled in a big heap with the grease paint still on their faces—a line of men blind with eye wounds sitting by the roadside—the waxen faces of lone figures lying in pools of blood. Twenty dead infantrymen lying behind a hedgerow as if on the verge of going into attack.

"No. 4 Commando formed up ready to join the rest of the brigade. We took the Caen road leading up to the Pegasus Bridge. On the side of the road lay many dead German snipers. One chap had been hit in the back of the head; his false teeth dangled on his chin. Further on we came across six Commandos who had been ambushed on their cycles. Bikes, Germans, and Commandos lay all over the road.

"Nearing the bridges now, we could hear the rattle of machine gun fire and the single shots from the snipers. Black-faced, grinning glider troops greeted us—'Thank the Lord you're here, mates.' Unburied airborne and German dead still held a grim reminder of the ferocious battle which had occurred earlier.

"Smoke screens were still being laid on the bridges, because hidden machine guns and snipers were still active on the riverbanks. We ran across in small groups. Men were getting hit every so often. My legs felt like lead, and I was glad I didn't join the still bodies lying on the bridge.

"We carried on four miles past the bridge to a village called Amfreville, then another couple of miles to Hauger. On some high ground overlooking the beachhead we were told to stay, hold on, and fight, not yield an inch. A Troop was placed about half a mile in front, waiting to make first contact with the enemy, a very precarious position indeed. As night fell the task of waiting, watching, and digging had begun. For those of us who had survived, it had been a very long day indeed."

The line established at Sword as well as Juno and Gold fell well short of the mark drawn upon maps at invasion headquarters in London. Montgomery had expected to take the pivotal city of Caen on the first day; it would be many weeks later before the ruin of that town fell to the Allies.

Horace Wright, in the 1st Battalion of the Hampshire Regiment, had lost only two from his forty-man platoon while rushing over Gold Beach. He quickly ran into fierce resistance at Le Hamel. "It was a complex of machine gun emplacements, and we didn't really take it until the midafternoon." The difficulty and opposition faced by Wright's outfit is summed up in the body count. "We had thirteen officers killed on D-Day."

Ambulance driver Bill Sadler, supporting the largely Canadian forces at Juno Beach, bedded down in German-dug trenches right at the edge of Juno, another sign of a lack of progress by the invaders. But at least the Allied armies striking at Juno and Gold linked up at Creully and could form an unbroken front line. The troops on Sword Beach, like their American counterparts at Utah and Omaha, only occupied pockets along the coastline.

William Ward, one of the King's Own Scottish Borderers, whose LCI had blessed him with a dry landing, insists, "When we got off the beaches in strength and moved inland about two miles, I knew we were there to stay. The Germans with the 21st Panzer Division put up very stiff resistance and could not be moved. If you gained a field, the cost was enormous."

While a few individual units remained highly vulnerable, by nightfall the possibility that the Germans might push the Allies off the continent was gone. Reinforcements were already landing, bringing with them massive amounts of armor and artillery. Eisenhower could toss away his memo of defeat.

# PART III

# AFTERMATHS

# CHAPTER 22

# BEYOND OMAHA

THE "BEGINNING," AS Churchill labeled Overlord, could be called a success if establishing a foothold were the sole criterion. By the morning of June 7, the Allied forces, with the fleet still lobbing ordnance at inland targets and only one hundred German planes operating against the invaders, controlled strips of land over a forty-mile stretch of coastline. More than 100,000 troops occupied positions in Normandy—the seaborne gridlock and the aerial-drop chaos prevented precise statistics—with the deepest penetration some eight miles in the British sector and the shallowest as little as one thousand yards for the American area beyond Omaha Beach. Inland, the pockets of airborne GIs and Tommies continued to beat back counterattacks, solidifying and enlarging pockets on the Cotentin Peninsula.

Casualties among the Allies for that first twenty-four hours included as many as 2,500 on bloody Omaha, fewer than 200 at the less fiercely defended Utah Beach, 2,499 among the U.S. airborne, and almost 4,100 for the British and Canadians, including 650 in the 6th Airborne Division. Several hundred sailors who went down with their vessels or were hit by fire as they reached the beaches added to the human costs. The total approached 10,000, decimation in the true sense of the word, loss of 10 percent. Since estimates of the dead, wounded, and captured had been pegged at from 50 to 90 percent for the airborne and from 25 percent up for the foot soldiers, the numbers were acceptable to the commanders, if not the kin and friends of those involved.

Back in the United States and in Britain, word of the invasion spread within hours of its start. The carefully couched communiqués issued from SHAEF hinted little of the carnage. Over the next few days, the correspondents' references to the malevolent reception in some areas were tempered by hopeful accounts of progress. To the neighbors and relatives of the young men from Virginia's Blue and Gray Division, it appeared that things were going well.

In Bedford, Virginia, on Sunday, June 11, Lucille Hoback, then fourteen, prepared for the family excursion to church services. "We got the first telegram telling us that my brother Bedford had been killed. Monday we received the second telegram saying that Raymond was missing.

"A month later, a package came from 'somewhere in France' and the soldier wrote he'd found a Bible on the beach with Raymond's name and address. He said that he did not know whether Raymond was living or dead but thought in any case the family would want the Bible.

"On the Bible, you could see where the strap of Raymond's pack pressed against it. The book wasn't wet or damaged; he'd probably kept it wrapped in plastic. We heard from someone that he'd been wounded, then placed next to the bodies of others waiting to be taken out to a ship, and that the tide had probably come in and drowned those there.

"Raymond was declared dead a year later and his body never recovered. Harold Baumgarten, who became a doctor later, told us that he saw a machine gun bullet hit Bedford, then ricochet off to wound Baumgarten."

Some on the scene knew little more of the fate of comrades than the folks back home. Roy Stevens could not locate his twin brother, Ray. "I asked a bunch of guys if they knew where he was, and then somebody suggested I check out the cemetery they'd made. That's how I found out Ray was dead. I got so mad I started to volunteer for everything. Col. Canham calmed me down. He said, 'The war isn't going to be won by one man. It will take all of us.' "

The achievements of June 6 fell well short of the goals on the planning boards. Caen, Montgomery's objective for D-Day, lay a good two miles beyond the outposts of the British positions. Another goal, Bayeux, the major city west of Caen, also remained in German hands until it was abandoned twenty-four hours later. The U.S. troops coming ashore at Omaha Beach were supposed to advance about four to six miles, establishing a line across the highway parallel to the coastline. Instead, they were still within yards of the Channel. At the westernmost end of the invasion, the combined assault of the airborne and Utah Beach GIs was expected to capture the territory beyond the Merderet River. But when June 7 came, the Americans were clustered in pockets and fighting desperately to cross the river and the inundated fields.

German losses in manpower and equipment on D-Day did not seriously weaken the ability to resist further thrusts. The end of what Overlord began, V-E Day, lay eleven months off, and those still on their feet in Normandy faced what would seem like an infinite ordeal by fire.

Richard Willstatter, as the engineering officer aboard LST 133, recalled that his vessel with its cargo of 1st Division troops never actually reached Omaha Beach on June 6 because of the chaos there. Instead, LST 133 settled in at a designated anchorage where wounded men arrived for treatment by medical teams. Shortly before dark, however, the officer in charge of the five 1st Division DUKWs packed with ammunition rolled out with his ducks and safely made it ashore.

Remembers Willstatter, "Around noon we received word to proceed to the beach and discharge our cargo. We grounded softly on the shore very soon after 1400. When I came topside, I found out troops ashore had waved frantically to keep us off the beach, because they knew many mines and obstacles had yet to be cleared from our path. The beach presented a picture of ruin and desolation. Directly ahead of us, about five hundred yards, LCI 92 lay broadside to the beach, high and dry. Her bottom had been blown out and the entire ship burned down to bare steel. On our starboard beam was LCI 91, another blackened hulk.

"As the tide dropped, many trucks, jeeps, ducks could be seen all over the beach. Hundreds of obstacles had not been cleared, and to each one were attached a Teller mine and other explosives. Bodies and pieces of bodies littered the area."

Trucks rolling off Willstatter's ship lurched across the beach, after the first one dropped a steel mat that enabled the others to proceed on a hard surface. As the ship emptied itself, casualties arrived, both as stretcher cases and as walking wounded. Some of the latter returned to their outfits after treatment. Willstatter observed a line of old merchant ships, the Gooseberries, being sunk to form a makeshift breakwater. Willstatter and his shipmates withdrew from Omaha shortly before dark and a day or so later sailed for England to disembark the injured men and load fresh soldiers and equipment for the coming battles.

On the morning of June 7, the LCM with Gil Miller as a member of the crew assisted in clearing the beach area for the resupply and infusion of more troops. "We used three LCMs to pull broken-down boats off the beach. We took them out into the Channel and sunk them. The army engineers with bulldozers shoved the debris out of the way for clear passage inland. By Day Three the army had in place the big floating docks [the Mulberries].

"We parked our LCMs and became beach cleaners. Sometimes I would sit up on the hill as the army troops walked in and talk to the guys going by. The most important question was 'Where are you from?' About the fourth or fifth day I even rode up to a town on a supply truck and then came back on an empty one.

"Then the weather got real bad; rain, wind, and waves drove everything up on the beach. For three or four days nothing moved. The storm did more damage than the 88s. We lost all five of our LCMs, which piled up like logs. When the storm hit us, we had no place to go but up on the beach. For a bunch of us, our only protection was an upside-down LCVP, a thirty-foot landing craft. It was one helluva mess. No supplies came in. We had only whatever we had on our backs. All our stuff, which was on the LCM, was gone. The army supplied us with pup tents to live in."

Bill Hughes, the young electrician aboard LCI 491, marked his first year in the navy on June 7. He noted in his diary delivery of a load of troops to Omaha Beach and the opening of a landing strip for planes. Hughes settled into a routine, taking prisoners out to larger ships and towing barges with four hundred tons of ammo or gasoline.

Entries for his June 8 diary note, "LCI 497 hit a mine and sank. Air raids every day and night. Some German shells land so close to barges we are splashed with water."

Ten days later, Hughes wrote, "Very rough, 60 mph gale. Lost all starboard stanchions off deck. Beach is covered with destroyed landing craft, tanks, trucks." Miller, Hughes and his shipmates had weathered the worst Channel storm in years. But the massive Mulberries were swept away.

The weather on June 6 had been bad enough to seriously compromise the landings. However, the tidal schedule for the month meant that even more violent outburst of wind and water, June 18–20, fell during the only alternate dates to June 5–7.

The combat responsibilities for the Allied navies ended within a few days as the beachhead widened and tanks and artillery landed to take over the responsibility for the long-range hits. Ken Almy, whose LCI had struck a mine just short of the beach, had joined a group of sailors at a "survivor base" before reassignment to another LCI that began to ferry fresh troops to the continent. Some amphibious teams went to the Mediterranean for Operation Dragoon, the invasion of southern France in August, and others took part in the Rhine crossing in March 1945. Crews also journeyed to the South Pacific to participate in landings there.

For the soldiers on Omaha Beach, June 6 indeed was only a beginning. The 116th's Bob Sales, sole survivor from his B Company boat team, says, "Every day was a D-Day, jumping off from the hedgerows. I would have this sick feeling, lying in a foxhole, finding it difficult to eat or sleep knowing we would jump off the next morning."

Sales served as a sergeant, earned a Silver Star, and jumped off in the Saint-Lô breakout, pursuing the enemy through Belgium and Holland. In November he accompanied a tank seeking to knock out a machine gun on the German border. A shell exploded against the side of the tank. Fragments struck Sales in the face, destroying one eye and blinding him in the other. Two years in army hospitals and a series of operations restored partial vision in one eye.

For the next forty-four days, Bob Slaughter endured the life of a combat infantryman. Until his outfit was relieved temporarily, he could not change his clothes, which deteriorated into a tattered, foul remnant of the impregnated uniform he had donned just before the start of Overlord.

Says Slaughter, "Isigny was the division objective, and we suspected we were between the 1st and 2nd Battalion sectors. Our puny group hooked up with others who were separated, and we organized a previously leaderless, rabble force that had served merely as psychological support. Any friendly rifle or machine gun was welcome. I felt extremely vulnerable and lonely during the early hours after the invasion."

Disheartened and uncertain though they were, the patchwork bands of GIs inched doggedly toward designated objectives. Those innocent of combat received instant educations if they survived.

"Snipers, machine guns, and 88s interrupted movement on the road into Vierville," remembers Slaughter. "The column took cover and waited for an officer or noncom with the initiative to collar a few riflemen and clear the obstacle. While lying in the warm sunshine, the rabble smoked K-ration cigarettes or rested. A young rifleman accidentally pulled the pin on one of the many hand grenades hanging on his belt. The explosion and shrapnel blew most of his buttocks away. He screamed in agony until an aidman gave him a shot of morphine. Word spread that heat from the sun had ignited the grenade. Many began discarding their precious grenades.

"As we entered the tiny resort village of Vierville-sur-Mer, less than a mile from the beach, sniper and burp gun fire came from the bombed-out Norman chateaus. We were trained to make every shot count, and German targets were hard to find. Smokeless powder was a tremendous advantage. Gunsmoke billowing from our weapons like cumulus clouds helped Jerry spot our positions. We fired in the direction from which sound came, but camouflage and smokeless powder made it difficult to locate the enemy.

"Following an exchange of fire, three or four enemy soldiers appeared waving white flags, hands over heads, yelling, '*Kamerad!*' With them appeared a young French female civilian whom we suspected of collaboration. Thinking she was one of the deadly snipers, we didn't treat her or the other prisoners gently. I doubt they made it back to the beach alive.

"After the Omaha Beach massacre, I vowed never to take a German prisoner. During the fight for the beachhead, hatred intensified." Slaughter says he was steadfast in this resolve until a few weeks later when he encountered a young German paratrooper. "His right trouser leg was bloody and torn, the limb almost severed by shrapnel. Remembering my pledge taken back at the beach, my first reaction was to put him out of his misery. I believe he sensed what I was thinking. He said, tearfully, '*Bitte* [please].' He was an impressive-looking soldier and I just couldn't do it. Instead, I made sure he was unarmed and then I cut away his trouser leg and applied a pressure tourniquet. I gave him a shot of morphine and a drink from my canteen and then lit an American Lucky Strike cigarette for him.

"As I departed, he smiled weakly, and said in guttural English, 'Danke very much, may Gott bless you. Gut luck.' That changed my mind. I still hated the German soldier but I couldn't kill one at close range if his hands were over his head."

A few weeks after his torment at Omaha Beach, Slaughter escaped serious injury as a sniper's bullet pierced the bill of his steel helmet and inflicted a bloody graze. He also recovered after a mortar burst drove a jagged piece of metal into his back. Both injuries fell short of the million-dollar variety, and he was sent back to duty. Slaughter continued with the 116th. Its once familiar faces were severely thinned out by enemy and even self-inflicted fire. He had just been rotated to the States when the regiment finally reached the Elbe River to meet Soviet forces advancing from the east.

Fellow Virginian Felix Branham, a squad leader with Company K of the 116th, also hiked through Vierville toward the German strong-point at Grandcamp on D plus two. "As we began the attack, we found some 2nd and 5th Rangers digging in. They told us they had been stopped cold by a heavy concentration of German fire and two of their support tanks knocked out. There was a company of German infantry in an elaborate communications trench from which they directed heavy machine gun fire.

"Several attempts by our company and some Rangers failed to neutralize this fire. Sgt. Frank D. Peregory stood up and began firing his rifle from his hip as he moved in the direction from whence the enemy fire came. Upon reaching the trench, he leaped in while firing his weapon, with fixed bayonet. He paused only to reload and throw hand grenades. Frank soon emerged from the trench with three German prisoners. [Peregory had killed eight of the enemy in the course of his charge.] After handing them over to someone else, he leaped back into the trench. After what seemed an eternity, he again emerged from the trench, this time with thirty-two German prisoners.

"For his action at Grandcamp, Frank won a Congressional Medal of Honor. But six days later near Couvains, while attempting to capture a German machine gun nest single-handedly, he lost his life.

"It was in front of Couvains that I was wounded. I should have known better, but we kept moving from hedgerow to firefight to the next hedgerow. Then it became dig in, set a defense as night fell, next morning send out patrols, and in two or three hours the shells from mortars would come in while German soldiers were nowhere to be found. The ground was awful hard, and as soon as we dug in, we'd have to leave again. I decided the next time we stopped, I wasn't going to dig in.

"Three of us were on watch—two guys would sleep while the other stood guard. We figured if we heard incoming mail, we'd just duck down against the hedgerow. I had just seen a medic not far away, and I asked him about a friend of mine from his company. He told me the guy had been killed that morning.

"I was starting to feel bad and then everything went black for about ten minutes. You never hear the shell that hits you. A German 88 had landed. My face was streaming blood; my left leg had been torn and something was protruding from my thigh, a piece of shrapnel. I looked over and the other fellow was lying on the ground, his face quiet, his leg lying up over his shoulder. The third man was sprawled on the ground, covered with blood; I could see his lungs or heart on the ground.

"The medic came up and started to patch me up. He used a morphine syrette above my leg wound and wiped my face clear. There were small pieces of shrapnel in my ear and jaw. I told him, 'Go help the other guys, some are worse off than I am.' But he stayed with me until he stopped the bleeding, using a tourniquet above the leg wound.

"I was carried back to the platoon CP, then a jeep picked me up and a couple of others for a ride to the beach. As they got ready to fly me to England, Maj. Howie, who became the 3rd Battalion CO, said to me while I was on a stretcher, 'You're going home, son.' I answered, 'I'm going back to France.' 'No,' he insisted. 'The war is over for you.' I said, 'You're nuts, sir.' He looked at me and winked.

"I did get back to France, in time for the attack on Saint-Lô. Maj. Howie was killed there." Division CO Gen. Gerhardt ordered Howie's flag-draped body to be displayed on a pile of rubble that once served as a wall for the Sainte-Croix Church in Saint-Lô. Branham himself fought with the 29th until February 19, 1945, when rotation leave returned him to Virginia for thirty days. This time he did not return to the 29th.

Antitank squad leader Bill Lewis with Headquarters Company of the 116th's 1st Battalion watched a gigantic air raid by eighteen hundred Allied bombers that kicked off the offensive preceding the Normandy breakthrough. "We got up on the hedgerows and watched it. The first group dropped a smoke marker. They bombed on that, but it drifted back towards our lines. Later we found they killed Gen. Leslie McNair and they bombed our guys too." A total of 111 Americans were killed and another 490 wounded by mistake.

By September, Lewis had become part of the siege around Brest, the Brittany port city. "The thing I remember is the surrender, how many prisoners we had. [About 38,000 Germans were bagged.] You wouldn't think a body of men that size would surrender, but they had a hopeless situation. They all said they wanted to go to America. We had a sergeant who spoke German and told them all, no, we have a deal to give them to the Russians.

"We lay around the port for three or four days. Everything was blown to hell. What we didn't do, the Germans did. We sat around drinking pink champagne out of our canteen cups. We found a bunch of German 25mm pistols, such small things that everybody thought they were harmless. One of the guys was fooling with one and it went off. The bullet hit Balinski right in the heart, and old Jim turned blue in the face and said, 'You son of a bitch, you killed me.' He was a fine man and we hated to lose him."

Lewis was with the 116th as it formed part of the ring around Aachen. But while on the line he contracted pneumonia, and he sifted through a series of medical facilities as the result of a subsequent tonsillectomy and then chronic colitis. He served out the remainder of the war in a noncombatant role.

Frank Wawrynovic, having bolted across the exposed beach "like a deer when hunters are shooting at it," lasted less than two weeks in France. "When any special scouting mission was necessary, with my Ranger training, I either volunteered or 'was volunteered.' After many close calls, I was beginning to feel like the legendary buck back home who time after time, season after season, escapes the hunters' bullets. But I knew the deer was not eternal, nor was I.

"The morning of D plus twelve arrived and I was still alive. I was dirty and very tired. My trousers had been torn to shreds a week before. I had dived for the ground when the Germans opened up, and I had left part of my trousers and some skin on tightly stretched barbed wire that I didn't know was there. After much crawling on the ground in the days that followed, there wasn't much left to my pants. Since it was warm, I didn't consider taking a replacement pair from a dead man.

"Things were looking better this day. Our cooks finally caught up with us, and from one I got a new pair of trousers. We got our first cooked meal since before we left England and enough water to shave and wash ourselves. As we relaxed and cleaned our weapons, I felt very lonely. Most of my friends were gone by now, either killed or wounded. I realized it was only a matter of time until I, too, would be either killed or wounded."

The following day, the members of Wawrynovic's C Company of the 115th cautiously advanced toward an unseen enemy who they knew would sooner or later challenge them. "There were only two alternatives, one to be killed, the other to be wounded," says Wawrynovic.

As he approached one of the ubiquitous hedgerows, a loud noise started Wawrynovic. He dove for the shield of the earth-and-shrub breastworks. A machine gun spattered the ground less than a foot from his trembling body. A large body of enemy troops exchanged heavy fire with the C Company GIs. From his highly vulnerable position, Wawrynovic realized his only chance of survival lay in the darkness, still many hours off.

"From one of the patches of weeds and grass in the apple orchard nearby came a loud cry, so loud even the Germans had to hear it. 'Help! I'm bleeding to death!' In the movies I would have rushed to him. But this was the real thing. I knew the slightest movement would bring a volley of German bullets. After he called out again, I cautioned, in a low tone that only he could hear, to wait until dark for our only chance.

"Everything was quiet for a while. Then he or someone with him panicked and got up and ran towards me. As he reached the open alley between the last row of apple trees and my hedgerow, the Germans opened fire. His limp and probably dead body fell. My cover was broken and I had to act fast. Even as his body toppled, I rose to get over the hedgerow to my right.

"Fast as I was, the German bullets were faster. I felt their shock and pain. Fortunately, my momentum carried me over the shoulder-high hedgerow and into a ditch beside the road. I lay motionless, facedown, thinking that when the Germans saw me they might think me dead.

"I realized I couldn't wait for darkness now, because I might get weak from loss of blood and pass out. I remembered the advice of an old-time deer hunter back home. 'If you hit a deer and he doesn't go down, don't get too anxious and start tracking him, for he will just keep moving ahead of you. Give him some time and he will lie down and get so stiff and sore that you'll be able to walk right up on him.'

"Not wanting to get 'stiff and sore,' I understood the danger I was in. I had to get back to my company. I had lost my helmet and rifle. My feet were useless to me. My left shoe was full of blood and blood was running out the top of it, seeping through the bullet holes on each side of my ankle. I thought my lower right leg was broken; there was a deep wound across it. I didn't think I was hurt internally by a wound on the front of my stomach. I padded it as best I could with my first-aid kit, my handkerchief, and the lower part of my shirt, pulling up my trousers and belt. I didn't realize it, but the wall of my stomach had been cut all the way through.

"I removed my pack and cartridge belt as excess weight and started a slow, long, painful crawl back through the dusty ditch. By grasping the clumps of grass with my hands or digging my fingers into the ground, I slid along, inches at a time, my progress almost imperceptible. After many hours of crawling, daylight began to fade. I was getting very weak from exhaustion and loss of blood. I reached a wounded soldier lying in the ditch. He begged me to stay, but I felt I had to move on in case the Germans should counterattack. I remembered one night as we passed a burned-out German tank. Lying motionless on the road was a German soldier. We thought he was dead, like so many others. But just in back of me, one of our men saw him move and stuck him with his bayonet. Recalling his awful scream, I drew on strength I didn't know I had and continued on.

"When I reached a place where friendly forces were just yards away and with no shooting for several hours, I began to feel secure and got careless. I thought I had better let my presence be known, so I called for a medic. Very shortly two arrived, the Red Cross bands on their upper arms still very visible in the fading daylight.

"They stopped by me and the other wounded soldier, and both went back, saying they'd send up litter bearers. In a few minutes they returned, accompanied by Capt. Carter, our battalion medical officer, also identified by his Red Cross armbands. He said it was too dangerous to bring in litter bearers.

"They checked my wounds and went to the other soldier. I had my head turned, watching them, when from the woods across the road came a long burst from an automatic weapon and all three medics fell to the ground. The Germans had killed all three, who were protected under the international law of war. These men had answered my call for help and died on account of me. To them I owe a debt I can never repay.

"I was so weak, I knew I couldn't last much longer. But with possible help so close, I could not give up. I pulled myself up to where I was just across the hedgerow from GI voices. I saw a hole through the bottom of the hedgerow, quietly called out, and they pulled me through. It was dark now, and I continued to move back, inches at a time. Finally, some unfamiliar American faces came up. As they gathered around me, I felt they were going to help me and I lost consciousness. When I awakened next, I was riding in an ambulance and it was morning."

In a tent field hospital, medical personnel dressed Wawrynovic's wounds and then dispatched him by plane to England. He would spend the next nineteen months in military hospitals and undergo a series of operations until his discharge with a permanent disability.

Side by side with the hard-hit members of the 29th endured the foot soldiers of the 1st Division. Two days after arriving on Omaha Beach, platoon leader Dick Conley with Company E of the division's 18th Regiment was in the vicinity of Colleville-sur-Mer, one of those seaside hamlets that by plan should have been taken in the first few hours.

"There was a machine gun tying us down. As I moved forward to locate it, the German gunner saw me first and I got hit with a bullet in my left hand. My platoon runner sprinkled sulfa powder on the wound and bandaged me.

"I stayed put for about an hour. Nobody was doing anything, including all the other platoon leaders who were combat-experienced. I figured it was time for me to go. I turned over my compass, carbine, and maps to my platoon sergeant and told him he was in charge. I reported to the company commander. He gave me two enlisted men with identical wounds, bullets in their shoulders, to escort back to the battalion aid station. One man thought nothing of his injury, but the other one, with the same wound, was almost dead from shock. He could hardly talk or walk; the differences between the two seemed mental attitude."

After the preliminary medical treatment, Conley traveled to a field hospital and followed that with six months in England as doctors sought to repair his damage. "I got back in December '44, during the Battle of the Bulge. I was assigned to G Company. I visited E to see who was left from my original platoon. There were only three of them, two of whom had been wounded. The others were either killed or still recovering from wounds.

"Before the Normandy invasion it was stressed that we were platoon leaders who would lead our men. I had lasted three days in that capacity and was out for six months. Now, when I came back, I was instructed that I was to command rather than lead. They had just lost too many 'platoon leaders.'

"I lasted another thirty-five days. Towards the end of January and beginning of February, we were attacking, taking one little town after another. Then we pushed into the Siegfried Line [a series of German fortifications along the border of Belgium, Luxembourg, and France]. There must have been seven machine guns all firing at me, personally, I felt. A mortar shell landed fifteen feet behind me. Several men were killed and I was wounded again."

Conley earned a Silver Star for the valor exhibited June 8 when he was struck in the hand. His enlisted men had taken it upon themselves to write him up, which has always been a great source of satisfaction to him. Conley's World War II decorations also included a Bronze Star, the Bronze Arrowhead, signifying participation in an invasion, a pair of Purple Hearts, three battle stars for campaigns, and the Combat Infantryman's Badge. And when he came home, he decided he liked the military life and chose to make it his career.

Lawrence Zieckler describes his first week in France as "just defensive, trying to teach replacements how to handle their weapons, the mortars and machine guns. Other companies moved up while we got ourselves organized and up to strength again." Zieckler served through the 1st Division's long saga from North Africa, Sicily, Normandy, and the Ardennes and into Germany with the only mark on him that grazing bullet as he left the landing craft.

John Bistrica with C Company of the 16th Regiment had awakened on D plus one to find enemy soldiers only yards away, who surrendered quickly. "As we marched on, the French came out with wine, cognac, brandy, milk. We emptied our canteens and put in whatever they gave us. We were hugged and kissed as we went through the small villages.

"Mostly, we fought snipers; they did not bring up tanks. The mortars and machine guns from the German 352nd Division, whom we were not informed about, were bad. The hedgerows became bigger and thicker and we encountered more and more resistance. Finally, we stopped at Caumont and held. We dug holes in the sides of the hedgerows which were large enough for four men. We patrolled and swapped with the other platoon.

"A lieutenant, who was a ninety-day wonder, called me to his CP, gave me a sniper's rifle, told me to find a tree and start picking off Germans. That officer carried a tommy gun with a sawed-off stock and a drum, like a gangster, but you never could find him up front; he was always back.

"As I started to leave, Captain Briggs, our CO, saw me. 'Bistrica, where are you going with that weapon?' I told him. Briggs said, 'Give me that rifle and go back to the lieutenant to get your M-1 and tell him I want to see him.'

"While we were in front of Caumont, the Germans started to shell us. We all hurried back, but when I got to my hole, I couldn't get in. 'Get out of my hole and find your own,' I yelled.

"A voice replied, 'It's okay, Bistrica. There's room enough for both of us.' It was Captain Briggs, who'd just started up and been caught in the open as the shelling began."

Bistrica remained with the Big Red One through its extended combat run, finally returning to Youngstown in December 1945, six months after V-E Day.

Dick Biehl, the B Company, 26th Regiment, scout, one of the later arrivals on June 6, did not lose any close acquaintances at Omaha Beach. But in the days that followed, friends fell frequently. He recalls a kaleidoscopic vision of the aftermath of June 6. "Plenty of patrol activity . . . night guard duty even for noncoms . . . trying to stay clean, trying to rest when possible, eating when possible, dashing off a quick V-mail in pencil to Mom, assuring her and the family I was okay. . . .

"Sitting in a foxhole watching a flight of B-17s heading towards targets, suddenly one falls behind, loses altitude, and you begin to count the opening parachutes, hoping there will be ten. . . . Feeling very thankful that one of the guys just looking upwards into a tree observed a German and without hesitation fired his rifle from the hip—Hollywood-fashion—killing the German, who no doubt was waiting for the last GI in the platoon to pass by and would then open fire from the rear. . . . Having a British captain and sergeant pull up in a jeep and halt where you and a couple of GIs are trying to observe activity across a field. It happened to be teatime and they asked if we had any sugar without any concern for revealing our position. . . .

"The Saint-Lô bombing in July, while we were approximately a mile or so to the rear and our half-tracks were actually rising off the ground as the earth shuddered from the impact of the bombs. . . . On the move constantly, pushing inland, small villages with buildings burning. . . . French people greeting us, giving cider to those who would drink it. . . . No shaving . . . quick bathing out of the helmet . . . checking the M-1 each day . . . sometimes a hot meal before nightfall. . . . When the rains came, trying to remain as dry as possible. . . . Watching Caen in the British-Canadian sector on fire as we sat astride the high ground outside Caumont."

He was also among the very few in the 1st Division to continue without ever becoming a casualty. The only injury was a finger cut while hurriedly abandoning a crude ladder as German 88s probed his area.

George Zenie, the antitank company platoon sergeant with the 18th Regiment, was at Caumont about a week after his outfit brought in its 57mm guns on D-Day. "We were glad to see that they could penetrate a tank's armor, and we disabled at least one tank that day. We hit a few others, but they retreated behind the hedgerows so we never knew how badly they were damaged.

"This was the first time I used my .45 against the enemy," says Zenie. "I was caught without my M-1 while going from one gun to another. Around a hedgerow came three Germans. I dropped and fired a clip from my pistol at them. I know I hit at least one, because they dragged him with them when they scooted back behind the hedgerows.

"I was wounded for the first time on the outskirts of Aachen in October. Enemy artillery shelled our positions and shrapnel hit my left hand. I remained until the barrage ended, then was evacuated for treatment. Several months later, I rejoined my company, January 1, 1945, during the Battle of the Bulge. At Harz Mountain, Lt. Day, the tank platoon officer, and I went on a reconnaissance mission to find the positions of our tanks and antitank guns. We reached a valley, supposedly secure, turned down a street, and struck an antitank mine. Lt. Day was killed instantly. I was thrown from the jeep and blacked out. I awoke in a field hospital. My hearing was gone, and my body had cuts all over, and I had a concussion. But after two weeks' treatment, I returned to the company.

"On February 1, 1945, the regimental commander called me to headquarters, discharged me as an enlisted man, and pinned on my gold bars. With a battlefield commission, I was assigned to the antitank platoon working with the 2nd Battalion. It was no problem, since some of the men already knew me." By the time hostilities ceased, Zenie wore the silver bars of a first lieutenant and was executive officer of his company.

Tom McCann, as a member of an I&R platoon with the 18th Infantry Regiment, also halted at Caumont. "The division had penetrated further inland than any other one, and we stayed in the Caumont area for a week or more while surrounded on three sides by the enemy. In this static position we ran patrols both day and night into the enemy lines. You would be on one side of the hedgerow and the Germans on the other, going in an opposite direction. We had observation posts in houses, churches, on the edges of clearings, anyplace where we could see what the enemy was doing. A static position like the one in Caumont was hard on the soldiers. It's much better to be on the move. We lost one fellow to a nervous breakdown."

Struck down by a mortar burst a short distance inland on D-Day, Fred Erben, a rifle squad leader for C Company of the 16th Regiment, was patched up in England and then returned to the war as the 1st Division besieged Saint-Lô. "Eight of the twelve guys with me on my squad on D-Day were left; two had been killed and two had been wounded."

Erben continued with C Company as it pierced the Siegfried Line in the Hürtgen Forest. "We could hear the Germans directing fire on us from a pillbox. A tree burst sprayed us with shrapnel. There were three of us, one killed. I got hit in the leg and the other fellow in the arm. When I came out of the hospital, they sent me to a replacement depot to train some of the new kids. I was elated to be out of combat, but I missed a lot of the guys, some of whom never came back. When they put in the point system for discharge, I had 197." The point-system formula counted months in service, time overseas, combat campaigns, and awards, with 85 points enough to go home. Apart from his four years and three months in the army, Erben had collected a Silver Star, a Bronze Star with two clusters, and three Purple Hearts and had survived eight European Theater campaigns. He even had a Good Conduct Medal, although he had been busted twice for minor infractions.

"It was hedgerow to hedgerow at first," says Eddie Ireland, who drove a Sherman with the 745th Tank Battalion. The combination of tanks and bulldozers engineered the start of the great breakout through the hedgerows of Normandy, climaxed by the capture of Saint-Lô, according to Ireland. "The bulldozers buried a lot of Germans under the hedgerows, made openings for the tanks, and dug positions for them. When we got to the tiger teeth that would knock the tracks off the tanks, the dozers pushed dirt on top of the tiger teeth, making a road for us.

"The infantry walked alongside of us until we really got moving, and then they rode with us. They were great, acting as our eyes, going ahead until they found something."

Ireland and his tank were engaged in the battle to capture the first German city to fall to the Allies, Aachen, when artillery disabled his Sherman. "Commander Archie Ross said, 'Abandon tank!' I dropped through the bottom and ran to the woods. Archie said, 'We forgot about the radio.' I volunteered, 'I'll get it.' I went back and busted up the radio.

"I looked through the periscope and saw two German tanks and a half-track. I let 'em have it with the 75mm cannon and the .30 caliber machine gun, knocking out one tank and a half-track. I saw a German running away, and I let him have it with a round from the 75.

"Gen. Huebner [CO of the 1st Division] called us in, and in recognition of my efforts I got a Silver Star. I collected two others but I don't remember the circumstances."

However, in March of '45 an 88 set Ireland's tank aflame. "I was on fire. I dragged myself out, fell into a watery ditch that put the fire out. While they carried me off on a litter, I could feel the blood running out under me. I spent twenty-eight months in hospital, lost one leg, but the other was saved after a series of skin grafts."

The 741st Tank Battalion with John Barner, its numbers badly depleted by the sinkings on the way to Omaha Beach, mustered a bare two of its five companies for the post–D-Day assault. "We moved slowly," says Barner, "and at a small town on the way to Saint-Lô stopped for a good night's sleep and cleaned and serviced the tank. The next day we advanced to support the infantry and my tank was hit. I was sent back to Omaha Beach, en route to an army hospital in Cardiff, Wales, for two months of healing."

While Barner lay *hors de combat*, the 741st passed into the control of a number of organizations, and with the 28th Infantry Division ground through the streets of Paris in the victory parade when that city became liberated. Barner rejoined his outfit as it dug into the Siegfried Line. The 741st eventually crossed the Rhine and halted only after it entered Czechoslovakia, by which time Barner owned a Silver Star and a Bronze Star along with his Purple Heart.

The 1st Division's combat engineers accompanied the infantrymen in the liberation of France. Leo Des Champs, like John Bistrica and George Zenie, participated in the assault at Caumont. "Once there, we put out fires in burning buildings and ripped down brick walls to allow the tanks a clear field of fire.

"The journey across France during August was fast, sometimes covering as much as one hundred miles a day. Our combat team breached the Siegfried Line near Aachen about the middle of September. During the siege of Aachen, we placed antitank mines against one wall and blew it into the next building. The houses abutted one another, and we tore down an entire street so the infantry could secure it without exposing themselves.

"Toward the end of April we were facing young children and old men instead of seasoned troops. Some of the kids looked as though you wanted to take the weapons away and kick their butts and send them home." Except for a brief bout with gastric enteritis that hospitalized him, Des Champs remained with his unit long enough to perform occupation duty until his point score dispatched him to the United States. He brought with him a Bronze Star with V device for volunteering to carry messages despite heavy enemy fire after an artillery burst destroyed his radio.

During the eleven months of war that followed those first terrible moments on Omaha Beach, there obviously had been little surcease. The casualty figures for the 1st and 29th Divisions mounted into the tens of thousands. A steady flow of replacements refilled the ranks several times over; as many as forty thousand men put on the Big Red One.

# CHAPTER 23

# BEYOND UTAH

STIFF OPPOSITION RACKED troops from the 4th Infantry Division a few miles beyond the beach. The figures of KIA, WIA, and MIA rocketed upward, and by the end of June the Ivy Infantry had counted 5,452 casualties. Other outfits in the VII Corps, including the 82nd and 101st Airborne, as well as three more infantry divisions landed by sea, also sustained horrific losses.

"We got off the beach well enough," says Charles Mastro, from the intelligence section of the 2nd Battalion in the 22nd Infantry Regiment, "but then we hit a wall." The entire offensive that included the 4th Division shuddered to a halt as an entrenched enemy, backed by the dreaded 88s and Tiger tanks, fiercely defended its turf. Unhappy with progress, the top brass sacked commanders. "We had one battalion commander," says Mastro, "who was not a leader. Omar Bradley, watching our progress from a hilltop, relieved him on the spot."

Col. Hervey Tribolet, the regimental CO whom Mastro describes as a leader who talked to the lowest privates like a father, was relieved of his command on June 10, although most of his officers and enlisted men retained confidence in him.

The bodies piled up rapidly with no respect for rank. On

D plus five, Malcolm Williams as the outfit's runner received the onerous duty of carrying to regimental HQ the news that his battalion commander, Lt. Col. Montabano, had been killed. When Williams reached the CP he was shaky, having been only a few feet from Montabano when he was struck down and aware that the regiment's leader, Col. Russell P. "Red" Reeder, was a victim of a wound that would cost him a leg.

"It was a helluva trip. I was fired on by a machine gun, shelled by artillery, and traveled down a sunken road with Germans all over the place. I expected one to shoot me at any moment. Major Burk, whom I knew from stateside, said I should report to Gen. Roosevelt.

"The general had come from division HQ to help choose someone to replace Col. Reeder. He invited me in to have coffee to calm me down. He asked me where I was from, what was going on up there. I told him about Col. Montabano getting hit by a mortar shell that killed three at once and wounded five others. When he asked who was left in charge, I told him the exec, Maj. [Richard] O'Malley.

"Roosevelt said, 'You go back and tell all the men that they have the best man in the whole army. I would trust that black Irishman anywhere.'

"Maj. O'Malley led us until the first week of July, when he was killed by a sniper's bullet. In eleven months of combat we had eleven different battalion commanders. Of the 886 from my battalion that landed on D-Day, twenty-one of us came home together at the end of the war."

Much of battalion surgeon Morgan Adair's diary is a book of the dead:

"June 7: I set up an aid station in a field where two gliders have crashed and there are casualties. Meanwhile two more gliders of the 82nd crash within fifty yards of where I am and ten men are killed, as many are wounded. After taking care of this mess, I push on up the road, where there are a number of casualties including the colonel's runner, Tom Sullivan, who has been killed. . . . The woods are full of snipers, and a man next to me in the ditch gets shot.

"June 8: Jerry shells our area during midmorning and sets fire to our ammunition trucks and several vehicles.

Fortunately, only several men are hurt. I explore a nearby road and there are more than two dozen dead Germans. I also run across Lt. Vill, killed by rifle fire.

"June 9: . . . the battalion attacks about 6:00 P.M. and E Company suffers heavy casualties, including the death of Lt. Wilder. We work far into the night, on our hands and knees under blankets, with flashlights. It's grueling, tiresome, and the boys are really in bad shape. . . . This has been one of our worst days yet.

"June 11–20: We hold a defensive position west of Montebourg. We receive our first replacement. Lt. Wilson gets killed and Lt. Couch is wounded. Capt. Haley is hit. We shuffle places in the line with the 1st Battalion and then the 3rd. Capt. Watkins is wounded. I write my first letters home and receive my first mail. We get better rations, a chance to drink cider and clean up.

"We make a night attack [June 19] commencing at 3:00 A.M. It's rough going at first but we drive the Jerries out of a dug-in place. . . . Twice we go through an artillery barrage. Lt. Col. Steiner is killed, but our casualties are not too excessive.

"June 22: I am awakened at dawn because a German patrol sneaked in the CP and shot and killed Lt. Marquard. Our boys kill five of the Krauts and wound the officer. They reoccupy the crossroad behind us, and cut us off. We are having casualties, and I send some back in an ambulance, which is machine-gunned. I also send a jeep back, which is stopped and then permitted to go ahead after a Kraut casualty is removed. I accumulate about twenty casualties during the day which I cannot evacuate. We are shelled thrice, and one actually hits the top of the aid station. Shell fragments destroy several units of plasma.

"June 23: Our battalion attacks this afternoon, and E Company sustains about thirty-five wounded and fifteen dead. . . .

"June 25: Chaplain Ellenberg holds a service this morning and I enjoy it. The Lord has been kind."

Returning to the front, Adair passed through the site of one of the earlier battles, a meadow laced with drainage ditches. "There are at least forty or fifty dead soldiers partially buried in the muck and slime and a few dead Jerries in the rise near the swamp. This was the most depressing thing I saw in all of France."

The VII Corps sought to wipe out the remaining but still potent German forces from the Cherbourg Peninsula, the line running from Saint-Lô through Périers to the Channel. On July 26, Adair, somewhat to the rear of the action, chose a house suitable for an aid station. He dispatched his sergeant to bring up the rest of the medical section and battalion surgeon Sam Victor. His diary reports:

"About 10:00 P.M., I sit on a wall next to the road, reading my map and watching the vehicles go by. Suddenly, something slams behind me about ten feet away and blows me onto my feet. Then my right leg gives way, and it is bleeding. I have to lie in the ditch. I expect more shells but none come. When the smoke and dust clear a bit, I get my breath. I see a couple of men and shout for an aidman. They are too befuddled to help. But it doesn't matter, because Vic and the boys come running up.

"By this time, I'm hurting like hell, until I get the morphine syrette. The boys bandage up my thigh (right), left buttock, and back and make out the EMT tag. I'm put on a litter and start back on a jeep to the collecting station. We're slow going back because we are meeting 3rd Armored Division vehicles bumper to bumper. Some fresh replacements with their clean uniforms are going forward. One asks the other if I am a German, and I rise up and say, 'Hell, no! I'm an American.'

"I get to Company A station and Capt. Smith and Capt. Scuka see me. I get sulfadiazine and am then loaded into an ambulance and taken to clearing station. There Capt. Miller anesthetizes all my wounds and pulls the clothing out of them. He also gives me tetanus toxoid, clean dressing, and an initial dose of penicillin.

"June 27: . . . After an interminable ride I get to the 44th Evac. Hosp. about 2:00 A.M. At dawn they X-ray me and I lie around all morning, quite uncomfortable on a litter. In early afternoon, they take me to the OR and give me pentathol. I go to sleep easily and when I wake up, I feel good—almost inebriated.

"The surgeon who operated tells me no fragments were removed, only debridement done. I have five wounds on my back. He dissected into one as far as my right subclavian artery, then gave up the search for the fragment. I have a wound on my left buttock, and the one in my right thigh is fairly large. . . . None of the fragments were removed, as it would have involved extensive exploration into the remaining muscle. All the wounds are packed with petrolatum gauze. I am most uncomfortable. . . . Later they bundle me into an ambulance and off I go. I stay all night at an airstrip, and it's a tough night."

Flown to England with other casualties, Adair underwent months of work repairing the damage before his return to the United States for additional treatment. In December 1945, he received his honorable discharge.

Reed Jensen, the litter bearer, saw the ubiquitous Gen. Ted Roosevelt about a week after D-Day. "He was wearing a stocking hat and came riding up with a driver. He saw us packing our gas masks and said, 'I thought you had better sense than that. If I were you, I'd throw the gas masks away. We have to tell you to wear them, but the Germans would have to have air superiority to use chemicals and we'd wipe them off the face of the earth, so get rid of the gas masks." A month later, Roosevelt, fifty-six, quietly succumbed to a coronary attack while in his tent.

In September, as the 4th Division bumped against the Siegfried Line, Jensen was seriously wounded and his companion in a foxhole was killed.

Bob Meyer, with the 22nd Infantry, swung to the north as the post–D-Day offensive strove to roll up enemy forces toward the tip of the peninsula. The port of Cherbourg became more desirable now that the destruction of the artificial harbor at Omaha Beach had severely handicapped shipments of supplies and replacement troops.

"The Germans sent a bicycle battalion to hinder our advance," Meyer remembers. "However, their G-2 [intelligence section] apparently had no idea where we were. In their ignorance they were moving along in column with no caution, and they ran right into an ambush. Four tanks lay in wait. As the bicycle troops pedaled into this area, two tanks in the roadway and one on each side in a ditch beside the hedgerows moved against them, firing all forward machine guns as well as their 75mm cannons.

"It was a complete slaughter. They were gunned down and then ground up beneath the tank treads. We had all seen dead before, but none of us had seen what tanks were capable of. We felt sick as we walked through that carnage. It was hard not to feel sorry for them, even if they were German SS troops."

As the "Double Deuce" trudged forward, Meyer's closest friend fell victim to a malfunction of his own weapon that put a bullet through his own ankle. "After he left it was more difficult for me. We'd done everything together and now he wasn't there. My motivation was very dependent upon esprit de corps. As our numbers dwindled, that feeling faded and each casualty was a personal loss. I had mixed emotions. He was gone, but I also felt a sense of relief. I knew where he was and his wound was not life-threatening. Had he been killed, I would have probably gone completely mad before I did."

Subsequently, a German machine gun ripped away Meyer's pant leg before he turned his BAR on the nest; he survived a thrust by seven German Tiger tanks, constant shelling by the enemy, and occasionally the menace of friendly fire. Combat fatigue struck Meyer in the autumn.

"The 8th Regiment had moved up, and we were relieved. When we started the attack, we had 185 men in our company, and when we pulled back, we took twenty-seven men off the line. When we got to the rear, it was dark, and some guides led us to foxholes that were already dug. Two of us were taken to an elongated one that would accommodate both of us.

"Everything seemed great, but just as we were thinking all was serene, we were almost blasted out of our hole. We were located right under the muzzle of one of our artillery pieces. They fired missions all night, and by morning I was a crying, babbling idiot.

"At the hospital, the first thing I had to do was take off my clothes. I had changed socks and gotten a new pair of pants when the leg of my old ones had been shot off, but otherwise they were the same ones I had worn since June 6. The smell was terrible. After a shower they weighed me. I was down to 105 pounds; I had been 165 when we made the invasion.

"The treatment then for combat fatigue was a drug-induced deep sleep for seventy-two hours. They were supposed to administer twelve grains [of morphine] in the morning and twelve in the evening to keep the patient in a deep sleep. But someone misread the instructions and they also gave us another twelve grains at noon. When the seventy-two hours ended, we didn't wake up the way we were supposed to.

"The idea of total rest was supposed to restore your outlook as well as your body. While it went a long way toward the recovery of the fatigued body, the psychological problems remained. I had still lost all my friends; I had still experienced all that blood and gore; I had still been blasted by artillery, theirs and ours.

"I was only slightly improved but according to theory well enough to be sent back to my outfit. I vaguely remember being brought to the company kitchen to wait until I could go up front. The kitchen was well behind the lines, and they gave me a hole that was more like a den. It had a cover, and I recall huddling in there for what may have been several days. I don't remember coming out, even to eat. One of the cooks may have brought me something to eat. I had been brought up without a weapon and one of the cooks lent me a pistol, German I believe, and I had no idea how to fire the thing. I overheard the mess sergeant tell the cook to get the pistol away from me because he thought I was crazy. I gave it up without argument.

"A plane came over real low one day, and I don't remember whether it fired or not but I slipped into total oblivion. I have no idea of how far I strayed from the kitchen group, but I was wandering around in the roadway when a jeep driven by a guy from my company came by. He took me back to a hospital which was an 'exhaustion center.'

"They ran me through the sleep therapy again, but they were beginning to suspect there was much more to it [combat fatigue] than originally suspected. I and many others were sent out to provisional companies, where it was thought work would restore our sense of well-being better than drugs. We did have resort to amobarbital, and they sort of left it to the individual to decide when things were catching up to him and he needed the drug. I took it only a couple of times, just to sleep through the night."

The labor therapy failed to cure what ailed Meyer. He passed through a series of hospitals before finally being shipped back to the States. The army handed him his honorable discharge in March 1945 along with a 50 percent disability pension.

With the 8th Infantry Regiment, machine gunner Harper Coleman spent the first twenty-one days after the second wave deposited him on Utah Beach hiking, creeping, crawling—"one hedgerow to the next on your stomach"—and attacking toward Cherbourg. "We must have been a dirty, smelly bunch, since we didn't have much time to wash or clean. We did get clean clothing from time to time and wash in our helmets occasionally. We had very little hot food until we reached Cherbourg."

A three-or-four-day respite brought shower tents, new, clean uniforms, and kitchens with hot meals. Trucks bore Coleman and his colleagues to the area near Saint-Lô. "The Germans fought for every inch of ground. Everything was destroyed, all buildings, bridges, and equipment of all kinds. The roads and fields looked like a junkyard, dead animals in all of the fields. Some civilians had not been able to escape. Most days there would be some trying to make their way to a rear area. Occasionally we would find dead ones in buildings.

"During this period, we lost quite a few people. How anyone made it I still do not know. I saw one battalion commander killed by a sniper as he stood near our position. A member of our squad was killed by a sniper, and a bullet came across my shoulder, cutting the top of my hand. We came across a column of German troops caught in an artillery barrage and still on the road when our tanks went through. They did not have time or take time to move any out of the way. It was not a pretty sight, but I don't think we gave it much thought.

"Sometime in this period, I saw a wounded German begging for water. One of our lieutenants seemed to have lost all control. He said, 'Water, hell!' and shot him in the head.

"The breakthrough started July 25th with what is sometimes called the greatest air attack in history. We were about one thousand yards behind the line along the highway from Saint-Lô to Périers. As the bombs began to drop, the whole area shook as in an earthquake. This lasted for about an hour. As the dust blew back over us, some of the last bombs dropped on some of our division."

Wounded in the right arm at the Hürtgen Forest, Coleman passed through the medical system for about six weeks, which included more than a month in England. "I was back with the 4th Division by the first week of January '45. It did not seem like the unit I had left. Most everyone was new. The gun crew that I had served with was gone. I was told they took a direct hit on their position sometime during the Battle of the Bulge."

Coleman lasted about a month before a case of trench foot rendered him unable to walk. He sat out the remainder of the war in a hospital north of London.

As a member of Headquarters Company, 1st Battalion of the 12th Regiment, Nate Fellman's basic task after D-Day was to furnish ammunition to the replacements heading for the front. But occasionally he supplied the troops during the middle of a battle and for such endeavors won a pair of Bronze Stars. "I still think our outfit was very liberal with granting battle awards," notes Fellman. "I went on patrol with my lieutenant and three other men. It was dark and we went into enemy territory. We made our way back to our company area when suddenly a loud explosion blew me off my feet. I ran to the man ahead of me, who said he was hit. I supported him a short distance to a medic, and he complained he was getting weak. He died in my arms because some shrapnel had pierced his liver. The medic noticed I was bleeding from a slight wound in my elbow. I was tagged for the hospital and received a Purple Heart."

Fellman was still on his feet when the Germans capitulated. "Since I could speak some German, I considered a job in military government and was offered one with a promotion to warrant officer. But I was burned out on the service and declined, separating from the army in October of 1945."

Ollie Clark, the jeep driver for Company H of the 8th Infantry Regiment, earned a Bronze Star for hauling food to units isolated during the winter offensive by the enemy. "I came through unharmed even though the area was occupied by a large number of enemy. But while I was on guard duty one night, a shell struck right in front of me. A medic patched me up, and then they loaded me on a truck with others for a trip that took us through snow and water before we reached a hospital. It was really nothing more than a giant tent, filled with wounded men all in a great deal of pain."

In England, surgeons repaired Clark's arm. He finished the war as a hospital patient until leaving the service in 1947.

"On D plus one," says 81mm mortar man John Beck, "I had 338 more days of the war to come. The 87th Mortar Battalion supported, at one time or another, twelve divisions. If we were with an organization and it was pulled off the line, the corps would reassign us in support of the division going on the line. We finished up with the 69th Infantry Division, which linked up with the Russians. Of the six hundred men who went in on D-Day, sixty-seven were killed and four hundred wounded."

The differences in the initial losses incurred between the two American beaches had little effect upon the ultimate casualty count. When World War II ended, the 4th Division and the units attached to it were as badly tattered as the 1st and 29th Divisions.

# CHAPTER 24

# AIRBORNE AFTER D-DAY

ON D PLUS ONE, the 2nd and 3rd Battalions of the 505th PR in the 82nd Airborne continued to operate from Sainte-Mère-Eglise. Landing craft had deposited the 325th Glider Infantry, another component of the division, on the beach. These troops, accompanied by Shermans from the 746th Tank Battalion, marched inland to support their compatriots.

For the next week or so, Bill Dunfee with Company I pushed north and northwest to widen the penetration into the peninsula and shut down any opportunities for the enemy to threaten the still vulnerable beach zone. "Attacking at night to avoid exposure while you're between hedgerows is great, if you are not a scout. Horrible pressure fell on them. Two scouts would have to go ahead, from one hedgerow to the next, and if all were clear they would return and move the company forward.

"To make it fair, we took turns, rotating after two or three exposures. The plan misfired while Dussault and I were the scouts. We had reached the next hedgerow, peered through, saw no sign of the enemy. We returned and moved the platoon up. But when we were a few feet away from the hedgerow, the Germans opened up with rifles and machine pistols. We hit the deck firing and lobbing grenades. They answered in kind with potato mashers. Our fragmentation grenades were better than theirs; our side prevailed.

"Continuing the night attack, however, Almeida was shot through the armpit. The bullet severed an artery, and the medics couldn't stop the flow of blood. Since Al did not return to duty after Normandy, I didn't know if he had survived. I was pleasantly surprised to receive a Christmas card from him in the 1980s. Another casualty, one of the new men, had been shot through the forehead, an instant frontal lobotomy. What amazed me was he remained lucid and able to walk with help. His mental attitude could only be described as euphoric, but he was blind. I had the eerie feeling I was talking to a dying man, as I assured him he would be evacuated and all right. I'm afraid my voice conveyed my concern, because he said, 'Don't worry about me, sarge. I'm going to live. You guys may not.' I admired his guts but had no desire to trade places. I do not know whether he lived.

"By D plus ten, my twenty-second birthday, the division in its hedgerow-to-hedgerow fighting pushed the enemy steadily westward. That enabled the 90th Division to drive to the sea, cutting the peninsula in two. This action secured the release of Charles Lipoli, my dearest friend for forty years. On landing in Normandy, surrounded by the enemy, Chazz elected to shoot his way out. A machine pistol cut him down, with one slug penetrating his abdomen to lodge in his back and another passing through the calf of his leg. After hospitalization, he returned to duty, jumped with us in Holland, and fought in the Ardennes campaign to pick up a second wound.

"About three weeks into our operations, we were physically and emotionally exhausted. We became pinned down in the open by artillery fire and were drawing small-arms fire from our left front. My buddy Dussault, a machine gunner, picked up his weapon, and with the ammo belt draped around his arm and shoulder, yelled, 'Let's get the hell out of here.' He stood up firing, and we all joined him, moving forward to rout the enemy on our left. That got us out from under the artillery fire.

"This sort of activity continued until D plus thirty-two, when we were finally relieved. The major change from day to day was, as you looked around, fewer and fewer pairs of eyes stared back. The 82nd committed 11,770 officers and enlisted men in Normandy. We sustained 5,436 casualties. KIAs or deaths from wounds added up to 1,142. One company was reduced to a total of sixteen officers and enlisted men. During the campaign we engaged five German divisions, and post-battle estimates indicate the enemy 91st and 265th were virtually destroyed as fighting forces."

Dunfee returned to England with the rest of the 82nd AB. In September 1944, he jumped in Holland as part of the ill-fated Market Garden operation designed by Bernard Montgomery. Subsequently, Dunfee and his fellow troopers rushed to seal off the salient created by the December offensive of the enemy in the Battle of the Bulge. The 505th Regiment continued in the role of foot soldiers as it slogged through the wasteland of the Hürtgen Forest and deep into the heart of Germany, until the ultimate caretakers of the Third Reich surrendered.

Taken prisoner late in the afternoon of D-Day, Jim Irvin, the CO of B Company in the 505th, remained at the German-held hospital in Valognes for four days. Meanwhile, other captured GIs were marched farther behind the enemy lines. "Some were killed while on the roads by American aircraft," says Irvin. "I was moved by night. There were twenty-eight officers on a bus taking us to Germany. Some were from other divisions and regiments. Three from the 505th, Bob Keeler, B. Hendrickson, and I, escaped. We were the only ones who did; the others spent the rest of their time in Europe as prisoners of war.

"The three of us were fortunate in that a French family, M. and Mme. Frenais of Couptrain, supplied us with clothing and papers. Together, we started across to Brittany. The French would stop and watch as we went through small towns, but the Germans paid no attention to us.

"On July 1st, we separated, and on July 4th I met a young boy, Henri Brandilly, who took me to his grandparents' home. I stayed as a family member on their farm until the Brittany peninsula was cut off. On August 15th I returned to England and B Company. My exec officer had taken the company through Normandy, where approximately seventy percent were KIA, wounded, or captured, before it returned to the base camp in Great Britain. Hendrickson, the officer who escaped with me, was killed while working with the Resistance forces in Brittany."

Irvin jumped with his company in Holland on September 17, and five days later a wound brought hospitalization in England. Shipped back to the States, he continued under medical care until retiring because of his injuries, in November 1945.

Raider Nelson, with the 507th PR, who spent his first thirty-six hours fighting in the company of strangers, saw some familiar faces on his second day in France. "That was my first battle, and I had another thirty days to go in Normandy. Our unit suffered almost fifty percent casualties.

"I never witnessed any cowardice during that month in Normandy. But there was plenty of above-and-beyond-the-call-of-duty action. My buddy Alex Krusa kept rushing out, under fire, to pull or drag some wounded buddy to safety. On July 4th, while Ulrich Thompson and I were bringing some prisoners back, artillery opened up on us. Shrapnel killed the German and sliced into Thompson's neck and legs. Later, they tagged him and put him on a jeep to be sent to England. Our battalion was on a hill and on the verge of being cut off by the enemy. As the jeep starts to haul away the casualties, Thompson jumps off, limping, holding his neck and hollering to the medic, 'I'm not going to no damn England. My company needs every man they can get.' When he reaches us, he reports to our lieutenant, Jack Hughes, with this big card, 'EVACUATION,' hanging on him by a string."

The 507th was attached to the 82nd AB Division only for Overlord. Upon return to England, the regiment joined the 17th Airborne. "During the Bulge," says Nelson, "I was caught in a blizzard, alone on outpost. My company moved out before daylight but sent two guys to find me. They pulled me from a snowdrift just in time, because the freezing pain had left me and I was enjoying the illusion of lying in the warm sun on some beach." Nelson's active role ended at this point. Doctors diagnosed him as an infectious hepatitis case, and during his three months in a hospital, the war ended.

C. B. McCoid, Company B CO in the 507th Regiment, staggered through the first hours of June 6 with a crushed kneecap incurred during his rough landing. After turning over prisoners he managed to bag, McCoid dozed through his second night in France, then boarded a vessel bearing other injured men to facilities in England.

"I was heartsick to be squeezed out as early as D plus two, since it seemed that I was leaving in the middle of the final phase of Armageddon. I learned later that the last of our eight officers was killed by D plus eight, and only about a score of our men came through unscathed.

"My treatment took four months, and when it ended I was classified 'limited service.' With the regiment now attached to the 17th Airborne, there was little use for a supposedly disabled captain. I wound up in the division G-2 section. Wounded again in Luxembourg during the Battle of the Ardennes, I recovered to take part in the airborne operation across the Rhine. When the war ended, I was in Essen, in the Ruhr Valley."

Like the members of the 507th, the widely dispersed troopers from the 508th frequently engaged the enemy in a series of hit-and-run battles that had as much to do with survival as with the capture of strategic strongpoints. In the language of military communiqués, "the situation was fluid," a euphemism to cover instability and a lack of adequate intelligence.

But the Americans shut down the flow of German reserves, and command and control was established with increasing coherence. Frank McKee remembers, "Early in July there were a series of hills to be taken. We advanced from a wooded area out into open fields. We were easy targets for the artillery, and they zeroed in on us. It was murderous, and we were losing many men. I heard this one shell I was sure was coming right at my head as I hugged the ground. Two men who were right behind me always stayed together. The shell landed just beyond me and caught them. I scurried to the protection of a hedgerow and called a medic who went over to them. He soon came back, saying they were dead.

"We continued to advance and were soon up the hill and then started down the forward slope. The firing became too intense to go further. The 88s were firing point-blank. Men were being killed and wounded all around me. Lt. Goodale, I believe, gave the word to get back over the crest of the hill.

"When I got up I was suddenly hit by something and was flat on the ground. It felt like a horse kicked me in the back and knocked me down. I put my fist back there, expecting to find a big hole, but only felt numbness. I tried to get up but couldn't move my legs. I felt no pain. Looking up, I saw Bill Giegold at the top of the hill. I waved my arms and hollered, 'Bill, I'm hit!'

"He disappeared over the crest. No one around me was moving, but there were many men down. I figured I had had it. But Bill soon came back, dragged me back, and saved my life. A medic joined us, and we went down the back side of the hill. They placed me on a stretcher in a ditch beside the road. There were ambulances lined up on the road while German artillery tried to zero in. Fortunately, the shells overshot and landed in a field.

"Bill Giegold got me into an ambulance and I was off to a field hospital, which was like a scene from $M*A*S*H$. The place was loaded with wounded. The doctors and nurses looked as if they hadn't slept for days, and they were covered with blood.

"I was placed on the floor, on the original stretcher, and not looked at during the night. The problem was, my wound couldn't be seen, and while conscious, I couldn't walk. The medics were tending to men who bled badly and seemed near death. During the night, while pulling myself to the john, I realized I had some movement in my legs.

"On the following day, they dug into my back to try and remove what was probably a fragment from an 88mm shell. They had no luck, and I was taken by jeep to the beach and then out into the Channel to a British hospital ship. An English nurse asked if she could have my paratrooper boots, which hung over my bunk. I said no, but when I awoke in the morning, my boots were gone.

"They operated on me again at an American hospital. The shell fragment put a notch in the crest of my pelvic bone and cracked it in several places. My temporary paralysis was due to the shock as the shrapnel went through bone only a few inches from my spine. After rehab, I was eventually able to walk, and I rejoined my unit. Sometime in January, I was evacuated because of trench foot. By the time I returned to the 508th, the war had ended and the regiment was serving as an honor guard for SHAEF headquarters in Frankfurt."

Having spent an anxious night of June 6–7 in the farmhouse serving as an aid station, Bill Lord moved on to relieve a besieged group of troopers atop Hill 30. He took part in both Market Garden and the Battle of the Ardennes, although a severe leg infection barred him from the actual jump in Holland.

Lord missed out on a unique jump possibility, a father-son expedition behind the German lines in France. His father, a textile manufacturing executive, noticed that the priority boards allocating scarce materials, with which he dealt, included many military officers. He persuaded them to recommend him for an army commission. Impatient with the delay in approval, he lobbied his way into the Office of Strategic Services, and, in his mid-forties, he matriculated at the Fort Benning jump school.

While Bill Lord was recuperating from the rigors of Normandy at Nottingham, England, his father, holding the rank of major and scheduled for a covert mission in France, appeared. During their reunion, father and son agreed it would be wonderful to work together on an operation. "I got my clearance from OSS, and when I got Dad's phone call the last week in August that everything was on, I obtained Col. Mendez's release. He was reluctant because of concern for my mother if both of us got into trouble.

"However, when I picked up my personnel file to take for Gen. Gavin's adjutant's signature, I sat down under a tree and opened the file. There was a red-bordered piece of paper with a stamp in red, 'Political Influence.' The text read something like 'This is the man whose aunt talked to Stephen Early [the President's press secretary] about trying to get him assigned to OCS.' That shocked me. I did not want to have the reputation of a political operator. I quietly returned the file to regiment and explained to Col. Mendez that I'd thought over what he'd said and decided to stay with the 508. When Dad called, I told him, truthfully, I couldn't get my release. Dad jumped on September 1st, and when he returned from France on the 19th, we were involved in Market Garden."

Lord was never wounded, even though he continued with the outfit through the Ardennes and into the Hürtgen Forest. As the war ended, he earned a battlefield commission.

Jim Kurz, the lanky trooper from B Company of the 508th and head scout, had led the way across the Merderet River when a superior force attacked his group. On June 8, Captain Royal Taylor, recovered from his injury incurred on landing, included Kurz in a forty-man force designed to clean out the villages of Le Port and Carquebut, thus widening the corridor from the sea. "About 110 Germans were taken prisoner," says Kurz. "We turned them over to the 4th Division, who linked up with us that morning."

Kurz continued with the 508th until Market Garden. He had hurt his back and ankle on the jump into Holland. Nevertheless, he performed heroically enough for a Silver Star citation, which read: "Sergeant [then Corporal] Kurz . . . led one of two assault platoons . . . against strong enemy forces who had seized a field which was to be used as a landing field for gliders. The enemy's heavy 20mm and small-arms fire stopped the advancing squads. Realizing the necessity for positive action, Sgt. Kurz stood up, rallied his men, and continued across the field. They overran the positions, knocked out two MGs, captured twelve prisoners, and killed twenty Germans. . . ." However, two days later, friendly fire from British tanks broke his shoulder blade and lanced him with a chunk of shrapnel a quarter inch above his heart.

That eliminated Kurz from further combat. His best friend, Japhet Alfonso, the trooper who had comforted platoon leader Homer Jones just before the Normandy jump, was a KIA in the Battle of the Bulge.

Bud Warnecke, a platoon sergeant with the 508th's B Company, had been among those forced to withdraw through the marshes and the Merderet River, but soon joined an isolated group with whom he fought for four days. "All our initial objectives were taken and held by makeshift companies and battalions. We were placed in reserve, and there I learned our first sergeant who'd been hung up in the trees when he jumped, had been shot. I also was told our battalion commander was killed during the drop."

On July 4, Warnecke's battalion prepared for an attack near the strategic heights commanded by the town of La Haye-du-Puits, as part of the breakout from the now secure Cotentin Peninsula. Warnecke recalls, "Sgt. Call and I were standing behind a hedgerow being briefed by Lt. Jones. A German machine gun cut down on us. I went down as if hit by a sledgehammer, and as I fell a slug ripped through my canteen. I got up dazed and saw Lt. Jones had been hit through the neck.

"Blood was squirting out both sides, and he was in horrible pain. We called for a medic. Jones was saying, 'Let me die! Let me die!' Sgt. Roland Fecteau, who was nearby, immediately stuck two fingers in the lieutenant's neck and plugged the holes. When the medic came he shot Jones up with morphine. The spinal cord hadn't been severed, and the wound was directly behind it. As Lt. Jones was loaded on a stretcher, he was smoking a cigarette and said, 'I'll see you boys in Wollington Park [the 508th's home base in England].'

"My wound turned out to be much more superficial. It busted the skin, looked as if maybe two or three bullets just grazed me. The medic threw some powder on it, put a big patch over it, and said, 'Well, you got a Purple Heart.' I went on my way with our new company commander, Lt. Millsap. The shoulder turned black-and-blue, but it wasn't enough to get me evacuated.

"By the time the fighting stopped for us on July 9, we in B Company, which started with 148 troops, were down to thirty-three. I received a letter from my mother telling me she read the headlines and news reports about the 82nd Division jumping into Normandy and she was glad I was in the 508 PR and not the 82nd. I had to chuckle and was happy for her ignorance of where I was.

"I had a couple of days off to ramble about while awaiting orders. I came across a most gruesome sight, a grave registration detail with a deuce-and-a-half truck loaded with dead Germans and Poles in German uniforms. Most of the bodies were so bloated I almost vomited. I thought, my God, I hate the live Germans. These men are dead—at least cover their bodies with a tarp."

Returned to England and Wollington Park, Warnecke discovered the promise made by Homer Jones was fulfilled. He recovered from his wounds and rejoined the unit. (When Jones recalls the scene near La Haye-du-Puits, almost fifty years later, his voice trembles and he pays homage to Roland Fecteau, whose quick action in plugging the neck wounds undoubtedly saved his life.)

Given a battlefield commission, Warnecke led his platoon in Market Garden. "Compared to Normandy it was a cakewalk," says Warnecke of the Sunday drop, but hard fighting ensued, and he barely escaped death from an enemy hand grenade. He endured the frozen, snowy horrors of the Ardennes, coming through without a scratch, and after V-E Day entered the ranks of Eisenhower's honor guard.

The 508th PR battalion surgeon Dave Thomas, trying to evade capture after landing along the edge of the Merderet River and the flooded plain, looked across the shore toward La Fière. "I could see a helluva battle going on there, but we were surrounded, at the water's edge. I was digging deeper in a ditch when a bullet nicked a nearby tree and smacked into the bank in front of me. By shooting a back azimuth from the tree, I could see jackboots. I couldn't get any of the troops around me to make out the guy in boots. I bummed an M-1 from a soldier. I figured where the body of the man was and squeezed the trigger. The damn thing wouldn't fire, it was so damn dirty. I gave it back to the kid and suggested it might be a good idea to clean his weapon. I got a carbine from some other trooper and put a clip up to where the guy had to be."

Some hours later, Thomas, separated from the other troopers, saw a German coming along the hedgerow. "This was the hairiest time, the longest moment, for me. There were a couple of dead paratroopers there, and I lay face-down among them. The German stopped and looked at me. He put his toe under my ankle, brought it up. I held the rest of my body still. He let the leg go and flop back. My heart was probably going about 150 and I was taking very shallow breaths so he wouldn't know I was breathing. He finally walked on."

Still looking to break through, Thomas and a medic from another outfit tried to bluff their way through by walking along as if they belonged in the area. "But there was a German that had listened up in basic training. He was in the shade of a tree, and he challenged us, 'Hände hoch,' and that was all she wrote. I threw away the .45 I carried before they captured us, because it wasn't considered kosher for a medical officer to get caught with a weapon.

"When they saw I was a medical officer, they put me in charge of the aid station. They had very skimpy coverage. My entire entourage consisted of a sergeant who'd been in the Afrika Korps and been shot at too often. He was goosey, as goosey as can be. We worked in a barn, and in-coming artillery would pass over and land on a hillside. Every time a round came in, this guy sprinted to get under the stone spiral staircase.

"There was a soldier with a burp gun on me to make sure I didn't walk off. Near dusk one night, the guy who was watching me was digging a slit trench, covering it with branches and tied-up faggots from the hedgerows. While he was busy, I stepped through a gate, walked into a field, and urinated. Nobody paid any attention. I slowly walked on, until I reached a hedgerow. I squeezed through it. A group of German bicycle troops came along and stopped for a ten-minute break. I stayed still and quiet until they moved out.

"It was dark, and I kept my eye on the north star while I traveled. When clouds covered it, I would take a rest. I came upon a German sentry, but I think he was sleeping, and I backed up to take off on another tangent.

"I wound up in a shallow ditch. It wasn't too well chosen, because I was in view of the main line of resistance for people from the 90th Division. Every once in a while they would walk a machine gun down the hedgerow beside the ditch, just coming over old Dave's butt. That's when I learned of the condition called nervous polyurea. It seemed like I was piddling every fifteen minutes. I made mud out of it and smeared it over the red crosses on my helmet.

"There was a Schmeisser at either end of the hedgerow that returned fire. When darkness came again, I took off, following the stars. At first light I saw something that looked like a 105 howitzer. This country boy from Arkansas sneaks up on me and asks me for the sign and countersign. I answered, 'Look, buddy, I've been out of contact for days. Just take me to your leader.' The 90th then lateraled me off to the 82nd.

"I went back to my medical detachment. I had an opportunity to go back to the area where I emptied a carbine clip at someone who'd taken a shot at me. Sure enough, there was a dead German there."

The antitank crew of the 80th Antiaircraft and Antitank Battalion, for which Vic Allegretti acted as a feeder, dealt with a series of encounters. "The first seventy-two hours were very bad," says Allegretti. "The names of officers and enlisted men who had been killed in action came in, and we were being pounded steadily by 88s and mortars. Still, we continued to do our job, knocking out tanks and armored vehicles.

"On D plus four, June 10, we came under heavy machine gun fire. I was flat on my belly, legs spread. A bullet caught me in the right knee. They dragged me to a shallow trench. An aidman medicated me, and I was put in a two-and-a-half-ton truck for evacuation to the field hospital, then an LST carried me to England. The war was over for me."

Bernard McKearney, the E Company platoon leader for the 101st AB's 502nd Regiment, awoke on his second morning in France to the sound of aircraft. "What a glorious sight! Transports came rumbling over the village, each one mothering a glider. Then the gliders cut loose. Down they came in a large circle. The timing was beautiful. Lower and lower, then the last few hundred feet they would flatten out and disappear into different fields.

"One of them came swooping over our village. Whether the pilot was hit by small-arms fire or the controls gave out I do not know. But suddenly he banked and crashed about half a mile from us. Doc Loge and his medics prepared to go to their aid. I was to take a squad to provide security against snipers.

"It took us fully half an hour to reach the glider. Jerry snipers were still very active, and we had to proceed with caution. We could hear the screams of the glidermen before we could see them. They had crashed in a field surrounded by the inevitable mud fences. I sent the squad to set up an all-around defense and then climbed the mud to assist the medicos. It was a British Horsa made of plywood. The tail was completely folded over and rested on the nose of the ship. Other parts of the glider were strewn about. Two men had managed to get out. One's leg was broken, bent from his knee at a grotesque angle. The other was trying to aid the trapped men and crying over his helplessness.

"Doc gave him a shot of morphine to quiet him, and we went to work on the glider. Several men had axes and managed to chop a hole in the side. I started to climb into the glider but was nauseated and had to leave. After a bit, Doc Loge and I entered the glider. The men were piled to the front, a welter of arms and legs. The moaning had ceased, although occasionally someone groaned. The screams we had heard must have come from the fellow with the broken leg and others who had since lapsed into unconsciousness.

"Doc and I started to pass them out. There wasn't much bleeding, and we couldn't determine the extent of the injuries. Another medico captain had come along and was helping. There were eighteen wounded in all. Doc would stop, examine a man, and point to the wing he wanted them under—the living under one wing, dead beneath the other. At first the living had twelve and the other six. But then the horrible scale began to balance itself. As Doc would give up on one, aidmen moved him to the other side. The medicos were a wonder. They injected plasma and morphine, set legs, applied bandages, and did everything in their power to save the injured. But it was a losing fight.

"We were a very quiet group of men as we returned to our village base. Everyone brightened up, though, when we saw the place swarming with GIs. By their khaki green we knew they came from a line infantry outfit. There was much back-patting and handshaking. The inevitable ribbing between jumpers and foot sloggers followed. 'What's the matter? Go to sleep on the beach?' 'Nuts to you, Joe. You can stop hiding now. We're taking over.' Whenever two doggies get together, the baloney starts to fly. But we were never more pleased to see anyone in our lives.

"Early the next morning we moved out. A more colorful caravan never traveled the rocky roads of Normandy. The men looked more like gypsies than twentieth-century soldiers. With faces still blackened, heads wrapped pirate-fashion with pieces of camouflaged chutes, and roses behind their ears, they must have seemed very strange to the French.

"We had the horses and carts of the artillery outfit that we had captured. Loading up six wagons with rations and mounting our nags, we started out. About twenty men had horses; the rest rode in wagons. I myself had a huge bay. Being a subway kid, I had trouble handling him, but it was much easier than walking.

"The night passed uneventfully, but then occurred something that could only happen on a battlefield. Across the road from us was a field hospital, and I could see wounded lying on the ground. Maj. John Hanlon, our battalion exec, who knew both of us, told me my brother Jim was there among the wounded. I was granted permission to go and see him. But before I could leave, word came for the battalion to move. We were to go through Carentan and take positions west of town. Rumor had it that a liaison plane had flown down the main street without a shot being fired. The men were laughing and shouting. This was to be a setup."

To the east of the troopers and glidermen of the 82nd,

the members of the 101st Airborne indeed drove on the important hub of Carentan. With the beachhead established and reinforcements flooding ashore, the initial defensive posture against a German counterattack shifted over to an offensive one. Capture of the Carentan Causeway, a long stretch of elevated road that bridged rivers, canals, and a soggy marsh leading into Carentan, would unlock a gate through Normandy and into the heart of France.

The 502nd Regiment ("the Deuce," numbering Bernard McKearney, John Hanlon, Bob Kiel, and Wallace Swanson in its ranks) drew the dubious honor of winning the causeway. The rumor that buoyed the hearts of McKearney and his fellow troopers was pitifully false. Instead, they confronted elements of the crack German 6th Parachute Regiment plus pieces of an infantry outfit. The defenders occupied tactically strong positions under the command of a highly skilled German paratroop commander, Maj. Friedrich von der Heydte.

McKearney's fantasy of a walkover cracked and then shattered. "In a long column with our battalion at the rear we were strafed and bombed by German aircraft. Our ack-ack downed three of them, one falling end over end like a flaming leaf. However, one bomb landed smack on the road, costing I Company a lot of men. We moved slowly during the night. Shots could be heard up front. No one worried especially. Hadn't a plane flown down the main street? Didn't you hear the guy say there was no one in town? We're going to just hold them from the flank. Some other outfit's going from the rear.

"The stories passed up and down the column. Carentan is already ours. We were actually moving toward the beach. Then the word came, 'Dig in.' You could hear it increasing in volume as it passed back, 'Dig in, dig in,' and as it went on by us, it became softer and softer. Then the clink of entrenching tools, not a word while everyone was busy digging. Then another command, 'Moving out.' Muffled curses. 'Why don't they make up their minds?' 'If this is war, I'm turning them war bonds in.' Then the shuffling of feet and we trudged on.

"We had advanced about a half mile when, whoosh! An

88 was shelling the road. Everyone bit the dirt. To others, dirt's dirt, but to the foot slogger, dirt is home sweet home. The firing up front increased. You could hear the growl of our machine guns, then the snap of Jerry's machine pistol. The rate of fire is so fast it sounds as if someone is ripping heavy canvas. You could pick out two of our guns and three of the Jerries'. They would answer one another back. Then you could almost hear ours talking the Jerries down. The firing ceased. Back came the word, 'On your feet, moving out.'

"The column had no sooner started up than mortar shells began dropping around us. The firing up front had become a storm of sound. God help the 3rd Battalion, I thought. Now the wounded straggled back. At first just a trickle, but then in groups. Wounded men somehow cling together. By now we were moving from slit trench to slit trench. These had been dug every few yards by the troopers up ahead.

"We passed through Saint-Côme-du-Mont, a cluster of rubble that had once been a village. This was a regimental aid station. I heard someone call my name. It was a lad who had fought on the regimental boxing team that I had managed. I asked him how he was feeling. He said, 'Okay, doesn't seem to hurt much.' After he was evacuated, the doctor shook his head and said he hadn't a chance. His middle was all shot up. Ordinary boys do extraordinary things in the most ordinary manner. The wounded don't cry. They seem a little dazed. Many have a surprised, hurt look in their eyes, but they don't cry.

"Just as we cleared the town, we came to the first of the four bridges guarding the causeway to Carentan. The Germans had blown the first one. Mortars, 88s, and machine guns were zeroed in on all four crossings. The 3rd Battalion had repaired the damaged bridge to some extent. The bridges had to be crossed, and the only way was to jump up and run like hell to the other side. One at a time we went over. I timed the man ahead of me. It took him seven seconds. Why I did this, I don't know, but you do funny things in combat.

"Then my turn came. I sprang up and had started

tearing across when from the other side came a wounded trooper. He had been shot through the neck. In a dazed condition, he just stood up and started to walk back. He was still walking when we passed one another on the bridge. I yelled at him, 'For God's sake, get off this bridge!' He just looked at me with a crooked smile and walked on. The People Upstairs must have been looking out for that boy that day."

McKearney not only made it across all four bridges without a scratch but also managed to go through the entire war without ever qualifying for a Purple Heart. His supreme accolade came after he knocked out a pair of 88s and "Silent" Steve Chappuis growled, "Good work, Mac."

Actually, the battle for the causeway and Carentan continued from June 8 through June 12 before the combined efforts of the 101st AB's three regiments and heavy support from artillery units finally routed the defenders. John Hanlon with the 2nd Battalion of the 502nd describes the engagement as "the most devastating battle I saw. The turning point came when Col. Robert Cole, CO of the 3rd Battalion, led a bayonet charge. Because of the noise and confusion, not everyone got the word. And when Cole started to run while firing and blew his whistle as the signal to begin the assault, only a handful of troopers followed him at first. Cole was awarded a Congressional Medal of Honor for what he did at Carentan. He was killed during Market Garden by a sniper."

Hanlon, who leaped into Holland and then had been promoted to battalion CO, was among the Screaming Eagles trapped in Bastogne during the Battle of the Bulge. Wounded there, he earned a Silver Star.

Lou Merlano finally caught up with the remnants of Company A, 1st Battalion of the 502nd, on D plus two. "Our officers were still looking for a number of missing people. We had somewhere near sixty-five or seventy men, around half our complement, and we were trying to operate as a company. I was asked to be a squad leader for the remaining riflemen of the first platoon. On June 11, in support of the 3rd Battalion, who jumped off for a bayonet assault, we became committed to go up the causeway. I caught a few slugs from a machine gun, which put me out of action.

"Several days later, I was in a hospital in England. When I heard in August that the 101st had returned from France, I went AWOL from the hospital to find the 502nd Regiment. That's when I found out that half of my plane had dropped in the Channel.

"A lot of survivors from Normandy moved from squad to squad, platoon to platoon, in my company. Perhaps I suffered from survivor's guilt and that's why I stayed with the first squad, first platoon. I was squad leader for the Holland invasion and then assistant platoon leader for Bastogne and finally platoon leader through the remainder of the Ardennes, Alsace-Lorraine, and Bavarian episodes. I finished the war with three Purple Hearts, a Bronze Star, several unit decorations, and three foreign awards."

Eventually, glider pilots Pete Buckley, Vic Warriner, Irwin Morales, and Tip Randolph were shipped back to England to fly in other operations. Buckley remembers, "At our home base they rolled out the red carpet for us. I guess they didn't think many of us would survive. After three-day passes, the daily training routine began again. Most of us went to command ground school for further training in weapons and ground tactics. Many of us got in copilot time in C-47s on the resupply runs so the power boys who'd been flying around the clock got a badly needed rest." As a first pilot, Buckley flew missions in Holland and the Varsity operation, the drop across the Rhine. He emerged unscathed.

Tip Randolph, who guided a Horsa with a 75mm pack howitzer and its crew during the night of June 6, was among the pilots consigned to shepherd docile enemy prisoners to the beach. "After Normandy, we figured we knew all about combat glider operations. But my next mission, the terrain was different. It was vineyards and steep hills, part of Dragoon, the invasion of southern France. I went on the Holland drop and then the Rhine mission, which began badly. We lost two glider pilots even before we left Belgium. I watched one lose its wing about forty-five minutes out. It fell tail-first for what seemed like an eternity.

The pilot was a bunkmate of mine for three years. Everyone aboard perished." But Randolph completed all four of his combat operations without being wounded.

Vic Warriner, whose ship probably touched down first in Normandy because the ostensible leader, Mike Murphy (with Gen. Pratt as his passenger), was forced to seek altitude for his overweight glider, returned to the beach for evacuation on D plus four. "By the time of the Holland invasion I was group glider officer, replacing Jack Willoughby, killed in Normandy. Our group dropped paratroopers the first day, and I rode as a passenger so I could familiarize myself with the area where we would land gliders the next day. I had reason for concern. Gen. Anthony McAuliffe, deputy commander of the 101st Airborne, had requested I pilot the glider carrying him. He had pinpointed a schoolhouse near the landing zone he wanted for use as headquarters and wished a landing near it. I found it from the air that first day, but during the glider mission we came in from a different direction. By sheer luck and no skill, we ended up within one hundred yards of the schoolhouse." Warriner also took part in the last great airborne effort of the war in Europe, Varsity.

Irwin Morales and his copilot, Thomas Ahmad, were listed as missing in action as they continued to fight with an isolated band of paratroopers. During a firefight the Americans split up and Morales saw his copilot manning a position with a handful of paratroopers. Morales himself found a small boat and paddled to friendly forces near Carentan.

After the European war ended in May, Morales returned to Normandy and visited the area where he and the paratroopers had battled the superior German forces. Townspeople informed him that the toll among the enemy amounted to nearly five hundred. In retaliation, the Germans took two local priests and twenty-five airborne GIs who finally surrendered to a farm outside the village. The captives were lined up and shot in the head. Morales believes his copilot, Ahmad, whose body was later discovered in a nearby cemetery, was one of those executed.

The performance of the airborne soldiers fulfilled the

prescription drafted by James Gavin. He said that he wanted to create an elite fighting force who, "when combat comes, then there's not too much to ask from them . . . and we expected them to come through." Public relations hype heaped on paratroopers irks some valiant foot soldiers, but men who jumped on D-Day conclusively demonstrated the value of their training and skills.

# CHAPTER 25

# BEYOND THE POINTES

IN THE COMMAND post with Col. Rudder, Lou Lisko watched apprehensively as U.S. fighter planes circled overhead, uncertain who occupied Pointe du Hoc. One Ranger managed to display an American flag, and the aircraft then pulverized a machine gun nest harassing the conquerors of the Pointe.

"By June 8," says Lisko, "we were waiting to be relieved by the Rangers from Omaha Beach, who had run into a lot of German resistance. We had run out of ammunition and two Rangers were using a German machine gun. Close to about noon, Col. Max Schneider and his 5th Ranger Battalion heard the distinctive sound of the German machine gun and assumed we had been wiped out. In the confusion, they started to fire in our direction with mortars, and tanks attached to the 116th Regiment joined in. After two and a half days of fighting the Germans, now we were being attacked by our own troops.

"Col. Rudder was yelling as loud as he could to the Rangers to stop firing the German machine gun, but he was not close enough for them to hear. My buddy and I were trying to contact the friendly troops over the radio in the command post and tell them they were shooting at their own troops. Finally, we succeeded. Col. Schneider ran out into the open and told his men to cease firing.

"Toward nine that night, I went into my foxhole, planning a good night's sleep. I heard some shooting close to me. I sat up quickly and saw two Rangers firing at two Germans. They appeared to have been prisoners who tried to escape. One of them fell on his back in a ditch about ten yards from my foxhole. He sat up and a Ranger put two more rounds in his chest. This may sound like a cruel, inhuman thing. But this was the front lines. One of the Germans was dead and the other badly wounded. So the Rangers decided the best thing was to do away with him.

"As they were leaving, I noticed that the injured German was not dead yet. He brought his knee up and tried to rise. I decided I was not going to fall asleep with a German alive only ten yards away. He might be able to crawl to my hole and kill me. So I shouted to the Ranger, 'He's not dead yet.' The Ranger came back and emptied his rifle into the man's chest and head. He didn't move anymore.

"I tried to go to sleep, but sleep would not come for a long time. I was looking into the sky—two Germans—the picture of them lying the way they were was imprinted in my mind, and I could see them looking up into the sky. I wondered who they were, where they came from, in which German city they lived. I wondered whether they were married. I thought about their wives wondering where their husbands were, what they were doing. It made me feel so bad I could not sleep for a long period."

Wounded almost immediately after leaving the landing craft, Len Lomell, the first sergeant of D Company who tried to maintain the woefully thin line of defense at the coastal blacktop road, managed to stick it out until D plus two, when the 116th with elements of the 5th Ranger Battalion and remnants of A, B, and C Companies of the 2nd Battalion trudged up. "Gangrene developed in my side, and I was to be evacuated. I walked down the road to the beach. There were seventy-five to eighty guys dead, laid out. It was horrible to walk by and see Ranger buddies,

KIA. The colonel walked up and said how glad he was to see me. He ordered me to get to Doc Block for treatment. Along with other walking wounded, I got onto a boat that took us to a hospital ship in the Channel."

Lomell recovered and returned to the 2nd Battalion and D Company as the invaders mounted an offensive that would culminate with the capture of Brest. In October, the army honorably discharged him as a sergeant major and then immediately swore him in as a second lieutenant assigned to D Company.

Along with so many other units, the army flung the 2nd Battalion Rangers with its freshly minted Lt. Len Lomell as well as Sid Salomon, Robert Edlin, and George Kerchner into the maw of the Hürtgen Forest during November. All around them, much bigger organizations such as the 1st, 4th, 8th, 28th, and 83rd Infantry Divisions and elements of the 5th Armored Division retreated as the Germans methodically destroyed men and machines. The Rangers, however, would not back off but held their ground until relieved.

Sid Salomon, CO of Baker Company in the 2nd Ranger Battalion, saw his people chewed up during the first exploratory thrust into the bloody Hürtgen Forest and considers his men cruelly used. "After the invasion, there was no need for a 2nd Ranger Battalion as originally intended. We were used as an ordinary infantry company, attached to maybe ten different divisions. Those in command did not know what the Rangers were. They would send the Rangers out first in an attack and keep their own casualties down."

Critical to the German defense, and deadly to the safety of the Americans, was the town of Bergstein and Castle Hill, designated as Hill 400 on maps. The locale provided the defenders with a commanding view of any movement of U.S. troops. Says Salomon, "A combat command of the 5th Armored Division [ordinarily about three thousand men with tanks and other armored vehicles] failed to take Bergstein and strategically important Hill 400. The general in charge of the task force specifically asked Gen. Leonard Gerow, corps commander, for assignment of the Rangers to assist the 8th Division's assault on Bergstein and Hill 400. Three companies of Rangers [hardly more than two hundred foot soldiers] captured it, going past burned-out tanks with GIs hanging over the sides."

Among those who fell in the Hürtgen Forest was Sgt. Otto Stevens, Salomon's accomplice in conquering the German defenders atop Pointe et Raz de la Percée and winner of a DSC for his valor there. Salomon himself collected his second Purple Heart on Thanksgiving Day 1944, as an explosion lacerated his eyebrows and chin, necessitating stitches.

From the middle to the end of the month, well-sited German artillery firing from the town of Schmidt killed, wounded, and harassed the Rangers, who incurred further losses from mines, mortars, and small-arms fire guarding the forest itself.

Lomell and George Kerchner with D Company started for Bergstein on December 6. In the early-morning hours of December 7, three years after Japanese bombs pelted Pearl Harbor, the Rangers passed through Bergstein, rousting those Germans who resisted. At 0730, amid a fearsome artillery duel, the Rangers jumped off, sprinting up Hill 400 firing their weapons from the hip, their bayonets at the ready.

In short order, the enemy fled, but it was an onerous victory. Well aware of the importance of the highland, the foe now rained a murderous assortment of explosives upon the new kings of the hill. The rocky, tree-root-laced ground defied the best efforts of entrenching tools. The only shelter lay beneath toppled trees or in shell holes. According to Len Lomell, "Survival was a matter of luck. We were under constant bombardment. Wounded guys were lying all over the hill. Because we lacked medical supplies we couldn't even give first aid. We were told we would be relieved in twenty-four hours and just to hold on. How long can you tell a guy bleeding to death to hold on? My God, he knew I was lying to him.

"I had tears of frustràtion in my eyes. We had just stopped a third counterattack, but if the Germans had known how many men, or really how few, we had up there, they would have kept coming." Bleeding from wounds of his hand and arm, Lomell, the sole surviving officer in D Company and ranking officer at the site, offered a proposal to his noncoms. "If we retreat, they'll take care of our dying, untreated wounded. We can come back with more troops and take the hill back." The men adamantly refused to consider the idea. Hindered by his injury, Lomell placed a machine gun in the crook of his arm and triggered it from there. An explosion nearby caused a severe concussion. "I was bleeding from the anus and the mouth as a result." At 9:00 P.M., under the cover of darkness, he was evacuated because of his wounds.

Originally informed, says Lomell, by his CO that they would need to control Castle Hill for no more than twenty-four hours before infantrymen of the 8th Division would take over, the tormented Rangers endured more than forty hours on the heights. Of the sixty-five Rangers from D Company who started the charge up the hill, only fifteen came down under their own power.

Awaiting surgery to repair the damage, Lomell expected to be rotated home. But as he traveled to a holding area to await further medical treatment, the Germans broke through in the Ardennes. "I was in a truck convoy on the way to Paris. I was the only officer on my truck, and a major ordered me to take the men to hold a road intersection to prevent possible penetration by the Germans. They left us weapons for that purpose. I didn't leave for the States until after January 1, 1945."

On the morning after Lomell came off Hill 400, in a last spasm of attack, German artillery slammed into the positions of the Rangers just as battalion surgeon Walter Block left his dugout to supervise evacuation of the seriously wounded. A shell fragment killed him instantly. The assault by the Germans was repulsed by the few surviving Rangers.

As one of his last acts, Block spared his medical technician Frank South the worst of the battering around Hill 400. "The day before the battalion was sent into action at Bergstein," South recalls, "I passed out due to dehydration and a severe gastrointestinal problem. Not knowing we were about to be committed, Block insisted that I get to a hospital. I was unaware we were in action until wounded Rangers began to arrive. I immediately went AWOL from the hospital and hitchhiked back to the battalion, only to find the battle of Hill 400 over, the battalion decimated, and Block dead. He was the only medical officer we had that deserved the name of a Ranger. I still feel both guilty and somehow cheated that I was not part of that battle."

Lt. Charles Parker from the 5th Ranger Battalion, who received a DSC for D-Day, was heavily engaged on June 7 with counterattacks. "There was a very nasty fight three or four days later. We had to cross a flooded swamp area where they had the targets painted on their emplacement walls. They could fire two or three mortar rounds from trenches and pits with manhole covers without exposing themselves. They had four years to prepare for us.

"In the Rangers we practiced an elementary principle. Once you jump off, there's no place to stop until you arrive at the target. If you halt halfway there, then you become pinned down. So we were right among them very soon, working our way down in the trenches using fire and grenades. They started to surrender, and a lot of them had been gathered out of their holes, but there were several SS men among them. They began killing those who surrendered, and that brought chaos. The entire thing had to be done again. One SS officer held a grenade to his head and blew off most of his face rather than surrender. I lost my first sergeant and a dozen other men there."

Subsequently, the Rangers with Parker trekked to a bivouac, where they sought to replenish their ranks. "I interviewed hundreds of volunteers, and we rejected most of them. Regular army organizations always hate special units. They didn't know what to do with us. They would use us for smash-and-grab operations. We were to take positions, but we never had enough men or firepower to hold them for any length of time." He recalls at least four subsequent encounters with the enemy that struck him as equal to the perils of the invasion. "But I went through the entire war and never missed a day at the office."

While Parker had been stranded temporarily on Pointe du Hoc, others from the 5th Ranger Battalion, including

Frank Dawson, the D Company officer, advanced off
Omaha Beach in the drive at Vierville intended to lift the
pressure on the Rangers penned in on the cliff.

"With two medium tanks in support of C and D Companies from the 5th, plus about 150 men from the 116th
Infantry and another eighty from the 2nd Ranger
Battalion, it was attack time. Mines forced us to use the
road. Because of German artillery, we still hadn't reached
Pointe du Hoc at dark. Again we halted and settled in for
the night. Our battalion medic, an enlisted man, Alexander
Barber, secured a horse and two-wheeled cart to use as an
ambulance. No vehicles had yet come off the beach to us.

"On D plus two, Companies C and D moved across
country at 0700 and met no enemy but contacted the 2nd
Rangers on the Pointe. The two battalions from the 116th
and the 743rd Tank Battalion headed down the road towards Grandcamp-les-Bains and wheeled to the right when
south of Pointe du Hoc. They opened fire on the Pointe,
mistaking my company, and particularly my platoon, for
German troops. My runner, Pfc Robert Steinen, was killed
while I tried to remove the stones and dirt under me in order to burrow deeper. When the tankers realized we were
Americans, it all ceased."

Eventually, the firepower from the sizable U.S. infantry
contingent supported by tanks, artillery, and naval guns offshore broke the defense of Grandcamp. A few days later, at
an unexpected ceremony, with Gen. George S. Patton looking on, Gen. Omar Bradley pinned DSCs on Dawson, along
with Parker, the medic Sgt. Barber, and several others.

Recollects Dawson, "D-Day, my first combat, differed
from what I later experienced. My platoon fought German
paratroopers at Brest, and house to house after we crossed
into Germany, and in the streets of towns as we approached
the Rhine River. Landing and getting off the beach, finally
reaching the crest of the bluff, was my worst experience. It
was new; by the time other battles occurred, you sort of
knew what to expect and you had seen death."

Ranger Robert Edlin, struck in both legs on the beach
and evacuated to England during the evening of D-Day, recovered rapidly from surgery. "They began making deci-

sions about what they would do with people. They asked me if I wanted to be ZI'd, sent to the Zone of Interior, the States. I told them the only thing I wanted was to get back to A Company."

In July, having shucked his crutches, Edlin persuaded the attending physician to release him for duty with a promise that he would be treated by the battalion surgeon, Dr. Block. "When I saw Dr. Block he raised hell with the hospital for discharging me. But he put on a solution that he said would heal my legs faster, and it worked."

Edlin took part in countless small, deadly firefights as the Rangers among others sought to extinguish the stubborn flicker of resistance from some 200,000 Nazi soldiers cut off as the U.S. Third Army under Patton broke out in a dash toward Paris.

In one instance, Edlin, on the heels of the lead scouts, suddenly sensed trouble nearby. He could not at first figure out what had spooked him. Rudder and the commanders expressed impatience at the delay. "Then, I thought, damn! I've got it. I saw a pile of human crap in the road. It was steaming. There was nobody in front of us, and I thought, how far does a man go from his foxhole to take a crap?"

Edlin's suspicions proved correct. The Germans lay a few yards off with an antitank crew and small arms. The Rangers opened fire, and Edlin emptied his M-1. "Afterwards, I rolled over the man I had shot. I see his face at night, even after almost fifty years. I wondered then and now what happened to the beautiful little boy and girl in the picture that the proud father carried to show his friends."

The culmination of the campaign to capture Brest on the Channel coast saw Edlin lead a handful of Rangers into the stronghold of the Graf Spee Battery, a fortress at Lochrist. Although the situation for the German forces was hopeless and the massive guns in the Lochrist bastion could only point toward seaborne invaders, the defenders had ringed themselves with a formidable array of 88s, mortars, and machine gun nests that pounded the Americans.

Rudder nominated Edlin to take a reconnaissance patrol, locate the minefields, and bag a prisoner or two for intelligence about those still manning the position. "Along about dawn, September 10th, we came down to probably within two hundred yards of one of the largest pillboxes I had ever seen. The fort itself stood above us like a ten-story building. The big guns had been largely silenced, and we were in so close that not even the 88s or mortars could fire on us. Only machine guns and rifles could get at us.

"We ran into a patrol from the 5th Rangers, led by Lt. Parker. He was a good friend of mine but we were very competitive. He told me he had the same mission as I, to locate the minefields so the 5th Rangers could move in. I told him they weren't going to beat us there, and he said, hell, he'd just take over the whole fort. I answered, 'I don't think so. We'll take it over first.' We were both just joking.

"He moved to my left to chart the minefields. We paused at a high stone wall. I told my platoon sergeant William Klaus to hold the rest of the platoon there and cover us. Sgt. Bill Courtney, Sgt. Bill Dreher, and my runner, Warren Burmaster, and I came within fifteen or twenty yards of the pillbox. The minefield ahead of us was posted, but there were no signs telling us the path through it.

"Bill Courtney suddenly announced, 'I see a way through the mines.' He started forward. Dreher yelled for him to stop, but I said let him go, and we followed Courtney. There was an obvious path where probably French civilians brought supplies in.

"We went directly behind Courtney to the mouth of the pillbox. There was an open doorway, and we could hear Germans talking inside. I motioned to Burmaster to cover our rear. An excellent man, he would report back to the company if something happened to us. We entered the pillbox with no opposition whatsoever. They were surprised to see American soldiers there. They had no idea any of us were within several miles. We captured the emplacement with thirty-five or forty men, some machine guns, and the radio equipment before they could use it. There was no firefight at all.

"There I was, a twenty-two-year-old lieutenant, sitting with prisoners in the shadow of the strongest emplacement on the peninsula. I called in Burmaster and told him to have the radioman back with the rest of the platoon notify Col. Rudder and Capt. Arman that we had captured the pillbox and were within two hundred yards of the fort itself.

"I knew if I asked Col. Rudder if we should go ahead and try to enter the fort, he would likely say no. It would just be too much of a risk. I also thought, if I wait for permission and don't get it, there will be an all-out assault and a lot of men will be killed. There were only four of us and we had a chance to prevent it.

"I decided to go into the fort. Courtney had been speaking to a lieutenant we captured who spoke fluent English. He said he could take me directly in to the fort commander. I left Dreher and Burmaster to stay with the prisoners and to notify Rudder that Courtney and I had gone to the fort. They were to hold everything until they heard from Burmaster.

"The German lieutenant guided us through a minefield and to the entrance of the fort. We came down through a tunnel like in a football stadium, and when we opened the door, the German was in front with me directly behind him, a tommy gun in his back. We walked into a hospital room, the site of a large ward. There was an operating room in it and a lot of motion, white-clad doctors, nurses, and patients everywhere. When we showed up in American uniforms with guns in our hands it was just turmoil.

"Courtney, who spoke pretty good high school German, yelled, '*Hände hoch!*' All hands went in the air. The German lieutenant asked if he could speak to them in German, and I agreed as long as he spoke slowly enough for Courtney to translate. He told the Germans to remain calm, to sit down. He would lead us to the battery commander to try to negotiate a surrender and avoid more casualties.

"Everybody quietly went about their business, and we passed through the hospital section, the German in front, my gun in his back and Courtney behind me. As we passed several German soldiers on guard at the cross corridors, the lieutenant would speak to them and they would immediately lower their weapons. Courtney explained to me he was telling them I was being taken to their commander and not to cause problems or trouble.

"We came to a doorway, and the German started to open it. I stopped him when he told Courtney it was the commander's office. I instructed him to step aside. I turned the knob and stepped into the office with Courtney right behind me, both of us with tommy guns. A middle-aged colonel sat behind a large ornate desk with carpet on the floor, like a modern office of today. He was apparently surprised that anyone would enter without knocking. I immediately said, '*Hände hoch!*'—one of the few expressions I knew.

"He raised his hands, and we closed the door behind us. I told Courtney to talk to him in German, but he answered that wouldn't be necessary. He spoke English well. He seemed surprised and alarmed at our presence, and I said the fort was completely surrounded by American soldiers. The air force attacks and artillery had lifted to give him a chance to surrender. He should immediately go on his PA system and announce that the whole fort should give up.

"He reached for his telephone, and I said for him to leave it alone. He told me he just wanted to check to see how many Americans were there. It was a tough position. About the only alternative I had was to shoot him, and that wouldn't gain anything. So we let him call. He asked if we would care to have a drink. I couldn't have taken a drink or anything else. My stomach was upset, my heart up in my throat. I don't know who was the scaredest, me or Courtney. We were in a position which we couldn't back out of. If he surrendered, we'd have done a great job. If he didn't, then we obviously would become prisoners. The two of us with tommy guns could hardly defeat the whole garrison.

"The phone rang after a couple of minutes, and he spoke in German. Courtney looked over at me and shook his head. The officer hung up and said he'd found out there were only four Americans, two at the pillbox and us two, and we were his prisoners.

"For half a minute Courtney and I were prisoners, but

we were very dangerous ones. I had made up my mind we would shoot him, barricade the office with desks, and wait until either the Germans got us out or our guys attacked the next day, and when they came in, we'd still be alive.

"Something struck my mind. I don't know where the idea came from or why I did it. But I told Courtney to give me a hand grenade. Why I didn't use a knife or the tommy gun I don't know. I took the grenade, pulled the pin, walked around the desk, and shoved it into the colonel's stomach. I told him either surrender or he was going to die right there.

"He said I was bluffing. I said, 'I'll show you how much I am bluffing. I'll count to three, turn loose the lever.' It would flip off and the grenade would splatter his stomach and backbone all over the wall. He just sat there. I counted, 'One, two,' and he said, 'All right, all right. I believe you.' I told him to get on the phone, use the PA system to announce to his men he had surrendered the fort, given up, and the combat was over. We would immediately get word to our battalion commander and stop any action coming in.

"Over the PA system he spoke in German. Courtney understood him, and it was plain and clear that he had ordered his people to lower their arms and not take any hostile action against the American forces. He said he would prefer to surrender to a higher-ranking officer than a lieutenant. I didn't give a rat's ass who he surrendered to. I said I'd take him to my battalion commander and he could handle it."

By radio, Edlin informed Rudder what had happened, and the Ranger CO confirmed he had notified the 29th Division commander and the 8th Corps commander of what happened, and there would be no artillery or air action.

"We went back to the pillbox and took out the prisoners we had obtained there while Rudder entered the fort to deal with the colonel. When I looked back, the sight was unbelievable. There were 850 men coming out. I had figured maybe 150 or even 250, but 850 lined up in military formation, stacked their arms, and there was sort of an old-time formal surrender ceremony. While we were inside,

Courtney had talked the German into calling the Brest commander, Gen. Ramke, and advising him he had surrendered the fort and, on Courtney's suggestion, telling him he too might as well give up. That didn't work, and there was to be another ten days of bitter fighting.

"After the ceremony as we started to march off the prisoners, Col. Rudder congratulated the four of us and told us we had done a wonderful job. Then he called me aside and proceeded to tear me a new butthole. He was nearly crying about the tremendous risk we had taken. I asked him what he would have done, and Rudder answered he hoped he would have done the same as I did."

There was talk of a Congressional Medal of Honor for Edlin, who insisted that while he appreciated the tale of four Rangers capturing 850 men and four artillery pieces, the men of the 29th Infantry Division, the other Rangers, the artillery, the engineers, and the air corps were what brought the episode to its conclusion. The recommendation for the nation's highest military honor was knocked back to a Distinguished Service Cross, with Edlin's three associates inside the fort receiving Silver Stars.

During the debacle at Hürtgen, a blast from a mine blinded Edlin with dirt and mud and ripped some agonizing gashes in his left hand and face. He finished the war after being patched up.

Like the paratroopers, the Rangers were all volunteers, motivated to high achievement. The screening process winnowed out some less effective recruits. Col. Rudder provided the basis for excellent leadership, and a rigorous regimen of training honed the men into a superb fighting force. On D-Day, they played vital roles in the ultimate success at Omaha Beach. But on the debit side, the virtues of the Rangers earned them the short end of the stick, a series of deadly assignments that wreaked heavy casualties.

# CHAPTER 26

# THE U.K. WIND-DOWN

INEVITABLY, THE WAR in Western Europe would become dominated by the American presence. The British pool of manpower, always a fraction of what the United States could field and depleted after years of fighting alone, could not match the American effort. However, before the balance shifted toward the U.S. contribution, those who battled their way off Sword, Juno, and Gold, as well as the airborne arrivals behind the lines, met a defiant enemy defending Caen.

William Ward, with the King's Own Scottish Borderers, says, "I did not feel at any time that the invasion had failed. However, Caen was our objective that first day, but we did not reach the Boulevard des Alliés in the city until July 9th." Canadians, including Earl Kitching in a Sherman tank, took the crucial airfield at Carpiquet the same day as Ward's unit entered Caen.

Horace Wright, only a lieutenant on June 6, was a major by August as the ranks of fellow officers in the Hampshires thinned out. "In October, during the campaign in Holland, I was wounded and off the road for three weeks," notes Wright of his later adventures. When the enemy finally yielded in May, the mild-mannered Wright, "more like a bank clerk than a hero" in the words of an associate, wore the prestigious Member of the British Empire and Military Cross with bar to go with three separate mentions in dispatches.

The Commando units, like the Rangers no longer in fashion and short of replacements for their already meager numbers, also fought on. No. 4 Commando with Arnold Wheeldon left France for the United Kingdom in late August. Recommended for a commission, Wheeldon was posted to Burma with the 7th Ghurka Regiment in the Indian Army. No. 3 Commando was relieved, returned to England in September, and then likewise dispatched to Burma to oust the Japanese.

James Murray, the British intelligence soldier who was with the Canadians on Juno, says D plus one was worse than the landing. "It was the custom for our section never to be all together at any one time. The intelligence officer told me to take the corporal and go for a wash and shave in the stream nearby. Halfway through, I heard two planes. At first I thought they were ours, but then I heard the machine guns and bombs exploding.

"We dashed back to our section on the beach to find the officer badly injured and two others killed. The planes made another run, and although everything that could fire was used against them, they escaped. That was the only time we saw or heard the Luftwaffe.

"I learned our antitank platoon had been hit by a bomb while coming ashore, losing the officer, a sergeant, and five men. Also the raft bringing the motor transport was hit and on fire almost at the water's edge, losing the transportation sergeant and some men.

"Later, I took a patrol of three men and went up the exit road to the small village of Graye-sur-Mer. Lying beside a war memorial for the 1914–18 war was a Canadian's body. A woman ran from one of the houses and covered him with a French tricolor."

Everett Gorman, promoted to captain and company commander in the Canadian North Shore, suffered through the series of engagements aimed at Caen. His outfit was charged with capturing the airfield at Carpiquet.

"Our big show was on July 3 and 4, and because of a mixup we were bombed and shelled by our own artillery and naval guns while on the start line."

The objectives fell, but the casualties continued to pile up. "We received ten reinforcements late one night, and the next morning a stone wall which they were behind was hit and buried them. An officer reported just as we started out. A shell killed him. People would come in without the training we had and after a few hours they were gone.

"The loss of sleep, the wondering whether you're going to get it, so many buddies killed and wounded—I think I'd have cracked up if I hadn't been an officer with so many things to think about and do. But in March of '45, two majors and I were sent out as battle-exhausted. We'd lost our efficiency. I came back to take the company home, but the other two officers never returned."

Bill Sadler, driving for a medical unit, noticed a change shortly after the fall of Caen. "All at once it seemed that the Allied forces broke out and began to move at remarkable speed. So much so that we found it difficult to keep up. We stopped constructing our own bivvies and went back to sleeping under canvas. Our personalized clothing gave way to proper uniform." But the war continued its bloody toll. Sadler helped retrieve the shattered bodies of civilians buried in Belgian cities by German rocket bombs aimed at Antwerp and ministered to soldiers badly hurt when a load of captured mines exploded as the Allies penetrated the German heartland.

"Suddenly, but perhaps not unexpectedly, came the end of the war in Europe. For us it was a strange feeling. We did not indulge in the wild celebrations seen in places like London. We were in the midst of the former enemy, and the British became embarrassed at the prospect of rubbing the noses of the vanquished in the dust."

D-Day, the capture of Caen and the area surrounding it, and Market Garden in Holland were the final three campaigns in which the British ground forces played a significant role in Europe. The United States with its much larger reservoirs of men and supplies dominated the battle with

Germany during the final seven months of World War II. Many of the Britons who participated in Overlord had shifted to operations in the Far East, fighting the Japanese and preserving the shreds of the British Empire well before the Nazi surrender.

# CHAPTER 27

# AFTER-ACTION REPORTS

WORLD WAR II spanned almost three and a half years for the United States and nearly six years for the British. During that period occurred a string of battles and engagements often waged with relentless ferocity. Still, to most of the men who were there, June 6, 1944, stands as the most memorable moment of their military lives, if not of their entire time on this earth.

To Bob Sales of the 29th Division, who endured the holocaust on Omaha Beach, as to many others who lived to fight on after the landings, "Every day was D-Day, jumping off through the hedgerows time and again." The opportunities to be killed or maimed persisted until the last gun fell silent, and a number of soldiers and sailors, such as those who put in at Utah Beach, encountered far more deadly opposition after June 6.

There is for most veterans nothing to approximate the excitement, the exhilaration, that accompanies escape from terrible danger—"to be shot at and missed," in the words of Winston Churchill. Homer Jones, the 508th PR lieutenant who displayed conspicuous valor at the shootout at the La Fière Manoir, offers another explanation for the fascination with conflict. "War is a terrible thing, men killing one another, but at the same time individuals exhibit a kind of nobility. In a rifle company or any other unit in that arena, you fought for one another. You did it because they were there and you were there." Modern life offers few opportunities for surviving deadly peril or for witnessing the "nobility" described by Jones.

Both elements were abundantly present on D-Day. Some recall the experience with awe. "It will always be special to anyone who was there," says Bill Dean, of the 508th PR, "because it was a moment that can never be equaled, containing every emotion a human is capable of feeling."

"D-Day was one of the greatest experiences of my life," declares Tom McCann, an I&R man in the 1st Division. "I would not take anything for having been there, but never again would I want to go through the experience."

Others recall June 6, 1944, with dread. John Bistrica becomes choked by his emotions. "I just stare into space thinking about it."

The passage of time also lends an aura. "The experience means more now," says Sam Frackman of the 4th Division. "It meant little after I was discharged. My children never seemed impressed, even when I took them to see *The Longest Day* [the film version of Cornelius Ryan's book on the invasion] with commentary by me. Some twenty years later, my son went to France and retraced the route of the 4th Division back to the beach. He signed his name in a book at a museum, and when asked to whom he was related in the landing, he wrote 'father.' That made him feel it was an accomplishment."

Bob Kiel, from the 502nd PR, never doubted the stature of the event. "I felt our D-Day drop would be part of history, and the years have borne me out."

"I knew then I had taken part in a historic day," says the 508th's Elek Hartman. "It was truly the 'Great Adventure,' but I wouldn't want to relive it."

Don McCarthy, a member of the 29th Division and a victim of shrapnel within hours of setting foot on Omaha Beach, insists, "The D-Day experience changed my entire life. Call it a religious manifestation if you like, or call it merely a special awareness of life, but the feeling of mystery has been with me ever since that morning when I lived through the din and chaos of Omaha Beach, 6 June 1944. So close—so very close to death. Each year at this time [the first week of June] I relive each moment, each step, the sounds, the cries, the smell of war."

Dick Conley, the 1st Division platoon leader, admits, "I didn't realize the historic significance at the time, because I was more involved with my survival from day to day. But I am now very proud to have been part of D-Day."

Dick Biehl, the scout in the 1st Division whose combat tour before the invasion included Sicily, is one of many veterans who have made pilgrimages to Normandy for anniversary celebrations. "Now I understand the significance of D-Day, what it meant to those people of Europe, especially the residents of Normandy and northern France. Liberation was long awaited, and despite the anticipated civilian losses, we were welcome."

Frank Dawson, the 5th Ranger Battalion officer, harbors special feelings about the event. "For years while I was in the service [Dawson made the military his profession after V-E Day], there was not much interest in D-Day. But as the years have gone by, and the ranks of those who hit the beaches are dying out, more and more attention is being paid to it. I can always say I had an important part in one of the greatest invasions ever—five thousand ships gathered—and in an atomic age it could never happen again."

C. B. McCoid of the 507th PR, another who made the army his vocation, expresses similar sentiments: "I had the good fortune to survive eight years of battle in the course of three wars. Despite a lot of high points, D-Day remains the apex of my thirty-four-year career."

Even a GI like Bob Meyer of the 4th Division, whose postwar profession as a teacher oriented him to think in terms of the overall experience, singles out his personal baptism under fire. "Participating in the war, particularly the D-Day invasion, had been important because most other people I meet, even the kids who were in my classes, could relate to that event with awe. I have a sense of pride for having taken part in the breaking of Hitler's Fortress Europe. Some friends almost embarrass me by wanting me to tell someone about it. I usually just wind up telling them

I was there, because how can you describe it to someone who has never been through anything like what it was? For a number of years I couldn't speak of it at all."

For Britons, the meaning of D-Day was heightened by their unhappy memories of times past, the series of stinging defeats during the early years, the months of anxiety over a possible invasion of their homeland, and the devastating aerial blitz of London and other United Kingdom cities and towns. "D-Day will live with me all of my days," says E. H. Gibbs, who soldiered with the Hertfordshire Regiment. "It was the culmination of years of military training."

Bill Bidmead remembers, "The landing was a high point in my time with the Commandos, although the next eighty-three days were a nightmare."

Hindsight endows the event with its historical importance but does not address the question of why men submit themselves to the ordeal of a June 6, 1944, doggedly pushing toward likely destruction, against their most basic instinct for survival. For many, the initial stages of the invasion brought the greatest terror, total loss of control over their destiny.

"It was a helluva day," says Bill Lewis, the antitank squad leader. "The experience was terrifying. To keep alive was something else, beyond us. It was the first time we had been under prolonged artillery pounding. Just to hear that shit coming over where you couldn't see it, couldn't fight them. You stayed because there was nothing else you could do."

Those coming to Omaha Beach were buffeted by an unexpectedly unforgiving sea that sought to swamp their clumsy landing craft and to drown them. They ran a gauntlet of lethal defenses through the shallows and then across the exposed strand of beach, with only the cloth of their uniforms between them and the enemy fire.

Once in position, a man could perhaps improve his chances by digging in, hunkering down behind a hedgerow, dampening incoming rounds with his own weapons, or in the best case advancing with great caution while supported by tanks and artillery. But on the pitiless killing ground of Omaha Beach, there was no ally but chance—and for many even that deserted them.

Desperate circumstances likewise enveloped the first minutes of those who jumped from the C-47s. Ground fire downed planes and forced pilots into evasive maneuvers that ended with hapless men being dumped into the sea. During their descent, paratroopers had only hope and their jumpsuits between themselves and the bullets from defenders as they swung helplessly in the air. In the darkness, many snagged on trees or buildings and hung there until they were shot. Glidermen, swooping over the drop zone in their flimsy craft, could do nothing about the outpouring of antiaircraft fire. They could only hope the skills of their pilot, flying blind through the bursts of tracers and ack-ack, could manage a controlled crash that would not kill them.

Said Bob Slaughter, from the ill-fated 116th Regiment, "I realized it didn't make any difference whether one was a superior soldier, was more religious, of better character. People were being killed randomly and they could not help themselves."

Horace Wright had remarked that it was all a matter of luck, with perhaps a slight edge to the officer who knew what was supposed to happen. But for many, the knowledge cited by Wright was illusory and engendered a false sense of control.

An army, particularly one in battle, is an undemocratic institution. Conventional military wisdom taught enlisted men that someone else would think for them and direct them. They learned to have faith even in brass-hatted patriarchs. Belief that the senior people knew what they were doing provided a sense of security for those toward the bottom of the heap, the ones charged with carrying out sometimes inexplicable commands. But on June 6, 1944, command and control vanished during those first hours. Nothing Eisenhower, Bradley, Montgomery, or even the divisional generals and their staffs could do would help the efforts of the men in chutes or in the beach-bound boats to preserve themselves, let alone accomplish their objectives.

That applied even to the airborne outfits in which the

generals went in with their men. Upon landing, they had no troopers to direct. The dispersion of the ordinary soldiers and upper-echelon leaders was summed up by 101st Airborne commander Gen. Maxwell Taylor: "Never have so few been commanded by so many." The 29th Division assistant CO, Gen. Norman Cota, was conspicuous by his presence on Omaha, but his contribution was not tactical. His highly valuable role was more that of a cheerleader than coach as he urged the troops to get off the beach. His opposite number with the 4th Division, Gen. Roosevelt, made a vital command decision on Utah when he exploited the error that landed the troops in a lightly defended area, but beyond that he too served chiefly as a morale uplifter.

With many field-grade commanders out of touch with their units, and even company-level officers suffering enormous casualties, survival, to say nothing of the ability to fight effectively, devolved upon individual initiative, upon handfuls of determined men with the most junior people in charge.

Nothing prepares one for the indescribable maelstrom of life under fire. Naiveté about the terror of war vanished with the first hostile shell. Yet few men blame shortcomings in their training. The 116th Regiment survivors Bob Slaughter, Felix Branham, and Bob Sales do not complain that they weren't ready. Nor do complaints come from paratroopers like Bernard McKearney, C. B. McCoid, and Bud Warnecke, who says, "I knew we were the best trained, and capable of beating the Germans in battle."

There were mistakes in planning and in execution. Excesses, born of the wish to deal with all possible contingencies, added to the peril. "We carried too much stuff," says Slaughter, referring to the heavy loads borne by soldiers expected to run across an open area. Gas masks were an obvious impediment to the Americans. Extra batteries for cumbersome radios and other redundancies lessened the ability of soldiers to move quickly. The seventy-five to one hundred pounds of gear loaded on paratroopers—mines and other items—contributed to injuries.

Not enough attention had been paid to the difficulties of

a night drop. The troop transport fliers received inadequate training for their mission.

Insufficiency marked some aspects of intelligence. The presence of a highly capable full German division escaped notice. The aerial reconnaissance mismeasured the elevation of the hedgerows, information vital to the glider pilots.

On the other hand, the intelligence gatherers allegedly learned from French agents that no guns were located in the Pointe du Hoc emplacements. That information never was passed on to Rudder and his Rangers. But neither were the invaders aware that artillery elsewhere on Pointe du Hoc was trained on Utah Beach. In hindsight, the cliff ascent was the best way to attack this unknown gun position. Navigation errors by the sailors foiled what could have been a landing with few casualties.

The tools supplied for the job were often inferior. The GIs did not have smokeless-powder ammunition and so were highly visible to their foe, even though the American M-1 and the British Lee Enfield rifles were as good as if not better than those facing them. The Allied machine guns and tanks were for the most part not up to their German counterparts. "We watched the things we shot at Tiger and Panther tanks bounce off them," says Eddie Ireland. The Sherman tank possessed some mechanical advantages over the panzer opposition, but the refusal to deploy flail or flamethrower tanks cost the Americans. The decision to launch the flimsy seaborne armor, which had never been tested in seas of the magnitude experienced on D-Day, was another grievous error.

The enemy 88 was easily the most effective artillery piece in the war. The guns of the naval forces off the coast also performed outstandingly, particularly since the U.S. Army contingent never had the opportunity to deploy its seaborne artillery on the first day and the air corps, busy with its own agenda—strategic bombing and attacks on targets behind the lines—was not supporting the ground troops' tactical needs.

The deficiencies and mistakes, all of which surface in the accounts contained here, handicapped what in any event would have been a desperate affair. Gen. Omar Bradley commented, "Every man who set foot on Omaha Beach that day was a hero."

The general drew the widest possible definition of the word, making no distinction between those who were there largely because of circumstances and the men who performed beyond reasonable expectations. Indeed, it is difficult enough for a soldier in pursuit of an objective to advance under fire. In fact, as Slaughter and Rangers Len Lomell and Frank Dawson (among others) demonstrated, charging the source of fire may be the best hope for survival. But to expose oneself solely to aid a comrade or to risk one's life to eliminate threats to fellow troops is truly heroic. Many such genuine heroes never achieved recognition; they and those who witnessed their acts simply disappeared in the welter of battle.

Homer Jones speaks of another kind of heroism, that of command and responsibility. "Men like Royal Taylor [his company CO] were so intent on what they did, and yet so conscious of the people who were with them. They knew what they were doing and that people might be killed as a consequence. They could feel the weight of these decisions and still carry them out."

The America in which the GIs came of age was a closer-knit place than it is today. The population in small towns and rural areas, where familiarity came with the territory, matched the numbers in the big cities. Even in the urban centers, people occupied neighborhoods, and anonymity was not so routine as it is a half century later.

For the former national guardsmen like Bob Slaughter and Felix Branham, military life perpetuated kinships already in place from having grown up together. The sense of belonging, of a responsibility to one another, was also a natural outgrowth of the years men from the regular army 1st and 4th Divisions had lived together in confined areas, enduring unpleasant demands placed on them, sharing memories and expectations for a decent future. Thickening the bonds within the Big Red One and some elements of the 82nd Airborne was a history of previous combat experience.

Another form of community, fellowship in an elite, lay in what Gavin, Ridgway, and Taylor inculcated into the paratroopers and Rudder instilled in his Rangers. Paratrooper John Hanlon says, "I'm not into telling war stories, but I am really proud to have been a member of the 101st AB. It does something for my ego." Over and above the time with a unit, D-Day was a singular moment in the company of a singular group of men.

The same sort of cohesive influences were at work in the United Kingdom. Some regiments were raised from particular locales and traced their antecedents deep into the nation's history. Bill Murray felt he belonged in the Liverpool-based King's Own. Horace Wright found a home in the tradition-soaked Hampshires. Derrick Cakebread remarked on the Commando ethic of "me and my pal," which in one form or another permeated both British and American special forces.

Leo Tolstoy's *War and Peace* describes the Battle of Borodino in terms of phalanxes of foot soldiers and cavalry hurling themselves upon one another amid torrents of cannonfire in a sprawling open-air slaughterhouse. "But though towards the end of the battle the men felt all the horror of their actions, though they would have been glad to cease, some unfathomable, mysterious force still led them on. . . ." Tolstoy could be speaking for those who first engaged the enemy in Normandy. Training, of course, prepared men to respond automatically to circumstances as command and control collapsed on June 6, but the resolve that enabled the invaders to forge ahead must lie in the character of those who were there.

World War II was the last war in which the burdens were shared equally by sons of poverty and of privilege. Coming of age during the Great Depression, another regrettably shared experience, many men of D-Day had fought economic deprivation with considerable determination. They scrambled to find employment, filled odd jobs, worked their way through college. They strike one as resilient, outgoing, fond of sports. In the United States they seem to have bought the American Dream—that if a person tries, he can succeed. In the more stratified Great Britain, they

come across as accepting of conditions. Some, like Bill
Sadler, rue the limitations imposed on the basis of a single
examination at school age, but most offered no quarrel
even when obliged to end their education at age fourteen.

Although it was available to them, surprisingly few
D-Day veterans had been on the dole in Britain or accepted
a slot on the public works payroll that absorbed so many in
the United States. Yet that so many enlisted in the Civilian
Conservation Corps or the National Guard for the pit-
tances of a dollar a drill or the paid "summer vacation" is a
measure of how desperate times were.

Still, the fellows who donned the uniform early do not
seem to have been lured solely by an opportunity to pocket
the king's shilling or Uncle Sam's buck. Men enlisted in the
prewar period glad to associate with the traditions of the
Virginia militia, or relishing the honor of entering the Big
Red One—a prideful Bill Behlmer sewed the emblem on
his blouse shoulder—or delighted, like Alfred Sadler, to
wear the garb of the Territorial Army. The glamour of the
uniform, mentioned by Bob Slaughter when he joined the
116th Regiment, and the paratrooper paraphernalia that
drew men like Dave Thomas and Tom Graham were the
trappings of a powerful patriotism.

The media of the day, supplemented by the out-and-out
propaganda efforts of the government, sought to make
their cause holy, but there is no talk among these men of
fighting to preserve democracy. Neither is there any of the
skepticism voiced by so many soldiers involved in later wars.
There is no sense of a religious war, the God-fearing against
the pagan Nazi ideology, although many recall praying for
survival or to escape painful injury. Most speak of a hatred
of the enemy born during the excesses of battle or their
personal observation of atrocities.

On the ignoble side, some German prisoners undoubtedly were murdered. Inevitably, the heat of battle persists
into the first moments after a man hoists a white flag, but
there were numerous instances of cold-blooded killing.
Nathan Fellman, for one, witnessed an execution by paratroopers. If anyone in authority issued orders approving the
slaughter of those who surrendered, the orders have never

surfaced. However, too many former GIs recall a mandate of "take no prisoners during the first three days" for that belief to be self-generated. Company-level, even field-grade officers might well have passed on this interpretation of careless remarks by their superiors. Gen. George S. Patton, for one, prior to the invasion of Sicily, delivered a fiery address to the troops that was understood as encouraging or, at least, as countenancing such behavior. No urging was needed after some saw how the enemy treated some captives.

And there were men with no enthusiasm at all for the venture. This developed particularly among some United Kingdom soldiers who had grown weary of the struggle after five years of the war, twice as long as the Americans had suffered. They were a minority (and there were some GIs who, in subsequent months, would flag to the point of minimum effort).

Today, some critics, depressed by the condition of humanity two generations after June 6, 1944, suggest that the costs were simply not worth the results. Most of those who were there think differently.

"The sounds, the cries, the smell of war" noted by Don McCarthy cannot reach those whose names are inscribed on the inconspicuous monument at the Bedford, Virginia, courthouse nor touch the thousands of others who died on June 6, 1944. They, like the fallen from other wars, are largely forgotten, except among the handful of relatives and comrades who survive them.

But the Normandy D-Day veterans remember. They who outlived the day and came safe home, albeit perhaps damaged, feel the heavenward tug of Henry V's promise that they might forever "stand a tiptoe when this day is named."

# ROLL CALL

Through interviews and their personal papers, these soldiers and sailors provided the accounts that are the basic substance of this book.

**Adair, Dr. Morgan** C. Battalion surgeon, 4th Infantry Division. Honorably discharged in December 1945, he practiced medicine in the towns of Washington and Rome, Georgia, before retirement in 1990. The close friendship he developed with battalion surgeon Sam Victor, a Bostonian, continued as the latter became a physician serving Waycross, Georgia.

**Allegretti, Vic.** Antitank crewman with the 82nd Airborne Division. He settled in a New York City suburb in the building trades. "A day in my life doesn't go by without thinking of my lost buddies in Normandy."

**Almy, Kenneth.** Deck officer aboard LCI 497. Mustered out in February 1946, Almy embarked on a thirty-eight-year career in insurance, making his home in Philadelphia.

**Barner, John.** Driver in the 741st Tank Battalion. He spent his civilian career employed by a manufacturing concern. Forty years after D-Day, Barner and his wife toured Europe. "Wherever we went, when the people found out I had been in the invasion, the response was really great. The ones I was talking to would get their friends to meet us and thank us for getting their own lands back."

**Beck, John.** Sergeant in the 87th Chemical Mortar Battalion. He returned to his slot at Westinghouse, but when the plant closed in 1961 he embarked on a desperate search for work—"I did anything to make a buck." Following a series of odd jobs he became an electrician for a large concern.

**Behlmer, Bill.** Sergeant with a 1st Division antitank platoon. He was discharged from Lawson General Hospital in Atlanta with a prosthesis in place of his amputated right leg. He attended Georgia

Tech and Southern Tech before hiring on with Lockheed Aircraft in Marietta in supervisory and management slots. "The old 'peg leg' has not been much of a problem. I am lucky to be alive and proud to have served in the Big Red One." He is deceased.

**Bennett, Harvey.** Naval gunnery lieutenant. He embarked on a civilian career in which he became national sales manager for a manufacturer of anticorrosive coverings.

**Bidmead, Bill.** No. 4 Commando. Upon retirement from the army after seventeen years, he entered the building trades.

**Biehl, Dick.** Rifleman in the 1st Division. He accepted a position with the U.S. Postal Service and became a postmaster. "My wife and I have returned to Normandy for D-Day anniversaries and we have signed on for one in 1994, the fiftieth anniversary."

**Bistrica, John.** Rifleman in the 1st Division. He came home to Youngstown, Ohio, in December 1945 and after employment in furniture factories started his own business as a carpenter and cabinetmaker.

**Boies, W. H.** Platoon leader in the 4th Division. He rejoined his father's grain-dealing firm and then became a country banker.

**Branham, Felix.** Demolition sergeant in the 29th Division. After separation from the army, Branham used his GI Bill benefits to further his education and became a superintendent of construction. "I wanted to get to Korea so bad, but my wife said, 'I went through a thousand days and nights while you were in World War II and must have written a thousand letters. I'm not letting you go to another war.' "

**Buckley, Pete.** Glider pilot. Under the GI Bill, he studied commercial photography, which became his career. "I came home ten years older than I should have been, and I had enough of flying."

**Canyon, Harold.** Rifleman in the 508th Parachute Regiment. He worked as a tester for a chemical company, bought a dairy farm, and finally became a CPA.

**Carter, William.** Member of an I&R platoon in the 1st Division. He and his wife opened a drapery business in California. "I thought of looking for my friend Carleton Barrett but never did. I learned that he received a Congressional Medal of Honor for his work saving men from the 1st Division on D-Day." (It is almost unheard of for the troops of one unit to nominate for this award a member of another organization.)

**Clark, Ollie.**  Jeep driver in the 4th Division. He remained in army hospitals until 1947 for treatment of his wounded right arm and was discharged with a permanent disability. "I would sincerely love to forget about D-Day, but it is a memory that will always be with me."

**Coleman, Harper.**  Machine gunner in the 4th Division. He received a medical discharge in September 1945, worked for the Department of Defense as a civilian, and upon retirement settled in Tucson.

**Conley, Richard.**  Platoon leader in the 1st Division. He chose to make the army his career and retired as a lieutenant colonel.

**Cubitt, Bob.**  Sniper with No. 3 Commando. He plied the electrician's trade after demobilization.

**Dawson, Frank.**  Platoon leader in the 5th Ranger Battalion. Dawson opted to stay in the Army Reserve. When the Korean War began he was recalled. He volunteered for the Ranger training center, which involved qualification as a paratrooper, since all Ranger units were now airborne. Dawson served in Germany and then Vietnam before retirement as a colonel in 1968. He was a charter nominee to the Ranger Hall of Fame, along with James Rudder and Max Schneider. He is deceased.

**Dean, Bill.**  Radio operator in the 508th Parachute Regiment. After his honorable discharge he worked as a quality assurance specialist with the Department of Defense.

**Des Champs, Leo.**  1st Engineer Battalion. Employed by the New York State government, he served as a member of the state National Guard and rose to battalion commander.

**Dunfee, Bill.**  Heavy weapons company sergeant in the 82nd Airborne. He learned the lumber business in Columbus, Ohio, and became a top executive with his company.

**Edlin, Robert.**  2nd Ranger Battalion. Mustered out in 1946, he was a captain of police in Indiana for six years before migrating to Texas. After several business ventures, Edlin settled on auctions of European antiques.

**Erben, Fred.**  1st Division platoon sergeant. He used his GI benefits for additional schooling and served as a draftsman for the New York City Board of Education before becoming a mailman.

**Fellman, Nathan.**  Ammunition sergeant in the 4th Division. He married one week after his honorable discharge in October

1945 and worked at a variety of food sales jobs before retirement. He volunteers twice a week at a Veterans Administration hospital in California and is the chaplain for the local Veterans of Foreign Wars post.

**Frackman, Sam.** Rifleman in the 4th Division. Frackman became a traveling jewelry salesman. He is the commander of his Jewish War Veterans post in California.

**Gibbs, E. H.** Rifleman in the Hertfordshire Regiment. After demobilization, Gibbs worked for thirty years at Vauxhall Motors, a United Kingdom division of General Motors.

**Gorman, Everett.** Platoon commander, Canadian North Shore Regiment. He considered remaining in the service, but the necessity of accepting a reduction in rank drove him to civilian life. After his own business went bankrupt, he emigrated to California, where as a social worker he was involved in special education programs.

**Graham, Tom.** Intelligence specialist, 82nd Airborne. He returned to farming in Indiana.

**Hanlon, John.** Staff officer, 101st Airborne. Hanlon rejected a promising future in the army. "In a recent conversation with men from the 502," says his erstwhile subordinate Bernard McKearney, "we talked about why he left the military. We were all of the opinion he could have reached the rank of general. One incident explains why John would become a colonel and I stayed a captain. We were chasing Germans through some woods in Holland. John and I found ourselves together, out of breath, looking over the terrain. John said, 'Dammit, they got away.' I could only look at him and say, 'Oh shit, John. Let them go.' " In place of the army, Hanlon chose journalism, and at the *Providence Journal* he covered local and national sports and created his own column. He is deceased.

**Hartman, Elek.** Trooper in the 508th Parachute Regiment. Hartman picked up his prewar calling as an actor.

**Hughes, Bill.** Sailor on LST 491. He worked for an uncle in an electrical contracting business and inherited the firm.

**Ireland, Eddie.** Tank commander, 745th Tank Battalion. He became a railroad man and then did a long stint as a radio dispatcher for an Illinois sheriff's department.

**Irvin, James.** Company commander in the 505th Parachute Regiment. Irvin entered the sales and sales management field to eventually establish his own firm as a manufacturer's representative. "We've maintained contact with our French friends [who sheltered him after his escape from his captors]. We still have company reunions, and I attend as many 505 functions as possible."

**Jensen, Reed.**  Medic in the 4th Division. He abandoned farming after a short period and accepted a job with a steel company.

**Jeziorski, Ed.**  Trooper in the 507th Parachute Regiment. Jeziorski went into sales. "I wanted my income determined by myself through my own efforts." While full of praise for James Gavin, under whom he served in Normandy, Jeziorski drafted an eight-page statement correcting what he believes are Gavin's errors in describing the achievements of the 507th in the general's book, *On to Berlin.*

**Jones, Homer.**  Platoon leader in the 508th Parachute Regiment. Jones temporarily left the service for a company with offices in Mexico. "The people there had no idea of what had happened. The lack of empathy surprised me." The onset of the Korean War recalled Jones. "At best there were ten to twelve noncombatants for every man on the line. I missed being with a rifle company, and I was out of tune with a staff position in the States." Jones obtained a transfer to Korea and served as a company commander. After he retired as a lieutenant colonel, he taught Spanish in the public schools near Washington, D.C., before taking his pensions and settling in Williamsburg, Virginia, where he indulges in his hobby of bird-watching.

**Kerchner, George.**  Platoon leader, 2nd Ranger Battalion. He entered a family business and settled in Maryland.

**Kiel, Bob.**  101st Airborne sergeant. He was wounded on Christmas Day 1944 and hospitalized for two years. "I wanted out, out, out. But after I did get out and worked for eight months as the manager of a bar/bowling alley, I made up my mind to return to the service. I was sworn in as a tech sergeant, a damn good rating then, and retired in 1968."

**Kuhn, Jack.**  Sergeant, 2nd Ranger Battalion. Separated from the army in favor of the Altoona, Pennsylvania, police department, Kuhn then served as a marine in an amphibious reconnaissance outfit that remained in the States during the Korean War. "The marines were very close to the Rangers in *esprit de corps* and training, but they didn't go to the depth of the Rangers." Discharged again, Kuhn resumed his law enforcement career and rose to the position of chief.

**Kurz, Jim.** 508th Parachute Regiment trooper. He became a forester for a large lumber company. Upon retirement in Arkansas, he volunteered for a variety of church and community programs, with a particular emphasis upon slide talks to schoolchildren.

**Lewis, Bill.** Antitank squad sergeant in the 29th Division. He primarily involved himself in railroad and automobile businesses.

**Lisko, Lou.** 2nd Ranger Battalion. He set up a barber shop in his home in Breckenridge, Pennsylvania. Later, he was hired as a security guard at a local steel plant.

**Lomell, Len.** First sergeant and later platoon commander, 2nd Ranger Battalion. Lomell studied law under the GI Bill, then practiced in New Jersey, eventually establishing his own firm, and served as president of the Ranger Battalion Association of World War II.

**Lord, Bill.** Mortar squad sergeant in the 508th Parachute Regiment. Lord followed in his father's footsteps, becoming an executive in the textile industry.

**McCann, Tom.** Intelligence and reconnaissance platoon, 1st Division. McCann taught high school social studies and economics at the college level. He started a collection of autographs of Congressional Medal of Honor recipients and Aces (from the air corps). This pursuit led him to the trail of the only nonposthumous CMH winner on Omaha Beach, Carleton Barrett. McCann learned that Barrett had died in 1986 and his medals had been lost. Under McCann's goading, relatives retrieved the awards, and a group of vets from the I&R platoon, including William Carter, who went ashore with Barrett, presented the trophies to the 1st Division Museum at Cantigny, Illinois.

**McCarthy, Don.** Intelligence and reconnaissance platoon, 29th Division. After attending Boston University, he worked for a New England telephone company and then the Greater Providence Chamber of Commerce.

**McCoid, C. B.** Company commander, 507th Parachute Regiment. Granted a regular army commission in 1946, McCoid says, "I continued to serve until 1973, in a variety of assignments, many of which involved airborne units. Despite never recovering full use of my right knee, I continued to jump for twenty-three years."

**McKearney, Bernard.** Platoon leader, 101st Airborne Division. "I knew I had to get an education beyond high school," says McKearney. "The GI Bill changed my life. I went to the University of Missouri and enrolled in journalism. Then I remembered my happiest days were as an instructor in the army. I changed to education." His pedagogical career culminated in the post of superintendent of schools, Scituate, Massachusetts.

**McKee, Frank.**  Assistant squad leader, 508th Parachute Regiment. He attended New York University's School of Commerce under the GI Bill and held management positions with a large manufacturing concern until retirement. "F Company was the best group of men I have ever met. We still have company and regimental reunions where survivors, even some in wheelchairs, come."

**Martin, Dell.**  Coxswain, LCM. Martin held jobs in manufacturing and engineering before switching to sales.

**Mastro, Charles.**  Intelligence specialist, 4th Division. He served with the U.S. Department of Labor, operated a landscaping business, and then managed real estate.

**Merlano, Lou.**  101st Airborne Division paratrooper. After going back to school, Merlano tried the accounting profession but did not like desk work. For forty years he sold office machines, moving up the ladder to general sales manager for his company. "I believe my tour with the 502 PR probably had the greatest influence turning my life around after World War II."

**Meyer, Bob.**  BAR man, 4th Infantry Division. Meyer waited until 1947 before deciding to further an education that had halted eleven years earlier. After obtaining his degree, he taught school.

**Miller, Gil.**  Crewman, LCM. He returned to upstate New York and drove trucks for a dairy conglomerate.

**Morales, Irwin.**  Glider pilot. He attended college and then became a "jack of all trades" before settling on nine acres of Indian reservation land.

**Murray, James.**  Intelligence expert, King's Regiment. After demobilization, Murray was employed as a boiler engineer.

**Nelson, Raider.**  507th Parachute Regiment. Nelson worked as a wood patternmaker before opening a plastic fabricating business with a partner. His craftsmanship led him to abstract sculpture, and one of his pieces was accepted by the National Collection of Fine Arts.

**Parker, Charles.** Platoon leader and company commander, 5th Ranger Battalion. Parker dabbled in wildcat oil explorations before opening a pharmacy. He is deceased.

**Randolph, Tip.** Glider pilot. For a brief time, Randolph sampled postwar military life, but the paperwork discouraged him. He ran the family dairy and potato farm in New Jersey before moving on to the leasing of agricultural equipment.

**Sadler, Bill.** Ambulance driver for the Royal Engineers. Following several ventures, Sadler started a travel agency.

**Sales, Bob.** Radioman, 29th Division. He prospered as a businessman in Virginia. Behind his home in Madison Heights, Sales cultivated a garden with a memorial plaque dedicated to the 112 men from B Company, who were killed in action during World War II.

**Salomon, Sid.** Platoon leader and company commander, 2nd Ranger Battalion. He sold paper products for a large corporation and after retirement became a world-class competitor in senior rowing. Salomon is a past president of the Ranger Association.

**Seelye, Irvin.** Scout in the 82nd Airborne Division. Seelye accepted a job at a corn-processing factory in Pekin, Illinois. After seven years, he moved to Normal, where, under the GI Bill, he and his wife enrolled at Illinois State University. After graduation he taught high school social studies and then sociology at a Chicago suburban community college before shifting to a post in Arkansas.

**Slaughter, Bob.** Machine gun squad sergeant, 29th Division. Slaughter indulged in wild partying when he first came home while nightmares bedeviled him during sleep. After marriage he calmed down and started at the bottom in the composing room of the *Roanoke Times*. He furthered his education and rose to the post of production supervisor at the newspaper. After a British TV reporter approached him in 1975 for his memories of D-Day, Slaughter put together a large collection of accounts from the men with whom he served.

**South, Frank.** Medic, 2nd Ranger Battalion. He abandoned the study of medicine for a career of research and teaching in the fields of biophysics and physiology.

**Sulkis, Karl.** 1st Engineer Combat Battalion. Sulkis renewed a career in advertising design, but "my three years or so blowing things up and living in a mud hole changed me, and I felt terribly confined and restless. I quit and turned myself into an industrial manufacturer's rep."

**Swanson, Wallace.** Platoon leader and company commander, 101st Airborne Division. He had married a college classmate, a nurse, while stationed in England. After leaving the army, Swanson worked in the petroleum industry.

**Tannery, Fred.** Messenger, 4th Division. He studied photography under the GI Bill, then accepted a position with a chemical manufacturer.

**Thomas, Dave.** Battalion surgeon, 508th Parachute Regiment. The former prisoner in Normandy made military medicine his profession, rising to brigadier general. He named a son Normand in memory of his service in France.

**Ward, William.** Rifleman, King's Own Scottish Borderers. Ward accepted a position in sales for a catering business.

**Warnecke, Bud.** Sergeant and then platoon leader in the 508th Parachute Regiment. He elected the life of a professional officer. Regulations required him to earn a High School Graduate Equivalency Diploma and collect sixty hours of college credits. "I flunked a bunch of courses but passed enough, and also received my high school diploma with the class of 1948." He served as company commander and acting battalion commander in the Korean War. Disturbed by the intrusion of politics into what he considered military matters, Warnecke left the service in 1964 and opened a TV rental service.

**Warriner, Vic.** Glider pilot. "After one year of peacetime bureaucracy and inefficiency, I opted for *out*!" He returned to the University of Michigan to complete his senior year. After working for Sears, he became a partner in a real estate development company in Texas. "I've always felt that my glider experience has given me an attitude that helps me combat difficulties. I believe that after Normandy, I have survived on borrowed time, and it's made me appreciate every second of life."

**Wawrynovic, Frank.** Scout, 29th Division. He earned an advanced degree in forestry and wildlife management at Penn State. After being employed by others, he and his wife formed their own company to deal with rights-of-way for power and gas lines.

**Wheeldon, Arnold.** No. 6 Commando. He won a commission and continued in the army, serving in Burma and India. He held the rank of captain when demobilized. Wheeldon claims that by applying the drive forged in Commando and other units, he became managing director of his civilian firm. "Every year I return to Normandy on June 6 and relive memories with my old comrades. I look upon it as a vigil, and yearly, I walk along the rows of headstones in Ranville Military Cemetery, observe the names and ages listed—nineteen, twenty, twenty-one, twenty-two—thinking there but for the grace of God . . ."

**Williams, Malcolm.**  Battalion headquarters, 4th Division. Williams established an appliance business in North Carolina.

**Wills, Bill.**  Sergeant, 1st Engineer Combat Battalion. He won an appointment to the New York City Police Department. Promoted through the ranks to sergeant in the detective division, he retired after twenty-seven years as a cop.

**Willstatter, Richard.**  Engineering officer aboard an LST. He became an expert in nonferrous materials and served a term as head of the LST Association.

**Wright, Horace.**  Platoon leader and company commander, Hampshire Regiment. Wright remained with the organization and served in the last outposts of the British Empire until he retired as a major. He then took over a family business in Bournemouth.

**Zenie, George.**  Antitank sergeant and then platoon leader in the 1st Division. Zenie considered making the army his profession, but a stint training recruits and marriage persuaded him to ask for an honorable discharge. He used his GI Bill entitlements to attend a trade school and become a patternmaker in the garment industry. "I liked military life. I hated war. I like order, and war is the exact opposite."

**Zieckler, Lawrence.**  Rifleman, 1st Division. After an honorable discharge, Zieckler worked as a carpenter and in Pennsylvania steel mills and public utilities.

# SOURCES

Books:

Ambrose, Stephen. *Pegasus Bridge*. New York: Simon and Schuster, 1985.

Black, Robert W. *Rangers in World War II*. New York: Ivy Books, 1992.

Blair, Clay. *Ridgway's Paratroopers*. New York: Dial Books, 1985.

Bradley, Omar N. *A Soldier's Story*. New York: Henry Holt and Company, 1951.

Breuer, William. *Geronimo*. New York: St. Martin's Press, 1989.

Center of Military History, U.S. Army. *Omaha Beachhead*. Washington, D.C.: U.S. Government Printing Office, 1989.

Center of Military History, U.S. Army. *Utah Beach to Cherbourg*. Washington, D.C.: U.S. Government Printing Office, 1990.

Devlin, Gerard M. *Silent Wings*. New York: St. Martin's Press, 1985.

Durnford-Slater, John. *Commando*. London: Greenhill Books, 1953.

Eisenhower, Dwight D. *Crusade in Europe*. New York: Doubleday, 1948.

Gavin, James M. *On to Berlin*. New York: Bantam, 1979.

Golley, John. *The Big Drop*. London: Janes's, 1982.

Harrison, Gordon A. *Cross-Channel Attack*. Washington, D.C.: U.S. Government Printing Office, 1989.

Hastings, Max. *Overlord*. New York: Simon and Schuster, 1984.

Howarth, David. *D-Day*. New York: McGraw-Hill, 1959.

Keegan, John. *Six Armies in Normandy*. London: Pimlico, 1992.

Kosmaki, George E. *D-Day with the Screaming Eagles*. Sweetwater, Tenn.: 101st Airborne Division Association, 1970.

Lane, Ronald L. *Rudder's Rangers*. Manassas, Va.: Ranger Associates, 1979.

Liddell Hart, B. H. *The German Generals Talk*. New York: Quill, 1979.

Marshall, S.L.A. *Night Drop*. Boston: Little, Brown and Co.,
    1962.

Mason, John T., Jr. *The Atlantic War Remembered*. Annapolis:
    United States Naval Institute, 1990.

Milkovics, Lewis. *The Devils Have Landed*. Longwood, Florida:
    Creative Printing and Publishing, Inc., 1993.

Morison, Samuel Eliot. *The History of United States Naval
    Operations in World War II—The Invasion of France and
    Germany*. Boston: Little, Brown, 1957.

Ryan, Cornelius. *The Longest Day*. New York: Simon and
    Schuster, 1959.

Salomon, Sidney A. *2nd U.S. Ranger Battalion* [Bergstein-Hill
    400]. Doylestown, Penn.: Birchwood Books, 1991.

Thompson, R. W. *At Whatever Cost*. New York: Coward
    McCann, 1957.

Turner Publishing Co. *U.S.A. Airborne 50th Anniversary*.
    Paducah, Ky.: Turner Publishing Co., 1990.

Young, Peter. *Storm from the Sea*. London: Greenfield Books,
    1989.

### Private Papers and Memoirs:

Bennett, Gen. Donald V. Oral History, Archives, U.S. Military
    History Institute, Carlisle Barracks, Penn.

Branham, Felix. Unpublished memoir of military experiences.

Buckley, Pete. Unpublished account of 74th glider squadron ex-
    periences.

Dunfee, William T. First-person account of Normandy Invasion,
    prepared for the Columbus, Ohio, Roundtable, May 1, 1986.

Edlin, Robert. Unpublished account of military experiences.

Gavin, Gen. James M. Oral History, Archives, U.S. Military
    History Institute, Carlisle Barracks, Penn.

Lewis, Bill. Oral history given to J. E. Kaufmann, San Antonio,
    Tex., 1989.

Lisko, Lou. Unpublished, undated interview with French college
    student, Sylvie Chapelier.

McCarthy, Don. Unpublished memoir of Normandy experiences.

McKearney, Bernard. Letter from England to his family after be-
    ing relieved in Normandy.

McKee, Frank. Unpublished account of Normandy experiences.

Meyer, Bob. Unpublished account of military experiences.

Ridgway, Gen. Matthew B. Oral History, Archives, U.S. Military
    History Institute, Carlisle Barracks, Penn.

Sadler, Bill. Unpublished book on his military career.

Slaughter, Bob. Unpublished "Wartime Memories."
Taylor, Gen. Maxwell D. Letter to S.L.A. Marshall.
Wawrynovic, Frank. Unpublished memoir of military experiences.

In addition to the above, all of the men listed under "Roll Call" were interviewed by mail, telephone, or face-to-face and responded by letter, audiotape, or verbally.

# ABOUT THE AUTHOR

A freelance author for the past twenty years, Gerald Astor began his career as a writer and then editor at *Look* magazine and worked on the staff of *Sports Illustrated*. He also put in brief stints with *The Saturday Evening Post, Sport,* and *Time.* His most recent books include *The Last Nazi: The Life and Times of Dr. Joseph Mengele; Hostage: My Nightmare in Beirut* (with David Jacobsen); *A Blood-Dimmed Tide: The Battle of the Bulge by the Men Who Fought It;* and *Battling Buzzards: The Odyssey of the 517th Parachute Combat Team.*

Educated in the public schools of Mount Vernon, New York, he was a member of the Class of '47 at Princeton and attended the Columbia University Graduate School.

During World War II he was an infantry replacement assigned to the 97th Infantry Division and spent the final months of the conflict hauling ammunition and guarding prisoners before serving eleven months of occupation duty in Japan.

He now makes his home with his wife, Sonia, an artist, in Scarsdale, New York.